The People's Right to the Novel

The People's Right to the Novel

War Fiction in the Postcolony

Eleni Coundouriotis

Fordham University Press
New York 2014

Library of Congress Cataloging-in-Publication Data

Coundouriotis, Eleni.
The people's right to the novel : war fiction in the postcolony / Eleni Coundouriotis.
pages cm
Summary: "This study offers a literary history of the war novel in Africa and argues for the genre's distinct contribution to the literary culture of the continent. The war novel is a form of people's history that participates in a political struggle for the rights of the dispossessed"— Provided by publisher.
Includes bibliographical references and index.
ISBN 978-0-8232-6233-5 (hardback)
1. African fiction (English)—History and criticism. 2. African fiction (French)—History and criticism. 3. War in literature. 4. Literature and society—Africa. 5. Africa—In literature. I. Title.
PR9344.C68 2014
823—dc23

2014005590

Printed in the United States of America
16 15 14 5 4 3 2 1
First edition

CONTENTS

FIGURES

ACKNOWLEDGMENTS

I completed this project while I was a faculty fellow at the University of Connecticut Humanities Institute in 2011–2012. Thus, I want to thank the dean of the College of Liberal Arts and Sciences, Jeremy Teitelbaum, for his continued support of the institute at a time of tight budgets. The Humanities Institute provides an invaluable resource for humanities scholars and effectively nurtures a wide range of research projects. Without it the university would be greatly diminished. While at UCHI I benefited from the wise directorship of Sharon Harris and the able assistance of Jo-Ann Waide and Dorothy Lustig. I would also like to thank the Felberbaum family for the faculty grant I received during my tenure at UCHI. It provided me with much-needed funds to purchase copies of my primary material. The CLAS Book Support Committee also provided funds to defray the costs of publishing this study. Furthermore, I owe a big thanks to the Interlibrary Loan Office at the Homer Babbidge Library, University of Connecticut, which provided me with invaluable assistance in tracking down out-of-print materials, and to Richard Bleiler, humanities librarian.

The People's Right to the Novel owes much to the insights of my undergraduate students in the numerous sections of English 3318 that I have taught since my sabbatical in 2006–2007, when I first began reading for this project. Teaching different versions of the course (the contemporary African novel, African women writers, war fiction from Africa), I was continuously impressed by my students' insights and gratified by their imaginative engagement, which made the real in these novels come close to home. My students repeatedly remind me that teaching is always a great privilege.

This project has been undoubtedly deeply informed by my involvement with the Human Rights Institute at the University of Connecticut. My colleagues at HRI have been a constant source of inspiration, and the interdisciplinarity of the institute makes it a truly amazing place to think. I am deeply grateful to my colleagues who have participated in the long conversation of our faculty seminars on narrative and human rights, visual media and humanitarianism, and the history of the humanitarian movement: Kerry Bystrom, Françoise Dussart, Susan Einbinder, Emma Gilligan, Margaret Higonnet, Elizabeth Holzer, Kathryn Libal, Samuel Martinez, Glenn Mitoma, Michael Orwicz, Serena Parekh, Richard Wilson, and Sarah Winter. Several of the same colleagues read and responded repeatedly to drafts of this manuscript: Kerry Bystrom, Glen Mitoma, and Richard Wilson, in particular, never failed to challenge and encourage me at the same time. My ongoing collaboration with Sarah Winter in the English Department and the Research Program on Humanitarianism has nurtured the sensibility that informs this book.

Over the years I presented material from this project at several workshops and small conferences. I want to thank Mohamed Kamara and Susan Z. Andrade each for inviting me to their excellent symposia on the African novel at Washington and Lee University in 2005 and the University of Pittsburgh in 2006, respectively. Nancy Armstrong and Tejumola Olaniyan were my respondents at the University of Pittsburgh conference, and their insights on my early thoughts on Farah's *Links* were particularly meaningful. I also benefited greatly from the feedback at the symposium on literature and human rights organized by Lauren Goodlad for the Unit for Criticism and Theory at the University of Illinois in 2009. Many thanks to Berthold Schoene for his gracious invitation at Manchester Metropolitan University, where I presented a version of the introduction to this book.

Furthermore, I was fortunate to have significant feedback at symposia organized through the auspices of the Human Rights Institute at the University of Connecticut. I thus want to thank the visiting scholars who responded to my presentations on such occasions: Sidonie Smith, Joseph R. Slaughter, Diana Tietjens Meyers, Wendy S. Hesford, and Crystal Parikh. The guest scholars to the Narrative and Human Rights faculty seminar were especially generous with their willingness to travel multiple times to our campus and engage with us. These were all memorable conversations, and thus I want to extend special thanks to Bruce Robbins, Amanda Anderson, Susan J. Brison, and Ian Baucom. My interactions with our Gladstein Visiting Professors in Human Rights, in particular Zakes Mda and Ariella Azoulay, have also been influential on my thinking for this project, and I thank them for their sharp insights and optimism.

Simon Gikandi wrote me several letters of support during the years when I pursued funding, and I thank him for his faith in this project. Furthermore, I want to thank my readers for Fordham University Press for their thorough and very useful reports: Wendy Griswold, Annie Gagiano, and Joseph R. Slaughter. The Press, under the astute leadership of Helen

Tartar, has provided me with terrific guidance and support, undoubtedly making this a better book.

As always, my spouse and colleague, Thomas E. Recchio, is my most perceptive, patient, and faithful reader. Our son, Thomas George, grew up with this book as a constant presence in the conversation at home. I dedicate this book to both Thomases, thanking them for their love and support.

The People's Right to the Novel

Introduction: Naturalism, Humanitarianism, and the Fiction of War

War has always occupied an important place in the African novel and, in recent years, has arguably become the dominant literary theme of works about Africa read outside Africa. This study attempts a literary history of the war novel in Africa in order to delineate its formal features and argue for the genre's distinct contribution to the literary culture of the continent. As a subject war presents particular challenges. It brings to the fore the violence of imperialism and its aftermath, it displays the weakness of the nation state and its pull toward social disintegration, and, in its presentation of social anomie, it threatens to mire us in stereotypes of Africa as conflict-ridden and dysfunctional.

A close reading of the literature, however, reveals a great deal that counters these now static images. The war novel, I argue, attempts a people's history and sits outside the frame of the *Bildungsroman*, the genre that dominated the literature of an educated, assimilated class in whose hands the novel took on the confrontation of the individual and society as tradition, modernity, political corruption, religion, and patriarchy.[1] The war novel instead attempts to capture the people's perspective and give a collective account of ordinary people in the historical transitions from colonialism to independence and the post-independence and globalizing eras. It focuses on the politically marginalized, trying to imagine a perspective from below.

As a protest against the dehumanization it portrays, the war novel offers important analytical insights on violence and its representation. It addresses the dangers of reinforcing stereotypes by balancing its specifically historical project, located in particular places and conflicts, with the more universalizing discourse of war and humanity rooted in humanitarian discourse. Humanitarianism is not only a form of governmentality that seeks to take care of precarious lives, but a form of witness that gives an account of trauma "narrating war in the language of suffering" (Fassin and Rechtman 198). After Biafra, humanitarianism increasingly takes on a role of "proxy testimony," speaking of the suffering of others (194). A discourse of witness, humanitarianism can produce "histories without a history" (209) or stories of trauma that reveal the intimate details of victimization as the violent removal of agency. As the novel of war performs a reclamation of history from the perspective of the people, it bucks this tendency of humanitarianism to stay mired in the "wounds of the soul" (198), and in the process it creates portraits of more resistant subjects. The war novel similarly creates a "proxy testimony" that speaks for ordinary people but that also exceeds humanitarian discourse. Because of its political aims to redress inequality, the war novel goes beyond the self-limiting realm of humanitarian discourse and shapes the identification between the educated (the writers and readers of novels) and the ordinary people in order to galvanize a democratic movement.

This study, therefore, seeks to contribute to a broader discussion of the formal features of the war novel as a genre. The scholarship on the war novel is usually organized according to a particular historical grouping (novels of WWI or Vietnam novels, for example) and turns to the question of genre in its broad global sense only secondarily.[2] A first interpretive gesture is to locate any war novel in its particular moment and then only afterward to compare it with material from across the literature. Despite its tendency to pronounce on war as a general phenomenon, the war novel frequently insists on the particularity of the history represented within it. How this "real" history correlates with a literary history of the form and establishes a politics of the war novel is a central concern of this study.

The question "what does the African war novel teach us about the genre of the war novel more broadly?" performs a double gesture: it delineates a distinct tradition (the African war novel) and seeks to bring it into a global context. To begin to answer this question, I first situate the war novel in relation to the aesthetic of naturalism. The negotiation of universality and particularity in the novel of war takes place within an aesthetic of naturalism, which helps foreground a discourse of political and economic disparity, a look within and from within African societies.[3] By alluding to naturalism I claim a degree of continuity between the war novel in nineteenth- and twentieth-century Europe and America and the war novel in Africa. Such continuity is not a manifestation of a writing back to Europe, a mode that, as Evan Maina Mwangi says, "performs a marginalizing gesture that ignores the African peoples' attempts to dialogue with one another" (Evan Mwangi, 25). These novels are, as I elaborate later, addressed to African audiences. The discussion of naturalism situates the war novel in formal terms and within a globally circulating aesthetics to which African writers make important contributions. Such an argument builds from what Tejumola Olaniyan calls "the foundational premise of an irreversible imbrication of histories, and therefore cultures and cultural forms" that veers away from opposing European and African aesthetics (Olaniyan 4).

War is the topic of humanitarianism par excellence and naturalism one of the most common aesthetic practices for the representation of war. Naturalism, moreover, is historically entangled with the emergence of humanitarianism. The two come to the fore in 1860s Europe. Harry Levin identifies the emergence of naturalism in 1865 with an "age of expanding humanitarianism" (Levin 347). Significantly, 1862 saw the publication of Henri Dunant's *Un souvenir de Solférino*, the founding text of the humanitarian movement and itself a war narrative replete with naturalistic descriptions of the injured and dying.[4] Dunant's text had a profound impact on how the story of war is told by shifting the focus from an account of the battle (which he delivers quickly, albeit with explicit details) to the protracted narrative of the consequences, showing extensively the appalling degree of suffering caused by the fourteen hours of fighting. The transformed setting after the battle, littered with destroyed and abandoned property and the dead and dying, becomes the narrative's focus (Dunant 35). The aftermath is presented as an entirely new time and place, the landscape of emergency, where there is no norm and the extant communities must reinvent themselves as emergency care centers. Thus in Dunant's text we have a historical account that stresses not the strategy of the battle or the execution of the fighting, but the consequences of the battle. Much of the war fiction examined in this study echoes this representational strategy, especially as it tries to integrate the experiences of combatants and civilians.

The war novel as a genre has carried the burden of a humanitarian consciousness, intensified with the rise of naturalism in nineteenth-century Europe and complicated by its reaction to a "politics of pity" that emerged, as Hannah Arendt argues, with the French Revolution. "Politics of pity" highlights an unequal situation of power where the empowered look upon the suffering of the people with empathy yet at the same time see this suffering as occurring at some distance from them. Consequently, they cease to regard those who are suffering as individuals (Arendt, *On Revolution* 79–80). Arendt, who made a distinction between pity and compassion in her critique of the French Revolution and its construction of the people, argued that "Revolutionary governments were neither of the people nor by the people, but at best for the people" (69). Pity, she claimed, was the feeling that enabled sympathy for the poor as a collectivity, a relation that depends on distance.[5] Naturalism complicates the idea of distance to give an intimate account of the details of suffering.

Placing the African war novel against this backdrop highlights the shape of the discourse of inequality that structures it. What interests me is the way in which Africa's citizens view the suffering of its rural and urban poor.[6] Because the war novel treats with suspicion nationalisms that promote political myths of unity along ethnic lines, it lends support to ideals of democratic and ethnically diverse nation states, imagining the possible reconciliation of the warring parties. The project of reconciliation, however, is not feasible rhetorically within the angry tones of a naturalist cry of protest, which must give way to a sentimental discourse. The war novel in Africa, therefore, reveals a rift between naturalism and sentimentalism. The failures of reconciliation, its inability to deal adequately with the traumas of war, bring about a backlash, a renewed turn to naturalism, now focusing on the urban poor, made up of former fighters and the displaced rural population. The opposition of naturalism to sentimentality is rooted in the philosophical idealism of sentimentality that insists "against the claim that the universe and human history are governed by mechanical, or rational, or deterministic, or pragmatic forces" (Kaplan 6), such that naturalism depicts. The cycle of anger and appeasement and then renewed anger can be mapped on the history of the genre of war fiction in Africa. But we can also detect a democratic project in this literature that veers toward a rights narrative.[7]

This emergent rights narrative debunks a "politics of pity" and taps into the aspirational energy of a people's history. Thus, whereas I trace the prevalence of naturalism in the literature, I show where and how this paradigm cracks, setting in motion a complex discussion of reconciliation. By drawing the outline of the genre in bold terms, I hope to illuminate what is at stake in the various manifestations of the war novel in Africa and create an understanding that is capacious enough to reveal the similarities without collapsing the differences among novels produced over the extended history of the genre and in its multiple sites of national production.

In what follows I first define the war novel as an example of naturalist fiction and elaborate further on its entanglement with humanitarian discourse. Next, I outline the argument that the war novel in Africa up until the mid-1990s frequently articulates a people's history. Finally, I turn to the implications of this literature's orientation toward a national audience and identify four motifs that structure and delineate it as a distinct literary tradition.

Defining the Genre

Naturalism is usually characterized as proffering a deterministic worldview and insisting on the influence of environment. The argument that I make here is sharply focused on naturalism as a way of coming to terms with the experience of war and attempts to delineate the naturalist environment as the war experience. War, in other words, is a special case, an environment out of the ordinary that is governed by different laws, those that are explained through naturalism.[8] My investigation of the nineteenth-century antecedents to this literature is not for the purpose of tracing an influence. Rather, it is made in order to establish how naturalism and war converge and to highlight the mediating effect between the two of a humanitarian ethos that takes shape at the same time. Humanitarianism has an overt presence in this literature, as the war novel in Africa frequently represents humanitarians in the field. Overall, the literature is deeply skeptical about the role of humanitarians and foregrounds instead the deterministic, naturalistic negativity of war, looking to resolve it by making strong rights claims against the powers that instigate war. Writing from below, the war novel rhetorically captures a sense of democratic possibility when the conditions of war can be overcome. Several steps are necessary to establish this argument, beginning with a look at naturalism's engagement with the poor.

Naturalism was first a genre of urban fiction. In the text that is considered the popular manifesto of naturalism, the "Préface" to *Germinie Lacerteux* (1864), Edmond and Jules Goncourt warned their readers that their novel came from the street and that, although it was pure, it was not beautiful (Goncourt and Goncourt 55). Moreover, they complained that the people had been deprived of their "right to the novel":

> Nous nous sommes demandé si ce qu'on appelle les "basses classes" *n'avait pas droit au roman*; si ce monde sous un monde, le peuple, devait rester sous le coup de l'interdit littéraire et des dédains d'auteurs qui ont fait jusqu'ici le silence sur l'âme et le coeur qu'il peut avoir, nous nous sommes demandé s'il y avait encore pour l'écrivain et pour le lecteur, en ces années d'égalité où nous sommes, des classes indignes, des malheurs trop bas, des drames trop peu nobles. (55–56, emphasis added).

At a time "when society was expanding its suffrage" (Levin 347), Edmond and Jules Goncourt aimed to expose the limits of society's rhetoric of equality and demanded that the life of the poor be dignified by being taken up as the proper subject of the novel. The "right to the novel" does not refer to access, therefore. For instance, it does not refer to the literacy with which the people can partake of and shape the cultural life of the nation via the novel as form. Rather, it is a right of representation. The lives of the poor and disempowered ("classes indignes" or the undignified classes) merit artistic representation in their actual conditions of life. This right, not of access but of representation, is not only the weaker right, but the one that aligns naturalistic writing with humanitarianism by claiming to speak for others. Moreover, the Goncourts stress the goal of giving witness to the "soul" and "heart" of the people, or the class that lives "below." Naturalism, therefore, echoes Fassin's claim for humanitarianism to speak about the "wounds of the soul," conditions of indignity rendered now as protest and hence reinflected with the demand for dignity.

Although critics have been cautious about the Goncourts's sincerity, taking notice of their tendency to sensationalize the putrid and ugly (Levin 347), naturalism, after the Goncourts, continued to make a committed stance for the people, especially in the work of Émile Zola.[9] Arendt recognized this when she admiringly called Zola "that great lover of the people." Unlike his contemporaries, Zola did not confuse the idea of the people with the mob and understood that the people stood for inclusiveness and equality, whereas the mob was authoritarian (Arendt, *Totalitarianism* 113–14). For Zola naturalism gives shape to a people's narrative in which the people have the "smell of the people" (quoted in Levin 347). Inspired by *Germinie Lacerteux*, which he said portrayed a "bleeding and superb" humanity ("l'humanité saignante et superbe"), Zola stressed the materiality of the body as a key subject for naturalism (Zola, *Roman* 263).

Zola's progressive politics and solidarity with the people, moreover, complicate the distance implied in the spectacle of suffering. How to modulate the observer's distance is a key problematic of naturalism. Examining humanitarian discourse, Luc Boltanski speaks of this problem in terms of "naturalism or realism in the literary sense" (Boltanski 45) and describes the aspiration to an aperspectival reporting, "a description without a point of view" (43). In the description of human suffering such a stance is immoral, Boltanski claims, because it asserts an "asymmetry," or inequality, between the observer and observed that goes counter to the intention to bring about an amelioration of suffering (43). To correct this Boltanski creates the figure of the "introspector," the observer who describes suffering by talking about how it affects him as an observer and hence "by involving himself as subject in his own story he takes a step in the direction of involvement within a situation and points the way to action" (44). Yet, aware that this too may be problematic, effacing what is useful about distance, Boltanski warns that the "introspector" may turn everything into a story about himself, bringing attention back to the need for naturalistic description (47).

The idea that naturalism is an intensified, more myopic, but degraded form of realism is an old one. Georg Lukács denigrated naturalism in such terms and argued that, by losing its sense of distance from that which it describes, naturalism abandons realism's effort to be historical or to capture through irony the contradictions of capital made manifest in the realist author's attempt to create a comprehensive picture of a particular society at a particular moment (Lukács 92–93, 95). Joining naturalism with humanitarianism as Thomas Laqueur does gives us a different perspective on what naturalism's myopic, detailed perspective elucidates. Laqueur identifies in the eighteenth century a "new cluster of narratives [that] came to speak in extraordinarily detailed fashion about the pains and deaths of ordinary people in such a way as to make apparent the causal chains that might connect the actions of its readers with the suffering of its subjects" (Laqueur 177). By the middle of the nineteenth century, "humanitarian sensibilities are so much assumed that they go unspoken" in the "naturalist novel" (184). Laqueur's discussion of humanitarian narrative announces as its subject the "ordinary people," but it also registers a distance between these ordinary people who are suffering and the consumer, or reader, of the narrative. It points out the "theatricality" of humanitarianism and its reliance on a spectacle of suffering, which Lilie Chouliaraki urges we grapple with as a way of exploring the "uncomfortable but vital questions of power, otherness, and justice" implicated in humanitarianism (Chouliaraki 4). Although the object of the narrative, for Laqueur, is to reveal "the causal chains that *might connect*" the readers to the sufferers, it is hard to miss the conditional construction of Laqueur's phrase. Humanitarian narrative, bound as it is to the cause and effect structure of historical emplotment, deals with the anxiety about its own effectiveness by being prescriptive. It enunciates a "detailed matrix of cause and effect, specific wrong and specific action," and thus "an analytic of suffering exposes the means of its relief" (Laqueur 178).

Two features of Laqueur's definition need further clarification: the emphasis on how naturalism brings the particularity of the people into focus and the insistence on the mechanism of a causal logic. Both contribute to our understanding of the portrayal of war as a total environment and how determinism is simultaneously evoked and angrily defied. Laqueur was very cognizant that humanitarian narrative takes as its subject the suffering of "ordinary people" and that it succeeds in placing them at the center by accumulating lots of detail as "the sign of truth": "unprecedented quantities of fact, of minute observations, about people who had before been beneath notice become the building blocks of the 'reality effect,' of the literary technique through which the experiences of others are represented as real in the humanitarian narrative" (177). Unlike Lynn Hunt, who identifies in a similar moment in the eighteenth century the emergence of an identity of the human, a universal Man, on which a theory of moral sentiments is attached that provides the underpinnings for an ideology of human rights,[10] Laqueur insists on the term "ordinary people" rather than humanity and aligns this aesthetics with naturalism rather than sentimentalism (184).[11] Moreover, he consciously limits the scope of this discourse and argues that, although it has the ability to address a variety of circumstances, it does not address itself to the universal, but always to the particular: "humanitarian narratives created 'sympathetic passions'—bridged the gulf between facts, compassion, and action—in a wide variety of places and circumstances, *but by no means exclusively or universally*" (179, emphasis added).

The causal logic Laqueur highlights closely identifies humanitarianism with naturalism. This causal logic therefore does not universalize. Zola similarly emphasized naturalism's attention to cause and effect and went so far as to suggest famously that the novel be thought of quite literally as a scientific experiment determined by heredity and environment (Zola, *Roman* 61). It is worth lingering over Zola's formulation of naturalism's determinism in order to clarify what it attempts to illuminate. The novelist, like the scientist, wants to answer the question "how," rather than "why." He sets characters in motion in particular circumstances that are recognizable as real (natural) to his readers in order to explore their experience, much like a scientist observes an experiment in order to identify how phenomena unfold even when the end result is already a given (63–64). This emphasis on "how" reveals that what is required is not distanced observation, but the disinterested adoption of another's point of view. The ending or outcome is rarely in doubt (hence the charge of determinism), but the individual experiences of similar conditions become the variable stories of "how" that engage the novelist.

Because Zola drew his theory of the experimental novel from a medical text (Claude Bernard's *Introduction à l'étude de la médecine expérimentale*), it carries with it the implication that healing is the goal (Zola, *Roman* 59), which is similar to what Laqueur identifies as the goal of humanitarian discourse, to articulate "an analytic of suffering" that "exposes the means of its relief." Once we have discovered the laws of causality ("quand on possédera les lois"), we will be able to intervene on individuals and environments, Zola proclaims, changing things for the social good: "il n'y aura plus qu'à agir sur les individus et sur les milieux, si l'on veut arriver au meilleur état social" (76). The novelist's insight will contribute to the "sciences politiques et économiques" and intervene in social policy (76). Zola's variables of heredity and environment affect the outcomes of his experiment (72), but they also create the rich tableaux out of which he can draw insight about human experience.

Heredity as an idea features less prominently in the war novel, but environment is all-important. Zola uses the word "milieu" and not "environnement"; "milieu" carries with it the implications of setting, or "mise en scène," pointing to the intentionality of an experiment set in motion by the novelist. Moreover, in Zola, "milieu" refers more often to social environment, and hence it points to our interconnectedness with each other (78). The novels of war are defined by the "mise-en-scène": war is the determining environment. The fact that environment is defining comes across as a constitutive element, part of war's definition of what it is, an environment in which man appears as different from what he normally is, unmasking a self that he must subsequently struggle to disavow. War exposes a degraded, instead of a heroic, self that lies hidden by the softening touches of quotidian life now stripped away. However, insofar as war novels draw a distinct boundary defining the space of this particular environment apart from the time of peace, one cannot always generalize from the specific circumstances of war to man's condition as a whole. What war, like naturalism, shows about "human animality" (quoted in Levin 328) belongs to war, and the novels are at pains to fix that boundary.

When occupying the perspective from within war, the novels show the environment as all-determining. Thus, in Ken Saro-Wiwa's *Sozaboy*, war is explained by the oft-repeated tautology "war is war." Why do things happen in war? Because "war is war." We also find this in the classic text of World War I, *All Quiet on the Western Front*, where it is pronounced as self-evident: "After all, war is war" (Remarque 229). This (il)logic reflects naturalism's emphasis on *how* rather than *why* (Zola, *Roman* 61). The *why* of war answers itself ("war is war"), or perhaps it does not, presenting us with the circular logic of a closed environment. The *how* of war, what it means in practice and in the experience of those subsumed by it, however, is infinitely engaging and illuminating.[12]

Because war is proposed as an environment apart in this literature, the novelists make vivid a resistance to war, the intense desire to get outside it, which hints at a higher order of human aspiration and agency. Often, however, demarcating this separation of spheres is elusive. The problematic contiguity (and possible continuity) between spheres becomes apparent when, for example, the African novels portray the guerrilla war and life in the forest as acquiring characteristics of civilian life, thus literally overlapping with it.[13]

It is easy to see why naturalism lends itself to depictions of war. It can portray death and physical suffering exhaustively; it protests against but also documents a determinism that foregrounds the power of the environment (political, social, and biological) over individual will, and it is hyperbolic and angry (as in Festus Iyayi's phrase, "people were the vermin that fed on the vomit").[14] The focus on human suffering in war often forces us to look up close at the injured body and see from the almost hallucinatory perspective of those with horrific injuries. Wounds are examined in minute detail, but so is the activity of injuring, which places the reader in the uncomfortable position of engaging with the physical effort of maiming and killing. Compulsive behavior, another naturalist feature, is also amply evident, especially in the depiction of the victim-perpetrators, those reluctantly drawn into violence, who, after being traumatized, become compulsively violent. More broadly, the depiction of victimization, of individuals whose agency is severely compromised, is common, and adversely affects the ability for these characters to be written into tragic stories and elevated into hero or martyr status. Thus the literature posits a deeply skeptical, and even satiric, attitude toward heroism. Characterizing the endings of naturalist novels more generally, M. H. Abrams explains that the "protagonist of the naturalistic plot, a pawn to multiple compulsions, usually disintegrates, or is wiped out" (Abrams 159). The idea that war turns man into a "pawn," depriving him of agency and humanity, is reflected precisely in the title of Charles Samupindi's novel *Pawns*. The disintegration of the individual, moreover, is often literal as he is blown up, consumed by an injury, or otherwise destroyed by war.

Neil Lazarus cautions us not to conflate African naturalism with European naturalism, because the determinism that makes the characters in naturalist fiction seem to lack agency is not at play in a postcolonial literature that, for Lazarus, clearly functions as protest literature (Lazarus, "Realism" 342).[15] The African works, Lazarus argues, are "not fatalistic" even when they portray settings that are exceedingly bleak; the characters instead display a "resilience that is negative, contentless, illustrative only of sheer resistance," and point to the inevitability of some kind of implosion of the system (342). Their negativity is their agency (342). Lazarus's insistence on the message of protest is consistent with the war literature's aim to show that war is unproductive and wholly destructive. The war novel's resistance seeks to draw out the particular features of war and make the confrontation with its negative nature inescapable. The proliferation of detail that attracts Laqueur's attention characterizes a realism that seeks to uncover historical truth in minute details, often focusing on the body, and has a similar intent: to force a confrontation with the uncomfortable reality of suffering.

A People's History: Historiographic Method and the Novel

The war novel denounces through naturalism, but, as a second gesture, it also affirms by setting out to do a people's history, laying a claim on the nation for the people, grounded in their struggle and suffering. In Africa the war novel provides a vehicle for collective expression by portraying bodily suffering and injury to counteract the distancing effects of pity. By using the term "people's history" I explore what it means to write a literature about ordinary people and place their fate at the center of the nation's concerns. These are broad claims that are intended to delineate the direction of the momentum of this literature and cannot possibly encompass all the details of specific readings. My analysis draws from the national literatures of Kenya, Nigeria, and Zimbabwe to show how the novel of war is an imaginative historical project that engages with the people's suffering in war, hoping that its vision will yield a more just society. It first groups the literature from the 1960s to the mid-1990s in chapters organized by national literature and then discusses in a broader, more comparative way the contemporary war novel.

We can understand the genre of people's history as an attempt to bridge what Mahmood Mamdani has described as the "bifurcated state" inherited from colonialism, which created educated citizens in the cities where ideas of rights, democracy, and nationalism were introduced (citizens who struggled with their *dissensual* experience, as Slaughter has shown in his study of the postcolonial novel of education), and disenfranchised subjects in rural areas where customary law was codified by colonialism.[16] Thus the war novel seeks to advance the citizenship claims of African subjects. This bid is made on behalf of the people as the authors' political gesture toward a more inclusive and just society.

The people's right to the novel, a people's claim to representation in the narrative of the nation as historical agents, is a preliminary step toward breaking down the bifurcation that Mamdani identifies. The novel's effort to embody the voice of the people, to enact the people's "right to the novel," counteracts the distance that reinforces the permanence of the "bifurcated state."

Moreover, the historicity of this genre is entangled in its rights claims. In the works examined here we see that war fictions insist not only on the remembrance of the war itself, but often on an explanation of its causes, as well. They do so usually against considerable pressure to forget the war for the sake of reconciliation, or alternatively against the grain of official histories of the war. Thus war fictions function as critiques of the peace by seeking to revisit the grievances that brought about the war and evaluate how they have been redressed.[17] War fictions' memory of the violence is highly contextual and contingent and articulates political demands that link the "after" to the "before." Moreover, war fictions give the lie to theories of revolutionary violence central to postcolonial theory, which posit peace (often admittedly unattained) as a "tabula rasa" from which new citizens will spring (Fanon 35). Frantz Fanon spoke of the necessarily violent nature of decolonization and of decolonization's invention of new human beings in a nation that at independence "constitutes, from the very first day, the minimum demands of the colonized" (35). His uncompromising language in this phase of his thinking is captured well by Simon Gikandi, who explains Fanon's liberation narrative as "nothing less than the transformation of a 'Real' held prisoner by colonial governmentality into a space of freedom" (Gikandi, "Postcolonial Theory" 172). Writing during the Algerian war, Fanon was positing a horizon to reach for, and by "minimum" he means the full attainment of the goal without compromise. True national sovereignty can only be achieved with a simultaneous cultural decolonization that can shape new political formations (Fanon 35).[18] War fictions might reflect this "writerly attitude" toward decolonization (Gikandi, "Postcolonial Theory" 173), but they also resist the notion that out of violence you can create a "tabula rasa." They point instead to the troubling continuities that link the before and after, as well as the unfinished business of the war itself. A post-conflict situation is overburdened with memory, and making sense of it becomes the project of war fiction.

Because of the postcolonial context of my study, it would seem intuitive to turn to Subaltern Studies as a model for how to define a people's history. However, the connection here proves tenuous. The literature I examine begins in the 1960s and blossoms in the 1970s and early 1980s, then dies back a bit and reemerges in the late 1990s. Subaltern Studies begins in the 1980s with the publication of several key texts, among them Ranajit Guha's *Elementary Aspects of Peasant Insurgency in Colonial India* (1983), Gayatri Spivak's "Can the Subaltern Speak?" (1985), and *Selected Subaltern Studies* (1988), a collection of the journal's essays published by Oxford and edited by Spivak and Guha (Chatterjee 82–84). By this time the literature I am examining is well underway. Moreover, as I show in each of the national literatures, the literary imagination of history anticipates the historiographic projects of academic history.

As an academic discourse Subaltern Studies addressed imperial history and sought to uncover the silenced experience of the subaltern, first by embracing Marxism and then by turning to post-structuralism, which enabled it to parse the language constituting subjectivity and enabling power. Subaltern Studies was always interested in talking back to empire and was widely influential in the global South, especially Latin America (Morris 10). The war novel in Africa, however, is more properly a national phenomenon, and while war as a subject and the novel as a medium situate it in a global literary project, its historical specificity and performative aspects address the national audience rather than imperial discourse. This stems in part from the fact that civil strife is often the focus. Even the earliest examples, Ngũgĩ's novels of Mau Mau, put the emphasis on how armed struggle against the colonizer turns into civil strife. Ngũgĩ has said about *Weep Not, Child*, for example, "I was trying to capture what it felt like to live in a civil war" (Ngũgĩ, "Tolstoy" 51). In post-independence (the moment of the novels' composition) and in remembering the war, it is the problem of internal division that must be solved.

British cultural history also sought to define in the 1980s the methodology of a people's history. Raphael Samuel defined people's history as a historiographic practice in his seminal *People's History and Socialist Theory* (1981), a volume of essays from the History Workshop at Ruskin College, Oxford. In its attempt to define people's history as a global discipline, Samuel's project engaged specifically with the emerging discipline of African history. Moreover, Samuel identified privileged literary discourse as a source of influence on people's history. He named the realist novel as an antecedent to this historiographic method. Each of my three case studies places the war novel against the backdrop of a particular historiographic argument, provoking us to compare the novel and history proper.

To explore how the idea of the people is constructed, I rely on the notion that this literature is "oppositional"—that it bucks the state's ideology of the nation. Samuel notes that "people's history always represents some sort of attempt to broaden the basis of history, to enlarge its subject matter, make use of new raw materials and offer new maps of knowledge. Implicitly, or explicitly, it is oppositional" (Samuel xvi). Writing in 1981, he used "oppositional" to refer in part to people's history's orientation toward academic history and the "professionalized monopolies of knowledge" (xxxii). Located at Ruskin College, "a center for mature working-class students" (Peter Burke, *What Is* 18) and working under the influence of E. P. Thompson and cultural history, Samuel described people's history as "bringing the boundaries of history closer to those of peoples' lives" (Samuel xv). While Samuel recognized that people's history had increasingly focused on the "local in scale, taking as its subject the region, the township or the parish," it had been traditionally concerned with the "broad lines of national development" (xvii). The tension between the particular and the general is also found in the democratizing thrust of people's history, its "democratisation of historical practice," as Samuel called it (414), which, in addition to the increased focus on local subjects, staged "the recovery of subjective experience" and a validation of oral sources (xviii).

People's history was also buttressed by the convergence of cultural history and political history and the emergence of what is called the new cultural history, such as the work of Hunt on the French Revolution and more recently on *The Invention of Human Rights*. The convergence of cultural and political history is also evident in Subaltern Studies. But even as early as Samuel's 1981 volume, the international and Third World potential for this historiographic practice was evident in the prominent place given to African history in Samuel's book.[19] Samuel's receptivity to African history, still a young academic discipline at the time (Feierman 168), helped strengthen its role. People's history drew from African history's difference and its focus on the local and everyday as well as its heavy reliance on oral sources. Thus people's history validated and disseminated practices that were at the methodological core of African history.[20]

In African historiography people's history has come to be identified with the history of democratic struggle. In South Africa writing a people's history was a tool of the anti-apartheid struggle. In a review published in 1990 that reflects on the work of the South African History Workshop at the University of the Witwatersrand in the 1980s, David Anthony defines the workshop's mandate as "a unique task of historical reclamation, placing committed scholarship at the disposal of the social majority of that country. Knowledge of history—of the resistance to oppression before and after the imposition of *apartheid*—has become a weapon in the struggle for a new, more democratic society" (Anthony 411). Anthony pays particular attention to the showcasing of people's history in widely circulated journalistic venues, the most important of which was the column "Learning Nation" in the journal *New Nation* beginning in 1986 (412). Also writing in the late 1980s, Leslie Witz stressed that people's history is distinguished more by the manner in which the historical information is presented (to address the widest possible audience) than by the subject studied. People's history was an important educational tool by which "history is conveyed in such a way that develops questioning, critical awareness and understanding of the past" (Witz 92).

The link between war and people's history is more explicit in the work of Congolese historian Georges Nzongola-Ntalaja. The Democratic Republic of the Congo has generated intense historiographic interest since the fall of Mobutu in the aftermath of the Rwanda genocide.[21] Nzongola-Ntalaja's *The Congo from Leopold to Kabila: A People's History* traces the Congolese democratic struggle. Moreover, Nzongola-Ntalaja writes as a "scholar-activist" proclaiming that he "cannot be dispassionate or neutral in examining the political history of [his] country" (Nzongola-Ntalaja vii). This disavowal of distance and Nzongola-Ntalaja's experience as both participant in the democratic struggle and its historian legitimates his claim to speak on behalf of the people. His argument that the Congolese democracy movement has failed so far because of the class interests of its leaders highlights the importance of class analysis in a people's history (253). It also echoes Howard Zinn, whose *A People's History of the United*

States: 1492 to the Present emphasizes social movements because they showcase the people's struggle for justice against their national elites (Foner 6).

The novel has had a considerable influence on the methodology of people's history. In the nineteenth century, people's history was synonymous with national history. Much recent scholarship on the British novel, for example, has focused on how the novel helped constitute the idea of the nation.[22] Speaking more broadly of the European novel, Franco Moretti has called it the "symbolic form of the nation-state" (Moretti, *Atlas* 20). Samuel recognized that the nineteenth-century realist novel helped create the nation by meticulously describing the people (Samuel xix). In Africa we find a similar correlation of nation and novel in the ethnographic project of the novel, which played a role in answering back to the colonizer and defining the project of national literatures.[23] At the same time, however, one can also speak of an uncoupling of the people and the nation in the novel, made manifest in the African novel with its divided imaginaries of the city and the village, of modernity and tradition. This fragmentation brings to the fore the challenges of looking within.

Looking Within and National Allegory

As a people's history the war novel invites us to reconsider the literary history of the postcolonial novel in Africa and pay more attention to the form's specifically African address. Both nation and novel are colonial inheritances that point to the "exogenous origins of modernity" (Julien 670).[24] The main arc of this history, of the indigenization of external influence, has been captured by what Eileen Julien calls the "extroverted" novel, written while its authors are glancing over their shoulders at their Western readers and "characterized above all by its intertextuality with hegemonic or global discourses and its appeal across borders" (681). Heeding Julien's call, scholars have sought to break down this monolithic construction of the African novel, whose main preoccupation is the struggle with a modernity that is perceived as having occurred elsewhere first (670). In the "extroverted" novels, many of which have become canonical texts, protagonists who fail to integrate tradition and modernity into a "hybrid identity" suffer dire consequences (671). Although the war novel has been part of the development of the African novel from the novel's inception in the colonial period,[25] it has occupied a space apart and provokes us to rethink the relation between the nation and the novel.

Following Julien's desire to dismantle a monolithic approach to the "African" novel that only values its mode of writing back to empire, I propose to examine the war novel as Africa's introverted genre: it addresses a national audience, takes most often the rural poor as its subject, and, although it records violence that shakes the nation to its core, also recommits to the nation with less skepticism than the "extroverted" novel in which a deep malaise with both the West and Africa lingers.[26] Although it too is indebted to borrowed forms, the war novel is much less anxious about being considered derivative or secondary ("ornamental," in Julien's words) (673) and seems to take its modernity for granted. The point is not to argue for a greater authenticity of the war novel, but rather to illustrate the reach of the novel as a discourse that captures important cultural moments without necessarily referring them to the outside. Often published locally, the war novel looks within and addresses domestic audiences about a national crisis, the impact of conflict on the society, and its aftermath. Its intertextuality with other African novels, the way it self-consciously identifies its own tradition of writing, further announces its introversion. Whereas Julien's delineation of an extroverted literature may seem too tidy and underplays the influence of indigenous narrative forms on the African novel, it is a useful characterization for examining a mode of reception that has shaped the perceptions about canonical works.

Without focusing on war as a subject, Mwangi delineates a similar distinction between the canonized texts of African literature that take up as their subject anti-colonial themes and a broader, more popular literature that is created to meet the demands of domestic readerships and thus is addressed internally to national audiences. Such popular books published by African publishing houses, Mwangi notes, focused on "mundane issues such as prostitution, crime, and drunkenness" (Evan Mwangi 35). To any reader of naturalist fiction "prostitution, crime, and drunkenness" is a familiar list! Increasing literacy in the 1970s created a boom of local publishing (36) and the proliferation of such popular texts as I just mentioned alongside "educational novels tackling political and cultural themes" (26). The war novel straddles these two domains of domestically published literature, some of it catering to popular tastes and some presenting war more moralistically to school audiences. While there are exceptions (is *Sozaboy* an introverted novel, for example?), even the few war novels that have passed into the canonical literature and are placed alongside the texts with "heavily anticolonial themes" (35) on close examination reveal ties to this model of the introverted literature. Mwangi's reading, for example, of the first edition of Ngũgĩ's *Grain of Wheat* (1967) against the revised and now standard (and canonical) edition from 1986 exposes the links between the earlier text and the naturalist genre of more popular Mau Mau novels, edited out of the revised text.

Mwangi characterizes Ngũgĩ's revisions as "gendered" (Evan Mwangi 154). He highlights Ngũgĩ's removal in the revised text of the scene where Koinandu (Koina in the later version) participates in a gang rape of Dr. Lynd as well as his removal of such language anticipating the attack, where Koinandu says, "Man, I'll break her in. I'll swim in that hole" (quoted, 154–55). This is explained in the novel as vengeance for the suffering that Koinandu has experienced under colonial rule (155). Vengeance and sexual violence, and the guilt and dehumanization that they bring, belong thematically in the naturalistic universe in which compulsive, self-destructive behavior prevails. Thus, although *Grain of Wheat* has been read as modernist in its aesthetics (Gikandi, *Ngũgĩ* 106), it has ties to the naturalist novel of war and the more popular literature. Mwangi clarifies the politics of Ngũgĩ's revisions: "The revisions tend to reflect nationalistic concerns, and little attention is paid to the splintering differences within the nation and in the settler community" (158). Mwangi's insight further confirms how closely aligned Ngũgĩ's original text was to the naturalistic novel of Mau Mau, where, as I will show in greater detail in Chapter 1, the divisions within the nation are foregrounded. The novel of war in Africa for the most part comes back repeatedly to the problem of the fracturing of resistance movements. War feeds onto itself and turns even just causes into self-consuming, violent destruction. The solution lies in moving beyond war and giving the people political purchase in the nation.

The internal focus of this literature looks to identify how the disjunction between ideas of the nation and the people comes to be—a disjunction reflected in the dynamics of war itself, especially civil war. We can usefully turn to Giorgio Agamben here, who discusses the term "ordinary people" by showing how referring to the people as the nation always masks the existence of people who are left out of the nation (Agamben, *Homo Sacer* 176):

> It is as if what we call "people" were in reality not a unitary subject but a dialectical oscillation between two opposite poles: on the one hand, the set of the People as a whole political body, and on the other, the subset of the people as a fragmentary multiplicity of needy and excluded bodies; or again, on the one hand, an inclusion that claims to be total, and on the other, an exclusion that is clearly hopeless; at one extreme, the total state of integrated and sovereign citizens, and at the other, the preserve—

> court of miracles or camp—of the wretched, the oppressed, and the defeated. (177)

"People" signifies at once inclusion and exclusion and becomes the core term that captures the ever-present civil strife running as an undercurrent in the nation state.[27] The "incessant civil war" implied by the term "people," Agamben asserts, is also that which paradoxically "constitutes it [the people] more securely than any other identity" (178). For Agamben this is not an agonistic relationship in the sense of class struggle as much as an inherent feature of the people as such—not the people opposed to the more privileged, but the people in flux, trying to attain political status.[28] When this civil war comes to an end, the category "people" will disappear, because those who constitute it will no longer be the people, a "set" suspended between bare life and political life (178).

The idea of a people divided against itself finds its historical form in Mamdani's analysis, which shows how colonialism, as I noted earlier, created two synchronous but distinct political realms, one for citizens and one for subjects. In this "bifurcated state" a sphere of civil society was developed in urban centers where ideas of rights, democracy, and nationalism were introduced for the *colons*, the Western educated. Alongside it colonialism codified and rigidified a realm of customary law in rural areas it governed through indirect rule, which resulted in a "mediated-decentralized-despotism" (Mamdani, *Citizen* 16–17). Mamdani, moreover, asserts that in independence African states carried over this bifurcated structure, part of "the inherited impediments to democratization" (25). The "bifurcated state" created competing nationalisms: the nation as defined in the struggle of colonized against colonizer was different from the nation of another type of anti-colonial struggle—that of peasants in revolt against civil society, best analyzed by Fanon (Mamdani, "Black Man's Burden"). If during colonialism the local state came to be identified with the tribe and was legitimized through custom (defined by the native authorities), then resistance to its despotism took the form of civil war within the tribe (Mamdani, *Citizen* 183). According to Mamdani, the potential for this type of violence is constitutive of the colonial order of customary law. Tribalism, even "tribalism as revolt," contained the potential for its own division. "Local populations," Mamdani explains:

> were usually multiethnic and at times multireligious. Ethnicity, and at times religion, was reproduced as a problem inside every peasant movement. This is why it is not enough simply to separate tribal power organized from above from tribal revolt waged from below so that we may

> denounce the former and embrace the latter. The revolt from below needs to be problematized, for it carries the seeds of its own fragmentation and possible self-destruction. (24)

Mamdani's analysis pivots on his ability to identify fissures and discontinuities that are continuously manifesting under the pressure of the urban/rural divide fundamental to the colonial state. At the same time, he reminds us that "every movement against decentralized despotism bore the institutional imprint of that mode of rule. Every movement of resistance was shaped by the very structure of power against which it rebelled" (24).

Resistance to colonialism, and especially to its culturally denigrating policies, is portrayed in the postcolonial novel as the desired outcome of a developing civil society. After independence the outcry against authoritarianism and state violence captured the discontent of an educated middle class, which felt the promises of civil society had been betrayed. This was expressed most dramatically in the large number of anti-dictatorship novels, such as the works of Sony Labou Tansi or Nuruddin Farah's *Variations on the Theme of an African Dictatorship* trilogy. On the other hand, novels that focused on gender-identity historicized the changing notions of the individual (Andrade, *Nation* 118). Even when they portrayed traditional settings, these novels were a means for the educated to explore the parameters of their new identities in transition to an expanding civil society. Whereas Mamdani juxtaposes "citizen and subject" as synchronous and unequal historical entities, the novel as a form treats these distinctions more ideologically than historically, projecting a desired path from subject to citizen.[29] The novel of education, such as Tsitsi Dangarembga's *Nervous Conditions*, illustrates this point very well: Tambu's education transforms her from a peasant into an urban, educated professional, while all along Zimbabwe's resistance war against white rule is raging.[30] Dangarembga has been criticized for not bringing the context of the armed struggle to bear on her novel, but her omission is part of the point I want to make: that there is a fundamental discontinuity between the canon of the African novel and the novel of war.[31]

By questioning the relation between the novel and the nation and shifting attention to the people as an entity that does not coincide with the nation, the war novel also challenges our thinking on national allegory, which is not surprising, since national allegory is closely linked to the extroverted literature and its paradigmatic form, the *Bildungsroman*. In his seminal essay on Third World fiction, Fredric Jameson famously made two sweeping statements. First, he asserted that "All third-world texts are necessarily . . . allegorical, and in a very specific way: they are to be read as what I will call national allegories, even when, or perhaps I should say, particularly when their forms develop out of predominantly western machineries of representation, such as the novel" (Jameson, "Third-World Literature" 69). Second, he argued that in Third World texts, "*the story of the private individual destiny is always an allegory of the embattled situation of the public third-world culture and society*" (69, italics in original). Thus Jameson mapped the individual onto the communal very directly in what many of his detractors found a mechanical and reductive gesture. The assumptions that the nation as an idea encompasses all, that it coheres and maps the relations among its members in a way that holds, are problematic for my discussion. If there is a fissure between the idea of the nation and the people, then this mapping does not hold.

I want to draw attention first to a different aspect of Jameson's argument, however. Jameson intuits a kind of introversion in the literature he sweepingly labels "third-world literature." Third World literature, he tells us, invariably addresses a reader for whom the text "has a freshness of information and a social interest that we cannot share." In a Third World text readers of the academy become aware of their "own non-coincidence with that Other reader" (66). This difference places us (meaning Jameson's projected reader) on the outside looking in as spectators in a drama of storytelling and reception. It also hobbles us with a difficulty of attention, as it is not always clear to us what is important. To borrow Boltanski's term, the reader as "introspector" has trouble making the story he is reading his own. Jameson is positing a typical First World reader, however, and not an ideal reader. As Lazarus argues in his defense of Jameson, the ideal reader is the one who, like Jameson, awakens to the challenge posited by this literature and its provocation that he see himself in a new light, "from the outside" (Lazarus, "Fredric Jameson" 55; Jameson, "Third-World Literature" 68).

According to Jameson, all Third World literature "necessarily" takes the form of national allegory and reflects the absence of a divide between the public, political sphere and the private, libidinal sphere typical in Western literature. Critics have grappled in different ways with Jameson's thesis, questioning whether allegory is an imposition on this literature or organic to it. Is allegory a heavy-handed interpretation by an overconfident reader who must compensate for his newfound unease by regulating the meaning of this literature through a familiar paradigm, or is it a complex representational strategy that captures something important about the ambition of Third World writers to intervene aesthetically in the wider project of understanding the Third World experience? Most of Jameson's defenders take the latter position and try to sensitize us to the complexity of allegory against the grain of our aesthetic prejudices.[32]

The question that interests me here, however, is different and addresses allegory as the reading practice of those readers for whom this literature has immediacy and is compelling—readers who are affiliated with the nations from which my case studies are drawn. By positing, albeit reductively, distinct First World and Third World readerships, Jameson sketches at a distance the dynamic of an introverted literature. Along these lines Lazarus claims that Jameson shows how in the denigrating estimation of Third World texts as derivative, the Western canon functions as "a false universal" because, in fact, it is not the point of reference of these texts (Lazarus, "Fredric Jameson" 56). (Here Lazarus and Julien are in perfect sync.) "National allegory" is an organic term arising out of the literature, according to Lazarus, and if Jameson had not named it, we would have had to "invent it," as "these writings seem to *require* such a hypothesis" (58). Lazarus's emphasis, moreover, falls correctly on reading practice rather than on the essential nature of these texts.

The sense that somewhere in Jameson's essay lurks the model of an introverted literature surfaces in both critics and supporters of Jameson. Thus Slaughter faults Jameson for focusing too exclusively on the metropolis-periphery axis of First and Third worlds. Instead, Slaughter urges us to consider what a similar axis might mean for particular national contexts internally, which in Slaughter's own case study is Nairobi versus rural Kenya. From here we must take a different step to expand the context by looking at the global ties that connect the African metropolis to countries in Asia and elsewhere outside the metropolitan West (Slaughter, "Master Plans" 46–47). Insofar as Jameson focuses myopically on a linear axis between the Third World taken holistically as an undifferentiated space and the West, his allegory reflects the West's desire for mastery: "this correspondence is one of interested desire of the West for the rest" (47). Slaughter, however, does not dismiss the importance of allegory as such. He invites us to think about different allegories, authorized by a differentiated space called "Third World."

Andrade's feminist reading of African literature, on the other hand, looks to national allegory for a way to make palpable the political in African women's fiction, a body of literature that has been read persistently as outside national politics (Andrade, *Nation* 21). Andrade is empowered by Jameson's assertion that Third World literature is "always" and "necessarily" an allegory of the nation: "He saves the personal for the political by reading the private (or personal) as a necessary and exclusive allegory of the public" (26). Her language of rescue reflects the degree to which Jameson gives her license to show how women writers, like their male counterparts, "deploy one fiction to expose another" (34). The binary of novels by men and novels by women hints at yet another context for an introverted literature in which the female writers are responding to male African writers rather than the "false universal" of the Western canon. As we shall see, this is certainly true in the war novels of women writers who seem to be self-consciously shaping a literary tradition of female war fiction.

What does national allegory, the theory that according to Lazarus seems inevitable while according to Slaughter is too meddling and heavy-handed, mean specifically for the novel of war? National allegory in the war novel is invariably ironic, pointing to a failure of coherence and not to the potentiality for a radically alternative totality that Jameson's defenders wish to awaken us to. If the nation as political aspiration often leads to violent conflict, its ideology might be, in fact, *always* and *necessarily* suspect. The author of the war novel is not observing those suffocating in Lu Xun's allegorical "iron house" (Jameson, "Third-World Literature" 75), but writing from within the house. Thus the author is more like one of the sleepers who has awoken to find himself suffocating in that house with no escape.[33] The inevitability of this reality, its inescapable nature, defines war and generates the naturalistic aesthetic and its intimate details of suffering. This does not necessarily preclude allegory (arguably it makes it more urgent), but it makes it less convincing and hence ironic.

In their categorical rejection of war as a means to achieve political ends, the novels point to an outside, or beyond, of war, something beyond the all-determining environment rendered through naturalism. This outside, intimated while the author conveys the sense of being trapped inside, is frequently alluded to through allegory. However, telling one story through another, the work of allegory, is exposed as impossible or deeply inadequate when it addresses the events of war. When allegory is blocked in the war narrative, it becomes the occasion to draw the focus back to the literal as the plane on which it is most urgent to comprehend war. Allegory is necessary, however, when the war novel moves beyond war to sketch out reconciliation. In novels where some kind of reconciliation after the war is suggested, ideas of the nation play a crucial role. The outside of war is posited from within the national conversation, emanating from the account of war, reclaimed as national history.[34]

The national allegory of the Third World text is authorized from within and transposes one story onto another in order to disrupt. If one reads along the grain of Jameson's argument, it is clear that complex allegorical readings expose discontinuities and do not set up simple one-to-one transpositions (73). The war literature that is the subject of my study similarly assumes that there is no private/public divide. Indeed, the absence of this divide is constitutive of the condition of war. There is no "from without" except if one emerges into an aftermath, which, conditioned by trauma, extends the experience of the war, making it difficult to establish a retrospective gesture from beyond the war's end. War, moreover, encroaches into the space of ordinary life, leaving us with little sense of a distinct war front.

Although I am describing the war novel in broad strokes, not all war novels do the same things, nor do they represent a single type of conflict. The organization of the study as a literary history reveals shifts over time as well as competing contemporaneous practices of representation. At the core, however, we find repeatedly the same problematic varying in degree, which arises from the literature's introversion, its chief characteristic.

Four Motifs

Before I elaborate on the specifics of each of the three case studies that comprise the core of this project, I want to highlight four motifs whose repetition across national literatures and languages heightens the impression that the war novel forms a distinct literary tradition in Africa. I have named these motifs as follows: the "song of my country"; the male warrior as war personified; the ordeal in the forest; and the eternal landscape. These motifs capture something about the meaning of war and the ways in which we seek to make sense of it. Through their repetition they disrupt the novels' insistence on the literal and gesture toward allegory, suggesting momentarily how the literature's realistically rendered detail transposes its particularity onto a narrative of resistance and aspiration, the outside of war.

The paradigmatic instance of the "song of my country" can be found in Assia Djebar's early novel of the Algerian war, *Les Enfants du nouveau monde* (1962). The significance of this motif is that it foregrounds the scene of torture as a battlefield, a place of a public agon (instead of pathos hidden out of view), where there are now multiple participants and witnesses. Thus it endows torture with the theatricality of the humanitarian spectacle of suffering while also opening up the possibility for an agonistic kind of solidarity with the victim. In Djebar's novel the prison is a building with porous walls where the integrity of the torture chamber as a sealed-off space is compromised. The voice of the nation is discovered here.

Sitting in her prison cell, Salima, a young teacher, hears the screams of a torture victim in an adjacent cell. She cannot see him, nor can she guess his identity. Her first reaction is to try to block out the sound: "She covers her ears, and in a gesture recovered from childhood she begins to pray for the first time" (Djebar 112). Her self-protective gesture reveals that she understands her subjection to the screams of a victim of torture to be part of the terror inflicted on her. Yet after a while she changes her attitude and decides to listen carefully to the screams and not to block them out. Through this effort she forms a profound identification with the cries of pain:

> Why run away from it? One should listen! She is seized by a wild exultation. "This is the song of my country, this is the song of the future," she whispers, an upright silhouette in the center of the empty cell, quivering with zeal and joy. (Djebar 113)

When the voice falls silent, she becomes anxious, and when it starts up again, she listens once more:

> Jerky, brief groans at first, which then swell anew into a single endless scream, immense, and Salima rides it with all her willpower because it seems to her that at the end it will open a door into the heavens. Blue landscapes she sees, instead of the cell's gray wall, the noontime sun that blinds you, or the evening sun that reconciles, faces of smiling cherubs . . . of children she recognizes, of Suzanne walking . . . of the man. "Who is he?" she wonders, shivering again, yet from the first moment on transported well beyond compassion. (Djebar 113)

Salima listens not out of an imperative to bear witness to this man's suffering, but because of the expansive consciousness she gains through the experience. Salima was "transported well beyond compassion" to a vision of Algeria as place ("blue landscapes," "sun that blinds you") and people, specifically the children of the future, her students, in whose name the struggle goes on. Powerless to intervene and change the course of the torture, she seeks to learn from the sounds of torture, to intuit from them a vision, or conviction, about the nation.

In the novelistic account of torture in war, the victim's body becomes the site of war. In the near absence of scenes from the battlefield in this literature (indeed what is the battlefield emerges as a key question), torture is often the surrogate site for war. Synecdochically, therefore, torture is a moment when the fate of the individual victim becomes identified most closely with the collective story of the nation. In fictional form the narrative of torture transforms individual suffering into a narrative of nation from the perspective of resistance to the colonial or state order. In the novels of anti-colonial wars the depiction of torture is emblematic of the wrongful violence of the colonizer. The prevalence of torture, especially in the novels of the Mau Mau, should not be surprising, as the techniques of torture in common usage today are derived from the "policing and military operations in French and British colonies" (Rejali 4).[35]

The second motif, the "male warrior as war personified," finds its prototype in Thomas Mofolo's *Chaka*. This most influential text, which was completed in 1910, revised in the early1920s, published in Sesotho in 1925, and translated into English and French in 1931, stresses the transformational power of violence and its capacity to radically reinvent identity. Mofolo's great achievement is to have shown how war is human (war personified) and that we cannot disclaim it, but must understand it historically. As Lazarus has pointed out, Mofolo seeks to "retrieve Southern African history and culture from the depredations of colonial historiography." Without excusing Chaka for his violence, he portrays him as an "intelligible if still exceptional individual . . . render(ing) his actions meaningful against a background of lived culture" (Lazarus, *Postcolonial Unconscious* 116).

A mission-educated African, Mofolo wrote the novel at a time of important transition in South Africa's complex and multifaceted national emergence. The year 1910 marks the establishment of the Union of South Africa and the beginning of the "segregation era" that lasted till 1948, when the National Party was elected to power and imposed apartheid rule. Mofolo created an enduring, if often misread, portrait of a proto-nationalist African figure. Chaka encapsulates the destructiveness of war in which Africans and Europeans are complicit. The witch doctor Isanusi functions as an allegorical figure for British treachery in South Africa. Isanusi arrives from a distant place. His origins and real name are unknown, making the magic he brings appear all the more powerful. He facilitates Chaka's rise with his drugs ("vaccinations," according to Kunene's translation) and political and military guidance. At the end of the novel, however, he confronts Chaka and demands his due, in effect robbing Chaka of the kingdom he created. One can decipher here a historical argument about the *mfecane*, or scattering, the wars that profoundly disrupted Southern Africa in the early nineteenth century and for which Chaka is usually held responsible. The *mfecane* are shown in the novel to have been instigated by the meddling of a foreign power, which exploited Chaka's sense of injustice and desire for redress in order to provoke a war that would increase its imperial influence. Isanusi's allegorical meaning as a symbol of British treachery does not exonerate Chaka of responsibility for his actions. At each turn Mofolo depicts Chaka struggling with his conscience, yet choosing to follow the path of power and brutality.[36] Not so much a moralizing religious portrayal of individual conscience, Mofolo's depiction of Chaka is rather an exploration of political choices that point repeatedly to the synergy between Chaka and Isanusi and thus the entangled histories of Africans and Europeans in South Africa.

As Chaka descends into greater depravity, however, he is transformed into war personified, both in his appearance and deeds. When Chaka first emerged as his people's leader, they saw in him "a beautiful young man with piercing eyes, with a powerful arm, ready to lift up the spear and the shield" (85). His lover "saw in him the perfection of manhood" (Mofolo 86). As he becomes more deeply implicated in war violence under Isanusi's guidance, "Chaka underwent a frightful change both in his external appearance and in his inner being, in his very heart; and so did his aims and his deeds." He loses the "last spark of humanity" (127). Following Isanusi's injunction to "let your spear be your hoe," Chaka becomes addicted to war, succumbing to compulsive violence.[37] When Chaka is at the zenith of his power and no longer needs to go on the battlefield himself, he lusts for bloodshed and turns against his own people: "he longed to see people dying by his own hand. He craved to witness death. Whenever he did not see that spectacle he became truly sick, and he desired that as his armies were shedding blood in battle, his right arm should remain steeped in gore here at home" (155). This rhetoric of denunciation highlights the similarity between Chaka and characters from more recent works, such as Emmanuel Dongala's Johnny and Nuruddin Farah's Caloosha (discussed later in Chapter 4), both of whom come to embody in their grotesque and eccentric physical appearance the transformational power of war.

Chaka's first encounter with Isanusi happens while Chaka is wandering in the wilderness, grieving his orphan status. His father has cast him out, depriving him of his position as a successor to the chiefdom, and even of his humanity: "a homeless wanderer . . . he is not a human being, but a hare hunted by the hounds" (Mofolo 49). This sojourn in the wilderness sets in motion the third motif, the "ordeal in the forest," a phrase borrowed from the title of Godwin Wachira's novel of the Mau Mau (discussed in Chapter 1). War fictions often send their protagonists on a sojourn in the wilderness where, literally lost, they become spiritually unmoored and improvise a changed orientation to war. This usually takes the form of a deepened engagement with war whereby they are no longer satisfied to let war happen to them, but want a role in its outcome. In Chaka's case this means adopting Isanusi's aims to have Chaka restored to his rightful throne and expand his kingdom. From being cast out, Chaka learned that "here on earth people live by might only and not by right" (35). Suffering a social wrong led him down the path to war. As we will see, the motif of the "ordeal in the forest" does not necessarily entail the moral degeneration of the character, but it does invariably constitute a passage through which war's regressive force reveals itself in terms that make it impossible to deny. We can call this a passage to the real now seen as profoundly other than ordinary life.

Finally, the fourth motif, the "landscape of eternity," can be found in exemplary form in Boubacar Boris Diop's novel of the Rwanda genocide, *Murambi*, and then read backward into the earlier texts. The landscape of eternity is in some senses a cliché allusion to the allegory of Africa as mother. It recurs in the war fiction with the specific purpose of inspiring healing by providing a counterweight to the devastation of war. Calling up the image of a pristine landscape that stands outside of history evokes a sense of identity that seems to transcend the war's destruction.

In his novel Diop evokes a deeper past and an almost mythical landscape to open up a discursive space within which the genocide can be examined objectively. Renewing a sense of one's attachment to place without ethnic overtones is key to Diop's hope for the future. One of the few symbols of the nation left untainted and capable of reclamation after the all-encompassing conflict of the genocide is the landscape. Although the genocide generated an iconography of Rwanda as a landscape littered with the dead and maimed such as we have already encountered in Dunant's description of the aftermath of Solferino, a sense of Rwanda as place—its particular, mountainous landscape—endures and is available to recall as what Diop calls the "eternal" (Diop 179).

In the war fiction that I examine in this study, landscape endures. It repeatedly becomes a symbol of the nation (the "blue landscapes" of Salima's vision) that can reconnect a devastated population to an idea of the nation that seems to transcend the historical vicissitudes of the moment. If ideas of the nation have always depended on mythical ideas about its antiquity, the landscape fosters this sense of continuity and endows it with particularity. A recognizable landscape is bestowed with the capacity to encompass the people. This mystical relation of landscape to human community can become a source of renewal at a time of despair. Situated in this evocative landscape, safe in its embrace, the writer can propose an examination of the recent history of violence. He can then appeal to reason and purpose in remembering the genocide.

In *Murambi* the wise figure, Siméon, is called "a real novelist . . . a storyteller of the eternal," because he holds onto both the historical and the mythical Rwanda (Diop 179). Siméon successfully inspires his nephew, Cornelius, to a renewed sense of belonging in Rwanda by communicating to him the necessity of a double gesture: a commitment to the truth of the genocide ("to call a monster by its name" [179]) and an investment in the future of Rwanda by committing to the work needed to bring about "the resurrection of the living" (181). Cornelius is reminded that Siméon had given him as a child the "scene . . . which had nourished his years of exile" (141). On a trip to Lake Mohazi twenty-nine years earlier, Cornelius had been captivated by a perfect pastoral scene and the "pure sound" of a boy shepherd playing his flute (140). Siméon had described the mountain and the lake to the child Cornelius as the birthplace of Rwanda: "This is where Rwanda was born" (140). Cornelius recalls this postcard landscape replete with smells and sounds to evoke his own coming to consciousness of the place called Rwanda and its power to renew itself through memory so many years later and after such devastation (140).

These motifs—the "song of my country," the male warrior as war personified, the ordeal in the forest, the eternal landscape—set in motion allegories to break up the deterministic drive to self-destruction brought about by war. Their recurrence helps delineate this literature, spanning from the 1960s to the present, as a tradition that has something important to teach us about the narration of war. The three case studies that form the main body of my project (the novels of Mau Mau, the Nigerian Civil War, and Zimbabwe's liberation wars) represent an array of high and low genres that resonates across the anglophone tradition so that we find echoes of Kenyan Charles Mangua's *A Tail in the Mouth* (1972) in *Sozaboy* (1985), a novel of the Nigerian civil war, for example, and echoes of *Chaka* in Farah's *Links* (2004). Chapter 4 examines the contemporary war novel with material from Nigeria as well as other literatures, most notably Nuruddin Farah's *Past Imperfect* trilogy and examples from the extensive child-soldier genre.[38]

In Chapter 1, "'No Innocents and No Onlookers': The Uses of the Past in the Novels of Mau Mau," I use Fanon's phrase, which refers to everyone's complicity in history's messiness, to reflect on Kenya's experience of a war on two fronts: the guerrilla war in the forest and the civilian war of razed villages and detention centers. I focus on the tension between the desire for reconciliation and the task of historical narration. These competing aims divide the literature into distinct aesthetic registers of modernist irony, sentimental reconciliation, and naturalist anger. I focus on the narrative reclamation of the peasant-turned–guerrilla fighter not for national myth-making, but for history. The recent histories by Caroline Elkins and David Anderson have reignited the debates about Kenya's Emergency, contributing significant new archival research. However, especially in the case of Elkins's study, with its focus on detention and torture, much of the history was already in Ngũgĩ wa Thiong'o's early novels. The novelty of Elkins's study is less palpable to readers of the Kenyan novel, inviting us to think critically about the relationship of the novel to an emerging genre of human rights history.[39]

Moreover, Ngũgĩ's *Weep Not, Child* (1964) and *A Grain of Wheat* (1967) offer a rich ethical and psychological exploration of torture within the context of a national struggle. Whereas Ngũgĩ focused mostly on the experience of civilians, many novelists looked at the fighters in the forest. I examine four such novels: *Ordeal in the Forest* (1968); *Carcase for Hounds* (1974); *Taste of Death* (1975); and *Dedan Kimathi: The Real Story* (1990). Although these novels pay less attention than Ngũgĩ does to the experience of civilians, they share with Ngũgĩ the concern with leadership and the problem of responsibility. Ngũgĩ asks Kenyans to take responsibility for their history as the only way forward. But, unlike Ngũgĩ's novels and their modernist irony, these works shuttle between naturalism and sentimentalism. They share with the war novel more broadly the tension between the determinism of naturalism and a hopefulness that is manifested in a kind of sentimentality that belies the "human animality" of naturalism, pulling the dehumanized fighter back to the community.

In Chapter 2, "Toward a People's History: The Novels of the Nigerian Civil War," I develop in greater detail the book's thesis that the war novel enacts a people's history. The literature on the Nigerian Civil War is large (upwards of twenty-nine novels) and I trace through key texts an evolving conception of the people that ends with Chimamanda Ngozi Adichie's revisionist account of the war in *Half of a Yellow Sun* (2006), discussed in Chapter 4. At the end of her novel Adichie places an educated peasant in the role of people's historian. Ugwu's sympathetic attitude toward the intellectual middle class suggests the potential for a more inclusive history, one that reconciles the social cleavages entrenched by colonialism and aggravated by civil war. Adichie's idealism reclaims some of the positive momentum of decolonization, despite the tragedy of the war. My reservations about how well Adichie fulfills her goal are developed in the context of the varied corpus of the civil war novels that came before and that are the main focus of Chapter 2. Here I look at the conception of the people in the works of Chinua Achebe, Flora Nwapa, Cyprian Ekwensi, Eddie Iroh, Wole Soyinka, Festus Iyayi, Ken Saro-Wiwa, and Buchi Emecheta. These novels explore the ways in which the war makes the fate of the people newly visible to a class whose modernization has distanced it from the everyday life of the majority. The novels, furthermore, propose a revised national politics.

Chapter 3, "'Wondering Who the Heroes Were': Zimbabwe's Novels of Atrocity," examines the war literature of Zimbabwe. The liberation war of 1966–1980 produced an extensive war literature that is usually described as "heroic," or as a "literature of cultural affirmation" (Msiska 92–93). Yet alongside these heroic narratives we also find a number of anti-heroic narratives that engage with the problem of atrocity and the guilt of former combatants, key among which are the works of Alexander Kanengoni, Chenjerai Hove, Shimmer Chinodya, and Yvonne Vera. These novels dissent from the official history promoted by Robert Mugabe's regime and provide a critical space for a people's history. Hove and Vera evoke the legend of Nehanda in an affirming way, but then redirect it to critique rather than to uphold the appropriation of the narrative of liberation by Mugabe. Chinodya is most interested in the theme of atrocity and the responsibility to be borne for it. Telling an unidealized history of the guerrilla war is a step toward the elusive goal of successful reintegration of the fighters into civil society.

My claim that the war novel presents us with an introverted genre might seem surprising to readers of recent African fiction. Since approximately the mid-1990s there has been an explosion of African war fiction published by both established and emergent writers, many of whom live and write in the West.[40] This contemporary literature is the subject of Chapter 4, where I begin by placing the child-soldier novels that became popular at this time in the context of their literary antecedents. I contrast the child-soldier novels to Adichie's *Half of a Yellow Sun*, which I read both as a response to the older novels of Biafra and as a revision of the form of the domestic novel. Last I turn to Nuruddin Farah's *Past Imperfect* trilogy, which treats the theme of returning emigrés to war-torn Somalia to bring to the fore the problem of environment once again.

The politics of pity are restaged in the contemporary literature, bringing the spectatorship of suffering closer and complicating the problem of responsibility. Adichie and Farah set in motion a historical narration that insists on its legibility in its own terms. Achille Mbembe has argued that most discourse about Africa falls into orientalizing that "flows from there being hardly ever any discourse about Africa for itself. In the very principle of its constitution, in its language, and in its finalities, narrative about Africa is always pretext for a comment about something else, some other place, some other people" (Mbembe 3). Writers in Africa have been dissenting figures historically, often persecuted by the state (Evan Mwangi 43). Writing about East Africa, Simon Gikandi notes that "novels of disillusionment . . . were an important mark of the parting of ideological paths between writers and nationalist politicians" (Gikandi, "Introduction" 16). The war novels are often grouped with the "novels of disillusionment." The intellectual is not only alienated from the political establishment; he is also viewed as distanced from the people because of the cultural and economic gap created by education and literacy. The intellectual's marginalization often becomes literal in the experience of exile.

As I have argued, in the novel of war, a strong sense of obligation to tell a history from below overwhelms and breaks down the citizen's sense of being disconnected from the people. Naturalism attempts an aesthetic solution to this problem of bridging the gap between high and low.[41] The world stage on which the contemporary African novel is received presents an opportunity to intervene and shape politics on a larger scale, yet war as a topic presents a danger of renewing the association between Africa and anomie.

The war novels construct power in politically complex ways. Lazarus has described the disciplinary difference between postcolonial studies with its "*culturalist* emphasis" and the social sciences ("sociology or political economy or development studies") by drawing a contrast between a project of answering back to empire and a project focused inward on Third World societies. This inward-looking project performs "the recovery and adequate theorisation of popular consciousness and popular practice" and thus has a focus on "the people" or "the disenfranchised sectors of society—actually a majority and typically an *overwhelming* majority of the population" (Lazarus, "Representation and Terror" 84–85). This distinction repeats the contrast between an extroverted cultural project and the introverted tradition of the war novel. War fictions seek to intervene in the discussion about popular consciousness rather than answer back to empire. There is a danger here that in following Lazarus's mapping one might be, as Mbembe warns, duplicating the "persistent dichotomy between the objectivity of structures and the subjectivity of representations—a distinction allowing all that is cultural and symbolic to be put on one side, all that is economic and material to be put on the other" (Mbembe 6). But the goal is to arrive at the point where the representations of experience engage with the structures and intervene within them.

Mbembe describes the postcolony as a composite space of different temporalities that are entangled with each other: "As an age, the postcolony encloses multiple *durées* made up of discontinuities, reversals, inertias, and swings that overlay [*sic*] one another, interpenetrate one another, and envelope [*sic*] one another: an entanglement" (14). As a theorist he proposes a kind of naturalism: to observe and describe this complex of temporalities for what they tell us rather than passing them through a sifter that enables us to separate the strand of progress from the strand of superstition, for example. The postcolony as an encompassing environment, its web of historical complexity mapped out as multiple simultaneities, helps theorize the reality depicted in the war fiction. It explains why, although popular, much of this war fiction has remained outside a canon that has favored texts that are more adept at sifting and separating rather than showing the "entanglement" of postcoloniality.

CHAPTER I

"No Innocents and No Onlookers": The Uses of the Past in the Novels of Mau Mau

Reading Caroline Elkins's Pulitzer Prize–winning *Imperial Reckoning: The Untold Story of Britain's Gulag in Kenya* (2005) is an ironic experience for those familiar with the early novels of Ngũgĩ Wa Thiong'o, where Ngũgĩ sketched much of the same history. Elkins's revisionist approach to the historiography of Kenya's Emergency (1952–1960) aims to shift the focus away from the campaign against the Mau Mau and onto the war against civilians (Elkins 55). Mau Mau, who called themselves the Land and Freedom Army, demanded the return of land taken by the British in forced removals.[1] The British declared a state of emergency in 1952, when the rebellion was just beginning. Thirty years before Elkins, *Weep Not, Child* (1964) and *A Grain of Wheat* (1967) characterized the British repression of the civilian Gikuyu population in all the ways that Elkins claims require a revisionist approach: Ngũgĩ depicted punitive detention camps, the wide use of torture and harsh labor, and the creation of "enclosed villages" to detain women and children.[2] Moreover, he focused primarily on the experience of civilians. In his novels the forest fighters cast a long shadow on other characters, but occupy the margins of the main action.[3] Similarly, Elkins portrays the Emergency as a total assault on the Gikuyu people, as

90 percent of the population had taken the Mau Mau oath for "land and freedom" (Elkins 90–91). Between the detention camps and the "enclosed villages," the British detained nearly the entire civilian Gikuyu population of one and a half million (xiv).[4] "Screening" and "rehabilitation" were used to identify Mau Mau sympathizers and force them into disaffiliating themselves with the movement.

The impact of Elkins's history was reinforced by the appearance in the same year of a second history of the Mau Mau, David Anderson's *Histories of the Hanged: The Dirty War in Kenya and the End of Empire*. Taken together, the two works greatly amplify the record of British brutality in Kenya.[5] Anderson sets out to examine the use of capital punishment by the British, and thus he focuses on the Mau Mau trials.[6] His attention to the legal system provides a detailed account of British colonial governance, and, by foregrounding the stories of torture, he corroborates Elkins's account. He agrees with Elkins that the conflict should be characterized as a war, a "dirty war," as his title indicates. Moreover, because "histories of the hanged" alludes to the traumatic narratives of those accused of capital crimes arising from their affiliation with Mau Mau, Anderson's work illuminates for us the gap between the experience of the many ordinary people who were detained and the few (although still shockingly many, upwards of 1,000) who were hung (David Anderson 7). Another recent history, Daniel Branch's *Defeating Mau Mau, Creating Kenya: Counterinsurgency, Civil War, and Decolonization* (2009) focuses on the role of Gikuyu loyalists (Gikuyu, who opposed Mau Mau), shedding light on a phenomenon that preoccupied many of the novelists of Mau Mau (Branch 4–5). The fiction of Mau Mau was written in the shadow of the legendary captures, trials, and hangings (recounted in numerous popular memoirs), but it focuses on the experiences of ordinary people and the complexities of their political alliances.

The expanding historiography of Mau Mau has sparked a conversation about how the rebellion fits into the larger narrative of decolonization. In their study of colonial disciplinary practices, Steven Pierce and Anupama Rao understand the Emergency as an extension of colonial logic, a temporary rule of exception to steer the narrative of progress back on course. They note the rapidity with which the British repression of Mau Mau undid the progress narrative of the civilizing mission: "Sixty years of the civilizing mission could be swept away in a night, as formerly docile peasants returned to murderous barbarism" (Pierce and Rao 1). In these circumstances "colonial discipline," Pierce and Rao argue, was perceived as "justified" and as an extraordinary measure: "as exceptional, a *necessary disregard* for metropolitan norms of justice and civility" (2, emphasis added). Rehabilitation, which included forced agricultural labor, among other harsh methods, was pursued by the British as a means to reclaim the colonial subject back into the state. The violent practices attributed to Mau Mau, especially as they related to oath taking, "seemed sufficient to destroy utterly the government's ability to rule, which could, however, be restored by forcing detainees to mimic the motions of disciplined agricultural work" (2). Forced labor, a disciplining of the body, was supposed to reassert the colonizer's authority and reincorporate the colonial subject into the state.

The novels of Mau Mau, written in the immediate postcolonial era, extend but also revise, often radically, this agenda of reincorporation. They examine the problem of impaired citizenship following a civil conflict and seek to address it, as we will see later, by means of sentimental allegories of the family as nation. This project, however, has numerous fissures. Most importantly, the works of Ngũgĩ (which are the earliest in the literature) do not fit comfortably with the other examples I discuss: Godwin Wachira's *Ordeal in the Forest* (1968); Charles Mangua's *A Tail in the Mouth* (1972); Meja Mwangi's *Carcase for Hounds* (1974) and *Taste of Death* (1975); and Samuel Kahiga's *Dedan Kimathi: The Real Story* (1990).This second group of novels is more representative of the popular literature. "Popular" here designates a distinction in form between high and low art that also roughly maps onto the distinction between extroverted and introverted literatures. Stephanie Newell, for example, points out that popular literature in Africa can be distinguished by the fact that it is locally published: "bookstores and market book-stalls within Africa are filled to the brim with locally published and less internationally renowned authors, whose publications can be found side-by-side with the 'big names' of African literature" (Newell 1). Evan Maina Mwangi confirms this, especially for the period that concerns this study: "The indigenous publishing that thrived in the 1970s was to provide an alternative canon, especially in Nigeria, Ghana, and Kenya. This popular literature was primarily for local audiences" (Evan Mwangi 35). "Popular" has a different designation in Africa, where it does not refer to mass-marketing (circulation is still relatively small) and, as Newell clarifies, it designates a "non-elite, unofficial, and urban" literature (Newell 4).

Ngũgĩ's fiction is ironic, pitting unfulfilled expectations against reality. His works seek to inspire his readers to recommit to a struggle for economic justice ongoing after independence[7] and remain deeply critical of the new era when an educated, urban Kenyan elite took power with what E. S. Atieno-Odhiambo has called an "ideology of order" that suppressed dissent (Atieno-Odhiambo, "Democracy" 177). The popular works, on the other hand, stage a confrontation between the sentimentality of reconciliation and the war narrative's naturalistic aesthetic. David Maughan-Brown has called these the "novels of the freedom," as opposed to Ngũgĩ's "novels of the not yet freedom," and he criticizes them for substituting a vaguer idea of freedom for the more contentious demand for land and economic justice (Maughan-Brown 221–22).[8] The popular fiction narrates the people's suffering during the Emergency retrospectively from an already achieved independence. Yet, it is also paradoxical. It gestures to history against the grain of Jomo Kenyatta's injunction at independence "to erase from our minds all the hatreds and difficulties of those years which now belong to history" (Kenyatta, *Suffering* 241), while attempting to justify Kenyatta's desire for forgetfulness through a mostly negative portrayal of the forest fighters (Maughan-Brown 207). In this literature we find, therefore, a conversation among three modes of writing about Mau Mau: the ironic, the sentimental, and the naturalist. Each remembers the conflict differently, anticipating the historiographic debates that were to follow.

Before turning to an analysis of the novels, however, we need to address two key historiographic problems. First, what kind of war is this? War is a contested term in the historiography, with the terms emergency, counterinsurgency, peasant rebellion, anti-colonial revolt all used more often than war to characterize the conflict. I will focus on the tension between "emergency," which is deployed both as a designation of a historical period and as a form of colonial governance, and "war," the preferred term of recent historiography. Second is the problem of Kenyatta's legacy. The political history of Kenya is of critical importance to the novels of Mau Mau, which are haunted by the towering figure of Kenyatta. I will look specifically at his political rhetoric, which the novels frequently echo, not always ironically.

What Kind of War?

"Emergency" masks the term "war." By insisting on war, Elkins explains the Emergency differently from Pierce and Rao, seeing it as a break from rather than a continuation of colonial practices. At stake are the human rights claims of Kenyans, recently vindicated by the British government's agreement to pay reparations to 5,228 victims of the detention camps (Cowell). The war revealed the rifts between settlers and colonial authorities. The Emergency Declaration was interpreted by settlers as a "sort of open season on Kikuyu" (quoted in Maughan-Brown 40), and several contemporary observers acknowledged the genocidal character of this violence (Elkins 49, 60–61). Colonial authorities failed to restrain this violence and imposed their own. Thus Elkins frames her history as a narrative of rights violations and argues that the hesitation of the British to call the conflict in Kenya a war stemmed from their refusal to acknowledge the status of their detainees as that of war prisoners with rights.[9] Despite being a signatory to the Nüremberg Principles, which stipulate that war crimes and crimes against humanity should be prosecuted,[10] the British persisted in treating the Mau Mau as "subhuman and thus without rights" (Elkins 97). Moreover, Britain was a very vocal critic of the Soviet Union and its detention policies, the gulags (Cobban 117), which provokes Elkins into naming Kenya "Britain's Gulag." She quotes Governor Baring's statement that "[Mau Mau suspects] are a type who in another form of action, would become prisoners of war" (Elkins 97) and interprets this as an unintentional admission of the illegality of colonial rule. The other "form of action" Baring alludes to would be a war between parties of some parity, although this would not have to be military parity; political parity as sovereign nations is the missing ingredient here. According to the logic of colonialism, the colonized are not a legitimate party to war. Anderson draws our attention to the inadvertent ways in which the British did indeed recognize the conflict as a war but sought to disguise this fact. Aware of the constraints on them, they first avoided the language of both rebellion and war, using instead the term "civil disturbance" (David Anderson 238). However, the arrival of General "Bobbie" Erskine in June 1953 to take military command and the formation of a "War Council" implied that the British understood this conflict as a war and hence should have felt bound by the Nüremberg Principles (269).

By insisting that the Emergency is a war, Elkins links her narrative to an authoritative legal framework. However, the obfuscation of what constitutes war (what types of action) is a common characteristic of war narratives. The novels of Mau Mau grapple precisely with war as a problem of description, especially when "real" fighting is assumed to take place in the forest, but direct depictions of such action are rare. In fiction and memoirs we see mostly the hardship of living in the forest rather than conventional battle. Elaine Scarry grapples with the obfuscating language used to describe war when she clarifies a distinction between the "outside" and "inside" of wars. She defines war as a form of "reciprocal" injuring in a "contest" that seeks to determine who can "out-injure the opponent" (Scarry 63). What she calls the "outside" and "inside" of war elucidates the narrative structure of stories of war. The "outside" of war is made up of the political justifications for war, the verbal articulation of grievances, which lead a people or a party to resort to the contest of war. These rhetorical constructs are present, Scarry argues, "before" and "after" the war, and are hence "outside" the event of war, which is made up of the activities of injury and contest (63). If a story of war is emplotted through its political justification, the more intimate and immediate realities of injury and contest are obscured. Indeed, Scarry's elaboration of the many euphemisms for talking about war and its activities highlights precisely this narrative obfuscation (64ff), a pattern we also see in accounts of Kenya's Emergency. Scarry is interested in the question "what is the relation between the obsessive act of injuring and the issue on behalf of which that act is performed?"—which, she explains, is a question "about the relation between the interior content of war and what stands outside it" (63). The aim of war fiction is arguably to answer this question, while it tries to keep the "interior" of war at the forefront of our attention. Moreover, the mismatch between the inside and outside of war lends war fiction its irony.

Because the "obsessive act of injuring" that happens in this conflict is torture rather than fighting on a battlefield, the definition of war is stretched further. In fact, Scarry defines war in contrast to torture; war depends on a "reciprocal" injuring precluded by torture's one-sided force (63). If the Emergency, as narrated by Elkins, reveals torture as a form of war, it also reveals a war with extraordinarily unequal adversaries. Thus the pervasive use of torture as a weapon of war complicates the task of narration. The number of civilians detained and tortured in Kenya far exceeded the number of freedom fighters who were captured, making the suffering of civilians the primary scene of the war. The contest plays out most vividly in confrontations with settlers at their farms or over incidents of torture. The two are often linked, since the white farmer is frequently depicted as a torturer. In *Weep Not, Child*, as we shall see, this takes on an allegorical dimension; the body of the African victim becomes a symbol of the land usurped by the British and now being fought over. Body is land, and torture is the site of the national struggle.

The answer to the question "what kind of war?" also addresses the identity of the antagonists, sometimes African against African, which helps explain why Kenya after independence in 1963 was "as much a post-conflict society as a post-colonial state" (Branch 180). Contained within the British war against the Gikuyu was a second war, a civil war between Mau Mau and Gikuyu loyalists (Elkins 69).[11] This contention has been made before Elkins and Branch, but it has been controversial. David Maughan-Brown explains, for example, "Being able to classify 'Mau Mau' as a Gikuyu 'civil war' . . . lays the onus for the violence on the Gikuyu and thereby enables settler and administrator alike to slough off responsibility" (Maughan-Brown 21). He refers to the movement as a "peasant revolt" (22–23). Tirop Simatei has resisted the characterization of Mau Mau as civil war because it undermines the nationalist character of the uprising (Tirop Simatei 156). The claim, however, receives a new emphasis and wider scope in Elkins and Branch. Elkins rejects the colonialist propaganda that sought to blame the conflict on tribal hatreds, and she contends that the civil war reflects the complexity of the Gikuyu society and the damage inflicted by colonial rule and education, which divided Kenyans against themselves. By foregrounding the role of loyalists, Branch similarly stresses the "bloody conflict between Mau Mau and loyalists" and insists on its central role in Kenya's postcolonial history (Branch 208).

The loyalists, according to Branch, are not a group whose political leanings were apparent before the Emergency and who act predictably during the conflict; instead, loyalists defined themselves in the moment as they confronted the violence of both the counterinsurgency and the Mau Mau (223). Before Branch, John Lonsdale highlighted the importance of the loyalists, rejecting the diminished role attributed to them by the official historiography of the Emergency: "The official portrait of Mau Mau was drawn in a series of denials that shifted the blame of the crisis from the peculiarities of Kenya to the abnormalities of the Kikuyu" (Berman and Lonsdale 273). Moreover, both this official account and its critics overlooked the role and extent of "Kikuyu resistance to Mau Mau" (291). This might seem to contradict Elkins's portrayal of the near-total assault of the British on the Gikuyu, but here Branch further clarifies matters because he emphasizes the fluidity of these identities and the fact that individual Gikuyu changed allegiances during the conflict in response to their fears (Branch 209).

Thus understanding the conflict as a war that upends the political order enables Branch to show how new political dynamics were generated by its events. The logic of insurgency and counterinsurgency has wrongly been conceived as dualistic (insurgent nationalists against counterinsurgent colonial power), when in fact counterinsurgency deeply polarized the Gikuyu population itself with its "programme of sanctions and rewards," turning the conflict inward and in the process giving shape to the new postcolonial order and its instability (Branch 212). How fighting the colonizer becomes a divisive political situation for Kenyans themselves is precisely the topic of the war fiction and exemplifies the kind of preoccupation central to a literary project that looks within.

Kenyatta's Legacy

The political history of Kenya is of critical importance to the novels, which are haunted by the towering figure of Kenyatta. It was not the nationalist politicians who came to power at independence, but the moderates and loyalists aided by what Elkins calls the "reinvention of Kenyatta" (Elkins 357). Kenyatta, once vilified internationally as the purported leader of an atavistic movement, was celebrated as the messenger of "anti-violence" (his own words) upon his release from detention (quoted in Elkins 359). The British helped bring about this change of Kenyatta's image, although Kenyatta in fact "had never been the oath-taking revolutionary he was purported to be" (358). Simon Gikandi describes Kenyatta in the 1920s and 1930s as a cosmopolitan figure, anxiety-ridden and alienated, who tried hard to map the values of his colonial education onto his political reality as an African subject (Gikandi, "Pan-Africanism" 4–6). In the 1920s he was known as "Muigwathania," "The Reconciler," which was also the title of the newspaper he edited. When he came out of detention, he reclaimed this identity (David Anderson 335). Branch explains Kenyatta's political self-positioning in the 1940s as anticipating the difficult choices that pushed many to loyalism during the Emergency. When he returned from England in 1946 after a fifteen-year absence from Kenya, Kenyatta was welcomed as a "hero across ethnic and class lines"; he advocated "non-violent protest," going "against the tide of Kikuyu politics." Constrained by the suspicious attitude of the British toward him and his own mistrust of more militant Gikuyu who thought he "would undermine their support," Kenyatta had to negotiate a hard-to-find middle ground. This effort was trumped by his arrest (Branch 180). After being tried and then detained for the duration of the Emergency, however, Kenyatta emerged as the undisputed national leader in 1961, his ex-detainee status lending him important credibility in the eyes of the people, so many of whom had also suffered detention (181).

At independence, his message was "'to forgive and forget,' and 'to bury the past'" (David Anderson 335). He "acknowledged the part the freedom fighters had played in the struggle," but stopped short of recognizing that they deserved any form of reparation. "Mau Mau was a thing best forgotten," he declared (335), despite the fact that "just below the surface of public life, Mau Mau was being talked about all the time" (336). Thus it is not only the meaning of the Emergency that was contested, but the terms of reconciliation. The politics of memory are entwined with the politics of reconciliation. It is around the challenges of reconciliation that the rifts in the war fiction manifest themselves rather than in the debates over the status of the Emergency as a war, an assessment about which the literature achieves coherence, seeing it indeed as a war.

Moreover, Kenyatta's political rhetoric shaped the allegorizing tendencies of the sentimental novels of reconciliation. "The great reconciler" (Elkins 361), Kenyatta used the family as a unifying metaphor for the nation, thus writing that "nationhood and familyhood must and can be contrived out of our many tribes and cultures" (Kenyatta, *Suffering* ix). The phrase "suffering without bitterness" is paradigmatic of the sentimental attitude in the politics of reconciliation; bitterness would shape the naturalistic ethos instead. "Suffering without bitterness" acknowledges pathos, but also seeks to restrain it so that it does not spill into the future. As a frame for telling the story of the struggle for freedom, it is an effective "strategy of containment" (Jameson, *Political Unconscious* 53–54). I evoke Jameson's term in my readings of the novels to describe the ideological work performed by these texts. Such a strategy is evident in Kenyatta's frequent allusions to the discourse of abolitionism. Speaking on Kenyatta Day in 1967, he described the struggle against colonialism in such terms: "I am just letting you know that people were chained, and that in time all those chains were broken" (Kenyatta, *Suffering* 341). The reference to the chains of slavery glosses the past in a universalizing language that alludes to a just struggle in unspecific terms rather than making reference to Kenya's historical particularity. Kenyatta's evocation of abolitionist rhetoric, moreover, incorporates the narrative of the colonized's resistance within the imperial power's own progressive narrative of enlightenment, its enactment of abolition. Hence Kenyatta suggests that a larger, more universal project of freedom encompasses the progress and historical transformation of both the old imperial power and the new independent nation. The two are aligned in the narrative of human progress. Deeply suspicious of such a historical narrative, Ngũgĩ positions his retrospective account, especially in *Grain of Wheat*, as a counterpoint to Kenyatta's vision of history.

Kenyatta's call to "Let us agree that we shall never refer to the past," reflects anxiety about vengeance, a theme central to the naturalist novels, such as *Carcase for Hounds* and *Taste of Death*. For Kenyatta, remembrance serves vengeance rather than reconciliation: "Never has there seemed any purpose in arguments about the past, or any nobility in motives of revenge." He asked the people to commit to a future "that is living" instead of "the past that is dead" (241). At the same time he also erected a fiction of the independence struggle as an effort in which everyone had participated. Thus in 1967 he spoke as follows: "We were all seeking freedom (together), and therefore it is not right to discriminate, saying that one man served to bring freedom while another man did something else" (342). The naturalist novels especially do not succeed in eliminating the kind of discrimination Kenyatta refers to and remain interested in the "something else" that many ordinary people succumbed to. Moreover, those who brought "freedom" were not always heroic, and their legacy is not necessarily self-evident.

Since 2002, when Mwai Kibaki was elected and democracy seemed to take hold, there has been an "explosion of interest in Mau Mau," officially sanctioned by the new government and thus openly discussed (Branch xii).[12] Elkins's text has featured prominently in this debate and as a result has been mired in controversy, criticized by senior historians in the field and tainted by its appropriation by the Kibaki regime in Kenya.[13] Official interest in the history of Mau Mau is part of an active "politics of reclaiming" Mau Mau and provides an intriguing backdrop for revisiting the literature of Mau Mau (xiii). Although historians are paying more attention to the internecine aspect of the conflict, the political interest in Mau Mau is going in the opposite direction, silencing the conflict with loyalists in the interest of exploiting the widely held but misconstrued belief in Mau Mau as a *national* war of liberation (xiv). In this new context the fiction from the 1960s, 1970s, and 1980s provides an important counter-argument that illuminates the historical process by which the remembrance of Mau Mau was politicized. The novels, which participate centrally in a project of remembrance against the grain of an official policy of "forgive and forget" (179), contain a record that only recently has been foregrounded by historians.

Torture and the Narrative of Re-membering in Ngũgĩ

Thirty years before Elkins, Ngũgĩ put torture at the center of his depiction of the war.[14] He brought together the war's distinct scenes (forest, detention camp, farm, village) by looking at the impact of torture in all these domains. In the absence of conventional scenes of fighting, torture is the surrogate site for the injuring of war. As narrated in these novels, it is an instance when the fate of the individual victim becomes identified with the collective story of the nation. Torture, witnessed by others or its cries overheard, instantiates in Ngũgĩ's novels the "song of my country" motif. In fictional form the narrative of torture transforms individual suffering into a narrative of nation from the perspective of resistance to the colonial order.

The particularity of British policy in Kenya needs to be highlighted. Unlike the French in Algeria, who used stealth torture techniques, the British in Kenya "did not care whether they left scars or not" and made torture into "a public spectacle in many cases" (Rejali 158). This open practice of torture was exceptional in the 1950s, since most repressive regimes by this point were practicing stealth torture, and Britain had done so "in India and Mandatory Palestine before World War II" (408). Although torture was perpetrated openly in the detention camps in Kenya, it remained invisible as a crime due to the impunity with which it occurred (Elkins 156). This impunity contributed to the intense humiliation endured by the Kenyan people and adds poignancy to the manifestation of the motif of the "song of my country," which aims to dignify the suffering of the individual by highlighting the people's collective awareness of the injustice of torture. The narrative of torture aspires to be a form of "redress," a setting right or narrative justice that by gaining recognition can bring about a recalibration of the historical narrative.[15]

In *Homecoming* (1972), Ngũgĩ lists the autobiographies and novels of the war to show that they comprise a substantive literature.[16] Echoing Fanon, he characterizes these works as a "literature about the small man: they show the dignity of the poor and the wretched of the earth, despite the violence of the body and feeling around them" (Ngũgĩ, *Homecoming* 71). When Ngũgĩ asks whether the peasants who fought the British have benefitted from independence, he is foregrounding a perspective from below: "What have the peasants gained from Uhuru [independence]? Has our ruling elite tried to change the colonial social and economic structure? Are the peasants and workers in control of the land they fought for?" (49). His historical novels keep visible the stories of the peasantry and aim at promoting social justice through historical remembrance.

In his lecture at Makerere University on August 8, 2004, one of the events that marked his return to East Africa after a twenty-two year exile, Ngũgĩ reaffirmed his commitment to historicism and joined the task of history symbolically to the reclaiming of the body after torture, what he called the body's "re-membering."[17] Using as his example the decapitation of the Xhosa King Hintsa by the British in 1839, Ngũgĩ described colonial violence as an attempt to "dis-member the colonized." Although this violence is enacted literally on individual bodies, it acquires an allegorical resonance as the dismemberment of the "social body" of colonized people, which Ngũgĩ describes further as an "act of disconnection and relocation." Colonialism fragments society through the literal breaking of bodies of individuals within that society. Ngũgĩ urges re-membrance as the "sacred duty" of intellectuals so that the fragmented body politic can be stitched back together again and made vital (Ngũgĩ, "Role").[18]

Ngũgĩ's description of historiography as a rejoining of the severed parts of the body provides an evocative set of associations for considering how the narrative of torture, and more specifically of torture in the context of war, functions as a historical narrative. The re-membered body symbolizes the reclamation of the point of view of the victim rendered incoherent by torture. Early in his career Ngũgĩ stressed the importance of point of view and talked about the way it shapes the story that is told: "What the African novelist has attempted to do is restore the African character to his history" (Ngũgĩ, *Homecoming* 43). "Restore" like "re-membering" suggests making whole again, a completeness that evokes the larger community beyond the individual's story.[19] In his critique of neocolonial historians Ngũgĩ draws attention to their inadequate treatment of the "history of the common people" (Sicherman, "Kenyan History" 351). "Making whole" refers to the successful reintegration of the peasantry in the community of the nation. Individual stories of Gikuyu, who suffered in the war and who moreover were in conflict with each other as well as with the colonizer, need to find a place in a larger coherent narrative.

Elkins's demonstration of the extent of the torture against the Gikuyu makes it easier for us to understand how torture can be an assault on a whole community. Because it was displayed in public in the detention camps, those who witnessed torture were also terrorized, as many testified to Elkins fifty years later (Elkins 80). In Ngũgĩ's fiction the imaginative identification of the writer with such figures, witnesses to terror, inspires the story of the nation. The novel as form provides the public forum for this witness. But the novelist, Ngũgĩ argued in *Homecoming*, must be both in the "mainstream of his people's historical drama" and "able to stand aside and merely contemplate the currents" (Ngũgĩ, *Homecoming* 39). From a critical distance, he is plagued by doubt: "Has there been a mainstream, anyway? . . . He frantically looks around and asks: where is my past, where is my history?" (39–40). This constant questioning perpetually renews the project of historical retrospection. It also highlights the introverted nature of its concerns. Everything the writer needs to achieve must be accomplished in a struggle against the history of the suppression (through fragmentation and violence) of his own and his people's point of view. The most extreme form of this suppression is the obliteration of the individual under torture and the terror this inflicts on the entire community.

In my discussion of *Weep Not, Child* and *Grain of Wheat* I focus on Ngũgĩ's vision of the nation. Torture is a key motif, but so is the family. Three fathers die in *Weep Not, Child*, signaling that Ngũgĩ sees the repression of the Gikuyu as also fundamentally challenging patriarchal structures. The key to moving beyond the destructiveness of the conflict is in whether the community can work through its grief and find a way into a new and different future, revising the hold of patriarchy on society. The problem in the novel, however, is that the sons have been traumatized by the conflict. War's impact is felt in how it renders the new generation profoundly pessimistic. In *Grain of Wheat*, a novel of greater narrative complexity, we end on a more optimistic note, marked by a family reconciliation. This ending is tempered by anxieties over structural changes and justice. However, the intense suffering generated by the conflict has found a narrative mechanism that can accommodate its complexity, and hence the novel empowers the reader, allowing for a nuanced understanding of history that frees us to imagine a future even in bleak circumstances. The non-coincidence of this reader with those who are the subject of the novel, however, troubled Ngũgĩ a great deal, and his awareness shows that the intent was to write for the people. In a 1971 interview before he committed to writing in Gikuyu, he declared, "I felt that people who fed the novel, that is the peasantry as it were, will not be in a position to read it. And this is very painful" (Ngũgĩ, "Tolstoy" 48). I take each novel in turn to flesh out this reading before turning to the more popular literature, the naturalist and sentimental novels, which tackle two themes not addressed by Ngũgĩ: life in the forest and performing, through fiction, the forgetting necessary for a reconciliation in the sense Kenyatta promoted.

Weep Not, Child: *Fathers and Sons*

Weep Not, Child and *A Grain of Wheat* are set in two different moments: the first as the Emergency is unfolding, the second on the eve of independence.[20] Thus the two novels exhibit different historical sensibilities, with *A Grain of Wheat* affording the fuller retrospective gesture. *Weep Not, Child* examines the destructive impact of torture on both individual lives and the community. It is partly an interrupted *Bildungsroman*; Njoroge's education is interrupted by his arrest and the intrusion of the conflict into his family life. As an interrupted *Bildungsroman* this novel reveals the interpenetration of different novelistic forms and shows how the war narrative self-consciously veers away from the *Bildungsroman*. As such it also prefigures other novels of war that begin with the interrupted education of their protagonists, such as *Ordeal in the Forest*, discussed later in this chapter, and

Sozaboy, discussed in the next chapter. *Weep Not, Child* also contextualizes the Emergency in a longer history of war that encompasses the two world wars, situating this African war in a global context.

Weep Not, Child shows how issues of land tenure radicalized the Gikuyu population and were the origin of the Mau Mau insurgency. What had been piecemeal appropriation of Gikuyu land was systematized after a 1921 colonial court ruling, dispossessing Gikuyus completely. Forthwith: "all land—even that which had previously been put aside for African 'reserves'—was now Crown land and . . . all natives were to be considered tenants-at-will on land that they had owned for generations." Gikuyu were "herded" into crowded reserves, became "squatters" on European farms, and were forced to work to pay their taxes (JanMohamed, *Manichean* 187–88). African veterans of World War II had little to no education and few opportunities for employment, and they became a generation adrift.[21]

What is war in *Weep Not, Child*? It is first a traumatic memory. Boro, one of the sons the novel focuses on, witnessed the death of his brother during fighting in World War II. Uncommunicative and withdrawn, all Boro will say about that war is that it "had been a terrible waste of life" (Ngũgĩ, *Weep* 10). Like his peers, he had fought with little understanding of what was at stake and not much investment in the war's outcome. Going to war was servitude to the colonial power. Seeking recourse in violence after the war (most commanders of the Mau Mau were veterans of the world war), Boro acted on what he had learned from his experience as the colonized: "The ripe hour of his youth had been spent in bloodshed in the big war. This was the only thing he could do efficiently" (102). Whereas his younger brother, Njoroge, has ambitions as a student in the best secondary school, the only education Boro received from the colonizer was in how to kill. The extent of Boro's disaffection contributes to his involvement in the Mau Mau, as seen in this conversation with one of his lieutenants in the forest. His lieutenant asks him, "Why then do we fight?" and Boro answers:

> "To kill. Unless you kill, you'll be killed. So you go on killing and destroying. It's a law of nature. The white man too fights and kills with gas, bombs, and everything."
>
> "But don't you think there is something wrong in fighting and killing unless you're doing so for a great cause like ours?"
>
> "What great cause is ours?"
>
> "Why, Freedom and the return of our lost heritage."
>
> "Maybe there's something in that. But for me *Freedom is meaningless unless it can bring back a brother I lost*. Because it can't do that, the only thing

> left to me is to fight, to kill and rejoice at any who falls under my sword." (102–3, emphasis added)

In one of the hints of the naturalist universe in Ngũgĩ's early fiction, Boro refers to the killing of war as a "law of nature," inevitable. His bitterness and unresolved grief show that he perceives himself as dispossessed by the colonizer of something irretrievable (his brother, now dead). The conditions for the struggle for freedom to become purposeful are impossible to meet, and the compulsion to keep killing leads to a future as endless revenge: "If he killed a single white man, he was exacting a vengeance for a brother killed" (102).

Dispossession from the land is linked directly to the aftermath of World War II and the sense of injustice, such that Boro feels. Josiah Mwangi Kariuki, who wrote the most influential memoir of Mau Mau and was a significant Gikuyu political figure,[22] noted the sharp sense of unfairness felt by black Kenyans after World War II (Branch 204–5):

> During the last war we sent our young men to sacrifice their lives in helping the British people to fight and conquer Germany. The white officers had been rewarded with farms on which to settle in our land and loans with which to stock them. The African soldiers had been rewarded with the colour bar, unemployment and the *Kipande* (registration card). There had been no colour bar to prevent us dying for Britain in the war. (Kariuki 11–12)

To maintain hope against this bleak sense of dispossession, the Gikuyu believed in the prophecy of Mugo wa Kibiro, who predicted the coming of a savior to free the Gikuyu from the British. Kenyatta came to be seen as this savior against the backdrop of the mood sketched by Kariuki (JanMohamed, *Manichean* 193).

Both Boro's father, Ngotho, and his brother, Njoroge, are tortured in the novel. Njoroge is taken for questioning after Boro is accused of the murder of Chief Jacobo, a Gikuyu loyalist and one of the three fathers who are killed in the novel. Thus, while Boro is in the forest with the Mau Mau, his family suffers under the punitive terror of the British. Njoroge is unaware both of the accusations against Boro and the fact that their father has incriminated himself in the murder of the chief in order to protect the third son, Kamau, whom he fears committed the murder.

Njoroge is handed over to his torturers by his schoolmaster. Taken from the idyllic setting of his school, now "a lost paradise," he learns that the school is no sanctuary from the war (Ngũgĩ, *Weep* 117). There Njoroge is just as vulnerable to colonial violence as any other Gikuyu anywhere else.

Holding to the widely held belief in the prophecy of restitution, his mother had encouraged education in the hope that it would somehow lead to a reclamation of the land. Ngotho's generation had been emasculated because of the loss of land, but for his son's generation a colonial education held the promise of dignity restored (Gikandi, *Ngũgĩ* 85–87).[23] Thus, Ngotho reasoned, "education was good only because it would lead to the recovery of the lost lands" (Ngũgĩ, *Weep* 39). In his memoir Ngũgĩ cites a song that children of his generation sang:

> If these were the times of our ancestors Ndemi and Mathathi
> My father, I would ask you for the feast due to initiates
> Then I would ask you to arm me with a spear and a shield,
> But today, Father, I ask you for education only. (Ngũgĩ, *Dreams* 123)

Even though the opportunity to be educated was controlled tightly by the colonial government,[24] the "messianic fervor" of the Gikuyu embraced the promise of education (JanMohamed, *Manichean* 187) and, as we see in this song, opposed it to violent resistance as a means to attain justice.

One detail stands out in the scene of Njoroge's torture. Rendered through the District Commissioner's point of view, the scene depicts the boy as a victim, yet he retains a point of view, expressed in his poignant "supplication":

> He still screamed. Mr. Howlands watched him. Then he saw the boy raise his eyes and arms as if in supplication before he became limp and collapsed on the ground. Mr. Howlands looked down on the boy and then at the officers and walked out. The red beard and the grey eyes laughed derisively. (Ngũgĩ, *Weep* 118)

Howlands's actions condemn him to evil; he becomes devil-like with his red beard and laughter. But, more significantly, Njoroge's supplication is recognized before it is denied. Njoroge makes a claim on Howlands's humanity to have pity on him. We find a similar emphasis on the victim's plea for mercy in other war novels.[25] It would be wrong to read such scenes as only displaying the demonic nature of the torturer, because the victim's supplication interrupts the portrayal of torture as a one-sided act. Although we do not see the stuff of myth, a heroically resistant victim of torture against the odds, the scene retains an awareness of the victim as an agent because the victim inserts his point of view to make a claim on the torturer, insisting on his own (the victim's) humanity. For the reader, moreover, the image of Njoroge supplicating turns into a moment of identification when the suffering inflicted by torture becomes an instance of the "song of my country." This association is amplified later in the same scene. Although alone in his cell, Njoroge is not isolated. He knows that his mother and his father's second wife are also under arrest, and, when he hears a woman screaming, he presumes it is one of his mothers. A witness to their suffering, his sense of his own predicament widens to include the community.

The climactic scene of the novel, Ngotho's (the father's) death scene, recalls but also subverts the sentimental register of reconciliation. Ngũgĩ complicates the convention of the sentimental death scene by focusing on the death of the father rather than the child. The Victorian sentimental aesthetic, an important influence in African literature of the 1960s, asserted that "fictional representations of the deaths of children had extraordinary corrective potential" (Kaplan 50). The scene in *Weep Not, Child* is gutted of this "corrective potential" because, focused as it is on the father's generation, it makes the reader acutely aware of the historical impasse in which this community finds itself. To understand the dynamics of Ngotho's death scene, it is important to look first at the circumstances under which he was tortured.

As I already noted, the novel pits two alternative reactions to colonialism against each other: peasant rebellion (the "spear") against education. Whereas the ostensible reason father and son are tortured has to do with Boro's being suspected in the death of the loyalist chief, Ngũgĩ deliberately sets out to complicate this cause-and-effect explanation by showing how the person Njoroge was turning into because of his education also posits a threat to the status quo. Njoroge's education placed him in the position of cultural mediator and gave him the opportunity to reach across various social divides (Ngũgĩ, *Weep* 121). He had a childhood friendship (and later a romance) with the chief's daughter, and at school he was friends with Howlands's son. These alliances open up his family to the scrutiny of colonial authority just as much as his brother's Mau Mau affiliation. Njoroge is shaken by the turn of events because, after being tortured, he understands that his role as mediating figure exposed his family to the disciplining intervention of the authorities. Once he imagined himself as the future savior of his family, but now he sees himself as the source of their suffering.

With Njoroge's sense of direction blocked and the other sons embroiled in a violent conflict that holds little promise, Ngũgĩ turns to the father to understand the historical origin of this impasse, which lies unsurprisingly in the politics of land. Ngotho viewed his alienation from the land as temporary. Because he believed in the Gikuyu prophecy that colonialism will end and the land will be given back to the people, he retained his sense of stewardship of the land. He justified working on Howlands's farm because he viewed his role as custodian of his own family land: "Ngotho felt responsible for whatever happened to this land. He owed it to the dead, the living and the unborn of his line, to keep guard over this *shamba*" (31).

When he begins to lose hope in such restitution, Ngotho struggles to find an appropriate path or action. Significantly, he does not take the Mau Mau oath, refusing it twice (71, 74).[26] Instead, he finds the appropriate action by turning himself in for the murder of the loyalist Jacobo. Thus he hopes to save his other son, Kamau, who is arrested for the murder. Tragically, this sacrifice turns out to be largely meaningless. Howlands tortures Ngotho without revealing that he already knows he is not the murderer.[27] Although Ngotho submits bravely to torture, the confrontation is not about what he thinks it's about. Irony here threatens to render the suffering meaningless. Moreover, Howlands is particularly vicious: "he became mad where Ngotho was concerned. Even the homeguards who worked with him feared to be present when the D.O. was eliciting information from this man. But Ngotho had stuck to his story" (120).

Howlands "was determined to conquer and reduce Ngotho to submission" (119), because he recognizes the African's claim to the land and, more importantly, the land's enduring appeal as an idea to Ngotho's sons. Earlier in the novel the two men had walked the land together, appreciating its beauty. Howlands solicited Ngotho's admiration by asking him, "You like all this?" and Ngotho confirmed: "It is the best land in all the country" (32). In this scene, Howlands's anxious thoughts turned to the future and his younger son's lack of interest in the farm. His older son, who would have farmed, died in World War II. Howlands and Ngotho, both fathers who lost sons in the war, derive their sense of belonging from the same land. Ngũgĩ echoes Alan Paton's *Cry, the Beloved Country* in this scene. In Paton's novel Kumalo and Jarvis share an appreciation for the same landscape; the African and the white man both identify with the land across the divide of apartheid and despite the black man's dispossession.[28] The absence of bitterness is notable. In *Weep Not, Child*, the similar circumstance fuels Howlands's animosity toward Ngotho. He resents Ngotho's superior knowledge of the land and understands it as constituting a special claim that Howlands cannot equal.[29] While he tortures Ngotho, Howlands reasserts the sense of "victory" he derived "whenever he walked through it all" (31). Ngotho's body is symbolically the land over which Howlands asserts his claim of possession. However, by aligning the torture of the individual with the struggle over land, Ngũgĩ reminds his reader of torture's collective national implication. The home guards, normally inured to such violence, are unnerved ("feared to be present") by this particular torture, responding to the foundational nature of what is at stake in this confrontation.

As a result of his torture, Ngotho dies. At home, surrounded by family and seemingly restored to respect in the eyes of his sons, Ngotho almost achieves the stature elusive to him. As the deathbed scene unfolds, it seems as if the "crisis point of colonialism" that "casts fathers such as Ngotho in the role of worthless symbols, subjects who have lost the capacity to hold their houses together and to ensure the success of their progenies" (Gikandi, *Ngũgĩ* 84) has been overcome by the restorative powers of sentimentality.[30] Yet the scene is so full of irony that it works against the sentimental convention of the deathbed scene by reasserting with devastating effect the diminishment of patriarchy. The impact of Ngotho's martyrdom is deeply compromised by the lies that surround it, which interfere with the reader's investment in the scene's sentimentality. Ngotho lied and put himself in danger to save his son Kamau, and this is undoubtedly courageous. But the lie's efficacy as an action is unclear. It does not save Kamau. Instead, Kamau and Boro have more time to act, and they do, showing up at Howlands's door and killing him. Subsequently they are arrested, and we are led to believe they will be hanged (Ngũgĩ, *Weep* 127). Thus Ngotho unwittingly facilitates the murder of Howlands and sacrifices the son he set out to save. At his deathbed he also naively encourages Njoroge to return to the pursuit of his education as an effective form of resistance, but the promise of education is now hollow (123). Lies buffer this scene all around, since Njoroge has also hidden the fact of his own torture from his father (123). The memory of Boro's dehumanizing experience in the forest, his and Kamau's anticipated arrest and execution, and Njoroge's shattered sense of self are the new reality.

After his ejection from the "paradise" of school and his experience at the place "popularly known as the House of Pain" (116), Njoroge loses his mooring. Violence "had showed him a different world from that [sic] he had believed himself living in" and "these troubles seemed to have no end, to have no cure" (120). His loss of direction is compounded when he sees the effects of his father's torture and castration. Profoundly humiliated, he tries to commit suicide. His mother calls him back from the brink of death, and it is only his filial allegiance to her that saves his life. The son's allegiance to the mother is a recognizable trope of national allegory (mother Africa calls back her son), especially potent in a situation where political leadership, the patriarch's domain, is bankrupt (Boehmer 243). None of the progressive promises of colonization bear fruit, and, by the end of the novel, when independence has not yet been posited as a historical possibility, colonialism is seen as an increasingly regressive historical force.[31] The mother's steadfastness hints of future possibility, but one that still lies beyond political reality.

Yet the future still lies inevitably with Njoroge, and the key component of his future is his relationship with Chief Jacobo's daughter, Mwihaki, his love interest. The two youths share the experience of the violent deaths of their fathers, experiences whose exact circumstance illuminates their "entanglement" with each other. As Sarah Nuttall has elaborated, "entanglement" describes the historical condition of "being twisted together," entangled in a historical circumstance that may be "resisted, or ignored or uninvited" yet yields a certain kind of "intimacy," captured here by the suffering of families on different sides of the political question (Nuttall, *Entanglement* 1). "Entanglement," therefore, can illuminate a kind of common ground that exists not despite division, but as a result of sharing the experience of division, albeit from different perspectives. It is an "idea which signals largely unexplored terrains of mutuality, wrought from a common, though often coercive and confrontational, experience" (11). Thus, in the circumstances of the novel, the violent deaths of three fathers (Ngotho, Howlands, Jacobo) illuminate the "entanglement" of their children, who are not necessarily bound to a narrative of self-destruction. Their reality does not have to be "Manichean," opposing colonizer and colonized, but an "entanglement" that overrides binaries.

Mwihaki recognizes that the violence that took her father's life has the features of a civil war. The meaning of her father's death "broke upon her like a revelation," and she came to understand "the horror of the calamity that had befallen Kenya" (Ngũgĩ, *Weep* 130). Mwihaki sees her father's death as a national "calamity" (130). The climactic confrontation between her and Njoroge places the personal squarely within the political and highlights the divisions among Kenyans and the violence they have inflicted on each other. Njoroge is the brother of Mwihaki's father's murderer. Mwihaki's father, who as a British loyalist became an instrument in the repression of the Mau Mau, facilitated the arrest and torture of Njoroge and his father. If Mwihaki and Njoroge can nurture their attachment to each other despite the history of violence that divides them, then a future is discernible. But alas, although the novel suggests this possibility, it does not depict it. Njoroge wants to escape with Mwihaki and start a new life in Uganda, but Mwihaki is horrified at the implications of this idea, seeing it as a betrayal of their "duty to other people"—specifically, their mothers (and by implication, Kenya). She urges Njoroge to be patient and "wait for a new day" (134). Personal happiness must be sacrificed for the good of others. Mwihaki's rejection is the final blow for Njoroge, who feels he has no future, "for now I know that my tomorrow was an illusion" (132). When Njoroge's mother saves him from suicide, Njoroge becomes the beneficiary of someone's else love and sense of duty to others. A different sentimental ending—that of romance, however—is aborted. What remains, through the symbolism of the mothers, is Kenya as land and idea.

A Grain of Wheat

In *Weep Not, Child*, Ngũgĩ relies on the family to create community and ultimately an allegory of nation. In *A Grain of Wheat* his aesthetic solution is more complex, a weaving together of multiple confessional narratives focalized through different characters, all of whom are part of a peer group, but not a family. The novel is deeply engaged with the problem of historical retrospection at the moment of transition, and although it is a novel of postcolonial disillusion, it also makes a commitment to continued struggle. Ngũgĩ echoes Fanon: the past should be used "with the intention of opening the future" (quoted in JanMohamed, *Manichean* 209; Sicherman, "Kenyan History" 350).

History as redress, the problem of responsibility, and the individual seen through the question "who is a hero?" are the key preoccupations of this novel. The humiliating experience in detention is paired with the strain of everyday life in an enclosed village. The focus is almost explicitly on civilians, most of whom are what Branch calls "risk averse actors" caught up in events and forced to enter history (Branch 222). "Risk averse actors" contrast with the idea of heroes, and this contrast engages Ngũgĩ because of its distinct modernist overtones and what he learned from his study of Joseph Conrad while he was a student at Makerere (Sicherman, "Kenyan History" 17). Who is a hero in war? Or, more aptly, are there heroes in war? The answer, as the novel's ironies suggest, is not obvious and points ultimately to a collective rather than individual identity. Articulating a national history also helps make manifest the nation's historical coming into being. Ngũgĩ's objective is to show how this narrative emerges organically from the community's narration of its experiences. Justice is a big preoccupation, both as a duty of memory (how will those who struggled be remembered?) and as an ongoing political matter, drawing attention to entrenched economic injustice.

To understand Ngũgĩ's engagement with the national and the historical, it is necessary to turn to Fanon, who discusses the "search for truth" as a problem of responsibility. The "search for truth" is a "collective" enterprise that requires the recognition of everyone's complicity, or "entanglement"—the way in which peoples' lives are stitched together, as we saw, not only in conscious solidarity, but through the vicissitudes of history and its violent conflicts (Nuttall, *Entanglement* 5–7). Violent events create intimacies, and from there a collectivity emerges. Fanon explains:

> The search for truth in local attitudes is a collective affair. . . . The collective struggle presupposes collective responsibility at the base and collegiate responsibility at the top. Yes everyone will have to be compromised ["il faut compromettre tout le monde"] in the fight for the common good. No one has clean hands; *there are no innocents and no onlookers*. We all have dirty hands; we are all soiling them in the swamps of our country and in the terrifying emptiness of our brains. Every onlooker is either a coward or a traitor. (Fanon 199, emphasis added)

Fanon's language is uncompromising and totalizing. Yet recognition of such participation in history, which is neither easy nor clean, yields a more just foundation for the nation. The retrospective ownership of such a history involves the taking of responsibility, a process of educating the people whose goal is "to make the history of the nation part of the personal experience of each of its citizens" (200). The didactic project of *A Grain of Wheat* attempts such a totalizing gesture.

Two stories of torture haunt the events of the novel, one historical (it took place in the 1890s), the other fictional, although rendered as a "history of the hanged." These stories paint an evil picture of the colonizer, yet Ngũgĩ uses them to open up the discourse of history to an introverted examination of Gikuyu responsibility in the conflict. The older story, rendered as part of the community's collective memory, does not merely repeat itself in the more contemporary instance. In the differences between the old and the new lie the possibilities for historical narrative as a taking of responsibility. The past's implications for the future are key in Ngũgĩ's repetition of these common motifs of martyrdom.

The torture of Waiyaki, a Gikuyu martyr of anti-colonial resistance from the 1890s (Kariuki 21; David Anderson 117) gives the novel its title, which is at the same time a biblical reference to 1 Corinthians 15:36. We learn that Waiyaki "was buried alive with his head facing the centre of the earth" and that his death came to be seen later by the Gikuyu as a prophecy of Mau Mau: "looking back we can see that Waiyaki's blood contained within it a seed, a grain, which gave birth to a movement whose main strength thereafter sprang from a bond with the soil" (Ngũgĩ, *Grain* 12).[32] The passage from Corinthians also refers to a grain of wheat but is an admonition, rather than a promise: "Thou fool, that which thou sowest is not quickened, except it die [unless it dies]. And that which thou sowest, thou sowest not that body that shall be, but bare grain, it may chance of wheat, or of some other grain" (quoted by Ngũgĩ as an epigraph to *Grain*). Ngũgĩ's use of this epigraph has been interpreted as Fanonian. In *The Wretched of the Earth* Fanon describes the transition to independence as an incomplete realization of the revolutionary promise of national consciousness articulated during resistance.[33] The novel's biblical epigraph complements its other epigraph, a note to the reader warning of injustice in the postcolonial order: ". . . the problems are real—sometimes too painfully real for the peasants who fought the British yet who now see all that they fought for being put on one side."

In his masterful reading of the novel, Gikandi concludes that the emphasis is on failure: "Ngũgĩ's novel is guided by a powerful image of a grain that wilts and dies instead of growing into 'that body that shall be'" (Gikandi, *Ngũgĩ* 98). But he also suggests that too much has been made of Ngũgĩ's preoccupation with the failures of decolonization in the novel and that more emphasis needs to be put on the novel's endorsement of cultural nationalism. The novel presents "a powerful story of national *retour* and restoration that lies hidden under the rhetoric of failure that dominates the novel" (101). The repeated interchange between "allegory" (the narrative of nationalism) and "irony" (the narrative of disillusion) makes it possible for Ngũgĩ to hold on to the promise of anti-colonial struggle while condemning the failures of decolonization (126–27).

Gikandi's reading captures the introverted energies of Ngũgĩ's historiographic concerns; "national *retour* and restoration" point inward to conversation about the nation. It is important to stress, however, that the concreteness of Ngũgĩ's historical engagement with the Emergency is not undermined by the allegorical. Ngũgĩ aims to deepen postcolonial society's awareness of history. The suppression of the people's history, through either the erasure of memory of the Mau Mau struggle or the mythologizing of heroes, is a corollary of their continued disempowerment after decolonization. There is a need both for a critical approach to the past and for the construction of a narrative that makes the nation imaginable.

Moreover, Ngũgĩ's allusion to 1 Corinthians 15:36 reflects the motif of anti-colonial prophecy and sounds a warning about the renewal of resistance in the future (Wenzel 8–9). The verse quoted by Ngũgĩ is preceded by the question, "But someone will ask, 'How are the dead raised? With what kind of body do they come?'" (1 Cor 15:35). Less about the death of the grain than about resurrection, this passage draws attention to the future's uncertainty. The relation between what you sow and what grows is not one of equivalence. The grain is transfigured by growing, and we cannot tell what it will be. When Waiyaki was buried vertically into the earth, no one could have known what would come as a consequence. By opening up the past's future, Ngũgĩ disrupts the sense of defeat that comes from contemplating such a horrific act of torture.

The second story of torture that haunts the novel is the story of Kihika, a fictional Mau Mau commander:

> Believe the news? The man who compelled trees and mountains to move, the man who could go for ten miles crawling on his stomach through sand and thorny bush, was surely beyond the arm of the white man.
>
> Kihika was tortured. Some say that the neck of a bottle was wedged into his body through the anus as the white people in the Special Branch tried to wrest the secrets of the forest from him. Others say that he was offered a lot of money and a free trip to England to shake the hand of the new woman on the throne. But he would not speak.
>
> Kihika was hanged in public. . . . (Ngũgĩ, *Grain* 17)

This condensed narrative provides a "histor[y] of the hanged" from the perspective of the people. The Mau Mau commander's mythical exploits in the forest are demystified by his arrest and demeaning death, punctuated by his rape. His refusal to speak under torture, however, emerges as a different dimension of heroism. He holds back his story, "the secrets of the forest," because they belong to the people and their telling.

In *Weep Not, Child*, Ngũgĩ shows us how Ngotho's torture, the violence against his body, was a synecdoche for the British appropriation of Gikuyu land. The story of male rape and public hanging that haunts the plot of *A Grain of Wheat* captures a typical element in this history. Sodomy, as shown in the wealth of evidence in Elkins's book, was the most widely used form of torture by the British, along with castration.[34] Such profound emasculation acquires a symbolic association with the loss of land. Being driven off the land was perceived as an attack on masculine identity, as Gikuyu manhood was measured traditionally by the ownership of land (Elkins 14). The violence of forceful removal from the land is inscribed literally on the body of the Gikuyu by the British.[35]

A Grain of Wheat is a record of what the Gikuyu people endured and an exploration of the meaning of political complicity and whether one can expiate for it and how. These are key questions for post-conflict societies and, ahead of the development of a human rights discourse, Ngũgĩ explores a solution in the form of a taking of responsibility through historical narration. Kihika's story of martyrdom is complicated by the suspicion that he was betrayed by a fellow Gikuyu. *Weep Not, Child* alluded to "entanglements" evoking ties that bind even in conflict, especially civil conflict. *A Grain of Wheat* shows that "entanglements" make it so that no one is innocent.

The plot is driven by a "who done it?" question, more typical of the thriller genre from which the popular novels draw. Using irony to position the reader where he always knows more than the characters, Ngũgĩ exploits the "who done it?" plot and its incremental revelations to chip away at all obvious explanations, showing at once how they come to hold sway and how they are challenged and revised by the community. By the end of the novel a complicated historical narrative has been articulated. Mugo, Kihika's betrayer but also a hero of the detention camps, is a "risk averse actor," the very opposite of the Mau Mau stereotype. A peasant who fears that the war will disrupt farming, he betrays Kihika to the District Officer, Thompson, in hope that his action will end the conflict. Instead of rewarding him, Thompson humiliates him and threatens to hang him. Mugo's betrayal of a fellow Gikuyu is perceived not as a sign of loyalty to the British, but as confirmation of his inferior moral status as an African. Mugo's self-realization that he was dirt in the eyes of Thompson is crushing:

> He was nothing. Tears could not help him. With a choked cry, his body smashed on to the broken stones and jutting rock, at the white man's feet. The shock of discovery was so deep it numbed him. He felt no pain, and saw no blood.
>
> "Do you hear?" [the threat that he will hang]
>
> "Yes."
>
> "Say Effendi."
>
> "Yes—"
>
> The word stuck, blocked the throat. His open mouth let out inarticulate noises. Foam had collected at the corners of his mouth. He stared at the whiteman, a watery glint in the eyes, without seeing him. Then the table, the chair, the D.O., the white-washed walls—the earth—started spinning, faster and faster again. He held on to the table to still himself.

> He did not want the money. He did not want to know what he had done. (Ngũgĩ, *Grain* 200)

His rage blocking him, Mugo cannot call Thompson "master" ("effendi"). More importantly, we learn that, ashamed of his action, he does not want to "know" it. This avoidance proves impossible, and Mugo eventually claims the implications of his actions, but only in front of an audience of his community at the independence-day celebration. This is indicative once more of a turning inward that takes precedence over a writing back to empire.

There are no witnesses to Mugo's betrayal of Kihika other than Thompson. When Mugo reencounters Thompson in detention, however, they are not alone, and others see their confrontations. Thompson at first does not even recognize him. He tortures Mugo, whose defiance now is also an act of despair: he "was indifferent to his fate. . . . Let the sword come quickly" (133). Because he did not take the Mau Mau oath, Mugo refuses to give a false confession. His defiance makes Thompson more persistent: "like a tick, [he] stuck to Mugo," repeatedly seeking him out to beat him (133). Mugo does not cry out in pain: "Beyond despair, there was no moaning" (134). His resistance is not explicitly ideological or political; it appears self-destructive, even suicidal, the expression of his deep shame at his act of betrayal. Yet it enables him to claim something back from Thompson, who had destroyed his sense of self. The other detainees who witness the torture are not privy to Mugo's guilt and see him simply as courageous, drawing inspiration from his stoicism. The gap between the private meaning of his actions and the public perception of them creates the space in which Ngũgĩ comments on history. To be true, the public perception needs correction; it must to take into account the private story. The purpose of this exposure is not to tar Mugo, but to understand his entire psychological journey and his struggle with his own sense of responsibility. This for Ngũgĩ is the stuff of historical narrative.

Ngũgĩ most certainly places a high degree of responsibility for the violence on the British and holds them especially accountable for their lack of remorse. The intransigence of the detainees, inspired by men like Mugo, drives Thompson over the edge, and he commits an atrocity that, according to the narrator, became known worldwide: "The now famous beating went on night and day. Eleven men died" (134).[36] World opinion casts shame on Thompson and eventually drives him and the British out of Kenya. However, as an individual Thompson is not punished for the violence he committed. On the eve of his departure from Kenya, he is held in high regard by the settlers as a "martyr," an example of how the British government "abandoned men she had encouraged and sent abroad" (163–64). He went safely back to Britain. Even more unsettling is Thompson's personal view that independence is not the end of Europe's influence in Africa: "'Perhaps this is not the journey's end. . . . We are not yet beaten,' he asserted hoarsely. 'Africa cannot, cannot do without Europe'" (166). This prophecy of neocolonialism proves accurate, and, as Ngũgĩ said in *Homecoming*, "they later returned through the back door" (49).

But Thompson's words echo in an unnerving way the rhetorical pattern of anti-colonial prophecy, as well, which similarly asserted that the peasant rebellion is not done and will return. This kind of thinking carries into the future the sense of injustice that needs to be corrected, crippling the ability for a full accounting of responsibility for past action and falsifying the history on which the future is built. Knowing the true story matters for how we go forward. Mugo is most important as the vehicle for making that full history known. He exposes his guilt in a voluntary act of claiming responsibility. When asked to speak at the independence-day celebration as a hero, he refuses, and instead, surprising all, he steps forth in response to the call for the betrayer of Kihika to come forward. Mugo's public confession becomes the independence-day speech he had refused to give, dramatizing to great effect the imperfect history of the struggle. His confession displays his desire to expiate his wrong by offering the truth. His community had already made up its mind that Karanja, the loyalist among them, was guilty, but must now change course and punish Mugo. Because there is no truth-telling process to hold Karanja accountable for his multiple betrayals, he is deemed innocent, and the harm he did as a home guard and chief go unpunished, whereas Mugo's fate is harsh. After his public confession Mugo is tried in secret by the Mau Mau on the eve of independence, and it is strongly insinuated that he is executed. This settling of scores for the old historical era "casts a long moral shadow" over the promise of independence (Gikandi, *Ngũgĩ* 126). Ngũgĩ thus illustrates the importance of a missed opportunity to claim the history of the struggle in its full complexity, to unify Kenyans against their colonial and neocolonial masters and establish the grounds for redress. The novel as a genre can suggest this possibility, but is constrained by Ngũgĩ's sense of obligation to stay close to the historical truth, which is that independence fell short of its promise.

In the absence of a public solution, Ngũgĩ turns to his characters' private lives and to the allegory of family reconciliation to suggest what should take place in the larger public sphere. Mugo inspires a transformation in Gikonyo, another former detainee, who recognizes the moral value of Mugo's action. Speaking privately to his wife and his mother, Gikonyo declares that Mugo "was a brave man, inside. . . . He stood before much honour, praises were heaped on him. He would have become a Chief. Tell me another person who would have exposed his soul for all the eyes to peck at. . . . Remember that few people in that meeting are fit to lift a stone against that man. Not unless I—we—too—in turn open our hearts naked for the world to look at" (Ngũgĩ, *Grain* 233–34). Gikonyo's statement is an explicit condemnation of Mugo's punishment. Moreover, his call to "open our hearts naked for the world to look at" argues that it takes this kind of candor and taking of responsibility to create the possibility of a just society.

Ngũgĩ's main commitment in the novel is to understand history. The ending of the novel suggests the potential emergence of a collective point of view, but this is achieved in the moments when individual suffering becomes understandable as part of a larger history. References to the hardship of detention and the beatings that took place there are ubiquitous in the novel, and thus the effects of physical punishment become diffuse, as much a collective humiliation as an individual one. This is not immediately apparent to the characters, who feel shamed individually and who slowly arrive at an understanding of the broader context of their individual stories. The reader comes to such an understanding by witnessing the totality of impulsive, spontaneous confessions the characters make to each other in private.

The novel's complex narrative strategy is organized around a sequence of confessional scenes where the characters come individually (and spontaneously) to Mugo to give testimony of their experience and confess the flaws of their actions, their less than heroic demeanor. The historical account is fragmented and out of chronological sequence; it is also marked by repetition, as the same events are narrated through different points of view. This cumulative process leads eventually (with the mediation of Mumbi's, Kihika's sister's, sympathetic presence) to Mugo's public confession and the discrediting of the heroic narrative. The multiple, overlapping retrospective accounts given in the novel also serve to complicate the "teleological narrative of nationalism" (Gikandi, *Ngũgĩ* 100). The process of history is not linear. It requires synthesizing different perspectives.

Confession, in the context of Mau Mau, is a very vexed practice, and to characterize Ngũgĩ's narrative strategy as confessional needs some explanation. So far I have put the emphasis on torture as the war's signature act. However, detainees were tortured in order to confess the Mau Mau oath. This was the key requirement for rehabilitation. The British believed that, upon entering the movement, the Mau Mau took an oath (or a series of oaths) of allegiance to the movement and that these oaths involved extreme rituals, even cannibalism.[37] The oath persisted as the focus of the British demonization of the Mau Mau, and confession became associated with the colonizer's response to the oath. Elkins and Anderson both explain confession as an invented tradition stemming from the dubious authority of ethnopsychologists, a colonial pseudoscience (Elkins 107–8; David Anderson 283).[38] Moreover, the influential Louis Leakey insisted that "traditionally among the Gikuyu the power of an oath could be removed if the initiate confessed having taken it" (Elkins 107). Thus the British came to believe that they were encouraging an indigenous practice and through confession would achieve the peasantry's disaffiliation from the movement.[39] According to both Elkins and Anderson, confession as exacted by the British was not intended to have Christian or missionary overtones, but to draw from traditional practice.

In order to show that taking the oath was not the sine qua non of being Gikuyu, Ngũgĩ portrays characters who have not taken the oath. Ngotho and Njoroge in *Weep Not, Child* are both tortured and asked to confess the oath, although they had not taken it. In *A Grain of Wheat*, when Kihika urges Mugo to join the movement, Mugo, who wants to remain apolitical, quickly replies that he has not taken the oath. Kihika is unimpressed. "But what is an oath?" he asks and explains that people of Mugo's moral character do not need an oath to stay committed (Ngũgĩ, *Grain* 192). Gikonyo confesses the oath in detention, although the reader is left to wonder if he had ever taken it in the first place. There is no scene in the novel in which he actually takes the oath or talks about taking it, although he repeatedly talks about having confessed to taking it. Karanja, who has become a loyalist, "sold the Movement and Oath secrets" in order not to go into detention and to stay close to Mumbi (209). Thus the only one who we know for sure took the oath is the character who turns up as a loyalist.

Ngũgĩ reappropriates confession and recasts it as a historical taking of responsibility. The novel shows how the community is reconstituted through its members' exchange of personal histories. Going against the grain of the British insistence that confession is a native tradition, Ngũgĩ deliberately exploits the Christian implications of confession and redemption by drawing repeatedly from biblical language. Located in the contact zone of colonizer and colonized, the biblical references draw on the cultural legacy of colonialism, and, in a classic rhetorical maneuver of resistance literature, Ngũgĩ turns the language of the Bible against the oppressor.[40] Each of the novel's three sections is prefaced by a biblical passage taken from Kihika's copy of the Bible and highlighted by him. The passages are used to demonstrate how the moral and political bear on the theme of confession and the promise of redemption, articulated here as the fulfillment of a nationalist aspiration, a people's freedom from oppression rather than an individual redemption. For example, the third section of the novel begins with two biblical epigraphs that prophecy a new historical era. John 12:24 repeats the image of a seed: "Verily, verily I say unto you, Except a corn of wheat fall into the ground and die, it abideth alone: but if it die, it bringeth forth much fruit." From sacrifice (Mugo's, presumably), the new will be born. The other passage, Revelation 21:1, also promises rebirth: "And I saw a new heaven and a new earth: for the first heaven and the first earth were passed away." The hopefulness suggested here is tempered by the vexed conclusion of Mugo's story, yet it draws attention to the "utopian" impulse that shapes Ngũgĩ's vision (JanMohamed, *Manichean* 220).

How the novel achieves its collective vision is a problem that has preoccupied critics for some time. JanMohamed argues that the reader comes to understand or "to experience the dynamics of a viable organic community," one in which social interactions are "based on sympathy derived from a communion of purpose." Ngũgĩ teaches us the "inescapable interconnectedness of concrete individuals" (209). But this "viable organic community" is suggested rather than manifested by the end of the novel. Moreover, in his eagerness to endorse this reconstitution of community, JanMohamed downplays the effects of violence. Gikandi finds the emphasis on the communal in Ngũgĩ's endorsement of the national (family) allegory at the end of the novel. Thus he argues that Ngũgĩ paradoxically uses irony to launch again "the allegorical narrative of national independence at a time when its ideals are threatened at their foundations" (Gikandi, *Ngũgĩ* 112). Ngũgĩ, in other words, sets in motion a new revolutionary agenda to fulfill the incomplete struggle for land and freedom.

Fanon's discussion of responsibility is framed by his idea of "a people conscious of its dignity," where "dignity" stands for sovereignty: "a free people living in dignity is a sovereign people" (Fanon 198). Dignity is needed as an aspect of the collective, and thus national, identity. But the violent nature of the struggle for self-determination can rob individuals of dignity, shaming them. As we have seen, "everybody will have to be compromised" (199). Thus it is in the construction of a national story, in the retrospective taking of responsibility for the coming into being of the sovereign nation, that dignity is realized. The narrative of *A Grain of Wheat* is dignifying, therefore, not despite the imperfections of the history it tells, but precisely because of the flaws that are marks of the people's participation in history. There are "no innocents and no onlookers" in the nation.

Sentimentalism and the Politics of Reconciliation

In Ngũgĩ's ironic novels allegory is the counterweight to disillusion, helping keep the idea of the nation alive. Historical narration works toward justice and truth, with the idea that only these provide the foundation for a peaceful society. The sentimental and naturalist novels by Wachira, Mwangi, Mangua, and Kahiga engage instead with the idea of reconciliation and Kenyatta's "forgive and forget," wrangling with the implications of "suffering without bitterness." They create imaginative scenaria of reconciliation and accommodation in order to enable the reintegration of alienated individuals (former combatants, civilians who are victims of atrocities) into the post-conflict society. To do so they first tell the story of their participation in the conflict, with the aim of familiarizing the reader with the particulars of this experience. By following the characters in and out of the forest they give a more intimate look at war and demarcate it as a distinct environment. Thus these novels remember the war, raising the question "what kind of history do they tell?" Some attention to story is necessary here because these novels compete to construct a national memory, weighing different explanations of the past against each other. Moreover, they exemplify the publishing history of an introverted national literature, having been read mostly by a Kenyan audience.[41] In their stories are embedded arguments about the implications of the past for the future.

Wachira's *Ordeal in the Forest* is the key text in the fiction of reconciliation, and like the other novels in this group it focuses on combatants instead of civilians. As its title suggests, much of the novel narrates the difficult experiences in the forest, yet this "ordeal" takes on allegorical meaning, as well. In what follows, I begin with an examination of Wachira's vision for reconciliation, shaped by the experience of the ordeal as a spiritual journey, and then turn to his and the other novelists' portrayal of the experiences in the forest, where the causal, deterministic logic of revenge prevails.

Sentimentalism is the aesthetic of reconciliation, the discourse of accommodation to the difficult experience of postcoloniality. However, sentimentalism is not a well-developed topic in postcolonial criticism, perhaps because the influence of F. R. Leavis on writers who were educated in the

British colonial system seems to have precluded it. Leavis's *Great Tradition* famously left out Charles Dickens, for example, as insufficiently serious because of his sentimentalism, although later Leavis changed his mind and added an epilogue on Dickens's *Hard Times* to his study. Attention to Leavis's influence has led to an underestimation of the importance of sentimentalism in African fiction.[42] The same colonial education that taught the Leavisite aesthetic, however, also exposed its students to Victorian ideas of sentimentality (Sicherman, "Ngũgĩ's Colonial" 15–16). Thus, Ngũgĩ, usually recognized as a modernist, begins his childhood memoir by drawing an analogy between himself and Oliver Twist. He represents his own hunger as a child by quoting Oliver's plea, "Please sir, can I have some more?" (quoted in Ngũgĩ, *Dreams* 4).

More attention has been accorded instead to the didacticism of African novels.[43] But didacticism is intimately linked to sentimentalism, which as a genre "exploited its consumer's appetite for feeling, taking a pedagogical role and training its readers in emotional responses through the exemplary responses of characters" (Keen 46). The emphasis on how readers respond to sentimental literature is on influencing their moral judgment. Kaplan's useful distinction between Victorian sentimentality and Romantic sensibility can illuminate this aspect of sentimentalism further: "Sentimentality is the possession of innate moral sentiments; sensibility is a state of psychological-physical responsiveness" (Kaplan 33). For our context here we can push the distinction and say that naturalism is a form of sensibility, which examines the responsiveness of characters in extreme circumstances. I will turn to this after the discussion of sentimentalism.

Understood as a fictional "strategy of containment," sentimentalism creates a usable past, a selective memory that can aid the unfolding process of national constitution. Jameson's term "strategies of containment" puts the focus on the ideological work of fiction, which seeks to create an independent and apparently self-contained coherence. "Strategies of containment" work to naturalize rather than historicize in Jameson's sense of critique (Jameson, *Political Unconscious* 193–94). The creation of a usable past that can stabilize a post-conflict social order is facilitated by sentimentalism's ability to articulate closure for a traumatic past.

The best example of Wachira's sentimentalism can be found in the extended scene of his protagonists' chance reunion in detention. Mrefu and Nundu, combatants coming out of the forest, tearfully recognize each other when they are shackled together in detention (Wachira 226–31). Nundu was once Mrefu's student; Mrefu considers Nundu an adopted son. In this new circumstance Mrefu fails to recognize Nundu, who is blindfolded, his face distorted from the beating he has suffered. Nundu, moreover, believes that Mrefu was killed: "Kifaru (Nundu's *nom de guerre*) had received the message that his beloved Mrefu was dead, and he had wept bitterly. But Mrefu, still surmising who could be next to him, could never, in the wildest stretch of his imagination, have thought him to be Nundu. He fell to thinking about his adopted son, his heart full of affection" (226–27). Reuniting, the two address each other as "my father" and "my beloved son," shedding "tears of joy" (231). When, tearfully once more, they share their regrets over the divisions that plagued their armed struggle, they locate their suffering within the narrative of the failed quest for national unity. Nundu recognizes his misplaced ambition to rise above his former teacher:

> "That was where I made my mistake, and I regretted it deeply later. If only I had stayed with you. . . . I'm sure that neither of us would have ended up here . . . instead of fighting our enemies, we fought amongst ourselves; because of greed and ambition, we forgot that unity is strength. Oh, Mrefu, I never thought it would end up like this. Why, why did we do it?" He broke down, overcome by emotion. (238)

Nundu not only admits the destructive infighting among the guerrillas, but he also draws attention to the intergenerational aspect of this conflict. The son rebelled against the father. This is what he regrets. The answer to Nundu's question "why did we do it?" is not forthcoming, because a full historical accounting of how the struggle took the shape that it did is not what the novel is driving at. Instead, the novel stages a scene of regret for past actions, which can be addressed by committing to a new course in the future. "Why did we do it?" with its implied negative judgment is as far as it is necessary for accountability to go in order to renew the sentimental ties and put everyone back on course, restoring the authority of the fathers.

The transformative experience, allowing for the regeneration of the sentimental ties, occurs in detention. This is where a unity of purpose emerges in Wachira's novel. Kenyatta claimed something similar: "Freedom came (to us) through AFRICAN UNITY. It was all of us being united: those in prisons and detention camps, in the towns and in the country. We were all seeking freedom (together). . . . All we Africans were in a state of slavery, and all of us (together) brought our freedom" (Kenyatta, *Suffering* 341–42). Notable here is the lack of reference to the forest, absent because its memory is divisive. If the novelist can show, however, that the fighters in the forest were also in the prisons, detention camps, and enclosed villages, then their suffering can be represented.

It is hard to miss the irony of this claim, since the British also envisioned "rehabilitation" in detention as the remaking of community through confession. Wachira thwarts this analogy by stressing the offended dignity of the people under colonial rule, especially in enduring torture and the razing of villages. Like Kenyatta, he stresses the victimization of the people. Njogu, the third figure among Wachira's leaders, tells a group of fighters, "The whites who call themselves police, security forces and so on, have no regard for our human dignity. . . . The tortures they use are too ghastly to describe" (Wachira 120–21). The same characters who tearfully acknowledge their bonds for each other also share a common enemy from which they get their unity. Yet the irony that the forest divides and detention unites demonstrates that the claim against the colonizer is made more effectively from the point of view of victim, not resistor, thus allowing for a postcolonial order where the victim will depend on the reparative actions of the new political dispensation, which was historically created under the influence of the former colonial power. Wachira's privileging of detention as a setting is a more politically expedient way to stage "suffering without bitterness" and attempt closure to the narrative of the conflict, compared to Ngũgĩ's emphasis on the negative impact of detention and an incomplete sense of justice.

The novel does not end with the military defeat of Mau Mau, however. It goes on to depict the subsequent political struggle as it accelerates toward independence, facilitated by the growing international criticism of the British for their human rights abuses. "World opinion," we learn, has rallied to the Kenyans' nationalist cause (Wachira 281). The nation imagined as family is the new configuration for the anti-colonial struggle, now taking place in a changed field of action and with a different moral map. Wachira seeks to legitimate the passage from Mau Mau to national politics through Mrefu's homecoming from prison. On the last page of the novel he reflects, "I was sent to prison and then home; here is my home, my people" (288). Wachira performs this legitimation by having Mrefu both disavow further violence and assert the value of the past struggle: "'our blood has not been spilt in vain'" (281).

The goal of national sovereignty, achieving an identity in the international order of nation states, obscures the economic and class struggle that is ongoing within the nation. At the end of Wachira's novel the vocabulary of struggle is no longer about land as it was at the beginning (139). Asked to lead the new political coalition that will struggle for Uhuru, Mrefu at first hesitates, burdened by an awareness of his past failings. Upon reflecting on his life's experiences, how he "changed from that pig-headed schoolboy who decided to take up teaching as a career" (287), he concludes that he has suffered a lot, "paid [his] debt," and expiated his guilt. He interprets his people's request that he lead them as evidence that he has "been forgiven" (286). In *A Grain of Wheat*, as we saw, Mugo was given a similar chance to lead, but his guilt got the better of him; his public confession reflected a commitment to historical accountability. Mrefu makes a more politically expedient choice to take on the leadership without making full disclosure of his own history. As a consequence, his suffering in war remains private, and, by implication, its sphere of action (the forest) stays outside public scrutiny.

It is hard to like Mrefu as a character, which gives us pause about the sincerity of Wachira's endorsement of Kenyatta's "suffering without bitterness." Our understanding of Mrefu's rationalization that he need not disclose his failings before assuming a politically powerful position is complicated by an earlier instance in the novel where, through dramatic irony, we see Mrefu's insincerity. When Mrefu and Nundu are reunited in detention, they have the opportunity to disclose to each other their stories from the time of their falling out in the forest to their present reunion. In a scene that recalls the multiple confessions of Ngũgĩ's characters to each other in *A Grain of Wheat*, Nundu pours his heart out to Mrefu, sincerely acknowledging his shortcomings (Ngũgĩ, *Grain* 238–46). In contrast, Mrefu is untruthful. He does not reveal that he left his unit in the forest because he had decided to surrender, and lies about his continued commitment to the fight: "I never was a power seeker, and I had no wish to bring the struggle to a head. For this reason, I decided to select my very best men and start my own battalion like you did—and I too was caught in the process" (248).

Mrefu misleads Nundu, inwardly "chuckling with joy" that he has manipulated him successfully (248). "Caught in the process" is the phrase that hides Mrefu's accountability for leaving the struggle. Although Mrefu is later remorseful about his decision to surrender (the regret is not surprising, since it resulted in his capture and torture) and about lying to Nundu, he never confesses his remorse. In the end it is his suffering in the hands of the British authorities (his debt paid) rather than his prowess as a Mau Mau fighter that legitimates him as a leader in his own and his people's eyes. The suffering is real enough, but it facilitates a forgetting of the political lessons of the forest, which need to be remembered to create a just political order after independence.

Wachira's novel, however, successfully stages such a remembering against the grain of his protagonist's intentions. The novel gives a full account of what "caught in the process" means; the "process" is a euphemism for the armed struggle. Indeed, the episodes in the forest that lead up to Mrefu's defection from the struggle and his "ordeal"—in which he and his men get lost and must fend for themselves in the wilderness before getting captured—provide a counterhistory to the narrative of unity, which constantly resurfaces even though it is segregated as part of that separate history of the forest.

Before I turn to this narrative of the forest, I want to compare briefly the treatment of the father and son theme in Wachira's novel to *Weep Not, Child*, where the sentimental scene at the father's deathbed attempts the political rehabilitation of the father figure. Ngũgĩ's irony makes it evident that this is a futile gesture, as the father is dying and being relegated to political irrelevance. The problem for Ngũgĩ is that the sons too have become politically handicapped. Wachira's novel seems to do the exact opposite. It elevates the father, whose standing was compromised during the war, into a leadership figure of the new establishment. The novel ends with Mrefu's autobiographical narrative, which interprets his war experience, as we saw, in terms of individual development and growth. Thus the novel's ending recasts the story of the father as a *Bildungsroman*, displacing the son's story of development with which the novel begins. (The opening is set in the village school, and the main focus is on the students). Nundu's maturation is deferred indefinitely, a symbol of the impending problem of "arrested decolonization" (Gikandi, *Ngũgĩ* 72). Thus we find here not only the interrupted novel of education as it applies to Nundu and his peers, but also a substitute *Bildungsroman* of an inappropriate figure, the father rather than the son. The war novel once more distorts the novel of education.

Ordeal in the Forest gestures to the *Bildungsroman* at the key moment when it enacts the individual's "incorporation" into the nation, the assumption of citizenship. The novel's substitution of the demand for land with the vocabulary of dignity, political freedom, and national sovereignty places it firmly in the mainstream of an ideology of human rights that emphasizes civil and political rights.[44] The novel asks us to imagine the father figure as having now grown up and matured politically. Figuratively, the colonized subject is a child; the new citizen of independent Kenya is a grown man. Wachira opportunistically borrows the *Bildungsroman*'s political capital and misattributes its symbolic terms. This representational strategy backfires, perhaps intentionally, because, instead of succeeding in making a convincing case for the father's belated political legitimacy, it reveals more shockingly the new political dispensation's war on the young and its selfish hold on the reins of political privilege. The novel begins with the schoolroom, but tells us of the teacher's journey to maturity and not the students,' who constitute a lost generation. Are we meant to think "so be it" for the sake of political expediency? Is the novel's introverted gesture also exclusionary? Much in the novel's account of the forest leads us to think differently, to see Wachira as masterfully ironic, gutting the myth of the individual's incorporation and leaving us with a good look at unfinished business.

In the Forest

So far I have discussed what happens in Wachira's novel after the combatants leave the forest. In addition to its exemplary alignment of family, national politics, and sentimentalism, *Ordeal in the Forest* is paradigmatic of war fiction because of the way it treats the transforming identity of the young male combatant, Nundu. Wachira's depiction of the forest war strains toward naturalism and is echoed in important ways throughout the genre, especially because of its evocative use of the "ordeal in the forest" motif. Written against the official rhetoric of insurgency, which seeks to diminish the impression that the conflict is a full-scale war, the novel shows that the dehumanization of the Mau Mau fighters is an understandable consequence of war rather than a reflection of savagery. The word "war" is repeated constantly, chipping away at alternative characterizations of the struggle. For example, when Nundu tries to win over his peers to the struggle, they confront him: "But Nundu, you are talking of war" (Wachira 74). And we are told that after the Emergency, "a declaration of total war against the whites" is made (101). Moreover, the many references to the two world wars make clear that this conflict created similar conditions. Countering stereotypes of the Mau Mau, the fighters are portrayed as disciplined and methodical, waiting patiently for the right moment to begin their offensive. In contrast, the settlers are in a "state of blind panic," and the colonial government prepares militarily by amassing troops and airplanes to "stop the rebellion" (107). Moreover, when Mrefu is captured he refers to himself as a "war prisoner" (217, 224).

At the beginning of the novel Wachira profiles the different background of each boy in the classroom. Poverty makes their situation precarious, and it seems unlikely that they will be able to stay in school. It is no surprise that Nundu persuades them to run away by appealing to their resentment of school discipline. The consequences of their rebellion are very harsh and play out in generational terms that inscribe themselves deeply in the way the war's story unfolds. After they run away the boys find employment with a white farmer, and when their fathers come looking for them, the farmer unfairly accuses the men of stealing his cattle. The fathers are sent to prison, while the boys continue to be employed by the farmer, Major Cook, a veteran of World War I, whose cruelty is explicitly linked to his war experience. Seething under the injustice done to their fathers and their continued maltreatment by Cook, the boys learn to hate. They become involved in the movement, take the oath, and receive instruction from the senior leaders in secret. Thus Wachira explains the emergence of the movement as a sequential process, progressing to its logical telos—war—by the growing distrust between settlers and Africans. The sons undertake to avenge the humiliation of the fathers by the colonial power. Wachira also represents the rift between the settlers and the colonial government that gives the forest fighters an advantage initially, since the colonial government is unwilling to believe that the Africans are capable of a full-scale war.

The forest narrative describes Nundu's downward spiral, the degradation of the young combatant, who is certainly not portrayed as a hero. Nundu leads the attack on Cook's farm and gets his revenge in a scene that is the most often quoted from the novel, because here Nundu seems to typify the savage Mau Mau. An example of the rage of the colonized, of Fanonian violence coming out of shame and anger, Nundu's murder results in the settler's demise, but also his own brutalization:

> Nundu sprang upon his victim, slashing his hated face again and again with the panga until it was nothing but an unrecognisable bloody pulp. He slashed until from pure exhaustion he could slash no longer . . . his savage joy, now that his long cherished desire was achieved, left him so weak and shaky that he was obliged to rest on the floor beside the man he had mutilated and killed, now so still and silent. (147)

Portrayed lying down next to the man he has just killed, Nundu is denied the posture of victor standing over his victim. Having unleashed his rage, he has now spent his moral capital, and indeed the rest of his story is one of progressive degeneration (he also becomes a habitual drug user, smoking his "bhangi" [183]), until his reunion with Mrefu, when he is redeemed in his new identity as adopted son. Nundu's is a story of arrested development, typical of the interrupted life stories of child soldiers whose induction to war completely disrupts the whole set of expectations about childhood and adulthood and places them in an ambiguous, liminal space.

As I noted, "ordeal in the forest" refers to the narrative sequence in the novel that recounts how the fighters get lost while trying to leave the forest. Wachira's novel initiates this sequence as a motif that has become prevalent in the African war novel. Wachira's Christian frame of reference evokes the spiritual condition of being lost in the wilderness, and "ordeal" alludes to a physical trial that must be addressed spiritually. While lost in the forest, Mrefu prays frequently, addressing the God of Kirinyaga (Mt. Kenya) in language that echoes Kenyatta once again: "Oh give us our freedom! Free us from the bonds of slavery—let your people go! Do not let our suffering count for naught!" (Wachira 219). The spiritual is the national. Pushed to the limit, Mrefu sets aside his selfish motivations and discovers his (genuine) commitment to the struggle. The prayer that suffering pay and yield tangible results expresses a wish for encouragement, for strength to stay the course, implying that the main danger is in disillusion and indiscipline. Thus the "ordeal in the forest," when one is lost and found again, brings the character out of an impasse and into a new commitment to a course of action, an intensification of his participation.

The problem for Mrefu will be determining a proper setting where he can act on this new commitment, which the novel shows us must be *uhuru*, not the Emergency, and hence also not the forest or the other scenes of war. This first entails a taking stock of the impact of the forest on his identity. The transformation of the combatants' appearance in the forest suggests that they regress: unwashed and unkempt, their hair and beards long, their clothing increasingly improvised from animal skins and whatever else they can find, their homemade weapons all symbolize a dehumanization and even a bestialization of man.[45] The ordeal in the forest importantly reframes the men's experience as extraordinary, an "ordeal" with spiritual and existential dimensions that elevates it to a universal plane. We are reminded of Henri Barbusse's claim in *Under Fire* (1916), the classic novel of World War I (a key influence on Ernest Hemingway and Remarque), that men in war are "men who have reverted to their primal state" (Barbusse 18). The problem is not Africa, but war. Thus, although the fighters look like beasts, their struggle for survival in the primeval forest humanizes them. They are lost, starving, thirsty, and are confronted by an array of wild animals. The British believed that the Gikuyu were familiar with the forest and had special survival skills, even a "forest psychology" (Carothers), but the fact is that the forest was alien to the Gikuyu who lived on its edges. As Anderson says wryly, "Gikuyu were farmers, not men of the trees" (David Anderson 236).[46] When one of Mrefu's men is injured by a rhinoceros, the narrator refers to this experience ironically as their "*safari*," reminding us that it is no more natural for them to be in the primeval forest than the settlers or the British (Wachira 199).

Like other novels that deploy this motif, the metaphor of the journey and the physical ordeal convey a process of psychic and spiritual transformation that helps motivate certain types of action necessary for survival once the characters reemerge from the forest. Afterward they invariably see the war with new eyes. The interlude of this journey enacts a shift in register to a more intense and active involvement with fewer inhibitions. In Mrefu's case this means first being forced to recognize that the war has another arena he had been unaware of: the detention camps and enclosed villages he knew nothing about while he was in the forest. Emerging from the forest, he stumbles upon a scene of the forced digging of trenches and is astounded:

> These people were being treated like slaves and they blamed the forest fighters for each day of slavery that they suffered, for placing them in this predicament. Those, and there were many, who sympathised with the fighters and would have done anything to help them given the chance, did not dare express their feelings.
>
> Neither Mrefu nor his colleagues had ever heard about this venture. . . . (221)

The combatants' story is here subordinated to the civilians' story of the war. The forest recedes further, and the primary scene of the war is detention, where Mrefu and Nundu regularly witness the torture of others. In a scene reminiscent of Djebar's *Children of the New World*, Mrefu and Nundu both listen as "the screams of the latest inmates echoed over the camp" (247). Mrefu finds a new purpose, discovering the "song of his country" in the people's suffering. Being witness to the suffering of others takes equal space as his own suffering and creates a group narrative and national consciousness from the isolating experience of torture:

> Yes, I've been forgiven [for betraying the fighters by surrendering and numerous other betrayals under duress in detention], and now I can start life anew, but with the same purpose—to free my people. We'll have to do it differently this time. Yes! Find a loftier, better, gentler way. No one people can keep another people in chains of bondage for ever! (286)

"Chains of bondage" focuses the problem on freedom and unfreedom without specifying who the struggle is against. This is a new beginning ("start life anew"), but also a renewal of the struggle "to free my people." The "loftier, better, gentler way" Mrefu vows to use in the future suggests a less violent path, understood now as possible because the injustice of enslaving a people will be inevitably resolved, even without violence. Sustaining such injustice is asserted as simply impossible; freedom will come inevitably, responding to the people's self-evidently just demand. Mrefu's rhetoric mimics Kenyatta's "AFRICAN UNITY," but sounds forced. The ordeal in the forest prepares Mrefu to recognize the war's multiple fronts, bringing into focus a suffering people. It takes time for him to realize what he learned. Under duress in detention, Mrefu is still scheming and conniving. Detention is a place where the logic of war is still operative, and, as Barbusse noted, "It's every man for himself, in war" (Barbusse 27).[47] Thus it is mandatory to break with war. "Forgiveness" is the formula for this break, and, whereas Kenyatta meant forgetting, Wachira goes against this, providing instead an accounting of the war that tells how such a forgetting could be justified without convincing us ultimately that forgetting is possible.

Mwangi's Naturalism

War is treated by Meja Mwangi as a determining environment that is nearly impossible to transcend. This is a mark of Mwangi's naturalism, where the historically specific becomes naturalized and, as such, an absolutely defining context. Naturalists "systematically represent contingent forms of historical determination as if they were absolute forms of determinism, and they mainly achieve this effect through figurative and narrative acts of metaphysicalization" (Moglen 32). Mwangi is doing something similar to "metaphysicalization" (especially, as we shall see, in the description of Haraka's wound), taking the contingent and making it absolute in order to illustrate the all-consuming nature of war. The forest becomes a hell of physical suffering and of mental and psychological confusion. Anger in particular is represented as a deformity that reveals a "human animality," the great theme of naturalist fiction (quoted in Levin 328), establishing a discourse of the unheroic. The manner of death and killing, the display of "human animality," are Mwangi's war themes, and they remind us of the war novel's central preoccupation as a genre: to demystify and condemn war. Making sure such condemnation is made from the people's perspective, rather than from that of those who came to power after independence, is the aim of Mwangi's depiction of the forest.

What this means specifically in *Carcase for Hounds* is that Mwangi exposes not only the suffering in the forest, but the politics of Mau Mau.

Thus he shows that, although subjected to the deterministic logic of war, the combatants in the forest were exercising agency through the politics of the movement, destructive as these were. Mwangi has been accused of avoiding the "taint" of politics by adopting a naturalist aesthetic (Maughan-Brown 220). His attention is on the "dramatic stories of war, love and betrayal" (Gikandi and Mwangi 350–51). Yet the novel's epigraph (and title) from *Julius Caesar* signals Mwangi's intent to write a political story.

Shakespeare's play about political assassination and revenge points to the novel's focus on power and the powerful. *Julius Caesar* is about civil war. In the epigraph of the novel, Brutus speaks of his intent to kill Caesar: "Let's kill him boldly but not wrathfully, / Let's carve him as a dish fit for the gods. / Not hew him as a carcase fit for hounds" (*Julius Caesar* 2.1.173–75). This is a comment on the appropriate demeanor of the assassin, suggesting he kill "boldly but not wrathfully," an attitude the forest fighters fail to live up to. The condemnation of war is thus part of the novel's politics.

Haraka is driven into the forest (like Nundu in *Ordeal in the Forest*) after a confrontation with colonial authority. A moderate village chief, who has tolerated the presence of Mau Mau in his village without committing to the movement (Meja Mwangi, *Carcase* 19), Haraka is targeted for questioning and humiliated. Reacting spontaneously, he assaults the District Commissioner and has no choice but to flee into the forest. Thus Haraka enters the forest a political moderate whose dignity has been wounded and his safety compromised by the terroristic colonial state. In the forest he transforms into a monster of vengefulness. The District Commissioner he assaulted is not far behind, however, as he too follows Haraka into the forest, gearing up to "hunt" his "elusive prey" (107). The two are equally intent on vengeance and destroying each other; Mwangi highlights a certain equivalence here. Having entered the forest, they are now subjugated to the logic of war, of reciprocal injury.

Haraka has other antagonists, as well: Simba, a loyalist chief, and even his own lieutenants turn against him when he blames them unfairly for the Mau Mau's defeat. The increasingly inward turn of the conflict (Africans fighting Africans) takes symbolic form in the gangrene consuming and destroying Haraka's body. An example of naturalist "sensibility," the wound is a vehicle for representing the "psychological-physical responsiveness" to the suffering of war. As he is dying, Haraka is aware that the "vultures were hovering, waiting, hovering and waiting for his carcase" (101). Once again we find echoes of *Julius Caesar*. Mark Antony in his reply to Brutus calls on Ate, the Roman "goddess of discord and moral chaos" (Bevington 1043):

> And Caesar's spirit, ranging for revenge,
> With Ate by his side come hot from hell,
> Shall in these confines with a monarch's voice
> Cry havoc and let slip the dogs of war,
> That this foul deed shall smell above the earth
> With carrion men, groaning for burial. (*Julius Caesar* 3.1.272–77)

Haraka becomes one of these "carrion men," living out the short remainder of his life as stinking, painful flesh. The bullet wound, which contributes to his long mental and physical decline, becomes a force in the novel. Described in minute, naturalistic detail, down to the "little microbes [that] ate their way into every tissue, every nerve," the wound's progression parallels the war's deterioration (Meja Mwangi, *Carcase* 132).

Consumed by hatred and his putrid wound (the "psycho-physical"), Haraka fantasizes about revenge incessantly. As he becomes physically and morally repulsive, he undergoes a transformation that makes him a personification of war, and recalls Chaka's transformation in Mofolo's novel.[48] Haraka:

> saw the face of the District Commissioner, tall, proud and white. White and hateful. D.C. Kingsley and his mascot Simba. The general's eye bored into the two and his hate was for them. His body was bathed in perspiration as the warm waves of pain and revenge washed over him, periodically making the veins on his face and neck dance excitedly. As he watched the two images the heads fell off one by one. (103)

Haraka's desire for revenge becomes a madness. Physically incapacitated, he insistently calls for his men to get him chief Simba's head. Importantly, it is not Kingsley's head but Simba's that Haraka wants; the internecine fight has displaced the anti-colonial war, which the forest fighters are losing.

Conditions in Mwangi's novel seem irremediable, but his characters defy the "totalizing, rationalistic progressivism" of realist narratives, and their "negativity" is their agency, as Lazarus has argued, for African naturalism (Lazarus, "Realism" 342). Mwangi moves the conversation about Mau Mau past the question of its legitimacy as an anti-colonial movement to inscribe in it a story about class, about the leaders and the led. The anticipated implosion suggested by *Carcase for Hounds* threatens the cohesion of post-independence society, its strategies of containment, if the divisions in the forest seem to be the same as those out of the forest.

The people, represented by Kimano and the others in Haraka's unit, are faithful followers who, in contrast to their leader's egotism, are motivated by noble ideals of loyalty, courage, self-sacrifice, and love of the land. Mwangi's characterization of the forest fighters, therefore, is not monolithic. He indicts the exploitative attitude of the leaders, who, in their egotistic self-destruction, expend the lives of their followers. But Kimano, as representative of the best of the people, is also flawed. He exhibits a fundamental political immaturity in his susceptibility to the charismatic appeal of his general, "that endearing, enslaving touch" of an authoritarian figure (Meja Mwangi, *Carcase* 123). As he realizes that he will need to take over the command of their unit, Kimano is plagued by uncertainty in his own ability to lead. He thinks nostalgically of Haraka "up until recently tough, clear-headed, a pillar of comfort, decision and confidence" (which is not how the reader has seen him) and feels paralyzed: "he groped hopelessly for something to do, something to decide, to break the encasing feeling of inadequacy" (116–17).

As the nurse of Haraka's wound, Kimano "had milked the wound of its weakening pus. . . . He had squeezed the ugly lips until the granite eyes watered, and a mixture of blood and water oozed out of the wound" (108). This role of tender to the wound captures Kimano's secondariness, his dependence and immaturity, which keeps him captive to the hate that defines Haraka. But it also enacts aesthetically that movement of expansiveness, where the novel peels back from the limit of war to reveal the human bonds that develop in the most extreme of situations. When Kimano succumbs to Haraka's "maddening" demands that he bring back Simba's head (119), he does so in despair. It is a suicidal gesture to prove that he has some worth left in the midst of failure, if only in his willingness to sacrifice all:

> There was only one thing to do now. Get the head as promised. He had no idea, no plan how to do that. But trying to do it was more helpful to his nerves than sitting in the cave all night worrying about everything. Now there was only one thing to worry about. And if he failed, if he got killed, better still. There would be no more mental torture then. (127)

Kimano's agency is asserted here through the negative path of a suicidal mission. It is necessary to act and use what agency he has to trump his lack of options. He fails in the mission to get Simba's head, and Haraka rages against him, threatening to execute him. Kimano, however, receives fatal injuries in an enemy attack before Haraka gets to him. Even so, forgiving his leader, he has a vision just as he is dying of Haraka leading him "as he had always done" through a gate (134).[49] This comforting vision is disrupted by the hyena's laugh, which mocks Kimano's naive faith in Haraka's authority.

The novel ends with an impasse, because war cannot produce its own solution. The novel's bleakness is most evident in its refusal of a future. In contrast to Wachira's gestures of reconciliation and forgiveness and Ngũgĩ's hope for Uhuru at the end of *A Grain of Wheat*, Mwangi's novel ends with the hyena's "sarcastic" laugh, a laugh that would be heard for "eternity," we are told, mocking the death of the novel's sincerest character, Kimano (Meja Mwangi, *Carcase* 134). One cannot imagine any good coming from the sacrifice of so many lives. Furthermore, the novel ends without offering an interpretation of independence and its meaning, thus refusing to credit the forest war in the transition. Having forced his readers to see a war they have refused to see, Mwangi simultaneously seems to be telling them it is best to abandon this realm and turn instead to the political, where some kind of resurrection of the people can be engineered away from the self-destructiveness of war.

Mwangi's second Mau Mau novel, *Taste of Death*, begins by deploying the sentimental as the genre of the middle road politically and ends with despair and disorientation. Thus it begins in one tonal register and moves to a totally different register, subverting the stock narratives of Mau Mau and showing the inadequacy of the reforming promises of home and hearth, nation and freedom. Two home invasions organize the plot and signal that the home is part of the war front. The allegorical implications for this attack on the family are fairly straightforward: war endangers the nation. But it also tells us that we have not yet overcome the war, and its poignancy continues to affect us. Mwangi sets up all the conditions for a sentimental reconciliation, only to show how this is an inadequate way to contain the trauma of the war. Instead of going home, his protagonist returns to the forest at the end of the novel. This rejection of the sentimental in a novel intended for secondary school students is of particular interest. Perhaps more of an appeal for rewriting the sentimental in some other way than an outright rejection of it, *Taste of Death* demonstrates the extent to which the sentimental plot was contested and revised over and over.

Once again, as in *Carcase for Hounds*, Mwangi begins with the premise of a politically moderate Gikuyu people. Kariuki belongs to the center politically. It is perhaps not a coincidence that he bears the name of the real historical figure of J. M. Kariuki and thus alludes to Kenyatta's political opposition. The fictional Kariuki is a World War II veteran who has not taken the oath, but is nonetheless targeted for reprisal by the loyalist chief because his independence is viewed with suspicion. Home guards invade his home in the middle of the night as he is sleeping with his wife, and we see Kariuki in an intimate moment: "Stop crying, darling," Kariuki tells his wife, stoically advising, "We have got to face it as it comes" (Meja Mwangi, *Taste of Death* 15). The reader understands, however, that the domestic space is not shielded from war. Since this novel was intended as a text for secondary students, it was printed as an illustrated edition (Figure 1.1). The illustration of this scene starkly portrays two masculinities, the loving, protective husband and the menacing armed male. The vantage point from the far interior of the room emphasizes the sense of invasion into the domestic space.

Mwangi renders this scene quietly, conveying its intensity with a restraint absent from his forest scenes. "[Kariuki] stood there in the semi-darkness of the room with his wife's head on his chest. She was weeping softly" (15). Although arrested and beaten, Kariuki escapes and flees into the forest in a sequence that repeats in reverse Wachira's "ordeal in the forest," which was an escape out of the forest. In a plot twist characteristic of this novel, Kariuki encounters the British despite going into the forest to find Mau Mau. Preparing the reader for this encounter, the narrator warns that the British are "naturally brutal" (27). After escaping from the British a second time and finally reaching the Mau Mau, he is in danger once again because they find his story "too pitiful to be true" and threaten to kill him. It is only when their general, also a World War II veteran, recognizes Kariuki that his life is spared and he is safe. This plot detail links the present to the past, underscoring the continuous war experience of Kenyans.

A few more twists in the plot rehearse various stereotypical situations. After the British defeat the band of fighters, they arrest and torture Kariuki, his general, and a fellow fighter, who dies from his torture. They are taken to Karima village, which has turned into a prison and is described as a "town of pain." Once again, the screams of victims of torture collectivize the experience so that "The cries of pain had grown in them, and they were one, the pain and the residents of the town" (162–63). Kariuki is (stereotypically) stoic and does not give up any information. He is sentenced to hang, but escapes when the van he is being transported in crashes.[50] After another harrowing trek in the forest he rejoins the guerrillas, but soon after learns the war is over. A former forest fighter and victim of torture, he is now poised to reenter civilian life as a hero of Uhuru, like Wachira's Mrefu, but with more legitimacy, as there is no ambiguity about his sincerity. The novel's ending, however, trumps this stock narrative.

The ending takes its shape through the profound consequences of the novel's two home invasions. The first incident, as we saw, propelled Kariuki into the forest. The second incident affects Kariuki's fellow fighter, Mbogo, and its consequences lead Mbogo to commit suicide in the last

Figure 1.1. In this illustration from Meja Mwangi's *Taste of Death* (1975), the novel's character Kariuki comforts his wife as he is about to be arrested. Illustration by Trixi Lerbs.

scene of the novel because, as he tells Kariuki with his dying breath, "I have done my duty. . . . It is finished. I lost everything. No home to go to. Nobody will miss me" (257). Despite the anticipation of peace at the end of the novel, Mbogo despairs. Several carefully selected details give Mbogo's circumstances particular poignancy: his wife was pregnant when she was killed trying to warn him not to cross the trench surrounding their village because the home guards were present (183). This tragedy is displayed in another illustration where the wife's body is catapulted into the air from the violence of the shot and strikes a strangely graceful pose (Figure 1.2). In the background we find once again the opposing masculinities: the distraught husband on the left and the armed men on the right. Mbogo was on his way to visit his wife in secret. To do so he had to cross from the forest into the enclosed village, defying the demarcation of the war's separate spheres; the couple was betrayed by a fellow villager, a woman whom Mbogo viciously kills, hence dehumanizing himself further (186). To preach a return to home and hearth as the appropriate transition to Uhuru does not address the aftermath of these experiences. The story of Mbogo and his wife inserts the civilians back into the narrative of the war, but by now the family allegory of the nation is spent, this too a victim of the war. A new paradigm of national cohesion is needed unless a significant effort is made to remobilize the national allegory of family and make it convincing.

Thus a second effort, Kariuki's return home, is attempted. As Mbogo is dying, he tells Kariuki, "Go back to your people, Kariuki. Enjoy freedom. We fought for it but we can't all have the same feelings after this. Remember what you told me. It is for the good of our children's children. Do not let the thought of me haunt you. Forget that we ever fought side by side or that you ever knew me. You will be alright that way" (257). "For the good of our children's children" recognizes the lost generation of sons and, instead of elevating the fathers, Mbogo wisely speaks of the grandchildren. However, with his own child dead in the womb of its murdered mother, it is unclear who will parent this generation of grandchildren. The familiar injunction to "forget" is repeated, but, ironically, it serves as a reminder of the strong bonds of the forest. Mbogo had been ambivalent about the struggle all along and had referred to it presciently as "suicide" (146). Echoing Mrefu's conclusion in *Ordeal in the Forest*, who had similarly been in favor of surrender, Mbogo did not believe armed conflict would drive the British away; time would do that on its own. Kariuki, on the other hand, had viewed surrender as cowardly (147). As it turned out, indepen-

Figure 1.2. Novel character Mgobo's wife is shot and killed in Meja Mwangi's *Taste of Death*. Illustration by Trixi Lerbs.

dence was achieved without a military victory in the war, leaving the former forest fighters to cope with the paradox of independence and defeat.

Mbogo urges Kariuki to return to his people, but "people" acquires a double meaning here. Although Mbogo meant family, "Go back to your people" gains a broader resonance, especially since Kariuki does not know if his family is alive or dead. By this point Kariuki has traveled far from the sentimental ethos of longing for home after his wrenching separation from his wife at the beginning of the novel. Emotionally disconnected from home, he is more anxious about missing the comradeship of the forest, what he called earlier its "sentimental solidarity" (128). In the novel's last paragraph, Kariuki "remembered things" against Mbogo's advice to "forget" (258). He remembers in particular the resilience of the fighters: "the Leader dying with a smile," the General tortured but still standing, another fighter who died of torture ("Njau was there too") (258). In his mind's eye he sees the "white soldiers stealthily moving in the forest" and "troops of forest fighters" firing their guns (258). Thus "Kariuki felt that he was missing something. He belonged to the world of his friends and firing guns, and not to a world of dead memories" (258). We have thus arrived at an impasse. Civilian life for the former forest fighter is full of dead memories, whereas the forest has a strong nostalgic attraction, a greater sense of belonging. The civilian life requires a divorce from the memory of the forest Kariuki is unwilling to make. The forest fighter resists being relegated to forgetting, although it is hard to know whether holding on to this identity makes him politically irrelevant by marginalizing him or whether it indicates a residual political power that at some point could reemerge. Ngũgĩ treats a similar theme in *Matigari*, where the protagonist returns to the forest because he comes to realize that "Justice for the oppressed springs from the organized armed power of the people" (Ngũgĩ, *Matigari* 160). Mwangi does not go so far, although he is clearly worried about the efficacy of forgetting, and its implied erasure of the forest fighters' voices.

The Role of Satire

Leaving aside the option of returning to life in the forest after the peace, what kind of life do the ex-combatants have? In contrast to the treatment of the fighters in the novels of the forest, the novels of urban life tend to satirize Mau Mau. Part of a genre of popular fiction that entertained large audiences of an urban, literate working class, these novels depict the underside of city life—prostitution, poverty, petty crime, heavy drinking—as the consequences of the former combatants' deracination from ordinary life and the family.

Like Mwangi, Charles Mangua was a popular writer. His urban fiction enjoyed considerable commercial success because of his humorous treatment of the seedy life of the city (Nelson 113). In his fiction he borrows from American slang, imitating in particular the dialogue of American gangster movies. American idiom reflects this type of novel's accommodationist politics.[51] "Americanness," a modernity apart from the punitive British colonialism and settler exclusionism, is adopted as the safe space from which to speak: masculine, self-mocking, and self-pitying, yet ultimately in control. This voice lacks the tone of rightful anger of neocolonial critique, but it only mockingly aligns itself with the narrative of "suffering without bitterness." Anxieties over masculinity, especially the fear of physical suffering and its potential to un-man, seem to displace political concerns. The threat of physical suffering is ubiquitous: colonial masters, Mau Mau, the home guard, urban criminals, accidents, relentless poverty all pose a threat to the physical integrity of the male subject.

The pervasive condition of poverty—both individual poverty and more broadly the condition of belonging to a poor country—is a constant threat to masculinity and an assault on the dignity of the people. The irreverence of Mangua's first-person narrator in *A Tail in the Mouth* compensates for the loss of dignity by asserting the independence of his point of view. The narrator's persona thus enacts a form of redress through his self-constitution in opposition to the political forces that marginalize him as one of the poor. This self-assertion, however, also requires an appearance of independence from any commonly held historical narrative. Thus the novel relegates the memory of Mau Mau to caricature.

The novel's humor and satiric bite are directed less at the Mau Mau as historical subjects and more at them as invented identities of the colonial and colonized psyches. Mangua's target is the representation of Mau Mau rather than their actual historical identity; they are referred to throughout the novel as "terrorists" (Mangua, *Tail* 63), "gangsters" (29), "a murderous lot" (41). His characterization of the Mau Mau has a cartoonlike quality as, for example, in the scene where the Mau Mau arrive at Moira's (the protagonist's) mother's hut after the funeral of his father. The flashback is rendered in the present tense:

> The first thing that gets in is a gun, then a beard and behind it a man. A giant of a man. He is wearing a wide brimmed military hat which has long lost its stiffness and therefore falls over his ears and the back of his head like a withered banana leaf that's been carelessly placed before the fire. His eyes are wild, sharp, sunken and red. His ears are hidden behind a mass of knotted hair that is the same blackbrown colour as his beard. It makes him look as if he was trying to imitate a gorilla. He is chewing something green that keeps popping in and out of his mouth and he smells like an oiled

> goat skin. He smiles broadly to reveal his broad brown teeth. Mau Mau gangster. It's written all over his face.
>
> "We have arrived," he says. "Get us something to eat. Some irio and make it fast. Always in a hurry you know. We never have time to rest. Can't rest as long as there's a white man on our soil." (77–78)

This caricature has all the trappings of cartoon hyperbole. The fighter's entry into the home is sketched in frames: the gun, the beard, the giant man with his ridiculous hat. He is drugged and hyper, but surprisingly nonviolent. His entry into the domestic space is not to kill but to eat, much like a husband returning from work and ordering his wife to get food. There is plenty of violence in Mangua's novel, but this first glimpse of the dreaded Mau Mau do not live up to their potential for terror. The five men who accompany the leader are pathetic, "like folks dug out of somewhere," dressed in tatters and very unkempt and dirty (78).

When the conversation turns to the oath, however, the Mau Mau can still intimidate. The "giant of a man" wants to know whether Moira has taken the oath. Because he talks too much (one of Moira's self-admitted faults), he lies that he has taken the oath when he hasn't. He embellishes his story with many stereotypes of ritualistic violence attributed to the Mau Mau and as a result does not convince the "real" guerrilla of his truthfulness. The "giant of a man" demands that he confess his lie and take the oath. This is the longest sustained comic scene in the novel, and it serves to underline Moira's lack of choice but also to demystify the oath, which has no extraordinary efficacy. Moira does not believe the oath "makes convictions stronger" and openly questions its power when he refers to the home guards: "But isn't something wrong with that institution if people who've taken the same oath, pledged to uphold the same cause are also fighting against each other?" (92). Thus, when Moira tells the story of his experiences in the forest to his friends, Kagwe and Kamau, he refuses to glorify them. His narrative of the "ordeal in the forest" deploys a shorthand of stereotypes that scale back the Mau Mau myths: "We knew nothing. No food, no direction, no shelter, wild animals etcetera. We just about lived on wild berries and water. It really takes an animal to live in the forest" (198).

When Moira leaves the city to return to the land at the end of the novel, he may be motivated by the urban dwellers' nostalgia for a "rural idyll" (Nelson 116), but the meaning of land has changed from what it was in the struggle, losing the strong national appeal it had in the contest between Ngotho and Howlands, for example. Moira returns as one of the urban poor restored to his rightful property of land and intending to farm a commodity crop: coffee. He has a role to play in the project of development and a new and, he hopes, more viable identity. The claim on the land is part of a progressive narrative that embraces modernization. As a forest fighter Moira had lacked conviction; he never said then, as he says now when he anticipates being a coffee farmer, "I am for the land" (Mangua, *Tail* 287).

Unsurpisingly, given Mangua's satiric vision, land ownership is not to be. Moira's friends are scheming to get the land from him. They urge him to borrow money so that he might default on the loan and the land will end up being turned over to them (285). The new dispensation, therefore, reinvents the rural in order to co-opt it into the capitalist order. Although Mangua's novel of disillusion restates the original grievance of the people's loss of the land in new terms, updating it as a claim against neocolonialism, it also withholds this awareness from its protagonist, who is perpetually caught in circular events that return him to the beginning. His life's story is a series of retellings, rather than a story moving him into the future. By giving the reader foresight of Moira's imminent failure, Mangua also bestows on the reader a responsibility to act. The novel creates the conditions to make recognition of the historical truth possible while requiring the assent of the reader to establish it as true.

Mangua's attention to land reform was prescient, as it is still today Kenya's largest challenge. Historians looking to explain the violence following the elections of December 2007 have stressed the importance of seeing this violence not as singular event, but as part of a larger problem of the consequences of policy mistakes from the independence era (Rutten and Owuor 320). Land continues to be a source of civil strife and competition among Kenyans after independence. The ending of Mangua's novel raises the alarm with its ironic treatment of the coming to power of Kagwe and Kamau and their anticipated usurpation of Moira's land: the opportunity to restore the land to its rightful owner is there, but the political weakness and destitution of the rightful owner make it unlikely. However, the novel's ending does not necessarily prophecy further civil strife. The tone here is different from the millennial prophecies of incomplete resistance movements (Wenzel 6–7). Mangua's humor provides an opportunity for his readers to recognize the terms of their own "impaired citizens[hip]," their complicity in neocolonialism.[52] It points to the potential to repair or restore citizenship damaged by the corrosive power struggles of decolonization and national constitution. Moira's lack of seriousness disarms his bitterness without exculpating his exploiters. It is they who lack self-understanding and to whom the idea of "impaired citizenship" applies as they fail to fulfill their duty. The ending affords the novel's readers with an opportunity to assent to the politics of land redistribution as redress for past and ongoing dispossessions and to escape the circularity that is the novel's key figure.

The novel's title alludes to an Egyptian motif: the snake eating its tail makes the shape of a circle, representing eternity. This symbol, the Ouroboros, has also been used in chemistry to signify a reversible chemical reaction. In poetics "serpentine verse" refers to poems that begin and end with the same verse. The title, therefore, makes a comment on the idea of "arrested decolonization," the difficulty of moving forward. Retrospection, the story's structure, returns over and over to the beginning, the moment that gave rise to the questions that need answering. Moira's retrospective account is shaped through his self-questioning: "I look back and wonder how it all started. How did I land myself in Nairobi? How come that I have sunk so low? How did I become so degenerate? What was the turning point? How did it all start?" (Mangua, *Tail* 26). In order to find the first cause of his decline, Moira must identify a beginning for his story. One plausible beginning is how he became a forest fighter. But the retrospective is not linear, and it is jumbled with the unfolding present in the city. Recovering the past does not create narrative coherence; it results in a series of disordered digressions into the how and the why that serve to entrench the impression of Moira's dead end life.

Why is this story so difficult to tell? Moira unmakes and then remakes himself in his own story, ending back where he began. Thus he claims the image of a tail in the mouth as a descriptor of himself when he tries to understand why, despite his ambition ("I have to do something for myself" [272]), he has gotten nowhere: "I've been chasing my tail too. I've caught up with it. I've got it in my mouth" (273). There it blocks him: the "tail" preventing the "tale" from escaping, unfolding with linearity into the future. His friend puzzles over this predicament: "you are the type that always wants to get somewhere—in principle that is" (218). The reader comes to see Moira's tendency to disclose himself fully as the problem: "I tell them everything from A to Z" (281). Mired in an endless recounting of the past, Moira is unable to seize the future. By the end of the novel he complains once again of his poverty and declares that he will give up speaking of the past. Punning once again, he says he "can't think backwards anymore" (263).

Moira's problem with coherence originates in his desire to remain apolitical. He is another of the "risk averse actors" (Branch 222). When he comes out of the forest and returns to the village (before he goes to the city), Kagwe advises him to join KANU, Kenyatta's party. But Moira does not want to relinquish his political independence and is skeptical of nationalist political rhetoric. Kagwe tries to persuade him otherwise: "We are supposed to be like one big family. . . . We are all brothers building one Kenya. One nation" (Manga, *Tail* 219). Moira is too cynical to buy into the sentimental rhetoric of nation and family: "When it comes to reaping the fruits of freedom, we are all one large family, but when it is a question of sweating for it, some of our esteemed brothers are ice cold" (219). He is unmoved even when Kagwe urges him to think of future generations and not himself, to be a "nation builder" (219). Moira protests: "To hell with nation building and your big talk. When I haven't got clothes, food, house, land, employment etcetera and my starting place is worse than where I left off, then I don't want to hear any high and mighty talk about brotherhood and nation building. I have to build my house before I can build a nation" (219). One constant, therefore, is Moira's acute awareness of his poverty. Rejecting the sentimental language of reconciliation and its use of family as allegory of nation, Moira insists on the literal: homeless and poor in the city, he needs his own house. The problem of poverty is such, however, that Moira's statement, although literal, reactivates the national allegory, now more sharply focused on the problem of who belongs in the nation's family and what this family home will look like. In the novel Moira is accused of "still hav[ing] the bitterness of the past" (189), but this refers not to memories of the forest, but to memories of who stole his land in the transition to independence. The forgetting that Moira is trying to speak against is the silence that is veiling the illegitimacy of power and privilege in the new post-independence era. His difficulty in finding the beginning of his story has to do with the fact that it is not to be found in the Mau Mau at all, but closer to now, in the new.

The self-hate evident in Moira's thinking as one of the urban poor is precisely what he needs to unlearn. Homeless and broke, but "no longer bitter" (264), Moira thinks his failure is his own fault: "I think that I am to blame for all that happened to me. I am to blame. I should be whipped. Really. I wish somebody would whip me" (265). The city's individualism and its modernity have not freed him yet.

Kahiga's Dedan Kimathi: The Real Story

It is not until 1990 that a novel openly takes as its subject a "real" Mau Mau.[53] Although *Dedan Kimathi: The Real Story* "rehearses familiar events in Kimathi's life" and aims at a popular audience by adopting "the style of a thriller with fast moving action and many melodramatic scenes" (Gikandi, *Encyclopedia* 255), the novel merits close examination within the larger body of this literature because it demonstrates how the uses of the past shift over time. It also develops further the naturalist theme of "human animality," although it suggests a different configuration of sentimentalism and naturalism by foregrounding the victimization of the young and their capacity for redemption. The order of naturalism in this novel, therefore, belongs to the world the fathers created, in contrast to the sentimental, which belongs to the young. The sentimental escape into national allegory and the family as motif focuses on the more egalitarian level of sibling relationships, a brother and sister and a new baby, thus shifting the generational focus and giving political hope for the future. This is in direct contrast to Wachira's empowerment of the fathers. Ironically, Kahiga's investment in the redemption of the fighters seen first as victims, as we shall see, undermines the novel's claim to be "documentary" or to be providing for its audience a journalistic scoop, "the real story."

Such are the claims on the novel's front and back covers. The cover illustration deepens the novel's ambivalence toward Kimathi (Figure 1.3). It shows a color photograph of the forest, taken from one hillside and focused on the opposite hillside. Kimathi's image is superimposed over the photograph of the forest. It is clearly demarcated with a black border. Boxed inside this border, Kimathi is shown in a black and white photo, lying down on his back, shackled, his hand visibly maimed. Instead of looking straight up (which would be at us), he is looking askance. He is shirtless and covered with a blanket up to his waist. This "real" photograph is the scoop, proffering the image of the elusive Kimathi with all the signs of the forest on him, unkempt and barely clothed. As he is lying down with his arms on his chest, however, he could be a body in a coffin, even though he is clearly alert, his gaze focused. Depending on the reader's orientation to the object of the book, Kimathi is either lying down (if the book is placed flat on a table, for example), or straight up, resurrected, so to speak, when the reader picks up the book and turns it upright to read. Kimathi, as symbol of the struggle for political freedom, can be launched anew into action by the very act of reading his story. It is this performative potential of retrospective narration that Kahiga's novel exploits. Thus its abundant naturalist details in the forest scenes are framed by constant reference to the ties of family, brother and sister, mother and son, which can legitimize the renewal of the struggle.

Although *Dedan Kimathi* proclaims to be the "real story," critics have noted that it reveals little beyond what was already known about Kimathi.

Figure 1.3. The cover of Samuel Kahiga's book *Dedan Kimathi: The Real Story* (1990) shows Mau Mau fighter Kimathi under arrest and shackled; the photo is superimposed over a photo of the forest.

Thus Kahiga's allusions to the known stories about Kimathi lend the novel a metahistorical feel.[54] He does not reconstruct the historical figure, nor does he try to create an intimate portrait of the man. This is a distanced portrayal, and only Agnes (who carries the sentimental perspective in the novel) sees him in an intimate moment when she finds him with a woman (Kahiga 220). The title's suggestion that the novel provides a journalistic scoop masks the novel's more urgent purpose, which is to use the Kimathi story to critique Kahiga's contemporary moment, the regime of Daniel Arap Moi (1978–2002).

As in the other novels, we see here how war reduces everyone to an animal condition.[55] Unlike Mwangi's naturalist novels of the forest, however, Kahiga attempts to revitalize the family as symbol of the nation. The novel ends with the birth of a child in the forest, a standard trope of the birth of the nation, while also showing the reunion of brother and sister (both forest fighters) to symbolize reconciliation. His emphasis on the younger generation marks a difference from Wachira's sentimental restoration of the father.

It is worth noting that Kimathi appears in the novel either through his written words, such as letters or diaries, or through giving speeches. Kahiga represents the leaders of Mau Mau as producers of the historical record (Peter Simatei 156–57), a record that can now be examined critically, perhaps. Like Kimathi, the other fighters write letters back and forth, keep diaries, and produce obituaries for their fallen comrades. This creates a couple of impressions. On the one hand, representing these practices of writing works against the mythology of Mau Mau, which demonized them as primitive. The leaders are presented foremost as historical figures, self-aware of the record they are leaving behind. However, historically, literacy in the forest was divisive, a mark of class difference. Not all fighters were literate, and "the bureaucratic authority of the word offended illiterate commanders, who found it alienating," seeing in it a symbol of the colonizer (David Anderson 249). Kahiga, therefore, begins a conversation in his novel about how class differences mapped themselves onto the social structure that developed in the forest.

In the novel Kimathi is often referred to with reverence, but he is also shown as deeply flawed because of his growing authoritarianism (Kahiga 256). He distrusts the people, the illiterate and uneducated, which creates a rift between him and Stanley Mathenge, the other important historical figure in the novel (258). The disagreement between Kimathi and Mathenge is rooted in their different interpretations of traditional political authority. Mathenge, the "wise elder," wanted to "bring back the glory of the African past" and restore the Gikuyu to their pre-colonial society (293). Kimathi, who grew up poor but had an education, is committed to modernity but has reverted to traditional religious beliefs, rejecting the Christianity learned in school (328).[56] Kahiga's portrayal is largely historically accurate, as we see from Lonsdale's account (Atieno-Odhiambo and Lonsdale 65–66). The fictional Kimathi disappoints in many respects, falling short of the reader's expectations, yet he is portrayed as able to inspire enduring loyalty, as we see from the admiration of Agnes and Theuri, the siblings who represent the people's perspective and who are the novel's real protagonists.

More than other writers, Kahiga makes reference to key events from the history of the Emergency: Operation Anvil (Kahiga 188); the Lari Massacres (200); the parliament in the forest; the British offer of amnesty (which is quoted in full (236). The political purpose of these references becomes apparent in instances such as when Stanley Mathenge complains to Kimathi, "How can you be the Prime Minister when nobody in Kenya has voted for you?" (256). The question also resonates against Moi's dictatorship in Kahiga's own historical moment. Moreover, in the novel Kimathi is accused of favoring his own people in the movement, a complaint that also resonates against Moi, who, when he succeeded Kenyatta, banned opposition parties and brought members of his own ethnic group, the Kalenjin, to power, keeping the Gikuyu out. The forest parliament shows how the people, represented by Mathenge, who is uneducated, confronted power (Atieno-Odhiambo and Lonsdale 66). To align Kimathi and Moi makes no historical sense, except that in a politically repressive environment, this might be an expedient way for Kahiga to veil his critique of Moi.[57] The emphasis falls on the rift among the leaders and their alienation from the people, which must be overcome. Moreover, Kahiga's fictional portrait shows how Kimathi as a historical figure, although stereotyped, can be fairly malleable as a symbol of what has gone wrong with the people's politics.

As I noted, the protagonists of the novel are not the historical figures but the fictional Theuri and Agnes, brother and sister who enter the forest as teenagers and reunite at the end, along with Agnes's baby, born in the forest from a relationship with the commander. All the horrible things that happen to them in the forest do not preclude a future. Agnes struggles to retain her grounding in "normal" (domestic) life, and it is through her perspective that we see the "human animality" of the forest fighters as a consequence of war:

> In their animal skins, they looked like creatures from an age gone by, and they rendered to her life in the cave an added quality of living in a dream. So this was it? Fighting for freedom? Had anybody foreseen all this, that in just a year of fighting, people would live like this? It was hard to believe that Baranaba had been a normal family man in a quiet homestead in Fort Hall. In his sheepskins, he now fitted in with the rocks and could have been born and bred a barbarian. (Kahiga 103)

War is transfigurative, and most importantly it removes the marks of family. What Agnes sees shakes her confidence in the war. To convince herself that the suffering is worthwhile, she turns for inspiration to the "landscape of eternity," available to her as a promontory view just outside the cave: "And the landscape was vast, beginning harshly in foreground and then softening with the distance to blend with the gentle sky. Beautiful cruel land. The land they were fighting for and dying for. She stood high up and surveyed it" (103). Inspired with a sense of national pride and ownership, of "land and freedom," Agnes prepares to brave the degraded conditions of the cave, yet she is distinctly hesitant, especially as regards the loss of family identity, which makes her question the war ("Fighting for freedom?").

Theuri's experience, which prefigures the narratives of brutalization we find in the more recent child-soldier fiction (see Chapter 4), is the severest test to "normal" in the novel. Instead of receiving an education, Theuri is coached to kill. Drawn to the forest after the death of his parents, Theuri is forced by his commander into a particularly brutal killing, hacking a man to death. We learn that "Theuri had killed men with bullets; he had even strangled them: but he had never hacked a man to pieces" (151). His commander, Kago, stokes his terror in order to motivate him to kill. His message to Theuri focuses on the threat to family:

> "You have a lot of sadness and very little anger, and that worries me. Try looking at it this way. These people are your friends and somebody wants to kill them. You are a mother, and someone wants to kill your child. Forget the already dead one. The murderer wants to kill the one in your arms. The only emotion possible then, besides fear, for which we have no room, is anger." (149)

Kago then instructs him to ignore the man's pleas for help and:

> "Finish off that bastard. Cut off his head, his arms and his legs. Let his friends bury him in bits. And Theuri . . ."
>
> "Yes?"
>
> "I want to see his testicles after you've finished." (151)

Thus Theuri is asked to imagine himself as the mother of a child whose life is threatened, while the very act of violence he is asked to perform robs him of the last vestiges of his innocence. He looks at his victim and sees a handsome "middle-aged man" for whom he can feel no anger (151), yet he performs the killing, albeit with difficulty, as we see from a detailed description of the messy, ugly work of killing. Kago pressures Theuri, and, with effort, Theuri decapitates the man and brings the testicles to Kago, as instructed. He is then asked to return to the mutilated corpse and stuff the testicles in the man's mouth. He follows through, wondering, "What a world we live in! What a war!" (152). These inadequate, perfunctory words distance him from his own acts and collectivize the responsibility. In what follows Theuri becomes particularly adept at killing, and, after Kago's death, he too becomes a commander, leading in a similarly brutal manner. Because we see the episode of Theuri's initiation in full, however, Theuri is also portrayed as a victim of the war, of circumstances bigger than himself, making it possible for us to believe in his capacity for redemption. His status as victim is further established when he is captured and tortured. He remains courageously faithful to Kimathi, does not betray the oath, and hence is, like Wachira's protagonist, rehabilitated in the eyes of the reader, someone who has paid his dues in suffering.

The sentimental brother-sister reunion with which the novel closes is a testament to the people's survival, the resilience of family ties and hence of nation. It is possible because, despite his violence, Theuri is seen as a victim who can be redeemed. It should be underscored that he is a victim of the fathers—the generation that has betrayed the future by its brutalization of the young and its willingness to sacrifice them. "You survived," Agnes tells her brother, and he responds, underscoring their bond: "Yes, sister. And you—embrace me again" (334). Kahiga is intent on restoring the dream of Uhuru and knows that to do so, the young must be inspired by its message. For Agnes, independence is the fulfillment of a dream: "Our dream has come true. We didn't suffer for nothing. We didn't die for nothing. Oh, this is a dream. I am free, I am here. I can't believe it" (334). Her use of the first person plural underscores the collective trauma of war, acknowledging that the survivors too have died in a sense ("We didn't die for nothing"). This is a statement in solidarity of the dead, but also a recognition that the living have suffered a kind of death in the war and that freedom must perform a resurrection of the living. The novel does not let go of Kimathi and ends with Theuri's testimony about Kimathi's arrest, trial, and hanging (336), testimony that enshrines Kimathi's martyrdom as a signature tale of anti-colonial resistance. Yet once again Agnes has the last word, reminding her brother that the struggle is not over, "Not yet" (337).

What does loyalty to Kimathi mean when Kimathi is portrayed as increasingly authoritarian? Although Theuri and Agnes admire Kimathi and remain loyal, Kimathi fails to lead the democratizing effort underway in the political struggles in the forest. The loyalty to Kimathi is more important as loyalty to the idea of freedom rather than as to the memory of the person. The novel closes with a celebration of independence, but also a pledge to continue to struggle for political freedom and, by implication, democratic rule. Thus Agnes cautions her brother not to celebrate prematurely: "'Not yet,' she said, 'You remember what [Kimathi] used to say? From the Cape to Cairo. All Africa must be free'" (337). This is a statement in memory (as he "used to say") of Kimathi, one that articulates his legacy for African aspirations to freedom broadly.

Kahiga's gesture to a Pan-African cultural and political identity is also arguably reflected in the novel's many intertextual echoes to other African novels that reveal its embeddedness in a tradition. For example, one of Kimathi's bodyguards who recognizes the intensification of infighting among the Mau Mau confesses to Theuri, "It's almost as if there's another war going on—among the members of Parliament themselves. Everything seems to be falling apart" (284). Achebe's phrase (borrowed from Yeats and a different colonial situation) is used here as a reminder that one of the reasons things fell apart in Achebe's Umuofia was a lack of cohesion against the white man. Another intertextual allusion is to *Sozaboy*.[58] Early in the novel Kimathi verbally attacks General Kabuku for lacking "daring and imagination" (59). Kabuku (one of several World War II veterans in Kimathi's army and the father of Agnes's child) is not convinced that the homemade weapons of the Mau Mau are adequate to fight the British. Kimathi insists on the importance of believing they can win, of having faith in the fight. Echoing a key scene in Saro-Wiwa's novel, Kimathi says, "If you have lost your faith you are like salt that has lost its flavor" (59). In *Sozaboy*, Mene puzzles over a sermon he hears in which the same biblical passage is cited to convince the young men to enlist in the Biafran cause.[59] The pastor tells the people, "You people are the salt in the soup," and from this Mene wonders if his identity is in crisis, since there is literally no more salt because of the war. "Can we be ourselves?" he asks, if the "salt not get salt inside?" (Saro-Wiwa, *Sozaboy* 42).

The third allusion is to Mofolo's *Chaka*. In the scene where Chaka stabs his pregnant lover, Chaka "felt somewhere inside him, in his chest, something falling down like a heavy stone, and settling heavily on his heart" (Mofolo 127). Noliwa gazes up at him as she is dying, and her eyes haunt him afterward. In *Dedan Kimathi* one of the fighters, Baranaba, is ordered to kill his forest woman because she was presumed to be a traitor. We learn this when he confesses it to Agnes: "it is a terrible memory I'll have to carry until I die. Whatever else I do is nothing compared to that—strangling a girl I loved while her eyes calmly stared at me, until she was limp and sightless." At the same time, Baranaba asserts the necessity of the action ("But I had to do it" [Kahiga 118]). Similarly, Chaka sees his action as necessary, exemplifying the determinism of the naturalistic vision that governs these war fictions.

The intertextuality of Kahiga's novel with other African novels is an expression of its introversion: a novel that situates itself in an already established African tradition rather than writing back to empire. It also illustrates the extent of the discursive construction of war. If any one incident of war examined on its own can appear absurd—like, for example, Theuri's brutal induction to the war, placed in a context of similar narratives and a larger discursive frame that may even include a telos (the attainment of Uhuru)—the individual incident acquires the appearance of necessity and inevitability. It is within the context of this kind of inevitability, one that reads the war backward from its outcome (an outcome already massaged to obscure the difficult return of the forest fighters to civilian life by inventing a narrative of carrying the family/nation out of the forest and into the polis), that Kahiga's novel circumscribes its use of naturalism. The war novel reveals war as deterministic and all-encompassing. But, although it presumes a total environment, it confines war to a particular time frame with a beginning and an end. The war novel, therefore, seems particularly preoccupied with setting these narrative limits, making its story out of varying attempts to position the frame around the war scene.

Thus we have seen how the novels of Mau Mau revisit the history of the conflict without presenting a unified position on whether the "negotiated bond of responsible nationhood" is endangered by remembrance or not (Berman and Lonsdale 267). The uses of the past are varied in this fiction and reflect another history, the history of the politics of memory in postcolonial Kenya. What does emerge as a point of consensus is a notion of "impaired citizenship"; the historical work done by these novels is the performance of this recognition, which draws the audience into history. Fanon's phrase, "no innocents and no onlookers," brings everyone into history as an agent, tainting them with complicity but also empowering them to act because their responsibility signals a degree of autonomy over the future, not recognized if the narrative of anti-colonial struggle is only reactive. Historical redress follows from the recognition of the problems of the present, a present that is performing compulsively the memory of the past. I turn next to the novels of the Biafran war, a body of work that similarly addresses an inadequate commemoration of the war and where the extent of the presence of its memory is uneven, suggesting an imperfectly realized citizenship.

CHAPTER 2

Toward a People's History: The Novels of the Nigerian Civil War

The sheer magnitude of literary works about the Nigerian Civil War (upwards of twenty-nine novels, in addition to plays, poetry, and memoirs) demonstrates that literature was key in constructing the memory of the war, especially since postwar Nigeria has largely repressed public commemoration of the war (Harneit-Sievers et al 1); the academic history of the war has been mostly military and political, not social or cultural (Nugent 98).[1] Writing in his memoir of the war published in 2012, Chinua Achebe asks, "Is the information blockade around the war a case of calculated historical suppression? Why has the war not been discussed, or taught to the young, over forty years after its end?" (Achebe, *There Was* 228). Yet every major Nigerian novelist has written about the war: Achebe, Flora Nwapa, Buchi Emecheta, Cyprian Ekwensi, Wole Soyinka, Ken Saro-Wiwa, Ben Okri, Chris Abani, Chimamanda Ngozi Adichie. A sizeable historical project addressing a plural national audience, the fiction about the war assumes that the war was experienced unevenly across Nigeria and that significant sections of the population do not know enough about it.

Despite the often conflicting points of view about the war articulated in the novels, two sensibilities permeate the literature and characterize it as a people's history: a sense of class injustice and dissatisfaction with the ways in which the stories of the war's suffering have been told. Class injustice is sometimes articulated as the middle class's awareness of the radical erosion of its own security, which coheres into a sense of betrayal by the political elite. At other times a sense of class injustice arises from the middle class's sympathetic awakening to the suffering of the rural poor. The unease with the war's humanitarian narrative, its story of suffering, reflects political suspicion of various official entities: the Nigerian state, the international community and media, and the Biafran government. This story of suffering is appropriated and rewritten to reflect the perspective and voice of the people. Although the novels mirror the record of starvation, displacement, and bombardment, they revise and complicate it in myriad ways.

The history of the humanitarian effort in Biafra has been told extensively and from several perspectives: in the pro-Biafra accounts of the war (Forsyth, De St. Jorre, and Jacobs); in histories of the humanitarian movement (Benthall, De Waal); and in histories of the humanitarian organizations themselves, most importantly of the International Committee of the Red Cross, for which Biafra was a crucial turning point in its own evolution.[2] Achebe's *There Was a Country* stresses the humanitarian crisis and looks at the tragedy of blocked humanitarian aid (Achebe, *There Was* 101). The novels, when they focus on humanitarianism as such, present a different perspective. Theirs is a corrective response that attempts to complicate the presentation of the Biafran people as spectral humans, the victims of famine. Makau Mutua has spoken disparagingly of the "Savage/Victim/Savior" metaphor of the humanitarian narrative in which victims are usually portrayed as "hordes of nameless, despairing, and dispirited masses" (Mutua 229). At its best, as in the photographs of Gilles Caron, the humanitarian lens on Biafra "particularized each person" and resisted creating the impression of "hordes" (Cookman 239), but the portrayal of Africa remained organized on the axis of savage and victim.

A distinction needs to be made, therefore, between a humanitarian narrative (exemplified by the journalism on the war) that treats war as a zone apart, in which human beings behave according to a naturalistic logic and in relation to which a humanitarian perspective negotiates a politics of pity, and, on the other hand, a narrative emanating from the war as experience, told from the perspective of one of its "victims" who can contextualize the changes wrought by the war in relation to what was before, thus revealing war as a transformation of the ordinary and quotidian rather than as a zone apart. This narrative from within also establishes a (critical) perspective on the humanitarians in action.

Although critical of the characterization of victims as "dispirited masses," the novels are undoubtedly similarly invested in the story of victimization, of those wronged and suffering. By seeking to make strong statements against war, they too foreground suffering. Moreover, even though the story of suffering in the war is the common ground between the humanitarian narrative and the novels, the two diverge, as the novels also significantly address a national audience for which they illuminate the war's political context, placing the spotlight on the responsible actors and agents of historical change. It is, of course, too simplistic to expect that all the novels of the war conform to this formula. The different politics of their authors certainly present variously nuanced versions of the war. However, there is a broad similarity in the way the novels insist on locating the narrative perspective "in" and "of" the war and as observers of the humanitarians. Aid workers, missionaries, NGOs, and journalists are frequently referred to in these novels as players among others in the arena of war.

In what follows I provide a reading of twelve texts, a large task, which is further amplified by my analysis of *Half of a Yellow Sun* in Chapter 4, as part of the discussion of contemporary novels of war (those published in the 2000s). The argument I lay out here prepares the ground for the analysis of Adichie, who self-consciously crafts her novel in light of the writing that preceded her, especially that of her female predecessors, Nwapa and Emecheta. Three generations of Igbo women have written about Biafra; my task is to distinguish this female tradition of war writing.[3] Moreover, I attempt to show the ways in which the story of the war gets woven into the literary project of the Nigerian novel begun around independence, both in its canonical expression in such figures as Achebe and Soyinka (in addition to the female writers) and its popular expression in Ekwensi, Iroh, and Ike. The discussions of Iyayi and Saro-Wiwa add important dissenting voices to this complex picture—dissenting both in their aesthetics and in their view of the nation. What I aim for in my selection of texts is to capture the breadth of different types of novels on the war; although large, this survey is not exhaustive. Furthermore, although I see a common purpose in much of this literature, the substance of the people's history is contested territory, fought over partly on aesthetic grounds over the form of the war novel as genre. We find once again the tension between the sentimental and naturalist, expressed in this case in different attitudes toward sincerity, a key term in my analysis especially of Saro-Wiwa. The novels of Biafra span high and low genres; satire, a characteristic of the popular novels, disrupts the morally serious, testimonial tone of the high literature.

The Idea of Biafra

In order to understand how the nation is imagined in these novels, it is important to understand something about the origins of Biafra. A nation cobbled together by the British, Nigeria had a precarious unity upon independence in 1960. Toyin Falola and Matthew Heaton describe it as "a state without a nation" (Falola and Heaton 159). During the First Republic (1960–66), the efforts of "artists" and "some politicians" to create a national culture were undermined by a tendency "toward consolidating power at the regional level" and by widespread "corruption, rigged elections, ethnic baiting, bullying and thuggery" (159). At independence Nigeria was divided into three regions (the North, the West, and the East), each dominated by political parties organized along ethnic lines, divisions largely cultivated by the British in the transition to independence.

The precipitating causes leading to Biafra's secession in 1967 were complex. Two military coups in 1966 and the outbreak of ethnic violence against the Igbos created a large refugee crisis, with Igbos fleeing to the East, their traditional homeland. The coup of January 1966 seemed to bring an end to the political dominance of the North and, although welcomed in the South, it was widely perceived in the North as resulting from an Igbo "conspiracy," because only one Igbo officer was killed (173).[4] This impression of a conspiracy was strengthened when the coup brought to power an Igbo general, Aguiyi Ironsi (who, however, had not been one of the coup planners), and shifted the balance of power in the army to the Igbos, who now held ten of thirteen senior positions, while previously they had held only five (De St. Jorre 78). Ironsi's reformist policies were perceived as ethnic (Nugent 93). In May 1966 he passed a decree abolishing the regions in the hope that he could neutralize the polarizing divisions in the country. The effect was the opposite, stoking fears of an Igbo monopoly on political power in a government that did not apportion power by region. Igbos in the North were immediately targeted, and thousands were killed (93–94). Another coup led by Northern troops took place in July. Many Igbo officers, including Ironsi, were killed.

A second, larger wave of violence against Igbo civilians followed, precipitating a massive exodus of the Igbos back to the East and the East's secession on May 30, 1967. This second wave of violence "bore significant indication" that the government was involved and the "army deeply involved." It affected a larger area of the country, "spilling out of the Muslim North and into Middle Belt areas where it was particularly savage" (De St. Jorre 84–85). Thus, for "much of September and October the

Northern government lay supine as the pogrom burnt itself out" (85). The violent unrest, which preceded the war and included reprisal killings in the East, resulted in an estimated 80,000 to 100,000 deaths (Osaghae 63; Falola and Heaton 174). War against secessionist Biafra broke out in July 1967, lasting until January 12, 1970. Biafra was blockaded, attacked, and ultimately defeated by the Federalist forces of Nigeria with significant help from the British (Jacobs 247–50).[5]

Victims of the pogroms, the Igbo came to see themselves as cast out of the nation, a people persecuted by genocidal violence. Writing in the *Times* on September 19, 1968, Chinua Achebe stressed his deep sense of betrayal and his understanding that the attacks on Igbos were genocide:

> I was a Nigerian and a great believer in Nigerian unity. I was until 1966 Director of Nigeria's external broadcasting. I had lived most of my life in Nigeria outside the Eastern Region, now Biafra. I knew and loved Nigeria. Now I do no longer. The change was brought about by a terrible traumatic experience that we call genocide. (Quoted in Ezenwa-Ohaeto 139)

Wole Soyinka (a Yoruba), who spent most of the war in a Nigerian prison for his dissenting views, concurred with the characterization of the violence as genocide (Soyinka, *Man* 20–22). To date there has been no official recognition that the killings were genocide. The Biafran government fanned the fears of genocide in its propaganda during the war; the official *Biafra Newsletter*, for example, ran headlines such as "Genocide Is Their Aim" (December 29, 1967) to describe the war itself as genocide.[6] Because there was no renewed ethnic violence against the Igbo in the immediate aftermath of the war, the charge of genocide was largely discredited, although pro-Biafra accounts of the war by Frederick Forsyth and Dan Jacobs mobilize evidence to uphold this charge (Forsyth 257–71; Jacobs 123ff).[7]

The Igbo experienced a "deep sense not of rebellion, but of rejection . . . they did not leave Nigeria, they were chased out of it" (Forsyth 95). In an interview given to *Transition* during the war, Achebe explains that the Biafran nation was born when the people came together in self-defense; the justification for secession, he argued, is the need to "giv(e) security to you and your people" (Achebe, "On Biafra" 31). The Igbos "were forced back" to the East, and Achebe reminds his interviewer that the nationalist ideology of "One Nigeria," used by the Federalists to attack Biafra as disloyal, was first articulated as Nigeria's national ideology by Easterners (33). Forsyth describes the Igbo attitude thus: "For most of them [secession] was the shattering of the illusions of their lifetime that after being the foremost of the 'One Nigeria' actors and thinkers, it was they finally who were not wanted" (Forsyth 95). The belief that secession was necessary to preempt genocide was very widespread among the educated and uneducated alike, as well as the "returnees," Igbos who fled the violence back to their home communities in the East (Harneit-Sievers et al 29). Easterners who saw injured and dying Igbos returning from the North and listened to Chukwuemeka Odumegwu Ojukwu's impassioned speeches about Biafra were convinced of the war's legitimacy. Secession was less understood, however, among minorities in the Delta region (32ff).[8] And, more generally, the people did not understand the implications of modern warfare; they underestimated the scale of violence, thinking of the war as "a war with matchets and local guns" (28).

In his speeches Ojukwu, the leader of the Biafran secession, stressed that the war was a struggle for "freedom, security, fair play, and justice" for the people "in their own homes and in their own way." Without the struggle, Biafrans would remain "a conquered, disgraced, and enslaved people" (Ojukwu, *Biafra* 216). Thus Ojukwu defined this as a people's freedom struggle, stressing the potent ideas of home and belonging. The promise of a just order, moreover, inspired hope of a political revolution and a new society that would emerge after what Ojukwu presented as an inevitable victory. His political manifesto, "The Ahiara Declaration: The Principles of the Biafran Revolution" (June 1, 1969) included a section also called "The Principles of the Biafran Revolution," which was mostly written by Achebe in his capacity as chair of the National Guidance Committee appointed by Ojukwu (Ezenwa-Ohaeto 146). The objective of this document was to rearticulate the meaning of independence and to turn secession into the narrative of true independence, setting the postcolonial state finally on the path of justice and equity for all and reestablishing the dignity of the African man. Biafra was to become an exemplary postcolonial African republic (147). As Achebe notes, the inspiration was Julius Nyerere's "Arusha Declaration," which was held in high regard by Nigerian intellectuals. Moreover, Nyerere as president of Tanzania was the first African head of state to recognize Biafra (Achebe, *There Was* 145). The "Ahiara Declaration" declared Biafra for the people: "In the New Biafran Social Order sovereignty and power belong to the People." But it also cautioned against empty promises: "it is no use saying that power belongs to the People unless we are prepared to make it work in practice. Even in the old political days, the oppressors of the People were among those who shouted loudest that power belonged to the People. The Biafran Revolution will constantly and honestly seek methods of making this concept a fact rather than a pious fiction" (Ojukwu, "Ahiara Declaration"). "Constantly and honestly" was a tall order, and the bitter edge of much of the war fiction illustrates how deeply disillusioned the people became with the Biafra government.

The war fiction of Biafra reclaims the people's perspective, narrating the story of the war as one of the failures of decolonization while desiring to see in its resolution a renewal of the promise of the nation. The literature, therefore, exhibits a tone of moral seriousness: "postwar Nigerian writing was marked by the quest for a strongly ethical framework by which to propound an urgent new vision for the endangered nation" (Quayson, *Aesthetic* 126). The novelists, middle-class and educated but politically marginalized by the failure of democracy in the post-independence nation, write as the war's survivors in a bid for recognition by the nation. Many echo Nwapa's determination to give testimony. In *Never Again* (1975), whose title is a deliberate allusion to the Holocaust, she exemplifies the stance of the moral witness often assumed by the authors. The task of testimony, however, is frequently complicated by the problem of identity and the clash among the discourses of class, ethnicity, and regionalism, which offer competing versions of the nation. In her sociological study of the Nigerian novel, Griswold recognizes the leading role that Igbo writers played in shaping "the literary experience of the reading class" nationally (Griswold 238). Out of the twenty-nine war novels that Griswold identifies, twenty-two are written by Igbos, leading Griswold to conclude that "in fiction, the story of the Nigerian civil war is being told by its losers" (235). For Achebe and Nwapa, key figures of Nigerian literature from before the war, writing to the nation was a familiar role. They picked up where they left off in the pre-war literary project, stitching together the before and after.

How the Other Half Lives

Division and how to overcome it are the key problematics of these novels. Division takes on many expressions: facing off across enemy lines, the demarcation of a boundary around blockaded Biafra making it the zone of war, but also class, whose lines of division are not always predictable, as we shall see. Although they often declare their intention to give testimony, the novels of the Nigerian Civil War make bold fictionalizing gestures. Dissatisfied with the journalistic narratives, the novels about Biafra deploy the literary imagination to burst into new narrative terrain, albeit similarly in a realist mode. They tend to elaborate large dramatic canvases with a variety (and often a significant multiplicity) of players who demonstrate the complexity of Nigerian society and the entanglements of its people. The intricate plots of these novels convey the impression of inclusiveness to overcome division. Their multiple perspectives embedded in a comprehensive narrative promote the recognition of a shared history to help heal the divided nation. Blame is often (not always) fairly evenly distributed: the Federalists are culpable for starting the military action, the Biafrans for continuing it too long. The novels, moreover, wage a war against war: no matter the righteousness of the cause, war is not worth the price. Indeed, the "most prominent theme" of the war novels, whether by Igbo writers or not, is "the utter meaninglessness of the war" (231).

The people's history of the war begins with the premise that the war was experienced unevenly across the nation, dividing the haves and the have-nots, as well as dividing the East from the rest of the country. Adichie wanted to capture "the mood of middle-class Biafra" (quoted in Cooper 135). Before her, Achebe recognized the gap between himself and ordinary Biafrans when asked to describe an "average day in Biafra," to which he responded with a question: "For me or for the average Biafran?" The interviewer, of course, wants to know about the "average Biafran," and Achebe explains: "millions by now . . . have no roots, no property" (Achebe, "On Biafra" 31). Achebe sees himself as apart from the ordinary people at the same time that he takes on the task of speaking for them. This posture exemplifies the writers' perspective on the war.[9] How to bring the two narratives of the war together, the suffering of the educated class and the poor, and then, furthermore, how to attach this narrative to a national narrative, either of civil war or of failed national—Biafran—aspiration, is the challenge.

In his short story "Girls at War," Achebe examines the ways in which different perceptions of the war divide Biafrans. The war does not homogenize or level, but rather tends to heighten social differences. "Girls at War" is narrated from the point of view of Reginald Nwankwo, whose name always appears in the story followed by his affiliation, "Ministry of Justice," a constant reminder of how social privilege and political power are coupled together. As a government official Nwankwo resents being searched at checkpoints: "if you were put through a search then you could not really be one of the big people" (Achebe, "Girls" 98). To make matters worse, on one such occasion he is searched by an attractive young woman called Gladys, whose response to his annoyance is to say in a disarmingly polite tone, "Sorry to delay you, sir. But you people gave us this job to do" (99).

When Nwankwo runs into Gladys again later in the war, she has changed from an upstanding militia girl to a prostitute, and he judges her harshly.

Overdressed in vulgar clothes at a time of famine, Gladys is now a symbol of a "society that had gone completely rotten and maggotty at the centre" (114). She responds to Nwankwo's disapproval by echoing her previous statement: "that is what you men want us to do" (109). Earlier she had addressed Nwankwo as one of "you people," referring to his social status; now she addresses him as one of "you men," showing that Nwankwo too has fallen in the war, becoming one of "you men" who frequent prostitutes. Nwankwo vehemently denies such complicity with other men and insists on recovering the Gladys he first knew, without the wig and the clothes. Thus he turns Gladys into his "saving operation" and offers her food so that she will not need to prostitute herself (115).

Gladys's responses reflect how intent she is on doing what's expected of her, part of her intense desire to do the right thing, which extends beyond conforming to men's expectations. She represents the ordinary people who, despite the degradation of the war, are still moved by ideals, whereas the elite are consistently motivated only by self-interest. Thus Gladys dies trying to save a disabled soldier, trapped in a car during an ambush. She and Nwankwo escape the car, but Gladys returns to help the soldier once she realizes he can't move on his own; they are both killed. Elleke Boehmer argues that Gladys's "emblematic role" in the story is fully apparent in this scene, where she symbolizes the "destruction of young Biafra" (Boehmer, "Motherlands" 232). The male soldier's disability and now death make him a positive symbol of national character, whereas Gladys, the militia girl turned prostitute, is the tarnished symbol. Nwankwo, moreover, stands in the privileged position of narrator who "index[es]" Gladys's various incarnations as a "girl at war" (231–32). Nwankwo's social privilege, which distinguishes him from both the soldier and Gladys, is the reason he is assigned the role of narrator. Thus there is more going on here than the gendering of the national imaginary. Achebe underscores the injustice of the representative of the "Ministry of Justice."

Although responsible for the soldier being in the car in the first place (he insisted on giving the soldier a lift), Nwankwo saves his own skin without hesitating. With his sense of entitlement intact, Nwankwo feels unconflicted about his own imperative to survive. In this (im)moral universe, Gladys's death, although principled, seems pointless, unless it can somehow redeem Nwankwo (and the reader) by making him recognize the people's worth. The idea of self-sacrifice is moving to Nwankwo, but Biafra's poverty and misery, as he perceives it, make it not worthy of sacrifice. Achebe, moreover, places this negative sentiment explicitly in relation to the humanitarian workers in Biafra. Nwankwo witnesses the outburst of a humanitarian worker and finds himself in general agreement with this angry white man who says that Biafra is a place that "stinks" (Achebe, "Girls" 110), where "even these girls who come here all dolled up and smiling, what are they worth? Don't I know? A head of stockfish, that's all, one American dollar and they are ready to tumble into bed" (111). By representing the humanitarian, Achebe shows that humanitarianism's script allows Nwankwo to continue to believe in his privilege and blinds him to his own degradation in the war. His "saving operation" to restore Gladys to purity shames her even more by underscoring the stigma of prostitution. Nwankwo's sense of entitlement, which remains intact even in the worst conditions of the war, is disquieting because it inhibits a broader identification with the people. Achebe, therefore, by placing the reader in a position to disapprove of Nwankwo, tries to foster such a salutary identification with the people.

Flora Nwapa echoes Achebe's concerns in her depiction of the uneven experience of the war, but her focus is on the divide between those who experienced the war in Biafra and those largely shielded from it in the rest of the country. Nwapa, who like Achebe experienced the war firsthand, writes from a deep identification with the suffering of Biafra.[10] *Never Again* is narrated from the perspective of middle-class Biafrans but addresses those outside Biafra who need to be educated about the war. Although Biafra is in the foreground, the larger Nigerian nation is evoked.

Kate, the protagonist and narrator of *Never Again*, declares on the first page of the novel that "I meant to live at all costs. I meant to see the end of the war. Dying was terrible. I wanted to live so that I could tell my friends on the other side what it meant to be at war—a civil war at that" (Nwape, *Never Again* 1). Kate is motivated to survive in order to give testimony to the horrors of war. In her testimony she wants to address "the other side" and expects a sympathetic audience ("my friends") that needs to be educated about the truth. Kate's insight about Nigerians' uneven exposure to the realities of the war correlates closely with the depiction of the war by Harneit-Sievers et al (1997). Striving to write "'a history from below'" or "the perspective of people 'below' the level of official positions" as well as a "history 'below' the level of official statements and announcements," Harneit-Sievers et al (3) understand that "only a part of the population—those who actually lived in the former war area—have gone through this profound experience in the fullest sense" (1). Speaking in the first person plural for all Nigerians, Kate also claims the history of the war as the people's history, a difficult history that Nigerians have a duty to remember:

> "What folly! What arrogance, what stupidity led us to this desolation, to this madness, to this wickedness, to this war, to this death? When this cruel war was over, there will be no more war. It will not happen again, never again. NEVER AGAIN, never again." (Nwapa, *Never Again* 73)

For Nwapa the war was a war from within rather than war against an enemy. But the "us" she refers to is not Biafra; it is Nigeria as a whole.

The mutual suspicion sewn deliberately by the Biafran authorities among its blockaded citizens creates another set of divisions, which Nwapa insistently refers back to the larger national narrative. These divisions are captured well in her portrayal of the practice of "combing," or searching for "saboteurs" (Nwapa, *Never Again* 33–34). "Combing" encompassed a range of different military activities (including guerrilla actions) carried out by able-bodied men who were too old (thirty to fifty years old) for the regular Biafran army. Often they searched the bushes for "infiltrators," arresting and even executing those they found on flimsy evidence, such as tribal marks. Harneit-Sievers called "combing" "outright witchhunting" (Harneit-Sievers et al 66–67). In the novel men arrive to search Kate's house. "We have come for combing," they declare, to search for "infiltrators" (Nwapa, *Never Again* 34). Kate and her husband, Chudi, are surprised and offended that they are treated with suspicion, but have no choice, and submit to the search. Afterward, Kate complains: "Nothing was private anymore. We had lost our freedom and democracy. We lost them the day that the army took over. January 15, 1966" (35). By pushing the frame of reference back to the January 1966 coup, Nwapa is creating a national context for the war. It began with the loss of democracy, when the nation went down the wrong path. Moreover, Nwapa understands that the Biafran leadership could have ended the war sooner and has Kate hold them responsible for the worst of the war.[11]

Through Kate we see the degradation of language as one of the effects of war. Lies, propaganda, rumor reflect society's frayed social bonds.[12] Speech is monitored closely so that any expression of dissent can be spotted. The degree of suspicion reaches such a point that Kate worries about why her mother asks her the type of questions that people ask of those they think are "saboteurs": "Am I not talking to my own mother? My God, is the propaganda affecting my mother?" she wonders, and the answer is "yes" because propaganda has poisoned human relations (26). Although we are told Ojukwu was trying to "win a civil war by mere words" because he had no resources and would not admit defeat, few believe Kate when she insists on the obvious, that "words were impotent" against bombs, and hence Ojukwu is lying to the people (23).

Middle-class and educated, Kate sorts through the confusion of the war intellectually, rationally. Her English name (the only character to have one) establishes her as Westernized, figuratively English, which puts her at a distance from the others, whom she criticizes relentlessly for their willingness to go along with the official reports on the war. Because of her skepticism she is positioned as an outsider, a figure analogous to the literary protagonists of the extroverted novels of African literature. The crux of Nwapa's story, however, is how Kate imaginatively reinvents her cultural identity, enhancing her sense of belonging among her own people through the awareness of shared suffering. Nwapa makes this point by showing how Kate embraces the traditional beliefs of her people at the end of the war, beliefs that she dismisses as superstitions before the war. Moreover, allusion to these beliefs links Kate to Efuru, the protagonist of that earlier novel with strong ties to the national literary project. Thus two types of divisions are repaired: Kate's distance from the people and the interrupted national literary project.

At the beginning of the novel Kate expressed her impatience with the peoples' belief that either the lady of the lake, a traditional goddess, or the Christian God of middle-class Biafrans will protect Ugwuta (5). After Kate flees from Enugu, Onistha, Port Harcourt, and Elele as each of these cities fall to Federalist forces, her attitude changes. When her flight from Ugwuta is imminent and she expects to become destitute and a refugee, she appeals in despair to the lady of the lake and the Holy Spirit in a jumbled prayer:

> Life was cruel. Life was meaningless. Was there no purpose, nothing? Just emptiness? The war. Who caused the war? The Woman of the Lake, why, why, why, did you allow this to happen to your children? We have sinned. All of us have sinned against the Woman of the Lake, against the gods and goddesses of the land. We were all guilty. But the punishment is too great, too severe, too crude, too raw for our offenses against the gods, the great woman. The Holy Spirit. Yes that. The sin against the Holy Spirit will not be forgiven, so the Scriptures say. What is the sin against the Holy Spirit? I do not understand. The world is a strange and mysterious place. . . . (59)

We see here that Kate is no longer satisfied with political explanations about the war. If in Ugwuta she kept her sanity by rationally questioning the official lies, the war has now become a more intimate reality and its dimensions apocalyptic, requiring a spiritual response.

Kate's description of the evacuation of Ugwuta reflects her growing sense of the unreality of things:

> The exodus from Ugwuta continued. My God, so there were so many people in Ugwuta! Old and young, men and women and children. Goats and sheep. They were walking out of Ugwuta to an unknown destination. Soon perhaps the buildings and the trees would develop legs and begin to walk. No it was not possible. It could not be possible.
>
> Everything that was happening in Biafra then was impossible. (55–56)

The exodus, as described by Nwapa, is a painful sundering of people from their physical surroundings as a community. Kate's commentary is nonsensical, "impossible," as she acknowledges. Even though trees and buildings are not walking, what is happening seems equally "impossible." The story of war becomes what later in Emecheta's *Destination Biafra* is referred to as a story no one will believe. Moreover, the war precipitates a change of consciousness, a more spiritual orientation, whereby testimony about the "deadly whine of shells" no longer captures adequately the experience of war (Nwapa, *Never* 1). Nwapa raises questions about the efficacy of reportage and signals that fiction can better express the truth about war.

The contrast between historical fact and story rests on different beliefs about the meaning of events. Ugwuta, like a few other Biafran cities, was captured by the Nigerians, looted, and then recaptured by the Biafran forces, allowing its citizens to return to the burned-out town before the war was over (Forsyth 137). In her novel Nwapa wonders about the meaning of this return. The people of Ugwuta use the occasion to reaffirm their belief that the lady of the lake has protected them as promised (Nwapa, *Never* 84). Historically, the recapture of Ugwuta was only a qualified victory in a war that Biafra was losing. In the novel, however, the people see it as confirmation of their inviolability: "[the goddess of the lake] had acted according to the belief of the people. No invader coming by water had ever succeeded in Ugwuta" (84).

The ethos of "NEVER AGAIN," the duty to memory, is shaped by the people's experience. How events were lived, their meaning to survivors, might not correspond with a strict accounting of events. The discrepancy between fact and fiction in novels of war that claim to provide a moral witness require that we understand their effort differently than a historical document. Describing war fiction in broad terms, Jay Winter has called it an attempt to sketch a representative circumstance, to tell us that "something *like* this happened." War literature "mixes the documentary and the melodramatic, the factual and the fictional, and refuses to distinguish between the two" (Winter xiv, emphasis added). War is so full of the "uncanny" and "bizarre" that it is hard to "reproduce it accurately" (xv).

Nwapa provides closure for her novel in a way that pronounces its fictional status, its narrativization of events. She depicts the people's belief in national allegory, in the idea that "no invader" will succeed. Inviolability is an enabling myth posited after the war is lost. At the end of the war, when the people return once more to Ugwuta, Kate is captivated by the beauty of the lake. Because the war has made her more receptive to her people's spiritualism, softening the edges of her rationalism, Kate's restitution is conveyed by Nwapa in spiritual terms. The natural environment (the lake where the goddess lives) becomes a sacred presence anchoring the people of Ugwuta to their town.[13] An instance of the motif of the landscape of eternity, it stands outside time as a source of cultural and spiritual renewal for the people:

> The only thing that stood undisturbed, unmolested, dignified and solid was the Lake. The Lake owned by the Woman of the Lake. It defied war. It was calm, pure, peaceful and ageless. It sparkled in the sunlight, turning now blue, now green as the sun shone on it. . . . Uhamiri [the goddess of the lake] was the people's hope and strength. Uhamiri be praised. (84)

As Kate and her husband look upon the beauty of the lake, they recover a sense of belonging that the town's destruction has severely challenged:

> The place was desolate. . . . The thatch-houses overlooking the Lake were all burnt down. There was evidence of mass graves beside the burnt down houses. The barns were empty. Bullet holes gaped from the walls of the houses that were still standing. (84)

Nwapa contrasts the devastation of the town with the natural beauty of the lake, despite the dead Nigerian soldiers floating in its waters. Although now "desecrated beyond description and imagination," the lake retains its mystical power (84). Nwapa's belief in the permanence of physical landscapes is a fictionalizing gesture, offering a path to renewal that is anchored in a sense of place that is not dependent on what people have built and destroyed, but on people's imaginative identification with a particular landscape.

Thus we have a powerful instance of the motif of the landscape of eternity. Homi Bhabha refers to "landscape as the inscape of national identity" that reveals the "power of the eye to naturalize the rhetoric of national affiliation" (Bhabha, "DissemiNation" 294–95). Nwapa's lake is a symbol of a people's resilience, their "dignified" (to use Nwapa's word) survival. The novel ends with the evocative image of villagers, who have lost everything, returning to the lake to offer a sacrifice of thanks to the goddess for her protection and thus renewing a spiritual practice from before the war. There is no trace of cynicism here toward those who have lost everything but still offer thanks. Kate responds to the people's healing gesture, which illuminates for her how the rich associations with place provide the source for continuity and resilience.

As I noted, Nwapa's treatment of the lady of the lake in *Never Again* is also unmistakably an intertextual reference to her seminal novel *Efuru* and a gesture toward the Nigerian literary tradition.[14] In *Efuru* the lady of the lake is depicted as the protector of women without children for whom the goddess provides alternative identities compatible with traditional culture. The widely cited ironic ending of *Efuru* is posed as a question to the reader, asking how come women, who supposedly want to bear children, pray to the goddess of the lake, who is a symbol of infertility? This question is a way of answering back to a gendered national imaginary shaped by the history of colonialism during which European beliefs of domesticity that restrict women's sphere of action reinforced traditional beliefs in the value of motherhood. By praying to the goddess, women demonstrate that they might also aspire to a different identity than motherhood and that traditional culture can accommodate this difference.

In *Never Again* the belief in the goddess enables the face-saving illusion of defeat as adequate self-defense, creating conditions for renewal after the war by fostering a sense of continuity with the cultural project of the prewar years.[15] If the people can attain cultural influence by providing the link to the spiritual life for middle-class Nigerians such as Kate, then they might be able to translate this power into a political voice. Later in this chapter I refer to Imre Szeman's reading of Soyinka's *Season of Anomy*, a novel that Szeman's sees as depicting the failure of Nigeria's literary project to keep the nation together. Perhaps we should read *Never Again* as a more optimistic text on the same theme, a text that shows confidence in the healing influence of Nigeria's cultural production.

The Figure of the Journalist

The fiction of the war returns frequently to the problem of how the other half lives by using a journalist protagonist, nowhere perhaps more successfully than in the work of Cyprian Ekwensi, who was himself a journalist. Because he has mobility and can move across the different arenas of the war, the journalist synthesizes the disparate experiences of the people's suffering on the one hand and the political struggles of the powerful on the other. The fictional journalist can also be a vehicle through which to criticize the journalism of the war. Ekwensi thought that journalists are biased because they write in the moment: "The journalists in their own way mirror the times but sometimes they do not hold the mirror very fully to the event for obvious reasons. The mirror is tilted to its side and it gives perhaps an image distorted in favour of a particular moment." In contrast, the novelist, although he enjoys less authority than the journalist, is freer to call out a warning about the state of society: "he pipes the tune which is the warning" (quoted in Nazareth 175). The writer is a "prophet" whom society must heed, because Africans, Ekwensi says, "are much in need of knowing themselves . . . and the writer who writes with immediacy serves to bridge this gap of self-knowledge, which I think is very vital to understanding ourselves and understanding our relationship with others" (Lindfors, *Dem-Say* 33). Thus the novelist is also explicitly identified with the introverted project of Africa's self-examination. Ekwensi's emphasis on "immediacy" and intersubjectivity, moreover, highlights the transactional quality of everyday life, the portrayal of action that displays agency and an ownership of history as the truth of fiction (34).

The most widely read writer on the war, Ekwensi achieved his success by being a "populist" writer who aimed to "speak directly to [a] 'lowbrow' group" made up of "literate and semiliterate working people, peasants and traders" (McLuckie 16). By trying "not to teach but to show," he avoided being didactic (44).[16] Ekwensi was also "controversial and enigmatic," a writer who gravitated to unusual topics and succeeded in breaking the mold of the canonical writer to "overcome the division of high and popular culture" (Gikandi, "Ekwensi" 170). Although Ekwensi grew up in the North, he considered the East his home (Lindfors, *Dem-Say* 27). During the war he was in charge of Radio Biafra and Voice of Biafra, so he bore a measure of responsibility for transmitting the distorting propaganda of the Biafran leadership (Ugah 56). In his war fiction, however, Ekwensi treated the role of the journalist with a significant degree of irony that reflected his experience mediating between government officials and the public. Although he insisted that war writing can only come from experience, he cast doubt on the effectiveness of testimony: "No one can explain it to you. No one can *tell* you about war" (Lindfors, *Dem-Say* 30). The novel afforded Ekwensi a way to write about war "with naked conviction" without having to tidy up the contradictions as he did in journalism (30).

Ekwensi acknowledged that he admired the "more naturalistic approach to writing" and that the "Americans, the French and the Russians were nearer to the African way of thinking" compared to the "English novel [which] tended to spend too much time on unnecessary description of setting" (34). He consistently describes the people's suffering in naturalistic terms: "From the areas under heavy shell fire, they would spill into the roads and footpaths, carrying headloads, their poverty and suffering too harrowing to contemplate as they beat a steady path, like human ants, into the deeper and safer areas and set up home under the trees" (Ekwensi, *Survive* 8). "Like human ants," recalls Zola's miners, "human insects on the march," their mine "a giant anthill" (Zola, *Germinal* 38).

Admitting that he liked adventure and action, Ekwensi consciously avoided sentimentalism and focused instead on what he called "contrasts of human behavior" (Lindfors, *Dem-Say* 34). This emphasis on "contrasts" creates the impression of irresolution and friction. If Nwapa puts Kate in touch with her traditional identity to redress the trauma of war, Ekwensi keeps the social cleavages in place even in the aftermath of the war. For him the war novel enacts a series of recognitions that relativize one's experience in relation to the experiences of others and, in the process, create a sense of a collective experience that is not homogeneous. Ekwensi's novels condemn the war, although they are written ostensibly from a partisan, pro-Igbo position. In them Biafra serves a symbolic purpose. Its shattered dream of sovereignty and democracy makes it a surrogate for the nation's betrayal of the people.

Who are the people emerges as a key question that can be answered only through a recognition about oneself. Ekwensi stages this critical moment in *Divided We Stand* (1980), where Chika, a journalist and a representative of the professional class, risks his own life by refusing to abandon an injured stranger during an air raid. This scene, an example of the classic moral dilemma of the good Samaritan, has a surprising resolution. Speaking through Chika's point of view, the narrator describes the injured woman thus:

> She was middle-aged, one of the millions of poor innocent peasants who must be victims of other men's iniquities, a woman who cared absolutely nothing about mineral oil, the unity of Nigeria, and the lofty aims of the British Government. This was the kind of Biafran woman whose life rotated around planting seasons, harvest time, the price of *gari* in the market. (Ekwensi, *Divided* 5)

The people here are seen as victims through the eyes of a privileged and educated person who feels removed not only from the normal life of this "ordinary person," but also from any association of guilt with the "iniquities" she and her people have suffered as "victims of *other* men's iniquities." Disempowered, the woman is subject rather than citizen and thus in some sense outside the nation. Ironically, the war draws her into the nation and destroys her. Chika's detachment, his conception of himself as primarily an observer, makes it seem as if this is not his war, either, but a war waged by those with real power and directed against those more vulnerable than himself.

Realizing that the woman will die in his arms, Chika asks out loud how come he is the survivor. The woman's simple answer leads him to reconsider his conception of the social distance between them: "It's not . . . your time . . . ," she tells him (6). Chika in her eyes has no special privilege in the war, just some luck at present. The woman's equalizing utterance forces the realization that Chika's time could come at any moment. He thus comes to understand himself as "homo sacer," the human subject who lives the "bare life" of those who can be killed by the "sovereign power" without their death being either "sacrifice" or "homicide" (Agamben, *Homo Sacer* 82), which is to say, he has no human worth, no dignity, and is powerless, insignificant.[17] In the biopolitical sphere Chika and the woman are quite equal and similarly vulnerable to the destructive power of bombs.

In this scene the narrative of class fails to explain the experience of war, and Ekwensi stages a rapprochement between the educated man and the "peasant" woman. The criterion of class inequality that underpins a politics of pity, making one class aware of its "luck" in relation to another equally meritorious but arbitrarily disadvantaged class, is debunked and replaced with a more existential kind of luck (Boltanski 5). The rapprochement between Chika and the peasant is possible because of Chika's empathy for the woman's suffering. In contrast to his colleagues, he does not abandon her. Chika's empathetic disposition at first reflects his awareness of their distanced class relation. Her statement, however, provokes a change of understanding whereby Chika sees his relation to the "sovereign power" waging war differently, realizing his own vulnerability and perceiving his equality with the peasant in this regard. Chika could also be killed at any time and is already living the "bare life" in this war. Thus he comes to a different awareness of his modernity, now perceived through a sharpened sense of insecurity rather than through the privilege bestowed on him by the colonial education that previously defined his modernity.

Ekwensi seems to be telling us that, chased out of one city after another into the rural areas and refugee camps, middle-class Biafrans developed both a bitter resentment against the small minority elite with political power who were safeguarded in the war and a deeper identification with the broader majority. Although this identification was sometimes tainted with class anxiety, it also held the democratic promise of a more inclusive nation. Agamben might give us a vocabulary for thinking of the heightened moments of emergency in the war, but the literature of the war also works contra-Agamben to display the myriad forms of resistance to the dehumanization of war that challenge his assertion of the absolute hold of the "bare life."[18] The protest against war reflects the belief that war is an aberration that we must come out of. Agamben's "state of exception" (the suspension of the law when the state is threatened by war or is at war) puts the emphasis on what he calls a "kenomatic state, an emptiness and standstill of the law," a vacuum, in other words (Agamben, *State of Exception* 48). The narration of the war's story correlates with the reimposition of the law, the reinvigoration of the distinction between justice and injustice.

The contrast between journalism and fiction is made in *Divided We Stand* by comparing the prologue to the main body of the novel. The novel is structured as a flashback, beginning with the scene where Chika stands by the dying peasant (which is in the prologue) and turning back to explain how Nigeria has gotten to this point. Ekwensi recreates the chronology of events from the coup of January 15, 1966, to the end of the war. His purpose appears didactic—to teach the history of the war—but insofar as he conceives of history only as chronology, the events put in order, the novel at first disappoints. We need to remember, however, that because of the ubiquity of propaganda and distortions of the truth during the war, many who lived the war did not know the sequence of events.

The prologue's lack of historical specificity is notable in contrast to the rest of the novel. The prologue imitates the journalistic accounts of the war. We are told this is a Biafran town, but the town is not named until the end of the prologue. The imagery is graphically violent, but also stereotypical. In the opening paragraph, Chika sees a truckload of bodies; he also visits the morgue where he sees the corpse of a mutilated pregnant woman, another cliché image from the war (Ekwensi, *Divided* 8).[19] The official journalistic reports composed by Chika and the others on his staff exaggerate the number of casualties, cheapening the lives of the victims (10–11). Defensive about his own role as director of the Biafran Information Service, Ekwensi offers the novel as an explanation of the history that shaped the journalism (Griswold 235).[20] Thus he shows how the history stands apart from the reportage and that the reportage is not an accurate record.

In *Survive the Peace* (1976), not only does Ekwensi suggest that journalistic lies helped to create social chaos, but he seeks to convey the novelist's "prophecy" for the people, thus contrasting journalism and fiction even more sharply. As a radio journalist Odugo has a significant degree of mobility, and he sees many aspects of the war. Yet this is the lesser experience when compared to his suffering as a citizen in flight at the end of the war, which brings him into intimate contact with the people and casts a critical shadow over the official portrayals of the war that he helped to disseminate in his journalistic work. Ekwensi thus emphasizes the gap between Odugo's professional and personal experiences, exposing the false picture of the war created by the journalism. The novel begins just as the war ends, but few realize the war is over, and fighting continues in a haphazard way, claiming victims after the peace. Indeed, Odugo himself does not "survive the peace." He dies a victim of crime in the new lawlessness after the war. The idea of a sharp boundary between war and peace is shattered.

Extended scenes of grieving democratize the representation of the national experience in the novel: the educated and the peasants mourn the war dead together. By revealing our vulnerability, mourning presents us with an opportunity to recognize our interdependence and create, or re-create, community (Butler 30). Ekwensi, writing in a climate of wounded nationalism, recognizes that the decision to go to war appears retrospectively as a huge mistake. Mourning entails not only working toward an acceptance of what has been lost, but also risking a commitment to new political alliances and community (Butler 28). Judith Butler describes mourning as a coming to awareness of our responsibility for the lives of others; the interdependence this responsibility reveals makes us also newly aware of our vulnerability; hence, it requires a certain kind of courage. Through grieving we are "returned to a sense of human vulnerability, to our collective responsibility for the physical lives of one another" (30).

Two deaths are mourned in the novel: Samson's and Odugo's. Samson returns home a hero in a coffin. The mourners assure his father, Pa Ukoha, that Samson "fought like a true son of Obodonta," and they grieve vigorously: "the crying now became an ear-splitting chorus of wails and shrieks and groans" (Ekwensi, *Survive* 53). Pa Ukoha, however, confronts the mourners with a question: "What was all this sacrifice worth?" (53) and asks the mourners not to eulogize his son, but to condemn the war instead. The war is an attack on families, he says, and if families are destroyed, then the nation cannot progress, nor can it be independent (54). Pa Ukoha's exhortation is an ordinary person's heartfelt sentiment. It is also a poignant reminder of the family as allegory of the nation, and through this allegory it raises awareness of the collective responsibility beyond the personal. His refusal to eulogize his son is a refusal of the heroic narrative of the war and of the moral certainty it could provide. The refusal of the heroic narrative is thus a recognition of "vulnerability" and an appeal to a morality that strives for greater inclusiveness in the nation.

This extended scene of grief (52–77) also brings about a change in the way Odugo relates to Pa Ukoha, a man from whom he has a substantive generational and educational difference. Thus it becomes an occasion for another scene of rapprochement between the educated classes and the people. Already dependent on Pa Ukoha for hospitality and protection despite his own once superior economic status and social means, Odugo begins to depend on Pa Ukoha's wisdom, as well: "They sat often and talked, and these sessions resulted in mutual self-revelation" (Ekwensi, *Survive* 55). The reciprocity of the exchange shows how war's trauma can create opportunities to repair the social rifts created by colonialism. The rapprochement between Pa Ukoha and Odugo is also notably generational, echoing the fictional circumstances of Achebe's *No Longer at Ease* (1960), which maps onto the rural-urban divide.[21] The full realization of such rapprochements hinges on the peace taking hold, whereas security remains elusive at the end of the novel, casting doubt on whether the promise will be fulfilled. When the war ends Odugo abandons journalism (and employment by the government) to work in the reconstruction of his home village. His commitment to work on rebuilding the East is foiled by the social disorder, as reconstruction, Ekwensi warns, is being sabotaged.

In the second scene of mourning Odugo's parents come together with the Ukohas to grieve, and while they mourn, the two families represent the nation. The common experience of grieving for a son bridges the social distance between them. Pa Ukoha declares, "Grief . . . it is everywhere since the war ended. My own son Samson Ukoha was brought to me in a coffin" (Ekwensi, *Survive* 172). Samson's mother "held [Odugo's mother]. She had known what it was like when Samson Ukoha's body was brought home" (173). When Gladys, Odugo's girlfriend from the war, gives birth, the absence of Odugo is felt acutely. He becomes a symbol of a generation of lost men and of a rudderless nation. Pa Odugo must console Gladys, who, in despair, declares, "We have already died, Pa. The war has killed us all. Imagine a person who had everything, suddenly having nothing—is that not death?" Pa Odugo responds, "My daughter, Gladys. . . . You do not survive, till you believe you cannot die" (181). The words, the novelist's "prophecy," make more sense for the nation than for Gladys individually. To embrace the future represented by the baby she is holding, Gladys should think of herself as mother Africa, eternal. It is not a matter of replacing the victim identity with the survivor identity, but of embracing a belief that one cannot die. The nation as eternal symbol is lurking in Pa Odugo's words.

Rupture and repair are also explored through the marriage plot in the novel. During the war Odugo was separated from his wife and children and had two extramarital relationships. At the end of the war he must come to terms with his obligations to both of these women, one of whom (Gladys) is expecting his child. His wife, however, also became involved with another man, an officer in the Nigerian army, and is expecting this man's child. Odugo's three women, like Nigeria's three administrative regions before the war, cannot be restituted. Odugo attempts to reconcile with his wife, Juliette, telling her that they have "endured" each other's infidelities in order to survive the war and be together again. Their reconciliation, he argues, will render their suffering purposeful (141–42). He acknowledges the difficulties they face: "We cannot start life again as if nothing has happened. The war has happened. The calabash has been broken" (142) and suggests that they reckon with the past in order to make it possible to accept their new situation, in particular the two children that will come into their family as a result of this history. But Juliette refuses Odugo's gesture, rejecting him both at this time and when he returns a second time after the birth of her child, a son. This time Odugo leaves embittered: "This woman was not his wife, but a strange product of the war. . . . Love grown cold. Family disintegrated" (155).

By following her new family Juliette allows Odugo to go freely to Gladys and their new baby. This failure at reconciliation is treated pragmatically by Ekwensi, who stresses the value of the new relations grown out of the war. All the same, he makes it hard to be optimistic about the future. New beginnings are full of peril, especially because they are never really new but play out the implications of the changes brought about by the war. As an allegory of the nation, Odugo's circumstance questions whether there is a national will to embrace a new path. His untimely death in a highway robbery makes the outlook even bleaker and reflects the continued insecurity after the war. The bleak ending of the novel is a nod to the naturalistic aesthetic for which Ekwensi has an affinity. The allegory of the nation proffered by Pa Odugo projects into the future, beyond the time and place of the novel where, we have seen, despite the peace, the dangers of war are ongoing. War has escaped its time and place, spilled over.

The Time of War

So far my focus has been on the divided nation and the framing of this conflict as a competition between different spheres. In the fiction I have examined, Biafra is a place of war whose reality is distinct because it is at war. In part because of their isolation in Biafra, the educated characters in these novels look inward and gain a sense of identification with the plight of ordinary people. There are novelists, however, who resist this characterization of separate spheres and distinguish between a *place* of war and a *time* of war in order to move away from the framing of the story of war as the story of a divided nation. The *time* of war brings the entire (divided) nation under the scope of the same, albeit multifaceted, experience, now posited as one of duration.[22] Festus Iyayi and Wole Soyinka both exemplify this way of writing about the civil war, and, notably, neither writer is Igbo. The time of war lends itself more easily to national history—the kind that requires a taking of responsibility for the conflict by all sides.

In *Heroes* (1986), Festus Iyayi breaks down the divide that separates Biafra as a war zone cut off from the rest of the nation by challenging the idea that somewhere out there exists a distinct war zone away from civilians. His protagonist, Osime Iyere, is unsurprisingly a journalist: "a political correspondent for the city's *Daily News*" (Iyayi, *Heroes* 1). Osime breaks ranks with other journalists and decides to report the war from the perspective of the common soldier. He embeds himself in the Nigerian army, lives with the soldiers in the barracks, and prepares to go to the front.[23] The novel is set in the West near Benin City, a region that was captured by the Biafrans in a daring military maneuver early in the war. At the beginning of the novel Osime is awaiting the Federal troops to liberate this area from the Biafran occupation. After witnessing atrocities committed by the Federal troops, however, he becomes disillusioned with the Federalist cause and adopts a more even-handed attitude toward the two sides of the war, eventually realizing that the war is evil. He becomes interested in the plight of the common soldier and the civilians, especially the Igbo, who face vengeful attacks after the recapture of this region by the Federalists. "A lot of things were propaganda in this war," Osime says, "but the maltreatment of the civilian population was not propaganda. That and the photographs of the hungry and diseased children. Those were not propaganda, they were true." He concludes: "How he would love to go to the war front, to see things for himself" (3–4).

Osime is aware that there is a general suspicion of the humanitarian narrative and sees it as his duty to dispel it. As a journalist he is in a unique position to cross borders and bear testimony to the suffering. By "war front" he means crossing over into Biafra. Having witnessed the atrocities committed by the Federal troops outside Biafra and their targeted killings of Igbo in the West, Osime, however, knows that the war is not confined to Biafra. As the place of war becomes the central problematic of the novel, Osime increasingly comes to understand that he is already in the war, even before he crosses into Biafra. Moreover, reaching Biafra proves to be difficult.

The place he is supposed to report from, that other place where the war is happening, is difficult to access. At first he is told that "there is no front really . . . what is a front is not a front but a town with people . . . the war goes on much further away" (43). Osime interviews a Federalist captain who shows him photos from the front (taken by journalists, "your own people" [61]), supposedly of Biafran atrocities.[24] In an effort to stop him from going to the war front, the captain encourages him to report the atrocities shown in the photographs and thus to give witness secondhand through the images. But Osime, intrigued by the photos, becomes more determined to reach the real war front. His effort is further complicated because he takes responsibility for returning the body of his murdered Igbo landlord back to the East for burial, an act that resonates powerfully with the plight of the returnees and further ties the actions taking place outside Biafra to the war, solidifying the impression that Osime already occupies the time of war and is not in its periphery. Osime demonstrates his solidarity by performing this act for an Igbo, at the same time underscoring the national bonds of shared customs and codes of decency, which he insists upon, even though they are frayed in the war.

Beyond the blockade Biafra is indeed a different place, where a naturalistic determinism has transformed the order of things: "War changes everything. . . . The grenades are used to kill the fish to feed the soldiers, and then the soldiers are killed with grenades to feed the fish. People are killed and dumped into the river. Here there are no burial grounds. . . . This is the war front, the front where death is commonplace and hope the only thread that ties the present to tomorrow" (79). Space and time are both alluded to in this last sentence. Indeed, they are collapsed into one, a place where death swallows up time and there is only a tenuous idea of what might lie beyond or after the war. Moreover, here there "are no burial grounds," and Osime's task of returning the body for burial threatens to go off course. Osime's revelation that Biafra is different is underscored by the realization that death is everywhere, disorienting the living. Being "*where nothing holds, even for a single morning*" (101, italics in original), Osime sees the destructiveness of war as a centrifugal force, scattering from the center and creating an undifferentiated time with no end in sight. Centrifugal force is paradoxical; indeed, it is not a force at all but the inertia of motion. Thus it is suggestive of dying, where something is happening only to become that which is no longer.[25]

Iyayi succeeds in bringing the whole enterprise of war reporting into question by showing that war is not recognizable or accessible as a demarcated space away from civilians, a "heroes'" zone of military action. Osime is constantly having to relearn what war is, and the journalistic paradigm of a place to go to, report, and return from does not hold. Instead, Osime immerses himself in the *time* of war, which spills out of the front, scattering its disorder.

Iyayi has been faulted for being strident, but he succeeds in creating a collective sense of responsibility for the war that overrides the ideological rift of competing nationalisms. The proper way to frame the narrative of the war is to affirm that the nation as a whole is in a *time* of war, rather than to blame the East for seceding and creating a zone of war. "War," Osime declares, makes us "answerable to ourselves": "We loot our neighbour's property, we set fire to his house because we say he is on the other side. We loot, we burn, we rape, we murder, lie and steal. We exhibit our vomit then, we show ourselves for what we really are" (95). This catalog aims to shame and pushes Osime's humanitarian narrative, his reportage of war suffering, into a different gear. Iyayi acknowledges the cost of the war to civilians as the collective responsibility of Nigerians in their "time," turning his novel's critical view inward.[26]

Thus Iyayi describes the filth in a town market during the war and concludes that the "people were the vermin that fed on the vomit" (28). This strong image captures for Iyayi the degradation of humanity in war, a war that he sees in class terms, caused by the greed of the privileged. He draws an analogy between the war and manufacturing ("soldiers are the raw materials" [166]) in order to illustrate the voicelessness of the people in decisions about the war. The people are used up as the others ("generals," "bishops," "politicians," "professors") seek to realize their ambitions through war (166). For the Biafrans, the war is a "swindle"; the Igbo man is promised autonomy without being given the choice of whether he wants a secessionist state or not: "the decision to create Biafra is not made by the working Igbo man, it is made by the Igbo businessmen and generals and politicians" (168). Thus "war is part of the whole business enterprise. And that means it must yield profits," not by producing anything, but through looting and stealing (148). War overwhelms so that individual action often seems futile.[27] Iyayi's fictional journalist-witness is a voice of conscience. He is not detached, because Iyayi "insists on implicating the observer in the events" and, by extension, the reader (Andrew Armstrong 179). Our repulsion at the naturalistic imagery of vomit marks a kind of contamination, a reminder that our distance from suffering does not hold. The time of war encompasses everyone; there is no other half, because upholding spatial boundaries is a fiction masking the responsibility of those who pretend to stand on the other side.

Soyinka similarly created a total environment in *Season of Anomy* (1973), where a time of war is explored, according to one reviewer, "through forest, mortuary and prison camp in nightmare visions of tyranny, torture, slaughter and putrefaction" (Mellors 136). The naturalist insistence on the details of suffering shapes the book's angry tone, written as it is in a "blazing fury" (135). Despite this degree of detail, however, it is notable that the novel is not set in a named, historical place, leading to some confusion among critics about whether it belongs among the novels of the war or not. Griswold, for example, discusses Soyinka's fiction under the rubric of the "intellectual novel" and overlooks this novel, discussing instead *The Interpreters*; furthermore, she makes no reference to *Season of Anomy* in her discussion of the Biafra novels (Griswold 214–15). Other critics describe the novel, however, as "a free adaptation and surrealistic transposition to fiction of the military crises and massacres of the summer of 1966 that led to the Biafran secession and civil war" (Wright, *Wole Soyinka* 127). The descriptor "surrealistic" is in reference to the novel's highly allegorical shape, which, combined with the intense naturalistic detail, produces something like an irrational, dreamlike reality. Using a fictional country is a fairly common practice in postcolonial novels of disillusion where the nation-state is discredited (Kortenaar 70). In *Season of Anomy* the reader is confronted with a geography she does not recognize and a society whose customs, especially its regulation of time, is unfamiliar. The setting is a violent dystopia divided into two regions: Aiyero, a "village utopia" with "communalist political ideas," and its parent state, Aiyetomo, governed by a "ruthless military-industrial ruling 'Cartel'" (Wright, *Wole Soyinka* 127). The plot is structured as a rescue narrative after the Cartel's repressive policies unleash ethnic violence against the people of Aiyero, whose more democratic and collective ideals the protagonist, Ofeyi, has tried to disseminate throughout Aiyetomo. The quest is for the abducted Iriyise, Ofeyi's love interest, and it leads Ofeyi through successive places of horror until he rescues her from the prison camp. Ofeyi turns from being politically activist to carrying the burden of testimony of what he sees, demonstrating how testimony in war becomes a form of activism. The names of Soyinka's characters deliberately echo the Greek figures (Ofeyi/Orpheus, Iriyise/Eurydice) from the Orpheus myth.

As I already mentioned, Soyinka was imprisoned for twenty-seven months for speaking out against the war and criticizing the Nigerian government. The "war," he said, "was morally unjustified." He blamed the Federalists but also the Biafrans for their greed for oil and their unfair treatment of the Rivers people, the minorities of the Niger Delta region (Soyinka, *Man* 48). The pogroms and the war were an extension of the logic of empire, a demonstration of Nigeria's incomplete decolonization. According to Soyinka, the civil war crisis was also a missed opportunity to articulate a genuinely postcolonial Nigerian nationalism and break with the colonial mentality for good. Tying the novel to the war, Imre Szeman proposes a different timeline and argues it represents "Nigeria after Biafra" (Szeman 140), but this begs the question what "after" means? Does it mean after the East's secession, when Biafra came into being, or does it mean "after" the defeat of Biafra, in which case "Biafra" names the war in retrospect? The confusion brings to the fore the problem of inhabiting a time of war. *Season of Anomy* unsettles the relation between the novel and the nation, furthermore, because of what Szeman refers to as the novel's preoccupation with the failure of the intellectual to intervene effectively in nation-making and thus the failure of a national literary politics (147–48).[28] Fanon's expectation that the intellectual must interpret the revolution and educate the peasant class is not met successfully by Soyinka's protagonist, Ofeyi (Pajalich 311). The violence that the dissemination of his ideas unleashes reactively makes him more influential than the ineffectual intellectuals of *The Interpreters*, but the results are nightmarish. The novel's unresolved question is how to act on one's responsibility in light of the extreme repression unleashed in reaction.

In Aiyero's egalitarian, agrarian society, men live according to ritual time and the natural seasons. The novel is divided into sections that allude to the growing season: "Seminal," "Buds," "Tentacles," "Harvest," and "Spores." These emphasize the novel's organization around concepts of time but also draw attention to the distortion of these in times of war, where "harvest" marks the peak of violence, for example. Those who leave Aiyero for their education return eagerly to settle back into the traditional life. Soyinka's narrator calls Aiyero an "anachronism," but it seems less a holdover from the past than a place out of time—eternal (Soyinka, *Season* 2). Szeman calls the place "an empty container for the concept of the perfect society" (Szeman 141), although we need to remember that its autonomy is illusory, as it belongs to the parent state, Aiyetomo. Moreover, the idealistic Ofeyi navigates this treacherous terrain with the help of Demakin, who is willing to be ruthlessly violent on behalf of the utopian Aiyero. Nicknamed the "Dentist" because of his skill in targeted, preemptive attacks, Demakin satirizes the notion of a nonviolent utopia and raises the question of how far one is willing to go with a violent intervention to rescue Iriyise.

Ofeyi is offered the leadership of Aiyero, but hesitates to take it on because he is an outsider. However, he returns later with a much more problematic mission—to disseminate the use of cocoa for the cartel, thinking that this will simply benefit the people of Aiyero. Ofeyi's return as an agent of the cocoa cartel sets in motion the catastrophic encroachment of capital, despite his intentions to balance this influence by using his skill in advertising to spread the culture of Aiyero, its communalism, to Aiyetomo. Soyinka's creation of a character who is an advertising agent is suggestive, as it echoes the real historical circumstance of Biafra by establishing a parallel between Ofeyi's skill in advertising and Ojukwu's skill in propaganda and the Biafra regime's reliance on a foreign public relations agency to gain sympathy abroad (Falola and Heaton 177). Ofeyi attempts to spread the ideals of Aiyero to revitalize the parent state, and in analogous fashion Ojukwu portrayed Biafran nationalism as progressive—less derivative of empire than Nigerian nationalism. The war in the novel is an all-out effort by the leaders of Aiyetomo to suppress the egalitarianism of Aiyero from spreading. Capital is much stronger, and thus no genuine dialogue takes shape, making a synthesis or resolution impossible. The result is the destruction of Aiyero.

The naturalist aesthetic used by Soyinka to depict dystopia and human suffering ties the novel to the mainstream of the war literature. Ofeyi repeatedly confronts the aftermath of extreme violence and the evidence of grotesquely mutilated bodies left behind and reconstructs in his imagination what must have happened. Hence his is a forensic imagination. For example, he comes upon evidence of a killing on the edge of the forest. At first he thinks it is the deed of hunters who have killed a monkey, but then realizes he is looking at the body of a man. He imaginatively reconstructs what happened: "A scene of stalking had surely preceded this" (Soyinka, *Season* 163). The victim is "the hunted" and is described in a desperate attempt to elude his killers: "his furtive breaks and exhausted crawl on all fours among the stunted camouflage of this scrubland. Feeding on roots, leaves, worms, retching as he ran, convulsing from unaccustomed juices and poisonous barks . . . how many days had they pursued this game?" (163). Ofeyi surmises that, exhausted, the man fell and was dying, decomposing into the ground while still alive. The effort to raise his head to save himself betrays him to the enemy and costs him his life: "His elbow sought a feeble leverage on the ground and the head, a matted trap of seeds, berries, insect life, pollen and earth rose a little way from the ground." As he raises his head, he is cut down, then castrated and his penis stuffed in his mouth. The killers' faces "betrayed neither thought nor feeling" (164).[29] The narrative is unsparing, and the reader is forced to stay with the victim till the end: "As the mouth was held open to receive its obscene fodder it dried out, a weakened gurgle and red froth accompanied a final spasm of the limbs. His eyes stared unblinking at the sun" (164). The use of the passive voice underscores the anonymity of the killers and contrasts sharply with the vivid presence of the victim. All of these details are conjecture, what Ofeyi imagines must have happened.

Focalized through Ofeyi and presented as a narrative recreation of what must have happened, this episode functions as an exemplary war fiction. Its vivid detail and depiction of the effects of extreme cruelty on the victim present the reader with the imperative to abjure war, to fight the war against war. Moreover, Ofeyi finds this victim at the edge of the forest from which he emerged, thus implicating the forest as the place of horrors. The conjectured narrative presents an ordeal in the forest, thus conforming to a key motif of the war literature. This victim's ordeal in the forest, during which he regresses to an animal condition ("feeding on roots, leaves, worms"), holds no possibility of a meaningful spiritual journey, but is transformative for the witness. Ofeyi's reaction to finding these remains at the forest turns the experience into Ofeyi's surrogate ordeal in the forest. His imaginative reconstruction of this man's suffering is analogous to the work of journalists, historians, forensic anthropologists, and sometimes novelists, all of whom must reconstruct atrocity in order to begin to redress the wrong committed. To do so they must enter the time of war; they must use the evidence of the remains to uncover retrospectively what happened. The naturalist aesthetic in which this reconstruction is rendered now appears fitting for an event that can only be told retrospectively through the deterministic logic of the evidence.

The bifurcated world of the novel (two regions, two economies, two societies) collapses, and we are faced with a dystopic panorama of maimed and suffering people, a landscape of war, which Soyinka, alluding to Dante, refers to as a descent into hell: "abandon hope all who enter," the narrator warns (282).[30] In the climactic scene Ofeyi is wandering through the "Leper's Ward" of the Temoko prison where Iriyise is being held. Maimed by disease and living in filth, the lepers create a revolting spectacle. Ofeyi is warned not to feel sympathy, however, because the lepers attack those who show sympathy for their suffering (298). What could have been a humanitarian tableau in the novel, the moral witness to abjection, amounts instead to a rejection of the politics of pity.

When Ofeyi comes upon the lepers, they are fighting over the little food that is being distributed to them. Echoes of the real Biafra abound in the depiction of famine, disease, deformity. As Ofeyi contemplates this scene, he hears "a guttural noise through twisted lips and words which approximate the phrase 'Beasts of no nation!'" He hears "Beasts of no nation!" repeated again, "fighting words," according to Ofeyi, uttered by one of the lepers to the group (296–97).[31] The leper's accusation that his fellow inmates are "beasts of no nation" (barbarians?) suggests his own struggle to hold onto a sense of belonging against their unbelonging. Nation is the humanizing reference here, and belonging to the nation must be claimed against the anomie of war. The other lepers in the group are beyond caring about the nation. Achebe used the phrase "beast of no nation" before Soyinka in *No Longer at Ease*, where it captures the anger of an ordinary man toward the educated Obi: "Foolish man. He tink say because him get car derefore he can do as he like. Beast of no nation" (Achebe, *No Longer* 138). Unbelonging to the nation is the accusation of the poor against the privileged who don't recognize their equal citizenship.

Ofeyi connects with just one person in the prison, the mute guard Suberu, whose job is to guard Ofeyi at the bedside of the comatose Iriyise. Suberu holds Ofeyi's last hope for the people, and Ofeyi sets out to radicalize him, but his unresponsiveness frustrates him: "Damn, I wish I knew how to reach you" (315). He urges Suberu to leave the prison, to walk out: "Why are you still here? . . . Why can't you see you've been trapped like her [Iriyise in a coma] in a capsule of death?" (315). He gets no verbal response, but in the novel's last scene Suberu walks out of the prison ahead of Ofeyi and the unconscious Iriyise. Suberu represents the people's predicament: devastated by hunger and voiceless, but capable of watching, listening, and acting. In what nation and under what leadership remains an open question. Can the rescue of Iriyise be considered a success when she is found in a coma? Her new condition symbolizes the indeterminate duration of the time of war, a symbol of the potential for political transformation that has not been stopped, nor is it advancing.

Iroh's Trilogy and the People's Satire

Soyinka's awareness of the failure to bring the people into history helps foreground that such an effort is one of the aims of a national literary politics. *Season of Anomy* situates the intellectual as an intermediary between the peasantry and everybody else: the nation, the state, capital, the military. Soyinka is considered a difficult writer who does not reach a popular audience. Iyayi, for example, has commented that, although Soyinka's Nobel Prize was a good thing for Nigeria, Achebe was perceived instead as Nigeria's most influential writer by other Nigerians: "Achebe has won our people because his writing is accessible. Soyinka tends to have a European audience" (Wendt, "Iyayi" 421). To read Soyinka as an "extroverted" novelist, however, is also incorrect, as he has always refused any notion of writing back. In the "Author's Note" that introduces his play *Death and King's Horseman*, he famously warned the reader not to interpret the confrontation in the play as a clash between the colonial authorities and the Yoruba protagonist, but to read it as the protagonist's coming into his own identity within a Yoruba cosmology.

The popular literature of the war addresses this concern of bringing the people into history and the failure to achieve this goal through a different aesthetic, deploying the subversive voice of satire. Satire depicts war as anomie, but its mocking juxtaposition of the exceptional status of war with the everyday and commonplace brings war under the lens of the law, custom, and conventional social behavior. Laughter is a regulating force, a reminder of where the social parameters lie even in the most extreme of circumstances. And coming from the perspective of the people, satire turns them into the law enforcers.

The most successful of Nigeria's satirists of the war is Eddie Iroh, who, like Ekwensi, worked as a journalist in Biafra during the war, although he did not depict journalists as his main characters. A very popular writer in the 1970s, Iroh is known for his "thriller style" (Ezeigbo 66).[32] He sought to develop a people's point of view against that of a corrupt elite, and the sharpness of his class critique makes him an important precursor to Iyayi, with whom he shares a similar naturalist aesthetic.

Iroh wrote in an attempt to salvage a popular memory of the war that he felt was being erased by a political atmosphere of paranoia after the war. *Forty-Eight Guns for the General* (1976), the first novel in a trilogy, focuses on the use of mercenaries in the war. This is an easy target, since both sides used mercenaries and were condemned for it (Forsyth 112). Iroh, who was himself Igbo, depicts the use of mercenaries by the Biafrans and calls them mockingly the "Christian Brothers." Mercenaries complicate the problem of distinguishing between war as a general condition and war as a discrete event, a particular conflict. If war is a way of life, an end in itself, as it is for mercenaries, war is not a crisis or a transition, but its own space and time without other parameters and without historical memory. It can go on indefinitely and happen anywhere. As the leader of the mercenaries in the novel, Jacques Rudolf, says, "if you are fighting to make a living, you fight to stay alive. . . . A good soldier fights to fight another day" with no end in sight (Iroh, *Forty-Eight* 61).[33] Rudolf's unbelonging to anything but war is reflected in his highly individualized dress, which signals his rogue status and carries symbols of his self-fashioning. This pastiche of military accessories speaks of idiosyncrasy and indiscipline:

> The beret and the pistol were no ordinary trappings of an ordinary soldier. Like his tiny personal pennant, they were more than testimonials: they were symbols of Rudolf's independence. It did not matter what country it was; what uniforms and colours its army wore; what personal weapons its officers were issued with, or what codes and regulations were mandatory, Jacques Rudolf always carried and used his personalised red and green emblem, his automatic pistol and, somewhat inappropriately for his chosen career, the Légionnaire's standard, *Honneur et Fidélité*. (39)

The eccentricity of Rudolf's dress is evocative of descriptions of other warriors in this literature (Thomas Mofolo's Chaka, Dongala's Johnny, as we will see in Chapter 4) and demonstrates how fighters become physically the personification of war. "Symbols of his independence" rather than his belonging to a disciplined corps, the accessories intimidate by signaling the rogue nature of his actions ahead of their execution. We know from his dress that nothing will hold him back; no rules apply. The mercenaries belong to war alone and thus come to be war, appropriating its meaning and highjacking the conflict for their own ends, the continuation of war. To confront them means to wage a war against war.

In the novel the mercenaries are ultimately defeated by Chumah, a Biafran colonel whose family perished in the fall of Port Harcourt, where Rudolf was the one responsible for the defense of that city. Chumah's mission to expose the duplicity of the mercenaries and remove them from the war becomes a mission of revenge for his family's demise. It is also an opportunity to exonerate himself from accusations that he failed in his own military duty to defend the Biafran capital, for which failure he has been imprisoned. It was only upon his release that he learns of the loss of his family. In a rare moment of sentimentality in the text, Chumah is portrayed crying, fists clenched (111).

Critics have read this novel as Iroh's attempt to restore military honor to the Biafran soldiers (Ezeigbo 72). Iroh uses the hated mercenaries as a foil to showcase the bravery of Biafrans so that Biafrans can be accepted as brave African soldiers. Rudolf, the white apostle of war, does not feel bound by the Geneva Conventions because he is in Africa: "it was not a white man's war. Germany against France or even France against the Algerians. It was not fought with sophisticated weapons, or according to the Geneva Convention" (Iroh, *Forty-Eight* 59). We know better than to believe the truthfulness of these claims about the French or the Germans, yet all the same we are reminded of the Geneva Conventions, as well as of the asymmetry between the two enemies in this war. The Federalists had a significant military force of 85,000 extremely well-armed troops and support from the British, whereas the Biafrans were blockaded and tried desperately to make do with significantly less firepower and homemade weapons (Forsyth 111–12). This unevenness between adversaries exacerbated the humanitarian crisis. The allusion to the Geneva Conventions is a good example of how satire works to bring the scene of war back under the purview of the law. The law may seem weak or irrelevant, but its evocation has a leveling effect: all parties to war are guilty, hence Chumah's revenge is also open to critique.

In addition, Rudolf alludes to stereotypes of African inhumanity: "The white man provided food and shelter for his civilian adversaries and his prisoners of war. He did not chop his enemy's head off, drink his blood, ritually gore his heart out and eat it alive to render his own heart stouter" (Iroh, *Forty-Eight* 59). The reader could respond here that the white man gassed Jews and burned their bodies in crematoria, and this kind of retort may not be beside the point, because Iroh can show that "war is war," no matter where it takes place.

Iroh pits militarism and humanitarianism against each other in the novel's most controversial scene, the rape of a Swedish worker for the Red Cross by a mercenary, who is a German with a Nazi past. Rape, a common war crime that implicated Nigerian and Biafran soldiers alike, symbolizes for Iroh the kind of war guilt that transcends sides and reflects instead the masculine culture of war.[34] Using European characters, Iroh makes rape tellable, distancing it enough to expose the misogyny that manifests itself in war. He also implicates his popular readership through the scene's quasi-pornographic structure. The scene's comic-book aesthetic, with its exaggerated gender identities and stylized action, renders it less real and more like fantasy. Furthermore, Iroh racializes the portrayal of the female victim, drawing attention to her whiteness:

> Wenda Britta was as strong a girl as she was a beautiful blonde.
> "Damn you, you bitching bastard!" Heinz cursed in a voice that sounded like air passing through hairy nostrils.
> "Now! Or I'll use that gun!" he glared.
> The gun!
> The mention of the gun . . . caused Wenda's stout head to tremble. She had put up a masculine fight against the brutal force of Hans Heinz as he had tossed his gun away along with his clothes.
> But now, the gun!
> Oh God! The gun! She moaned silently, her strength suddenly sapped by mortal fear of the maniac's threat.
> "My God! My God, Oh, Oh!" She was moaning ineffectually as Hans Heinz, his eyes aglint with the smile of evil lust about to be assuaged, tore her thighs apart and ripped off the last shreds of Wenda Britta's privacy! (200)

Read through Iroh's satire, the scene makes an ironic comment on the secondariness of humanitarianism's moral project. Humanitarianism is easily overwhelmed by the West's other favored practice, war. The scene's sexual violence, however, also arguably displaces the humiliation of the Biafrans onto the blond woman. The gun, a phallic symbol, terrorizes. Its presence clearly tips the balance in the scene and dooms the victim. It also alludes to the novel's title, forty-eight guns, the number of mercenaries in this group. Being victimized thus by the gun, she is turned into a symbol of the people. The popular readership that reads the scene through its comic-book aesthetic going along with its masculinist assumptions ends up somewhere different from where it began, now implicated in a scene of sexual violence it would rather disavow. The female humanitarian worker turns out to be of more value to the Biafran perspective, which realizes it has something at stake in protecting her, although, alas, this comes too late in this novel.

The second volume of Iroh's trilogy, *Toads of War* (1979), depicts the final days of the war. Biafra has turned into a degenerate place of sex and violence. While the elite are having parties and sexual orgies, bombs are killing the people (Iroh, *Toads* 127, 137). The public face of Biafra during the war was the humanitarian crisis, yet Iroh shows a different reality. Indeed, dualities govern the moral universe of Iroh. The novel has two narrators: Kalu and an unnamed narrator. Kalu, an epileptic who was forcefully recruited to fight despite his disability, ends up an amputee. As a disabled veteran Kalu leads a life of abject poverty, dreaming of the moment when he will successfully avenge himself against the man who sent him to war, Chima Duke, a rich businessman who had been his boss. Kalu's desire for vengeance foregrounds the theme of a people's vengeance, similar to what we find in *Heroes*, where Iyayi suggests that a revolution of the discontented, who will form a "third army," is imminent and will kill the officers on both sides of the war (Iyayi, *Heroes* 90).

The social divide, the gulf between the haves and the have-nots, is present here as it is throughout the literature. The novel begins on Christmas Eve by opposing soldiers who suffer against those who profit from the war. For those on the battlefield, "the piercing shriek of nerves of pain were an unlikely simulation of yule sound" (Iroh, *Toads* 1). But for those on the other side of the social divide, things are considerably safer:

> But the gloom and grimness existed not in the quarters of a few people—the war racketeers and profiteers, the disaster millionaires, the big shots, the toads of war, civilian and military, who fought their own war by proxy. (1)

"Toads of war" don't attach themselves to powerful people, but to war itself. A toad or toady is a sycophant or proxy to someone in power. Iroh lambasts the Biafran elite, who, not unlike the mercenaries of *Forty-Eight Guns for the General*, are men invested in the continuation of the war. There are two "disparate breeds of men":

> The one was middle-aged, privileged and powerful. He lacked nothing, wanted nothing—not even an end to the war. An end to the war would mean the termination of his influence and affluence. . . .
>
> The other was young, deprived and deformed. He was unemployed and, for now, unemployable. . . . Alone in his rat-hole . . . he would take off the sweet, silky veneer that covered his inner side. Then you could see the bitterness, the vengeance, breathing through his skin. (Iroh, *Toads* 5)

Kalu succeeds in killing his former boss and thus fulfills his desire for vengeance. This action presents us with a straightforward national allegory: the disabled Kalu represents the politically handicapped people (Nigeria as the "crippled giant" of Africa) who unleash their violence against the political class that led them to war without their consent.

Yet, despite offering this allegory, the novel does not satisfy us that justice has been done. When Kalu learns of Biafra's surrender, he is in prison for killing Chima. Because Ojukwu received asylum outside Nigeria, there is no justice for the people and, with the war over, there is no more possibility of vengeance, as vengeance belongs to the logic of war (141–43).

The novel ends with a poem that speaks bleakly of the future and continued destitution:

> dragged, rudderless
> we are lumbered home
> to reyouth in coldfisted darkness
> gilded with tepid rainbow colours. (144)

The injunction "to reyouth," which sounds like official propaganda, saps individual initiative. "Rudderless" and represented by the passive voice, Kalu and his generation have little hope of meaningful agency. The naturalist environment is no longer an attribute of war. Having escaped the bounds of war's place and time, naturalism is now attached to the quotidian realities of the urban poor. Like the trilogy's first novel, the second ends on a note of bitterness that contrasts what could have been, now realized too late, with what is. Perhaps there is an opening here for a hopeful intervention, to be proactive and avoid the pitfall of realizing too late that which was worth saving from the outset. The sarcasm and satire beg for a kind of sincerity, a more direct investment in a cause. Similar to the regretful reaction to Wenda's rape, Iroh's novels show us in retrospect what the value of what is lost and worth fighting for is.

The last novel of Iroh's trilogy, *The Siren in the Night* (1982) focuses on a more sincere character who tries hard to do the right thing. The novel borrows its title from a poem by Dennis Brutus: "The sounds begin again; / The siren in the night / the thunder at the door / the shriek of nerves in pain." The allusions to apartheid South Africa, state repression, and torture set a bleak tone for this novel about reconstruction and reconciliation after the war. The new Nigeria is not free. It is paranoid, haunted by the unfinished business of the war. The protagonist, Ben Udaja, is an advocate of the people who becomes the target of harassment and political assassination. His enemy, Colonel Kolawole, believes that Biafran "rebels" are plotting to overthrow the government, even though the war is over. In this atmosphere of deep mutual suspicion, the people's cause (reconstruction) is a non-starter.

In a scene that portrays torture as the surreptitious continuation of the war violence, Kolawole abuses a former Biafran fighter, who, physically and mentally broken, agrees to cooperate in a plot to frame Udaja. In Kolawole's view, Udaja is a dangerous Biafran "terrorist" (83), despite being employed in the relief effort organized by the federal government. He suspects Udaja is organizing a new rebellion, accusations that the reader knows are absurd (70). Udaja, a man of principle, defected during the war from Biafra to the Federalist side because he did not want to be complicit in the criminal continuation of the war. When the war ends, he receives the important assignment of chief of rehabilitation for the East. Although Udaja is a civilian official in the same state in which Kolawole is a colonel in the army, they are not joined in a common purpose working for the people. Udaja wants to do good; Kolawole wants to cling to power by all means.

The difficulty of getting the project of reconstruction under way becomes the butt of Iroh's satire. The plot is full of tragi-comic twists, misperceptions, and deadly errors. A war mentality of division and antagonism still predominates, and Udaja's sincerity stands no chance. Although he embraces his new role, he is inhibited by his lack of trust in his fellow Biafrans and convinced that he will be viewed as a traitor by them. When he becomes the target of harassment by Kolawole's agent, he believes erroneously that the Biafrans (not the Federalists) are out to get him. In a panic, he murders Kolawole's agent just as the agent is about to confess to Udaja the army's plot against him. Udaja's inability to read accurately the politics of post-war Nigeria causes such profound psychic upheaval that he ends up in a psychiatric hospital. He is politically neutralized and the effort of reconstruction and rehabilitation stymied. Iroh pits the militarist culture of unchecked power and secrecy against the promise of reconstruction and reconciliation, which is the opportunity that should not be lost and regretted later. Kolawole succeeds in getting Udaja out of the way, but he does not survive the transition, either, as he is tried in secret and executed for allegedly planning to overthrow the government. Thus he is victim of the culture of militarism that he cultivated.

The state's power is shown to be theatrical, making it possible to demystify and critique it. Earlier in the novel Udaja, already rattled by anonymous phone calls and other harassments, arrives at his apartment with his newlywed wife to find the electricity and phone cut off. Here the reader expects something awful to happen. Instead, Udaja finds a luxury coffin on his bed with his pajamas laid neatly inside. This macabre joke pushes Udaja further to the edge. The humor is less at Udaja's expense than the reader's, however, who, caught reading according to the thriller convention, is not quite satisfied by the gestural quality of the scene and its irresolution in terms of physical danger. Iroh's use of sensation and exaggeration, elements of the popular in his writing, position his readers to laugh at power (Ezeigbo 66), yet we don't really want to laugh at Udaja. Iroh intended his trilogy to be read as an accurate depiction of how things were (he called his work "historical fiction" [Ezeigbo, *Siren*, "Author's Note"]), and he provided a platform for an irreverent popular attitude toward authority, setting in motion a people's view of the history of the war. This perspective is captured by the satisfaction we feel in Kolawole's demise, but Udaja's ineffectiveness, his inability to overcome his own neuroses and work for the people, is ultimately disappointing. The satire of reconstruction makes it impossible to mobilize an allegory of the nation, reminding us of the precariousness of the people's point of view. It is important to save Udaja's project of reconstruction, even if Udaja himself turns out to be laughable. Thus we are reminded of the regulating power of humor, which brings to the fore an awareness of the expectation of lawful, constructive behavior.

Sincerity and the Critique of War

Whereas the early fiction cast a wide net to show that "the people" should encompass all Nigerians and that the novel could teach them how to understand each other's histories of the war, the satires of the popular literature made it clear that the post-war years failed to incorporate the poor into the nation and hence kept the war alive as a topic through which their economic and social justice struggles could find expression. Much post–civil war discontent is expressed by mocking the reconstruction efforts. The twelve texts that I discuss in this chapter represent a wide range of approaches to the representation of the people's point of view; hence I turn now to yet another, different configuration of this problem of representation with Saro-Wiwa's *Sozaboy: A Novel in Rotten English* (1985). Like *Season of Anomy*, this is a novel that does not name the war and whose specific engagement with the political realities of Nigeria is veiled, couching the plight of the Ogoni of the Niger Delta in more universal terms so that their story can constitute an antiwar novel with wide appeal.

Sozaboy is perhaps the most successful novel to deploy a literary pidgin (the "rotten English" named in the subtitle) as the voice of the people. It is also the most important precursor of the child-soldier narratives of the late 1990s.[35] Because it is stylistically unique and does not name the war, the novel has acquired the status of an anti-war classic, bridging the distances separating the national, African, and world audiences. Outside Nigeria, it is not known that Pitakwa is Port Harcourt, for example. Moreover, Saro-Wiwa's profile as a human rights activist helped launch this novel on the world stage.[36] This novel, therefore, does not easily fit the paradigm of the introverted text, although it is worth noting that it was published first in Port Harcourt by Saro-Wiwa's own press, Saros International Publishers.

It was republished by Longman in its African Writers Series nine years later, in 1994, and has remained in print ever since.

Saro-Wiwa's identity as an Ogoni gives him a unique perspective on the war. If the novels of the war have been written primarily by the war's losers, as Griswold pointed out (Griswold 235), Saro-Wiwa writes from a different perspective, as one of those who did not feel this was their war at all, yet got inevitably drawn into the conflict and suffered as a result of their political invisibility. Saro-Wiwa was born in Bori, near Port Harcourt, the major city in Nigeria's Rivers State. In his writing he remained committed to the people, keeping as a central theme of his work the problem of "how to resolve the class issue" (Ojo-Ade xxiii).[37] Before the civil war he held assistantships at Ibadan and the university at Nsukka, a hotbed of Biafran nationalism (portrayed, as we shall see, in *Half of a Yellow Sun*). Saro-Wiwa opposed the Biafran cause and joined the Federal forces during the war. He felt that the Ogoni were trapped by the accident of their geographical location within the borders of secessionist Biafra. In his war memoir Saro-Wiwa calls the Eastern minorities "the real victims of the war" caught in a "no-win situation" (Saro-Wiwa, *Darkling* 10). A witness to the fall of Port Harcourt, he saw firsthand how the Ogoni were "pillaged by both sides" (Ojo-Ade xiv).

Saro-Wiwa's invention of a literary "rotten English" works mimetically to capture the voice of the people, but also goes beyond mimesis to create a rich heteroglossia of literary genres. In addition to oral literary traditions, the novel alludes to: the epistolary in one of the text's often repeated expressions, "believe me yours sincerely"; the *Bildungsroman* as the story of Mene's interrupted education and his apprenticeship as a lorry driver; religious testimony in Mene's apocalyptic witness of Bullet's death; domestic fiction in his mother's appeal to the values of home and family as antiwar values; the picaresque in Mene's wanderings; and epic in the failed recognition scene of Mene's return after the war. Saro-Wiwa claimed that "rotten English" was meant to capture the limitations of illiteracy and the kind of chaotic, disorderly world of those who have a limited understanding of the language(s) of power (Saro-Wiwa, "Preface," *Sozaboy*). But this scrambled language turns into a capacious literary instrument that conveys the urgency with which Mene narrates and his coming into a political subjectivity in the very act of telling his experience of war. The text's heteroglossia reminds the reader of its literariness, its indebtedness to other forms to make meaning. It connects it to other literature by making us aware of the "transperiod narratives of genre," which demonstrate how form signals its "extraliterary significance," its historical reference (Robbins, "Afterword"

1650). We do not have to choose between language as mimesis and our own recognition of the literariness of Saro-Wiwa's text. It is by signaling his participation in a world genre, while at the same time using a language that signifies the local, that Saro-Wiwa accomplishes a translation of a historically particular African subjectivity and makes it politically visible. The literary brings about a kind of recognition that hopefully will spawn a political recognition leading to a more inclusive nation. Thus, although the novel is deeply pessimistic about war, its ending is not without hope. Having lost everything, Mene runs and runs to what can only be some kind of new, albeit difficult, beginning (Saro-Wiwa, *Sozaboy* 181).

A key instance of the novel's obvious switching of literary codes comes after the deadly aerial attack on Mene's unit, which kills his squadron leader. The tone of the novel turns at this point away from satire, banter at Mene's naivete and anger at authority, to a sincerity that culminates in the multiple appeals to the reader to "believe" Mene, who is "yours sincerely," a phrase repeated also as the novel's closing line. Mene resorts to the language of testimony, cast in Christian terms, the most solemn language he is familiar with:

> After the plane have disappeared, then I got up from where I was hiding. Oh Jesus Christ son of God, the thing wey I see my mouth no fit talk am. Oh God our father wey dey for up, why you make man wicked like this to his own brother? Oh Mary, mother of Jesus, pray for us to God to forgive us all our sins and not to kill us like fly because of our wickedness. Angel Gabriel, please beg God if he does not want us to live, make'e no make us only to kill us after like goat or rat or rabbit. Oh, I can never forget what I saw that morning. . . . And inside my pit, you will see the head of soza, and in another pit, the leg of soza and in another pit, the hand of soza. (111)

Mene adopts phrases from several common prayers (the Jesus prayer, the Hail Mary, the Lord's Prayer) to signal the apocalyptic nature of what he is witnessing and the sincerity of his words. After Bullet's death his voice becomes frequently "deliberative" in the Aristotelian sense, urging the redress of wrongs (Nance 23). This new seriousness reflects an enhanced moral authority as Mene realizes that war is not what you fight in, but what you fight against. He deserts, fleeing into the forest for his turn at the "ordeal." Here he comes into contact with Manmuswalk, one of those recurring characters in war fiction who personifies war.[38] Manmuswalk's name means "man must eat," and his unstable identity correlates with his total lack of values. He adjusts with his environment and appears alternatively as Mene's torturer and savior. Manmuswalk switches sides repeatedly in the war, confusing Mene and challenging him to think beyond the dualistic logic of war.

Sincerity is intimately linked to the novel's second-person narration. Mene frequently addresses the reader as "my brother," alluding to a human community not in evidence in the war. Michael North reads "my brother" as ironic, a "critique of the fratricide of civil war" (North 99), but it also refers to the imagined community of Dukana, Mene's village, whose inhabitants have dispersed. The epistolary form contributes to the novel's change in tone and strongly intimates the existence of a different space, the "where" to which the letter is addressed, outside and beyond the war-ravaged reality. This is a place where humanity and community can be recovered. Moreover, this other space projected through the epistolary is suggestive of Amanda Anderson's evocation of sincerity as the space of "the dual stance of critique and transgressive displacement" that "necessarily preserves the importance of the sincerity topos: it is not a simple rejection or eclipsing or replacement" (Amanda Anderson 166). Sincerity makes possible a certain way of arguing (which Anderson connects to Habermasian proceduralism) that assumes "the positive values of critique, transparency, and civic virtue" (167). And whereas it is also associated with negative qualities ("social conformity and disciplinarity" [167]), sincerity invites the well-intentioned participation of persons who feel connected to each other, the brotherhood in Mene's address to the reader, threatened during war and in an undemocratic society. Originating from somewhere beyond the novel's boundaries, sincerity, therefore, adumbrates the new nation that could be "actualized" (to use Saro-Wiwa's term) if war did not block it.

The theme of the people's political disempowerment has its most poignant expression in all the literature of the war in *Sozaboy*. By universalizing the perspective of a minority drawn by circumstance into this catastrophic war, Saro-Wiwa breaks down the entrenched view that everyone belonged to one of two sides in the conflict. "Everybody is enemy in this our war," a character says in the novel, indicating that the civil conflict ("our war") is not between sides, but pits everyone against everyone else (Saro-Wiwa, *Sozaboy* 137). Unlike the earlier novelists, Saro-Wiwa does not allude to an allegory of the nation. We are reminded instead of Agamben's description of the people as permanently divided against itself, of being in a constant state of civil war. The "people," Agamben says, contains "the fundamental biopolitical fracture within itself," the opposition between "bare life" and "political existence," or "exclusion and inclusion," for which the camp, set apart from the polis, is the paradigmatic structure (Agamben, *Homo Sacer*

177). As the war rages in *Sozaboy*, villages and communities are destroyed. Camps emerge that turn into crowded, makeshift cities.

For Agamben the always already thereness of the civil war in any conceptualization of the people makes it impossible to posit the people as a distinct entity because it is always already in an agon, playing out the struggle between the "people" and the "People," the bare life versus the political existence. Saro-Wiwa comes the closest to capturing Agamben's conceptualization of the people because, by totalizing the condition of civil war, he shows how it inhibits the articulation of any political rationale for the war. The novelist, seeking a way out, sees an opportunity to forge a new political struggle for the "People." Moreover, Saro-Wiwa never hesitated to assert the political role of literature; literature must be "interventionist," he said (quoted in Ojo-Ade xvii).[39]

The war in *Sozaboy* has a very weak, even nonsensical, explanation, and the people surviving the war are confused about which side they are on and why. Those who understand that there are two sides switch sides repeatedly, following their self-interest. The social disintegration is mirrored in a transformation of the landscape, erasing the characteristics distinguishing places from each other and replacing them with an uncanny sameness. In the words of Mene, war is always "useless": "all this suffering is total useless. And to fight war is even more useless" (Saro-Wiwa, *Sozaboy* 153). Saro-Wiwa's total war engulfs and tears apart the entire nation, changing its geography by erasing the identifying marks that link regions, villages, cities to peoples and histories. Towns and villages are destroyed, the people are uprooted, and new towns and refugee camps emerge where a chaotic Babel of suffering humanity prevails. Looking for his mother and wife, Mene wanders through a large camp where "everybody was just talking different different language" and, even though he stays a week, he feels that he had not seen everyone in the camp (150). He calls the camp a "black forest or a black swamp" because of its overcrowding and wonders if it is not more than a camp, a "new town, new dirty town born by the foolish war" (150). The war also creates a new economy where "many people were trading with the enemy" (150).[40]

War is the story of the loss of home and its attempted recovery. The new places, new economies, and new language function in the novel as a reminder of the loss of home, a loss that is profoundly destabilizing. Saro-Wiwa's surreal landscapes of devastation destabilize the allegory of nation as home, rendering the domestic more precious even as it becomes more insecure. The desire to escape a war-ravaged place creates a yearning for an elsewhere that could be the place where Saro-Wiwa's reader (Mene's "brother") is located. Whether this is the same place as the indeterminate place and time from which Mene tells his story retrospectively is unclear, but it can be seen as the place toward which he would like to move, a place that is intuited as that which could be "actualized" instead of war.

In contrast, the war produces potent rot in the novel, most significantly in Saro-Wiwa's description of the refugee camps. His fellow villager Zaza describes the refugee camp as a "compost pit." He tells Mene that a "refugee is somebody that they just throw away like rubbish, no get house to stay in, no get food to eat or cloth to wear. So the camp where plenty of them are staying is like compost pit" (147). For Zaza, "they" who throw away people are the same people who came to Dukana to recruit Mene and others for the war and then betrayed them: "we are among friends and they are hunting us like anmals [*sic*]" (146). The Red Cross saves them from being cannibalized: "If not for Red Cross, all Dukana people will have already dead." In Zaza's explanation, the Red Cross collects the sick and the weak so "the cannibals do not come to kill and eat them" (146).

Cannibalism is Saro-Wiwa's metaphor for what the war's leaders are doing to the people, a form of consumption symbolically associated with the exploitative practices of capitalism (Barker et al). It is also Saro-Wiwa's oblique reference to the politics of oil and world capital that lurk in the background. Zaza explains to Mene, "Friends? They are not our friends. They are our worst enemy. All the things you hear on the radio and from the D.O. who have come to Dukana before the war proper start, they are all lies" (146). Their own leaders have betrayed them, and corruption is rife in the camps, where the leaders from the village still find ways to profit from their own people.

Mene is tortured in the "dirty town" refugee camp because his story, the happenstance through which he found himself on both sides, seems suspect (159–60). His predicament is characteristic of Saro-Wiwa's satire of the war. In the refugee camp he encounters his former pastor and the chief of Dukana and is eager to tell them how he ended up on both sides of the war. Mene initially feels pity for their decrepit state, but soon realizes that they are corrupt and have been hoarding and selling the food aid, acquiring an interest in the war's continuation. They have "sold their eyes and their ears to the big sozas for their belly," turning in purported "saboteurs" to maintain their own protection (156). Chief Birabee insists this is a "war that we must win" (154), echoing the Biafran leadership who prolonged the war despite the famine. Since the chief and the pastor do not want to stop the war, they perceive Mene's antiwar feelings as treasonous, dissenting from the common cause they supposedly share as men from Dukana. The lack of tolerance of critique marks the absence of sincerity; hence the honest account of the war is displaced onto the epistolary, beyond the time and place of the war. The disillusioning reunion in the refugee camp also underscores the loss of Dukana for Mene.

Longing to escape the trap of "war is war," Mene longs for home, war's opposite. Saro-Wiwa presents the tautology "war is war" not as nonsense, but as a system with its own sustaining logic of self-gratification, or compulsion. Michael Walzer has described this perspective as a view of war as a "world apart, where life itself is at stake, where human nature is reduced to its elemental forms, where self-interest and necessity prevail" (Walzer 3). "War is war" is identified with Manmuswalk, a completely deracinated character, in the novel. Mene's dissent from war is also his proclamation of the value of home as he seeks to reclaim what he lost by going to war. Before the war his mother had warned him, "But if war is coming, it is better to be in your own house and fight it" (Saro-Wiwa, *Sozaboy* 67). The war was not fought for home, which would have been the only thing worth fighting for. Mene manages to return but finds the village burying its dead and in the midst of a smallpox epidemic. His house has been destroyed, and there is no trace of his family. The villagers shun him: "even in my own town I have no house" (175). The warrior's return is ironically comic as Mene's old friend Duzia tries to ascertain in a mock recognition scene whether Mene is a ghost (177). The ending of the novel offers no place for Mene to go, only the imperative that he leave Dukana:

> I just get up and begin to go. As I was going, I looked at the place where my mama house used to stand. And tears began to drop like rain from my eyes. I walked quickly from my own town Dukana and in fact I did not know where I was going. (181)

Home no longer exists, destroyed by the lack of trust, everyone an enemy. The novel closes with this: "But now if anybody say anything about war or even fight, I will just run and run and run and run and run. Believe me yours sincerely" (181). At the end of the novel Mene runs away from war itself. We are left only with the interpolated and indefinite place from which he narrates the story, a place that is projected beyond the immediate reality of the war and its consequences.

The Inconsequential Woman and Humanitarianism

This chapter began with attention to gender. Achebe's "Girls at War" and Nwapa's *Never Again* self-consciously contrasted the different war experiences of men and women, even though they focused on civilians. The combatants are distanced; the focus is on civilian experiences, and these are clearly gendered. A broader survey of the literature reveals that novels that center on women have more to say about humanitarianism. In "Girls at War" Achebe used the portrayal of a Western humanitarian worker to highlight the degree of Nwankwo's alienation from the people. The humanitarian worker could say that Biafra "stinks" and Nwankwo agreed, demonstrating his distance from the people but also the parallel roles of humanitarian worker and government official. Chukwuemeka Ike's *Sunset at Dawn* (1976) characterizes humanitarianism differently by explicitly identifying it as woman's work, relegating it to the politically weak and marginalized but not contesting its sincerity. Emecheta in contrast recognizes this alignment of humanitarianism and the feminine sphere and contests it from within, questioning its relevance to women's experience of the war.

A satiric novel of the war, *Sunset at Dawn*, is typical of the popular literature and seeks to mock how the elite cope with the war by illustrating how the humanitarian crisis enters the awareness of the elite. The wife of a doctor and Director of Mobilization for Biafra, Fatima is at first safely on the sidelines, bored in the village while the action is elsewhere. Her inspiration to commit to humanitarian work comes not from a devotion to Biafra—in fact, as Hausa she feels out of place—but from her identification with the suffering of another woman, a refugee from the violence of the North. This woman's story shocks the bored and homesick Fatima into action, motivating her to start a feeding center for children suffering from kwashiorkor. We are told that now she "found herself seeing everything with new eyes" (Ike 98), and, more importantly, "She . . . wept at the shocking discovery that, faced with similar problems, an illiterate, unsophisticated, inconsequential woman had proved better able to cope with the situation than she had, with all her education, professional training, easy life and world-wide experience" (100). Like Ekwensi's Chika, who stands by the side of an injured peasant and in the emergency sees things from her point of view, Fatima's new regard for an "inconsequential woman" challenges her own sense of self-worth. I will come back to the term "inconsequential woman" shortly.

Her husband, on the other hand, is incapable of seeing the people's suffering. He sees the war only in personal terms, as a plot against *him*:

> The Nigerians were not content with imposing a blockade against *him*, but they had dogged *his* footsteps ever since. The Nigerians had slaughtered *his* innocent son at Enugu. The Nigerians had driven *him* out of

> Enugu. The Nigerians had driven *his* family out of Obodo, *his* village. Now the Nigerians wanted to drive *him* out of Umuahia. Where to? Wasn't there a point at which one had to say an emphatic NO to the vandals? (209, emphasis added)

Everything revolves around him and his hurt sense of entitlement. His "emphatic NO," however, costs Dr. Kanu his life. After her husband is killed Fatima is poised to replace him in Biafra's government, but she is eased out by his male colleagues, who send her to work in a refugee camp, instead. Humanitarian work is seen by the patriarchs as a safe place to contain an inappropriately ambitious woman. Her ambition to transition from humanitarian work to a position in government is blocked, and thus we learn that class privilege does not guarantee a woman's consequence. The specter of the "inconsequential woman" attaches itself to Fatima herself.

Humanitarianism thus appears as a feminized sphere that exists on the margins of the political and contains the suffering of the people in a narrative apart. It is also, however, a vehicle through which the storytellers of the war bring in the experiences of women as actors in the war. Whereas earlier we examined novels that attempt to heal the bifurcation of the nation by showing how the other half lives, Ike's novel shows us how that other half is relegated to invisibility and how educated women are relegated to the same invisibility. To answer the question "who are the women in the war and what are their stories?" we need to follow the thread that connects women to the suffering of the people. And this is very much what Emecheta sets out to do in *Destination Biafra*.

Emecheta's protagonist is haunted by a sense of unbelonging in her own country despite (or perhaps because of) being an educated, privileged woman who aspires to be an ethical and influential actor in the history of her country. *Destination Biafra* is a transgressive novel because of its emphasis on female agency in a context where women are emblems in male stories of war. Emecheta was criticized for writing a feminist novel that purportedly gave a distorted view of the war. Thus the reviewer for the *Times Literary Supplement* wrote that the novel "does not convey the feel of the experience of Biafra" (Chinweizu 228). One of the few Igbo writers on the war who was in London, Emecheta was also attacked for her inauthentic politics, which alienated men and women readers alike. Her residence in London purportedly gave the novel "its distinctive, exilic sensibility" (Morrison 11).

Intent on creating a character that would stand up as a peer to the men who made the politics and ran the war, Emecheta portrays Debbie as exceptionally privileged. She returns to Nigeria from Cambridge and decides that, instead of marrying, she will join the army: "she wanted to do something more than child breeding and rearing and being a good passive wife to a man whose ego she must boost all her days, while making sure to submerge every impulse that made her fully human." As a result of her unconventional choices, however, "she felt more and more like an outsider" (Emecheta, *Destination* 45). At Cambridge she was a classmate of Abosi, the fictional Ojukwu and a man whose proposal of marriage she has turned down.

Moreover, Debbie has a clearly articulated political position and lofty ideals she is ready to act on. She believes that the war undermines the possibility of a "free" Nigeria, free from the neocolonial influence of the British. Her thinking echoes Ojukwu's justification of Biafran nationalism in June 1969, when he called the creation of Biafra a "true independence" (quoted in Morrison 11). However, the novel critiques the pursuit of this goal through war.[41] Debbie chooses the army because she believes that it stands for a nation without tribalism (Emecheta, *Destination* 76).[42] She breaks with the army, however, when she is ordered to participate in the killing of Igbo officers, which she considers a betrayal of the army's ideal of standing against tribalism (82–83). A few months later she accepts an implausible mission to travel alone to Biafra, find Abosi, and convince him to stop the war. In this improbable role as a one-person intervention for peace, Debbie anticipates characters in much more recent fiction. As we shall see, Farah's *Past Imperfect* trilogy repeatedly depicts lone savior figures on improbable rescue missions.

Humanitarianism once again helps bring into focus both the roles available to educated women in the war and the suffering of the people. The question of Debbie's belonging is explicitly raised by humanitarian workers. When she finds Irish nuns ministering to sick children in Asaba (a Biafran town that was just then surrendering to the Nigerian army), she is indignant that they should ask her what she is doing in such a place (Emecheta, *Destination* 218). Recognizing her for what she is, an educated daughter of the Nigerian elite, the Irish nuns wonder why she is among the destitute in Biafra. Angered by the suggestion that she does not belong in her own country, Debbie wonders to herself whether the Irish nuns belong in Biafra, either, and whether "these women sincerely believe in what they were doing, or did they still subscribe to the old idea of helping the savages?" (218). For Debbie, humanitarians are outsiders who represent the old colonial ideology. She articulates this question by referring to the nuns' sincerity. Yet it jars her that her own status could also be viewed as that of an outsider.[43]

This is one of many reminders in the novel that, because of her class, Debbie's place is always somehow elsewhere. Thus she is frustrated by the social distance that divides her from the people, even after their joint struggle to survive:

> It was at moments like this that Debbie really felt lonely, surrounded as she was by other women. Her education, the imported division of class, still stood in the way. She was trying hard to shake it off, to belong, but at times like this she knew that achieving complete acceptance was a formidable task. These women would only accept her if they did not know her real background. (211)

To belong among her own people seems almost impossible and requires that she efface much of who she is. The disjunction for the reader is a little different, however. We understand how Debbie is like the refugee women, because like them she is vulnerable to insecurity and sexual assault. She has no special "luck" on her journey across worn-torn Biafra. The problem instead is that we also witness how she falls into the people's zone of invisibility. She wants to belong, but it is also imperative that she have a sphere of action commensurate to her capabilities. The problem, which comes into view gradually through a very complex plot that gives Debbie many opportunities to make choices, is how Debbie can be an influential actor for the people without either taking on a humanitarian's distanced position or becoming invisible ("inconsequential") like the people. To answer this problem Emecheta has Debbie adopt the role of the people's historian, a role that passes to Ugwu in *Half of a Yellow Sun*, losing in that later novel the trace of the feminist politics that shaped it, as Ugwu receives this project from another man, the Englishman Richard.

Debbie's notion of Nigerians and foreigners with its neat demarcation of insiders and outsiders is inadequate in the face of both the humanitarian crisis and the global interests that fueled the war. In the novel we learn that control over oil reserves in the East was a major reason that Biafra's secession led to war (Emecheta, *Destination* 102–3).[44] The novel disrupts the neat narrative of the war as a war of secession and territoriality and problematizes the role of class and global capital. Thus the narrator complains that the Biafran elite, like the Nigerian elite, managed to send their sons out of the country so that they would avoid the war. Meanwhile, "the ordinary Igbo family still had to send their sons to the front to fight the war of liberation, their children and old people still died of malnutrition" (228). The gulf between the haves and the have-nots is the most significant political reality for Emecheta and demands a new history of the war.

Debbie comes to realize that the war is largely the story of refugees and displaced women and children. Womanhood and the vulnerability to rape change her sense of belonging. However, if she identifies her point of view with the people's, she carries the risk of rendering herself invisible, inconsequential. Humanitarian discourse (represented in the novel by the activities of the ICRC, NGOs in London, humanitarian workers in the field) presents a possible venue for Debbie's alternative history of the war, but Emecheta is troubled by humanitarianism's own assumptions about belonging.

Emecheta characterizes Debbie's journey across war-torn Biafra (which, as we shall see, also includes an ordeal in the forest) as a "war for her womanhood" (174). This journey is transformative. Traveling as an ordinary civilian with other women and children on a bus, Debbie finds herself in constant danger of attack and rape. Her circumstances are also complicated by her ethnic background. Her family, the Ogedemgbes, are part of the "small Itsekiri tribe, which claimed to be of Yoruba stock, and indeed their language was similar" (15). With a name that sounds Igbo and a language that sounds Yoruba, the Ogedemgbes are free to some extent to choose how to play the politics of the war. This freedom is an important element in Emecheta's characterization, as it foregrounds the subject's agency in creating her identity as well as the responsibility for political choices. On the journey Debbie is raped twice. After the first rape, a gang-rape perpetrated by soldiers from the Federalist side, Debbie's mother warns her that "nobody would believe" her story and advises her to say she was raped by Biafrans and hence is a victim of the "enemy." As a victim of the enemy she could hope to rehabilitate her reputation (159).

Being in possession of a story that no one will believe awakens Debbie to the fact that her own experience is part of what she *must* give testimony about. She insists on claiming her experience as it was lived and asserts that the history of the war should not be manipulated for political reasons. The strong motivation to bear witness, which Debbie shares with Nwapa's Kate, can restore a subjectivity compromised by trauma. As Kelly Oliver suggests, "Bearing witness works through the trauma of objectification by reinstituting subjective agency as the ability to respond or address oneself . . . witnessing can restore subjectivity by restoring response-ability" (Oliver 105). The parsing of responsibility into "response-ability" puts emphasis on the subjects' ability to respond to her own trauma while correlating this ability to her potential to act responsibly for the community. Debbie's realization that she must give testimony about her rape is the moment when her commitment to the people crystallizes. Thus she declares to her mother that she "do[esn't] want to be pitied" and will not accept the status of victim (Emecheta, *Destination* 160). She explicitly expresses her identification with the people's suffering, reminding her mother of the unjust deaths she has witnessed:

> Didn't you see what it did to our innocent guard in Lagos? Didn't you witness . . . that death of that Igbo woman? It is not a war between Abosi and Momoh [the leaders of the Biafran and Federalist sides respectively]. This is our war. It is the people's war. Our very first war of freedom. Momoh and Abosi started the purge, to wash the country of corruption and exploitation. Now there is a danger of the two men putting their self-interest foremost. If that is the case, the war will be taken out of their control and put into the hands of responsible leaders who will see the purge through and restore us to a new clean Nigeria. That is why I am going to Abosi, to warn him not to let himself be carried away by personal ambition to such a degree that he forgets his original aim. (160)

Debbie gives a political meaning to her rape and understands it as further evidence of the corruption that must be purged to save the nation. She also recommits to her mission to reach Abosi, because she is still a believer in the nationalist cause, the reunification of Nigeria, and the end of the war. Male and female actors are implicitly contrasted here, as Debbie knows she must warn Abosi "not to let himself be carried away by personal ambition." Acting selflessly is the hallmark of the woman actor. Debbie leaves her mother and travels alone until, in the course of her journey, she is thrown in with a group of Igbo refugees trying desperately to reach Biafra.

Once again, this time in Emecheta's novel, we find the motif of the ordeal in the forest, narrated in the chapter entitled, "Women's War." Indeed, Emecheta's deployment of this motif is paradigmatic: the experience is taxing, the danger extreme, and the forest itself the most alien of environments. Disguising her identity in order to fit among the refugee women and their children (211), Debbie treks through the forest pursued by Nigerian soldiers. Debbie and the women trudge through waist-deep water in the night, carrying the children above their heads (208). Although their experience is harrowing, Emecheta creates an idealized portrait of resilience and cooperation in the group. Brought together by chance and unaware of the social differences that divide them, the women cooperate and struggle as one, and Debbie's nationalism takes on an increasingly democratic tenor: "their common Africanness came to the fore" (212). In this sense the ordeal is transformative, and, whereas the group's experiences after it leaves the forest tests its cohesion, the democratic lessons learned in the forest serve to transform Debbie's sense of purpose for the rest of the novel.

The encounter with the Irish nuns closes the "Women's War" chapter and happens as they emerge from that space. Debbie aligns herself tentatively with the nuns as she admits that "in times as desperate as this any help was better than none." Her answer to the nuns' question of why she is in the forest is, "Like you, Mother, I want to see what help I can give" (218). Debbie's answer announces her alignment with the nuns as the advantaged party in relation to the disadvantaged. It contradicts, however, her own experience in the "women's war," which was more egalitarian. Her trust in the nuns is tested, and she learns the hard way that the protection offered by them carries significant danger.

Although well-intentioned, the nuns cannot really protect the women. They give Debbie false assurance, advising her that it is safe to bring the refugees out of the forest. Once in the nuns' compound, all the women (including Debbie) are attacked, two of the children are shot, the nuns are raped and killed, and the refugees go back into hiding. The nuns' assumption that they somehow stand on protected ground, outside the conflict, is delusional. Before the attack Debbie observed an officer put his gun away under the stern gaze of the Mother Superior. But unlike the nun, who seems to think this is evidence that she is protected from the soldier because she does God's work, Debbie becomes immediately suspicious that the soldiers are planning something bigger (220–21). Tragically, she trusts in the nuns instead.

Because the nuns are raped and killed, this encounter gives the phrase "women's war" a supranational connotation. War pits combatants against noncombatants regardless of nationality.

The women refugees feel sympathy for the nuns, especially the eighty-year-old Mother Superior, whose suffering they recognize as the "abuse of the helpless old" and consider it more shocking than even the shooting deaths of the two children in their group (225). In a reversal of the humanitarian relation of proxy testimony, the women are now in a position to claim the story of the nuns' rapes as part of their own witness, part of the people's story of the war. Thus it is the nuns' vulnerability rather than their "superior" status as white and foreign that reveals the true extent of their commitment to humanitarian work.

The "ordeal in the forest" typically results in a new commitment, a transformed type of engagement with war. Debbie emerges from this ordeal as a witness to atrocity and prepares for the time when a reckoning with justice or history can take place. Thus she has an even stronger motivation to survive: "She must try to live, not just for the women but for the memories of boys like Ngbechi [killed in the forest]. . . . She had to make it. She must" (224). Throughout her flight she has been keeping written notes, and, even when this becomes difficult, she stays focused on the goal of documenting what she sees: "a great deal of what was happening was too dangerous to write down so she had to make her brain porous enough to absorb and assimilate, writing down only key words to trigger off her recollections when she finally sat down to put it all into plain words" (224).

What form can Debbie's testimony take? Reinstalled within her class privilege at her father's London flat and speaking as a British-educated Nigerian, Debbie gives testimony to journalists in London about her experiences. The reader learns that "The moving talk went on for hours" (241). But Debbie cannot escape others' inscription of her identity. Her former lover and agent for the British, Alan Grey, is in the audience, and, although he compliments her on "her very moving" talk, he admits that he considered it all a performance rather than a truthful account (241). Alan goes on to question her about her whereabouts "all these months," implying that her testimony is fabricated and not a truthful account of her activities (241). Indignant, Debbie asks him why he cannot understand what speaking "from personal experience" means (243). Alan cannot bear Debbie's insistence that she was raped and urges her not to speak.

This censorship silences her "woman's war" experience and reinscribes Debbie within her class. There are assumptions at play here about who is the appropriate victim. Debbie can speak movingly about the people so long as her audience assumes that this is not her story. She is not a proper victim, being too educated and not helpless enough. Alan's reaction to Debbie also shows that sympathy for the people as victims poses no real political challenge to those in power in the developed world. Her witness to their suffering does not shake things up. Keeping the destitute as objects of sympathy subordinates them in ways that extend the neocolonial relation (Mutua 207). Alan appeals to Debbie's class identity to co-opt her into this project, but she has changed too much to be susceptible. She asserts her political autonomy instead, breaking with Grey and refusing to help Abosi smuggle arms to Biafra on planes carrying humanitarian relief (Emecheta, *Destination* 245).

Dissatisfied with the role of moral witness whose narrative she seems unable to shape, Debbie abandons the idea of writing a personal memoir and commits instead to writing the story of the people of Biafra. The "plain words" she sought are words that ordinary people can understand. She decides to return to Nigeria: "I am a daughter of Nigeria and if she is in shame, I shall stay and mourn with her in shame" (258) and refuses to align herself with her class and its tainted identity. Instead, she decides to devote herself to raising some of the war's orphans and to writing her book ("there is my manuscript to publish"), a people's history of the war based on her witness of the people's suffering (258).

Debbie escapes the fate of the "inconsequential woman" largely because she is intent on controlling her own story. What to make of the fact, however, that she ultimately turns away from telling her own story and embraces the more impersonal role of writing a people's history? The either/or dilemma that Debbie resolves with this choice leaves us worried that the shadow of the "inconsequential woman" still hovers, as her own story would likely be relegated to a zone of invisibility. The negative reviews of *Destination Biafra* and the resistance to Debbie as a character confirm this. This difficulty presents itself in particular because Debbie's story includes accounts of rape.[45] At the same time, however, we must also acknowledge the importance of her new role. A woman historian of the people breaks Debbie's association with the distanced humanitarian actor, a role to which her class insistently relegated her. Whereas the persistent problem of her lack of a "permission to narrate" the experience of sexual violence shows the limited gains in terms of gender (Said), her ability to speak as an educated woman in solidarity with the people is important. Emecheta is the middle figure in a gradual process of authorizing women's voices on war that took three generations, from Nwapa to Emecheta and finally Adichie. Adichie adopts the voice of the empowered, educated woman with greater ease, but she segregates the role of people's historian, bequeathing it to Ugwu, the representative of the ordinary people and, significantly, a man guilty of rape. A fuller discussion of the implications of these fictional choices follows in Chapter 4, but we can wonder here and in relation to Emecheta whether Adichie is more invested in the type of history that the novel can tell and acknowledges her advantages as the latest writer in a genealogy of Igbo women writers.

Conclusion

As we have seen in these twelve texts representing high and low genres, the project of a people's history remains essentially incomplete, often left only as a hypothetical narrative that could be articulated somewhere after the novels' endings to draw on the form of witness suggested by the novels. I enumerated several of these forms of witness: speaking from experience to the other half of the nation that is unfamiliar with the extent of the war's horrors; documenting the war with a journalist's eye; speaking of a time of war as a way of demarcating its otherness. Satire and sincerity establish different tonalities but similarly foreground a people's perspective that is critical of those carrying out the war. What we find in these texts is a growing engagement with the plight of ordinary people.

War is narrated as an experience that sharpens social divides. With insecurity there is a greater chasm between the reality of those who are protected (usually those in command) and the many who lack protection. At the time when the difference between security and insecurity is more absolute, the space within security is narrowed and accommodates fewer people. Insecurity creates downward social pressure, but in doing so it also opens up the possibility for new forms of solidarity that can encompass a greater sweep of people. These incomplete projects of a people's history attempt to create a kind of social cohesion that could create some democratic pressure in postwar Nigeria. One might ask, how come the novels of the Biafra war, mostly written by the defeated party, become mainstays of the national literature? It is their class politics, and not ethnicity, that resonates.

Speaking in another context about writing against oppression, Ralph Ellison claimed that the novel as a form "could be fashioned as a raft of hope, perception and entertainment." Aiming less at realism and more at a plausible interpolation of the "ideal" and the "actual," the novel can make "available that fictional vision of an ideal democracy" (xx). To follow Ellison requires a reading beyond the ending and shows how the novel can make perceptible to its readers a certain potentiality—what Ellison calls "vision." The novels of Biafra engage with history in complex ways. They set out to tell the history of the war, but also gesture to the necessity for more professional history, which they tell us, however, should be cast in the mold suggested by the novels with an orientation toward the perspective of the non-elite actors.

CHAPTER 3

"Wondering Who the Heroes Were": Zimbabwe's Novels of Atrocity

The novels of Zimbabwe's liberation war are focused on the problem of narrating atrocity and revisit obsessively the violence of war from two competing perspectives: one that presents the veteran as a traumatized war victim, the other that looks at civilians who are victims of the guerrillas, the purported heroes of the war. In both narratives the status of the hero is disputed. On the one hand, the traumatized veteran cannot reconcile his actions in the war with the expectation to be a heroic figure. On the other, the civilian victims of violence see the guerrillas as aggressors instead of saviors. The literature's ambivalence toward the figure of the hero troubles Zimbabwe's nationalist history and, what we have come to know in the twenty-first century, its hardened and exclusionary version, "patriotic" history (Ranger, "Nationalist" 215). As Alexander Kanengoni puts it, the literature leaves us "wondering who the heroes were" (Kanengoni, *Echoing Silences* 93).

This chapter teases out the implications of different historiographic paradigms for the narration of atrocity in the novels of Zimbabwe's liberation struggles and places the narration of atrocity in relation to the larger projects of a naturalist war fiction and a people's history. The figure of the hero is central to naturalism's politics of the people, or, as Levin put it, naturalism reveals the "two faces of the working-man, mean and heroic" (Levin 347). Because it showed ordinary man pitted against the most extreme exigencies, the effort heroic while also shocking and ugly, the naturalist novel claimed to give a truer picture of contemporary society in the nineteenth century (Auerbach 510). As we have seen, war offers rich possibilities for portraying the "mean and heroic." By casting doubt on the hero and the heroic, the novels I examine in this chapter seek to intervene in the idealized versions of Zimbabwe's liberation war. They portray war in naturalistic terms and hence share the antiwar sentiment of the Kenyan and Nigerian examples. In some instances they also redefine the heroic, dissociating it from the perpetration of war violence. Thus the "mean and heroic" can be posited alternatively as the suffering person, the victim of atrocity (frequently a woman), who, degraded in the assault against her person, appears "mean," but mentally and psychically exerts a heroic effort to preserve the self. Narratives of particular instances of atrocity, micronarratives of the war's violence, function allegorically as the motif of the "song of my country," broadcasting the people's endurance of war violence. The story of war given from the people's perspective is a corrective to the heavy emphasis on the "heroic" deeds of the liberation fighters that constitute the nationalist history. The literature's introverted focus is shaped by the effort to delineate the entanglement of the guerrillas' perspective and that of the broader, rural population on whose home front this war unfolded.

Moreover, Zimbabwe's war literature is grounded in the evocation of the historical figure of Nehanda, who is the emblem of Zimbabwean resistance to white rule. The treatment of Nehanda in these novels is not monolithic, however. It divides over a tendency on the one hand to masculinize her and turn her into a symbol of armed resistance and on the other to feminize and demilitarize her image, stressing a dignified autonomy and spirituality. Both are idealizations of sorts, and their historical importance is not in their realism but in how they code the stories of *chimurenga* (the Shona word for "flame," meaning revolt) told by the novelists. Zimbabwe's literature has often been referred to as "heroic," or as a "literature of cultural affirmation" (Msiska 92–93).[1] Some novels in this literature, moreover, anticipate the pitfalls of "patriotic" history and give us insights into the inspiration for the contemporary veterans' narrative and their agenda of cultural affirmation.[2]

In what follows I explain the key historiographic paradigms of Zimbabwe's three chimurengas and then turn to an analysis of novels that portray Nehanda before looking more in depth at the novels that represent the Second Chimurenga. I draw a contrast between the masculinization of Nehanda's figure for appropriation by the armed struggle in Charles Samupindi's *Death Throes* (1990) and her reclamation as a feminine figure in Vera's *Nehanda* (1993). The analysis of novels depicting the liberation war of the 1970s focuses on the treatment of atrocity and examines texts that query the status of the hero and destabilize the nationalist history politicized by Mugabe's regime. I divide these texts into two groups, man-centered and woman-centered texts, that correspond roughly to novels that take on the point of view of guerrillas who have perpetrated atrocities (Kanengoni's *When the Rainbird Cries*, 1987, and *Echoing Silences*, 1997, and Chinodya's *Harvest of Thorns*, 1989), and novels narrated through the perspective of female victims of atrocity (Hove's *Bones*, 1988, and Vera's *Without a Name*, 1994, and *The Stone Virgins*, 2002).

Writing History, Making Revolution

Academic historians have argued extensively over the merits of a national history, articulated first in Terence Ranger's widely influential account of the First Chimurenga of 1896, *Revolt in Southern Rhodesia* (1965). Ranger's history placed the disparate events of the First Chimurenga in a cohesive narrative that helped Zimbabwean nationalists conceive of their struggle in the 1970s as a revival of that earlier revolt. This national history was vigorously challenged among professional historians in the 1970s, who argued against the supra-ethnic character of the events as put forth by Ranger (Ndlovu-Gastheni 53–55). Moreover, because its nationalist narrative has been co-opted by the Mugabe regime and used to bolster the distortions of "patriotic" history, its project has become compromised. Ranger himself has revised his position in his reconsideration of the legacy of this nationalist history (Ranger, "Nationalist" 230). However, in his memoir of this period, he clarifies that he stands by his "liberal nationalism" and calls for its renewal, "a continuation of the ideals and practice of the 1960s" (Ranger, *Writing* 182).

Southern Rhodesia was first a British-chartered company (1890–1923), then a self-governing British colony until 1953, at which point it entered into a federation with two neighboring states (present-day Malawi and Zambia, formerly Nyasaland and Northern Rhodesia). When the British granted independence to Malawi and Zambia the federation fell apart, creating a crisis among whites in Southern Rhodesia who were reluctant to cede ground to African nationalists. In 1965 Ian Smith proclaimed the Unilateral Declaration of Independence, breaking all ties with Britain. Rhodesia as a white minority–ruled, independent state was boycotted internationally. In the 1970s it fought a protracted war against African nationalists led by two parties, Mugabe's ZANU and Joshua Nkomo's ZAPU, that together formed the Patriotic Front, even though they were constantly at odds. At the conclusion of the liberation war the two parties stood separately in elections, which Mugabe won (Sithole 336–38). In the following years Mugabe crushed ZAPU by waging an undeclared war in its stronghold in Matabeleland. Nkomo conceded in 1987, and a Unity Accord was signed (Meredith, *Mugabe* 73).

Ranger's history of the First Chimurenga of 1896 places the emphasis on the historical self-awareness of its African subjects. According to Ranger, during the First Chimurenga Shona and Ndebele religious leaders coordinated effectively to organize an armed rebellion against white settlers who, in six short years since their arrival in 1890 and after they failed to find significant amounts of gold, appropriated vast tracts of fertile land. Although the Ndebele settled with Rhodes within a year, it took two more years before the British subdued the Shona. The settlers seriously misunderstood Shona history, according to Ranger, and viewed the Shona erroneously as newcomers without roots in this area. Furthermore, they considered the Shona politically unsophisticated (Ranger, *Revolt* 2). Consequently, the settlers were surprised at the extent and intransigence of the uprising. Moreover, Ranger stresses that whites believed the Shona had an undeveloped sense of religion, a perception "extraordinarily beside the mark," since religion gave shape to the Shona sense of grievance against the settlers (17). To subdue the rebellion the British arrested and executed its two spiritual leaders, Nehanda and Kaguvi (also spelled Kagubi). Nehanda was charged with ordering the killing of Native Commissioner Pollard, for which she probably bore responsibility (209). Her enduring influence, however, came from being perceived as a prophet of the Second Chimurenga. It is widely believed that she used the phrase "My bones shall rise" at her trial in 1898 (Bryce, "Snapshots" 222). Bones were traditionally an instrument of prophesy in Shona and Ndebele belief.[3] As a medium, Nehanda's function was to communicate with the divine (Mwari) and the dead through the spirit of Mhondoro (lion). Thus Nehanda is not a personal name but a title that names her role: "the oracular spirits resided in chosen human beings for the duration of their life-span" (Lawrence Vambe 67).[4] This religious function enabled Nehanda, moreover, to express the grievance over land because the ancestors consecrated the land they were buried in.

The rebellion is also remembered for the brutal methods used to suppress it. Britain sent troops to help the settlers' cause. In some of the more controversial incidents of the war, which caused a humanitarian outcry in England, the British dynamited the caves where the rebel population was hiding, blowing up all those inside (Ranger, *Revolt* 277–78). In addition to dynamiting, British troops "pursued a scorched-earth policy," burning down villages and destroying agriculture (Lawrence Vambe 124). The effects of the crushing of the First Chimurenga were devastating:

> Rotting bodies upon rotting bodies, burning, charred huts and crops piled up all over the countryside were proof that all the prophecies of the Kaguvi and of all the other seers had been false. Perhaps for the first time in history, the Shona people were shaken out of their blind faith in the Mhondoro spirits and the protection of the ancestors. It was a shattering realization and . . . the disillusioned Shona for a time lost confidence both in themselves as a people and in their traditions. It also made most of them, especially the young, ready material for Christianity and gullible converts to Western materialism. (133)

The effects were material as well as spiritual. The appropriation of the land by the settlers had severe economic implications, but the Shona defeat also brought on a crisis of faith (95). Recognizing the suffering in this history of subjugation without losing a sense of dignity became a challenge. Nehanda's story provided the elements for a face-saving narrative.

Nehanda became a symbol of intransigent resistance by her refusal to communicate with her captors. According to witnesses cited by Ranger, on the day of her execution she danced and laughed; at the scaffold, she screamed and resisted. She also refused conversion to Christianity, whereas Kaguvi converted before being executed (Ranger, *Revolt* 309). She was believed to have said that "the African people should touch nothing that belonged to the white man" (quoted in Ranger, *Revolt* 210). This injunction, as we learn from Mutswairo's historical novel, *Mapondera: Soldier of Zimbabwe* (1983), was actually an order not to loot the settlers (66–67). Mutswairo explains that after initial success, the Chimurenga faltered because there was looting, "taking spoils of war." The temptation to loot was very real, especially since the settlers were perceived as thieves to begin with. Thus few heeded Nehanda's warning (Mutswairo, *Mapondera* 73), leading to the perception that the Shona were defeated because Nehanda's injunction was violated. This explanation left open the possibility for renewed resistance. If the Shona played a role in their own defeat, then there was something under their control that could be corrected, giving hope for a successful future rebellion.

The Second Chimurenga of the 1970s was interpreted as the fulfillment of the prophecy of the spirit mediums of the first revolt for the bones to rise again and kept the spiritual link to the land very much in play. It was not till the 1980s that ZANU-PF's discussion of land became more economic than spiritual and an extension of the government's socialist rhetoric.[5] This shift in terminology tracks the hardening of the narrative of the liberation war, turning the demand for land into a "fundamentalism" (Chan and Primorac 64).

The idea of an unfinished struggle that can be revived multiple times has become instrumental in suppressing a historical reckoning of the abuses of the Mugabe regime. It can be appealed to at any moment as a historical imperative that brings the nation back to ground zero of the anticolonial struggle, as if no history has transpired in between. Thus what has come to be known as "patriotic" history presents Zimbabwe as existing in an unfinished, ongoing struggle for decolonization. The politically motivated insistence on a lack of closure to the liberation war of the 1970s makes it difficult to achieve hindsight and move on. Moreover, a state-supported "patriotic history" is patently propagandistic, existing as politics and not in any "history text" (Ranger, "Constructions" 505). It contends that Zimbabwe's identity is one with its history of violent struggle against white rule, shaped around the stories of three revolts, or *chimurengas*: the First Chimurenga in 1896 against white settlers; the Second Chimurenga, the prolonged guerrilla war of the 1970s; and the Third Chimurenga, announced by Robert Mugabe in 2002 as his election campaign slogan and conceived as a struggle that would "finally set Zimbabwe free of its colonial heritage" by legitimating the seizure of all white farm land.[6] Patriotic history, a justification for the policies of the Third Chimurenga, "assumes the immanence of a Zimbabwean nation expressed through centuries of Shona resistance to external intrusion" (Ranger, "Constructions" 505). This emphasis on Zimbabwe's "immanence" constructs a story of *revelation* that suppresses the narrative of the historical making of Zimbabwe in its full complexity and diversity. It insists on a "simplistic notion of a pre-existing 'Zimbabwean' identity" and foregrounds one ethnic identity (the Shona), one party (ZANU-PF), one liberation war leader (Sabelo, quoted in Ranger, "Constructions" 507).

The ideology of the Third Chimurenga thus also deliberately collapses distinctions between colonialism and white settler rule, aiming to give

Zimbabwe "a new history in which it was a British colony until 1980" (White 97). Its narrative overlooks the complicated issue of the citizenship of settlers and Rhodesia's "renegade" independence as a white minority–ruled state from 1965 to 1980 (97). Seen through the lens of the Third Chimurenga's renewed struggle to seize white land, Zimbabwe's history takes the shape of an archetypal narrative: colonial conquest followed by the usurpation of the land and oppression (marked by physical violence, especially torture), then resistance and, at some point now postponed into the future, liberation. This sequence provides the frame into which specific events are fitted. Thus Zimbabwe's complex history is assimilated within the dualistic paradigm of colonialism and resistance, attempting to make invisible the complexities of internal political divisions.

Ranger has critiqued the development of Zimbabwean historiography post-1980, dividing it into phases that chart the turn from a "nationalist" historiography seeking to redress the unfairness of colonial history to a more critical "history of nationalism" that examines the pitfalls of the early independence years in order to explain the devastating implications of the rise of "patriotic" history during the Third Chimurenga.[7] Thus my question here is, do the historical novels written about Zimbabwe's wars before the start of the Third Chimurenga provide a counternarrative that we can marshal against its policies? Can these novels, many of them inspired by the nationalist history launched by Ranger, play a role in dismantling the narrative of "patriotic" history, or are they complicit in the conditions that gave rise to "patriotic" history? For example, does Vera's deployment of a "spiritual temporality" in Nehanda lend the novel more easily to appropriation by "patriotic" history (Christiansen 207)? If not, then how does Vera avoid this pitfall?

Within postcolonial studies we take the "oppositional" role of literature for granted (Said, *Culture* 196–99), but Zimbabwe presents us with a challenge. Zimbabwe's war fiction follows the pattern of using the symbolism of one war to speak of another and at times risks creating the impression of "immanence." This kind of repetition is typical of prophetic anti-colonial discourse that refuses to recognize failure and instead postpones the achievement of liberation into the future (Wenzel 7–8). Identifying the discourse of repeating chimurengas as a resistance discourse in the literature of the 1980s and 1990s seems fairly straightforward until we need to account for the similar discourse being used by Mugabe's regime to create a state of exception in which Zimbabwe, in the twenty-first century, justifies political repression in the name of the same anti-colonial struggle. If we are to buck the cynical use of "strategic references to internationally acclaimed names such as these [Marechera, Dangarembga, Hove, Vera] . . . used by government media to lend credibility to Zimbabwe's official nationalist ideology of the moment," we must do more to delineate the complexities of these authors' historical narratives (Primorac, "Echoing Silences," online source).

What kind of history, therefore, do the novels tell of the period between 1896 and 1987, from the first rebellion against white settlers to the end of the civil conflict that followed independence in 1980? Can we distinguish a different historiographic argument in the fictional historical accounts and, if so, what are its elements? By insisting rhetorically on the sameness of the present and the past, Mugabe has emptied the promise of arrival announced by independence, masking his party's interest as the state's and turning against his own people.[8] ZANU-PF placed the problem of self-determination at the center of its narrative in the period between 2002 and 2008 and deflected attention away from the impoverishment of the Zimbabwean people. Anti-colonial struggle has been used before to trump human rights claims. Referring to decolonization in the 1960s, Samuel Moyn has argued that national self-determination historically displaced human rights claims that could have advocated for the people's collective social and economic rights (Moyn 85). Thus heeding the narrative of the people embedded in Zimbabwe's war fiction can reclaim the human rights narrative entangled in this history and complicate in necessary ways the meaning of the struggle for the people's independence. The "afterlives" of these fictional narratives of traumatized veterans and peasants (the liberation war was largely rural) can contribute to revitalizing Zimbabwe's imagination of its future. I use "afterlives" in Wenzel's "worldly, nontheological sense" to highlight the uses to which narratives are put in addition to retrospection (Wenzel 9). New readings foreground the constantly renewed influence of texts over time, exerting another kind of historical influence.

Representing Nehanda

As I already noted, the war literature of Zimbabwe returns frequently to the stories of the traditional spirit mediums Nehanda and Kaguvi, who sparked the first rebellion against the British in 1896. Garikai Mutasa's *The Contact* (1985), a narrative of the 1970s war, for example, opens with an evocation of Nehanda's hanging by the British and the commonly held belief in the prophesy of resurrection: "The people know. There will be a resurrection" (Mutasa 7). The liberation fighters in the 1970s are described "as the makers of History" who continue the struggle begun in 1896 (28). Their heroic status is conveyed by their effectiveness, but also by their restraint. They witness the atrocities perpetrated by the Rhodesian Front (42) and bring the message of "justice" and "democracy" directly to a white Rhodesian lieutenant, whom they confront violently but, mercifully, let live under the condition that he leave Zimbabwe (58). Ranka Primorac reads Mutasa's novel as an example of the idealization of the guerrillas that answers back to the "Rhodesian discourse" demonizing the liberation fighters and "indiscriminately glorifying those fighting *against* the gueril-las" (Primorac, *Place of Tears* 141, emphasis in original). Primorac's reading makes sense. However, the concern that the absence of such restraint leads to atrocity is palpable in the novels of Kanengoni and Chinodya, especially, and gives shape to these novels' criticism of the heroic narrative.

Who are the "makers of History"? Zimbabwe's First and Second Chimurengas were both rural and involved its disenfranchised subjects and not its citizens. The question "who are the makers of History" leads us back to the people and the articulation of their aspirations, spoken in this literature through the figure of Nehanda. The story of Nehanda's death is retold obsessively in the fiction in order to define the moral terms of the struggle against settlers and colonizers. Moreover, since death by hanging is a form of torture, the story of Nehanda's death when told intimately with details of her suffering functions as an example of the motif of the "song of my country." The physical details of the experience of torture given in minute detail, such as we find in Vera's *Nehanda*, are broadcast widely and become a conduit for recognizing national identity. The emphasis on Nehanda's hanging, furthermore, shapes the literature's broader concerns with atrocity and its tendency, as we shall see, to see war through the prism of a single episode, a highly focused narrative of a particular atrocity.

Zimbabwe's wars figure in all of Vera's novels, either as memory or as her characters' present experience. In *Nehanda* the people grieve the loss of land: "In places where we have buried and worshiped, new owners have arrived and led us off with guns. How long shall we suffer this indignity?" (Vera, *Nehanda* 66). The humiliating loss of the land has spiritual dimensions, and Vera keeps us attuned to this nuance in the meaning of the land for the people. Furthermore, she is echoing a well-known text, Solomon Mutswairo's prayer to Nehanda in his Shona novel *Feso*, where the people are referred to in similar terms, characterizing the loss of land as an indignity: "They no longer have human dignity/They possess nothing" (Mutswairo, *Feso* 66).[9]

By returning to the familiar figure of Nehanda, Vera aims to recuperate her resonance as a feminist inspiration and to revise the appropriation of Nehanda by the heroic narrative of the Second Chimurenga and its strongly masculinist overtones—the object of her direct critique in another novel, *Without a Name*. Vera's feminist agenda goes even further, according to Maurice T. Vambe, who argues that in the novel "Vera re-appropriates the cultural symbols of a validating male-dominated tradition of spirit possession in order to weave into them women-centred meanings of independence and install these at the new nation's consciousness of selfhood" (Maurice Vambe 128). Thus *Nehanda* stands in contrast, for example, to Charles Samupindi's *Death Throes*, where the depiction of Nehanda's trial is clearly in the heroic tradition, contributing to the masculinization of Nehanda. For example, Samupindi renders Nehanda's prophecy "My bones will rise" as "'These bones will rise up one day and fight!'" (Samupindi, *Death Throes* 11). Nehanda is hardly human in his text, and her diminished appearance contrasts with her large symbolic resonance for the nation:

> Her hands were manacled at her deflated tiny tummy by heavy cinches and iron chains. Her legs were two little sticks with slight knots in the knee area. Knots of perseverance? They were leg-ironed. And all those chains for so withered a body! It was an affront to logic.
>
> She was the nation. A people. (10)

Samupindi describes Nehanda as she appears on the cover of his novella, a drawing that copies and revises a famous photograph of Nehanda and Kaguvi after their arrest (Figures 3.1 and 3.2). The "deflated tiny tummy" suggests an aborted pregnancy, a loss of progeny. He stresses the shackles and irons, the strength of the physical restraints, which are "an affront to logic" because the body they restrain seems incapable of any physical force. Hence Samupindi suggests that Nehanda's power lies elsewhere, in the spiritual realm and as a symbol of "a people" or "the nation." Nehanda is a powerful idea, not a body; to try to manacle her is to miss the point. National discourse even displaces the spiritual here, and Samupindi's reference to "a people" recodes the ethnic Shona narrative as the national narrative.

Samupindi's rendition of the trial proceedings is speculative, as the only extant records pertain to the preliminary hearings, where the evidence shows that Nehanda was uncooperative and refused to talk (Ranger, *Revolt* 388). In Samupindi's fictional account Nehanda answers the prosecution

Figure 3.1. The cover of *Death Throes: The Trial of Mbuya Nehanda* (1990) shows accused rebellion leaders Nehanda and Kaguvi awaiting execution. The artwork is based on the original photo shown in Figure 3.2; the nooses were added for effect.

Figure 3.2. The original photo of Nehanda and Kagubi awaiting execution, which was reproduced in Terence Ranger's *Revolt in Southern Rhodesia 1896–7* (1967); Ranger gives credit to the National Archive in Zimbabwe for its use.

by asserting the right of her people to kill in self-defense: "Killing!—in self-defense," she says emphatically, "How else does one defend himself against one who seeks his life and land?" (Samupindi, *Death Throes* 33). The masculine "himself" inscribes the struggle's gender against the evidence of her femininity. Samupindi, furthermore, showcases the anti-colonial argument, implying comparisons to other trials such as Kenyatta's in 1953 and Nelson Mandela's Rivonia trial in 1962–64, which also focused on the legitimacy of the use of violence. In *Long Walk to Freedom*, Mandela describes himself as "the symbol of justice in the court of the oppressor" (Mandela 317), and it is as such a symbol that Samupindi portrays Nehanda. The words fictionally attributed to Nehanda articulate the essence of the national resistance and transform her from an intransigent and unassimilable figure to defender of a people's rights.

We see more appropriations of Nehanda in other masculinist, heroic narratives. In Mutswairo's *Mapondera: Soldier of Zimbabwe*, Nehanda's story becomes the narrative model for the "soldier of Zimbabwe." A historical novel about the Rozwi confederacy, a pre-colonial centralized Shona polity, *Mapondera* is explicitly didactic. It juxtaposes Nehanda and Kaguvi with Mapondera, a secular hero who led his people's resistance to the Portuguese during the time of the First Chimurenga, only to return and find his own village destroyed (Mutswairo, *Mapondera* 90). Mapondera rises again from his defeat. He renews his people's revolt in 1900, but, as a result, he is imprisoned. Mutswairo highlights the fact that Mapondera was Nehanda's disciple as a youth. From her he learned all about traditional medicine (11), knowledge that later enabled him to transform into a warrior who had magical powers and was "able to disappear with impunity from sight in battle and to fly like a winged reptile" (18).[10] What makes Mutswairo's treatment interesting is that he recognizes the expectations for historicity and feels obligated to qualify this magical claim, characterizing it as a "popular belief" that "whatever it was" reflects Mapondera's reputation as an exceptional warrior (18). The heroic narrative is accommodated within the historical as evidence of "popular belief" and thus as a particular type of literary "afterlife" that sustains the cultural currency of the heroic.

Through the figure of Mapondera, Mutswairo also comments on the historical episode of King Lobengula's betrayal by Cecil Rhodes.[11] He creates an analogous scene where Mapondera, in contrast to Lobengula, proudly demands "justice" instead of "future relations" with the British South Africa Company (7). The depiction of Mapondera's death in prison makes allusion to Nehanda's similar fate, and his defiance echoes the popular belief that the first three attempts to hang Nehanda failed to kill her

(76). In analogous fashion, Mapondera struggles to keep as much control over his death as he can. He preempts his hanging by going on a hunger strike.The themes of autonomy and defiance shape the heroic in the face of conditions that are otherwise humiliating.

Distancing herself from the masculinizing appropriations of Nehanda, Vera emphasizes the spiritual as a kind of collective memory. She describes the personal source of her own inspiration, a "memory" that does not draw from the official historical record: "I wrote [*Nehanda*] from remembrance, as a witness of my own spiritual history" (quoted in Ranger, "History Has Its Ceiling" 204). The novel came to her "almost like a dream" (Bryce, "Snapshots" 220), although she alludes to the same photograph of Nehanda as a prisoner that inspired the cover of *Death Throes* and became widely known by being printed in Ranger's history and David Lan's influential *Guns and Rain* (1985) (Figure 3.2). In an interview with Eva Hunter, Vera talks about her desire "to write beyond the photograph, you know, that frozen image, beyond the date, beyond the 'fact' of her dying" (Bryce, "Snapshots" 77). The photograph represents only the idea of a historical fact and constrains the ways in which Nehanda is remembered. "To write beyond the photograph," Vera must marshal evidence that comes instead from "remembrance" and her "spiritual history." Furthermore, she appeals to Zimbabwean women specifically as custodians of the collective memory to provide alternative versions of the Nehanda story. Speaking to Bryce, Vera claims she understood something about Nehanda that "wasn't anywhere in a book where I could read it, and I didn't know why, except maybe the knowledge has become discredited by other ways of seeing" (221).[12] It is intriguing that Vera refers to "other ways of seeing," which can mean either other ways of understanding or, more literally and in reference to the photograph, other kinds of visual recognition.[13] "Writing beyond the photograph" suggests not only going against the grain of the photograph's presumed purpose, to capture for history the defeat of Nehanda and Kaguvi, but also to read against its heroic appropriation. Thus Vera explores Nehanda's interiority, imagining how Nehanda "feels within herself" (Hunter, "War Stories" 77), a quintessentially novelistic undertaking.

Vera's starting point is a paradox: "Our oral history does not even accept that [Nehanda] was hanged, even though the photographs are there to show it" (Bryce, "Snapshots" 221). The photograph of Nehanda and Kaguvi in captivity shows them standing next to each other, their backs against a brick wall, squinting in the bright sun and awaiting execution (Figure 3.2). The photograph provides a stark record of their imminent, but not yet achieved, death. The bright light is assaultive, pinning them against the wall and conveying their confinement. Against the brick wall they seem diminished, an old woman and an old man, poorly dressed. The differences between the figures, however, speak beyond the intent of the photograph to confine them against the wall.[14] Nehanda's hands are folded, her feet close together, her squinting eyes almost closed. She conveys self-possession. Kaguvi's arms hang awkwardly by his side, his feet apart with the weight shifted slightly to his right as if he is about to step forward. These subtle details capture the individuality of the figures and betray the fact that the two retain a degree of volition to choose their pose, escaping the photographer's complete mastery.

In the version of this same image on the cover of Samupindi's novella (Figure 3.1), the figures are drawn just as they are in the photograph, standing in front of a brick wall. Nehanda's figure is bathed in light, Kaguvi's obscured in the dark, possibly a comment on Nehanda's resistance to the last in contrast to Kaguvi's capitulation and conversion to Christianity before his execution. Both have shackles on their feet, and nooses hang prominently near their heads, details not in the photograph. Two skulls are drawn on the bottom of the picture, one next to Nehanda's feet, the other next to Kaguvi's. The drawing emphasizes the terror of the imminent execution, but the added detail of the skulls shifts the emphasis back to the spiritual and the mediums' connection with death and the ancestors. Most importantly, the spiritual is a reference to land, and agitating in the name of the ancestors is agitating to reclaim the land. The drawing superimposes on the photograph the spirit of nationalist resistance, transforming its meaning.

The appropriations of this image are many. For example, in another example the photograph is cropped and turned into a portrait of Nehanda, then used in an Independence Day poster for ZANU-PF, where it is placed above Mugabe's bust (Figure 3.3). This appropriation, which places Mugabe in the tradition of Nehanda, once again subverts the original intent of the photograph and performs the infinite reproduceability of Nehanda as symbol of national pride and autonomy, illustrating, moreover, the extent of the masculinization of Nehanda.

The masculinization of Nehanda is accompanied by the feminization of Kaguvi. A second photograph, also reprinted in Ranger's history, shows Kaguvi barely dressed and in shackles (Figure 3.4). Although Samupindi describes Nehanda as emaciated, Kaguvi is the one who appears emaciated in this photograph. This is a portrait of the abject, a figure diminished in contrast to Nehanda, who, with eyes almost closed, seems focused inward. Moreover, in this second image Kaguvi is standing next to an African po-

Figure 3.3. Zimbabwe's president Robert Mugabe is promoted in a poster that uses the image of Nehanda, who is considered a martyr and spiritual leader of the fight for independence. The author thanks David Lan, author of *Guns and Rain: Guerrillas and Spirit Mediums in Zimbabwe* (1985), for allowing the reproduction of this image.

liceman in uniform. The policeman is holding a rifle and has an ammunition belt draped diagonally over his chest. The photograph evokes a deep discord. Colonialism, with its instruments of violent control, is called forth as a divisive force. Both men avert the camera, their gazes focused in opposite directions to either side of the camera. The trajectories of their gazes cross, forming an X and exuding the potential for conflict, even though each figure by itself does not appear particularly imposing.[15] An interpretation of this image that stresses Kaguvi's status as a figure of abjection is evident in the use of Kaguvi's image on the cover of *Revolt in Southern Rhodesia* (Figure 3.5). Here the image is cropped to edit out the African policeman and then superimposed over a "contemporary drawing" showing the "arrival of the British South Africa Company in Matabeleland" and more specifically the "repulse of an Ndebele attack on a white laager during the march on Bulawayo." The cover conveys the message of African defeat twice over, in the original conquest and in the repressed rebellion. It also implies a narrative of the white colonizer against the African, eliminating the more complex narrative evoked by the presence of the African policeman in the original image. Vera's desire to "write beyond the photograph" means that she is holding out against the indexicality of the photograph. She sets out "to negate that hanging," to evoke the ways in which Nehanda endured to become the inspiration of the Second Chimurenga (Hunter, "War Stories" 79).

Nehanda, Vera tells us, "surpassed that moment when they took her body, and when they put a noose on it, she had already departed. Her refusal and her utterances are what we believe to be history" (Bryce, "Snapshots" 221). In contrast to Samupindi's, Vera's portrayal of Nehanda is more human, although intensely spiritual. She tells the story of Nehanda's education as a young girl and her initiation into her spiritual calling. The resulting narrative is a radical departure from tradition because it is a novelization of the figure. As Primorac notes, in the novel:

> the medium does not function as the mere "external" mouthpiece for the ancestral voice. Historically, the name Nehanda refers to a royal ancestor of the Shona people; her medium at the time of the first Chimurenga was a woman named Charwe. In the novel, on the other hand, a young woman named Nehanda becomes the transmitter of the collective, undifferentiated ancestral voice *which becomes a part of her person*." (Primorac, *Place of Tears* 151)

Vera's Nehanda is not a "role" that a historical person steps into, but the Nehanda of 1896 as a person called Nehanda. Moreover, I would argue,

Figure 3.4. Kagubi under arrest by a police officer. This widely disseminated image is from the National Archive in Zimbabwe; it was reproduced in both Terence Ranger's *Revolt in Southern Rhodesia* and David Lan's *Guns and Rain*.

Figure 3.5. The cover of Terence Ranger's *Revolt in Southern Rhodesia* adapts the photo of the captured Kagubi in Figure 3.4 and superimposes it over a drawing showing the armed arrival in Rhodesia of the British South Africa Company.

she is presented to us very intentionally as a novelistic character, drawn from the historical memory but distinct. Vera transposes the figure from memory in the present back into history, giving the features of Nehanda as remembered to a character in a historical fiction. This attention to novelization sharpens our awareness of the constructedness of the figure of Nehanda, exposing the inadequacy of seeing the photograph, for example, as historical fact when it, too, is a construction.

Vera alludes to the conventions of the novel of education less for its realism than for its association with the theme of disillusionment. She wishes to capture the contrast between the promise of youth and the disappointing reality of adulthood constrained by history. Moreover, the fictional Nehanda's life takes place in eight years, from 1890 to 1898, from the beginning of white settlement until the historical event of her execution (Ranger, "History Has Its Ceiling" 203), and is impossibly telescoped. The novel is written as a flashback and opens with the account of Nehanda's death in the third person, but focalized through her point of view.

The hanging is rendered ambiguously so that its finality is difficult to decipher, although we are told of "irreversible" damage. The intense focus on the violence done to the body and the demand that the reader follow closely renders this description similar to the "song of my country":

> She feels that gaping wound everywhere. The wound has been shifting all over her body and she can no longer find it. She raises her hands over her head as though supporting a falling roof. She gestures into the sky with frantic arms. She laughs. The skin tears away from her, and she knows that the damage to herself is now irreversible. Nothing will save her from this final crimson of death; it is too much like her inner self. (Vera, *Nehanda* 2)

Dying is described as Nehanda's collapse into herself (she is like the "crimson of death") and reveals that spiritual part of her that is in contact with the ancestors. At the same time, and in a somewhat contradictory fashion, the narrative perspective renders Nehanda continuously conscious as she is dying, making apparent a mind-body split that leaves her in control of her mind. Thus she maintains her autonomy even as her body succumbs to violence ("the skin tears away from her"). As the scene builds to the climactic passage quoted above, Nehanda's physical pain is described in naturalistic images:

> Rivers and trees cover her palms; the trees are lifeless and the rivers dry. Anthills move in giant elongated shadows while furious red clouds escape, swirl upward, thin into a haze. Grass trembles with the wind while ants vanish into the ground, over her waiting palms. (1)

The visual terms metaphorize her pain into an aerial view of a landscape, the body turned into land. The reference to anthills and ants recalls the familiar simile we use to describe the feeling of numbed limbs, yet Vera keeps us intensely focused on the visual so that the verbal painting displaces the gruesomeness of a different kind of naturalistic description that could have been deployed here.

A similar displacement occurs in my original example of the motif of "the song of my country" in Djebar's novel, in which the blue sky is alluded to while the torture victim screams. This aesthetic displacement deflects from the killing, the injuring of war, while it also seems to focus more sharply on the experience of dying. This is because it places emphasis on thinking during this difficult physical experience and hence asserts the presence of the whole subject while she is being assaulted, her skin tearing. The description's intensely visual terms are extremely different from the stark photograph, which, however, also stands in place of the hanging as a representation of the execution. Thus Vera has disrupted the purported obviousness of the photograph as a record of the execution and succeeded in producing a convincing portrayal of interiority and experience that reach from the individual to the collective.

In her prophesying, Vera's Nehanda takes up the suffering of the people. The prophecy is rendered as another variation of the motif of the "song of my country." Historical accounts of Nehanda's life construct her death as the end of a sequence of acts of prophesy: "Her body shook with paroxysms of horror. She cried like a child, unable to stomach the sight of blood, death, starvation and the subjection of her people that were to follow. She writhed in physical and mental anguish as she saw it all in her spiritual transformation" (Maurice Vambe 120). Nehanda "sees it all," and we see through her. Vera's description of Nehanda's hanging subsumes it as the last in a sequence of episodes of possession and thus defies the intention of her killers to impose their meaning on her life story. Her execution does not break the sequence of possessions but stalls it in an infinitely repeating pattern produced by the people's traumatic memory. Because we are told the "final crimson of death" is "like her inner self," we understand that Nehanda achieves her essence in death. Vera's portrayal goes beyond cultural affirmation to show Nehanda's self-awareness of her political agency. She consciously shapes her legacy, speaking the words that express the meaning of her death, figured here as a "legend-creating wind" that "gives new tongues with which to praise it, and new languages with which to cross the boundaries of time" (Vera, *Nehanda* 112–13). Wind is analogous to voice, a voice that Nehanda bestows to the future, connecting the people to their past.

Vera's sympathetic treatment of Kaguvi is another aspect of her critique of the masculinizing tendencies of the heroic narrative, which has cast Kaguvi in a negative light. Vera stresses his despair and sidesteps his shameful conversion to Christianity. Kaguvi is very much a human being, a historical actor who despairs. He experiences a deepening spiritual crisis that begins with the loss of the land and reaches a climax in his arrest. In prison he loses his spiritual powers completely:

> The prophetic cloud in the sky has burst for Kaguvi, and there is nothing strong enough left to shelter his dreams. His ancient spirit, which he now sees as something separate from himself, weighs sorrowfully on him. It is as though they now live in separate ages of time, himself in the present, his spirit departing further into the past. (107)

No longer capable of prophecy, Kaguvi experiences a loss of harmony, the disjunction of the self from the spirit. To perform as a medium, to interpret the sky and earth, Kaguvi needs to be outdoors, free to move. As a medium, his role is to bring the past into the future and thus shape the people's agency. As Vera suggests, imprisonment disrupts Kaguvi's relation to history—to the way he orients action in relation to time. In prison he is in the present only, severed from the past and without access to the future. Kaguvi despairs, because in the confines of prison he has been wrenched from history. Deprived of freedom, he has no meaningful agency.

Vera's Nehanda handles the predicament of her capture with greater success partly because she has time to prepare for it. The importance of this episode is heightened by Vera's use of the motif of the "ordeal in the forest." With her capture imminent, Nehanda flees into the forest, where she gets lost, literally going in circles. She remains resolved to create meaning from this ordeal:

> In each circle that she has woven, she sees the completion of something definite and unconquerable. Each circle is a word which will redeem the soil from the feet of strangers, a trap for those who dare follow her footsteps on the ground along the path to ancient wisdom. (93)

Thinking of her flight in the forest, Nehanda compares the paths she traced to words, willing them to have meaning. Thus she determines not only her own action, but her own myth, providing the resistant words that will survive her before the colonizer takes her life and appropriates its meaning. Words as prophecy transmit her influence. From the beginning of the novel, we learn that she "carries her bag of words in a pouch that lies tied around her waist" like a weapon (1). The women who hear her are inspired: "With words compelling them through the intersection of time, they recognize their future selves" (113). She sees herself as the custodian of a "seed," which has come to her from the spirit world, and which she plants "in the fertile ground" (93).

Thus, in the forest, Nehanda experiences a "second birth" during which she mourns for those killed in the war. Her mourning marks the shift or intensification of involvement resulting from the "ordeal in the forest." Her mourning is aided by "elegies" sent down to her by the spirits (92). By the time she is arrested, she has already withdrawn spiritually to a place where she is with the ancestors' spirits. Although she appears to the Englishman as mad, her only utterance a scream (116), she has eluded him, in fact. At this moment she also symbolizes the future: "Hope for the nation is born out of the intensity of newly created memory" (111). Nehanda makes herself into that "newly created memory," bringing the past into the future and signaling hope for the people: "Her death, which is also a birth, will weigh on those lives remaining to be lived" (112).

In this novel Vera speaks repeatedly of sacrifice, referring to the sacrifices of those fighting in the forest, to the villagers whose communities are burned down, to the grieving mothers and wives of the fighters. Nehanda's story proclaims that the people can retain their dignity even under physical assault and is intended to redress the humiliating sense of being a conquered people, expressed most cogently in Lawrence Vambe's important nationalist history, *An Ill-Fated People*. Writing in the early 1970s, when the nationalist struggle was intensifying, Vambe stressed the humiliations of white rule to promote the kind of unity against the settlers that had been undermined historically by the recruitment of African policemen, wielders of the hated *sjambok*. According to Vambe, the sjambok "fermented a great deal of hatred and trouble for the white man" and dangerously divided the African community (Lawrence Vambe 107). As an example, he gives the story of his grandfather, who was arrested for not paying poll tax on his dogs. A frail, old man, he was handcuffed, marched for twelve miles, jailed for two weeks, and punished with hard labor for a minor offense against an illegitimate law. This "act of monstrous injustice" taught Vambe the full implications of his family's subjugation to the authority of a single white officer, to whom they submitted "in a state of sheepishness and timidity," and made it plain for him that his people "were a conquered people" (18–19). As a "conquered people" they experienced settler rule through torture, an experience that became emblematic. In the preface to *An Ill-Fated People*, Doris Lessing also stresses this point. Drawing from her own experience growing up in Rhodesia from 1924–1949, she recalls witnessing an incident of torture that epitomized the "monstrousness of the society we lived in" (Lessing xvii).[16]

Vambe's narrative and its emphasis on torture feed a sense of outrage that in turn aims to inspire an alternative narrative of the people distinct from the settler's point of view. An "ill-fated people" must seize the initiative and turn its fate around. *Nehanda* is an attempt to rehabilitate the people's narrative from the distortions of its masculinization in the heroic narratives. Vera aims to give a more concrete sense of the lived experience through the intensity of the spiritual as conveyed by the Nehanda figure. In other words, she retrieves the spiritual as part of the lived experience and not exclusively as a code for the discourse of nationalism. As a result, the spiritual in her novel casts a wider net, capturing not only the potential for "a people" but the experience of the people. Her uses of motifs from the war novel (in particular, the "song of my country" and the "ordeal of the forest") indicate that she is trying to negotiate the boundary between the naturalistic portrayal of suffering in war and the allegorical investment in an idea of a national future. The novels that I examine in what follows reveal the doubts that creep into the heroic narrative and undermine it. Atrocity is not exclusively the white man's, but a feature of war more generally for which the guerrillas themselves bear responsibility. Kanengoni's and Chinodya's novels are presented as retellings of particular atrocities that aim to make sense of them as distinct episodes within the larger narrative of the liberation war. These retellings often fail, and, instead of explaining, they reveal the extent of trauma. But they also gesture beyond the protagonist to a fuller story that strives to overcome the limitations of the protagonist's memory and give an account of the people.

Atrocity as Narrative Paradigm

Rather than attempting an overarching narrative of the liberation war, many novels depicting the Second Chimurenga focus on a particular incident of extreme cruelty with lasting effects. Thus they suggest a narrative paradigm for atrocity. The dictionary definition of atrocity emphasizes "heinousness," "wickedness," and "enormity" (OED). In international law, the phrase "mass atrocity crimes" has emerged as a "unifying term" to describe the crimes named in the Rome Statute governing the International

Criminal Court, which are genocide, crimes against humanity, war crimes, and ethnic cleansing (Scheffer 91–92). Thus the International Criminal Tribunal for the Former Yugoslavia "was established by the United Nations in response to *mass atrocities*," a term used on the court's website interchangeably with "mass crimes" and shorthand for a group of legally defined crimes that share the descriptor "mass."[17] Enormity in this context is determined by scale, numbers of people targeted by the violence.

In contrast, the concept of an atrocity in these novels aims to delineate and differentiate individual incidents from the larger narrative of the war. It does not highlight enormity in terms of numbers so much as it does in terms of type of harm done, of heinousness.[18] The goal is to break up the larger sweep of narrative, slowing it down to account for a detail, a single incident, devastating to those involved, but easily swept up and buried in an end-driven narrative such as that of national liberation. Thus, for example, when the atrocity refers to the destruction of an entire village, the particularity of the event, its status as a single episode that needs elucidation is stressed.

Earlier I referred to the expectation that heroic behavior reflects restraint; in the absence of such restraint, the heroic falls away and heinous violence emerges. Echoing this line of thought, philosophers have tackled the problem of atrocity as an instance of evil unconstrained. Thus in Claudia Card's "atrocity theory of evil" (Card, *Atrocity* 5), evil is a secular term defined as actions that produce "foreseeable intolerable harms by culpable wrong doing" (3).[19] She emphasizes responsibility for such actions and the distinctions among the identities of victim, perpetrator, and survivor.[20] "Atrocities," she points out, "are both perpetrated and suffered"; hence they require a focus on both the "harm" and the "wrongdoing" (9). Suffering and wrongful action must be discussed in relation to each other, but they must also remain distinct. Card's aim is to broaden the discussion of the perpetration of evil by "giving victims' perspectives more of their due" (10). Victims, moreover, are not always innocent. Loss of innocence can even be a distinct kind of victimization. While "not the same as loss of virtue," loss of innocence occurs "when we become responsible through our choices for the undeserved suffering of others or when we betray their trust, even when we make the best decision open to us under the circumstances" (221–22). Innocence is defined in relation to our responsibility to others. Failing to meet this responsibility by harming others compromises our innocence and places us at risk to commit more evil, because it also causes us to "los(e) self-respect and moral motivation" (222).

Card's focus on the victim's point of view makes her philosophical discussion particularly useful for an analysis of literary depictions of atrocity, since most of these are written from the point of view of the victim, even when they expand that identity to include those forced to be perpetrators. When engaging with the consequences of atrocity as portrayed in a novel, we are invited to judge the account, to provide a moral response from a somewhat distanced, outside perspective beyond the war itself. The novel of war circumscribes war as a chronotope and situates the reader as a traveler through that time-space who belongs elsewhere, after and outside the war. War is what Primorac distinguishes as a "spatio-temporal category" as opposed to a "thematic" one (Primorac, *Place of Tears* 127).[21] But such a reading presupposing distance unfolds only in resistance to a powerful counterforce that pulls us in, threatening to contaminate us with a loss of innocence similar to that suffered by those in the war. This is particularly true of war novels whose narratives are organized around a specific traumatic event whose influence haunts the entire plot and complicates our notions of victim and perpetrator. Furthermore, the lack of closure in the repeating chimurengas suspends the kind of distanced reading that should be possible, postponing it into the future. Zimbabwe's literature about the Second Chimurenga, read now in Zimbabwe's fourth decade of independence, can resensitize us to the need to move to the outside and after the war.

Atrocity in Kanengoni and Chinodya

The impetus behind the retrospective to uncover the traumas of the war comes from the discomfort with the figure of the disgruntled veteran captured aptly in Charles Samupindi's *Pawns* (1992). In *Pawns*, former guerrillas are living a marginal existence in Harare, and Samupindi criticizes a post-independence regime that is ignoring the debt owed to the liberation fighters. The novel's title makes allusion to the naturalistic view that the common man is a pawn of larger forces, incapable of determining his own fate. Samupindi's protagonist, Fangs, is destitute on the streets, even though he played a larger-than-life role in the war. The heroic is alluded to in contradictory ways by reference to restraint and excess. Like the heroes in *The Contact*, Fangs had an experience during the struggle where he recognized the humanity of his enemy. Gripped in hand-to-hand combat with a white soldier, Fangs "suddenly felt that he loved him" (Samupind, *Pawns* 179).

The soldier, Fangs realized, could not really have understood the politics behind this war and must have been an unwilling combatant. However, this recognition does not stop him from killing the soldier and going on to kill six more of the enemy (180–81). Fangs fails to recognize the significance of his sense of kinship with the white soldier and to act on the restraint he intuited, but did not fully grasp. His willingness to engage the enemy without restraint makes him a hero in the popular sense, but does not prevent his pariah status as a veteran after the war. The novel thus introduces some doubt into the idea of the war hero and implicates this memory of the lack of restraint as a possible cause for tarnishing the hero image. The liberation fighter was perhaps not a hero but a "pawn," doing the violent bidding of those in power. However, as a pawn, the responsibility for his actions is not all his, and he is owed better treatment by those who sent him to war. Samupindi's cynicism is an attempt to draw attention to the injustice done to neglected war veterans, but today it contains a cautionary tale for the veterans agitating in the Third Chimurenga, warning that they too might be pawns, caught up in violence at the bidding of political powers.[22]

The unheroic takes the hyperbole of the heroic, larger-than-life deeds and turns them on their head to reveal wartime atrocity. Moreover, atrocity is often narrated from the perspective of the surviving perpetrator, who in retrospect sees himself as a victim of the war. Where to place this victim identity in relation to the "real" victims, those targeted in the atrocity, is one of the challenges presented by Kanengoni and Chinodya's novels.

Kanengoni's anti-war novels have been praised for articulating the guerrillas' disillusion with the internecine violence that persisted throughout the liberation war and for criticizing Mugabe's repression in Matabeleland after independence. However, Kanengoni also became a supporter of Mugabe's land policy (Chan 373; Ranger, "Nationalist" 221–22) and a recipient of a requisitioned farm (Primorac, Place of Tears 31). The evolution from disillusioned veteran to supporter of the current regime is an evolution that parallels that of a significant constituency in Zimbabwe. Although not unusual, critics take note of Kanengoni's political about-face as perplexing. The regard for his antiwar novels, especially *Echoing Silences*, remains undiminished, however (Chan 373). A careful reading of *When the Rainbird Cries* (1987) and *Echoing Silences* (1997) reveals perhaps a consistency in his political thinking that critics have not acknowledged and that pertains to his framing of the problems of atrocity and responsibility. Moreover, by placing Kanengoni in the context of other writers who seem to be responding to his work, we can identify the shape of a complex conversation about political responsibility.

When the Rainbird Cries appeared the year in which Nkomo capitulated to Mugabe and the civil war ended. The novel offers a sympathetic account of the sufferings of the peasantry during the liberation war of the 1970s, and its portrayal of the guerrillas is far from heroic. Their constant infighting makes them ineffective and unnecessarily violent. Thus the novel gives a cautionary message about the lack of political discipline. Furthermore, Kanengoni presents a Manichean world *manqué*, projecting the desire for a dualistic world, divided between bad whites and heroic Africans, when in fact he finds something else instead. His portrayal of Lieutenant Kruger of the Rhodesian Front more than fits the bill of a bad white, but heroic African fighters are in short supply. Thus the novel solicits a masculine response of "let's shape up."

Signs of masculinity in need of reform are everywhere. Stationed in a rural village far from the field of war, Kruger is bored and spends his time reading pornography (Kanengoni, *Rainbird* 25–26). When something finally happens (the guerrillas stage a small-scale attack, and their escape vehicle is spotted), Kruger is jumping at the bit to punish the villagers. He thinks of the prospect of torture with pleasure: "But it was the cringing of those faces, those contortions of painful endurance, the formidable stretch to breaking point and the final snap, then the deafening wailing, all this, offered a simplistic, unspoiled African beauty nowhere else encountered except when induced" (36). Torture and pornography are seen in a continuum; torture will provide the pleasures of a "simplistic, unspoiled African beauty," satisfying a lust for violence. In one of the most explicit scenes of torture to be found in the literature of the liberation war, Kruger goes on to terrorize and humiliate the village leadership for days (35–36, 48).

Evil is unambiguously present, but the guerrillas don't come in as the saviors. They make matters worse through their incompetence. They fail to pull off their operation, and the result is the tragic destruction of a village. The atrocity is described in detail: "Hewn bodies lay strewn everywhere, some burning in the collapsing logs and others hideously groaning away the little lives that still remained in them in the surrounding bushes. Corpses of school children scattered the gutted school buildings" (92–93). The novel promises to investigate the "tragic events that happened at Nyamutowa village" (1), but demonstrates instead why the investigation of atrocity comes up short because of an unwillingness to take responsibility. The reader also sees that the guerrillas are guilty of the torture and death of the head teacher, who was framed by a jealous subordinate as a "sellout," or traitor (78, 87). In this instance the guerrillas fail again to provide leadership because they prove incapable of seeing past the petty jealousies of a small village community. Instead, they divide among themselves, and their unit self-destructs.

A similar confusion seems to affect the spiritual realm, where things do not signify what they are supposed to, leading to a troubling disjunction between the religious and the historical interpretation of events. The novel ends with the resumption of a rain ceremony interrupted by the events of the novel. The ceremony serves as a reminder of the spiritual link to the land. Because traditional religion opposed rain to blood (where blood was spilled, rain would not fall), the spirit mediums' involvement in warfare is profoundly compromising (Lan 151). The mediums are responsible for protecting the land from drought, and hence they must avoid bloodshed (141). This casts doubt on the appropriateness of Nehanda and Kaguvi as leaders of the armed resistance in the First Chimurenga and unsettles the meaning of these references in the novel.

Mao, the guerrilla who survives, keeps asking for an account of "what exactly happened?" and thus for a historical explanation. "Revolution is a ravaging monster," he is told by the "Chief of Information" (Kanengoni, *Rainbird* 104). When Mao insists that he still does not understand, the Chief replies irritably: "Don't ask me to explain what I am saying. I wish I had an explanation but I don't . . . the only imperative is the justice of our cause and the certainty of the resultant victory" (104–5). If Mao is looking for some kind of accountability for the repeated atrocities he has witnessed and participated in, he does not receive it. "The justice of our cause" trumps all other concerns. As the Chief has the last word before the rain ceremony resumes, we are left with the impression that historical accountability is obscured behind the veil of the rain ceremony.

Mao struggles to stay focused on the "people's war" so that he can justify what he is doing. In a conversation with another guerrilla about the food that the villagers are giving them, Mao expresses anxiety over this relationship:

> A guerilla war must be a people's war. If it isn't one as yet, we have to transform it into one and only then, instead of being lonely soldiers, roaming the wilderness, making isolated and haphazard encounters with the enemy, fighting a grueling and losing war, let's become one with the people, sharing their burdens as well as their comforts and fusing our limited power with their endless resources. How can we lose? There is nothing comfortable about war, Killer, any war. (52)

Mao acknowledges that the guerrillas are "lonely soldiers" distinct from the people and expresses a desire to "become one with the people." The idealized vision of the relation to the people is most likely unrealizable, given the atrocities the guerrillas are responsible for. In trying to articulate his identification with the people and his understanding that the legitimacy of the war comes only from them, Mao refers to "sharing their burdens as well as their comforts," stating also that "there is nothing comfortable about war." Each statement makes sense on its own, but the important part is the logic that links them. The statements are linked by the rhetorical question "How can we lose?" which stipulates that only by aligning themselves with the people will the guerrillas be successful.

The guerrillas depend on the people for food, but they often coerce the people into giving them food, harming their relationship with the people. Mao recognizes that a more concerted effort needs to be made to win the hearts of the people. By explaining that there are no comforts in war, he is warning Killer not to expect the people to serve his needs. If he chooses to fight, then he must assume the hardships that come with the war and not use the gun to make himself comfortable at the expense of the people. Mao also observes that war "will always remain abnormal. People are not made for wars" (52). Thus Mao indicates that you have to buck the environment, resist its logic. There is a danger in what he says, however. If war is also a zone of exception where people don't belong naturally, there is little accountability; war "will always remain abnormal."

The kind of alliance with the people imagined by Mao was supposed to be forged during the *pungwe*, all-night meetings between guerrillas and villagers where "history" lessons were given and patriotic songs were sung. The *pungwe* is usually portrayed as a top-down affair where the guerrillas manipulate the people to coerce their allegiance. Mao, however, leads a *pungwe* where the people break down in grief:

> They were all crying for Zimbabwe. Almost every one of them here had a story to tell about this raging war, nasty encounters. Around them, death abounded. War was not life. War would never be life. They had flung themselves body and soul behind this raging monster, but inwardly they all wished that it would come to an early end. War was not something one could get used to. (68)

Mao's response is to recognize the suffering of the people before he urges them to continue with the war: "we are not afraid of war . . . especially when it means claiming back what rightfully belongs to us" (70).

Critics who praise Kanengoni's candid assessment of the guerrillas' shortcomings read the novel as a series of authentic tableaus that depict war as "abnormal," a "raging monster." In fact, Kanengoni is an authentic rapporteur, since he fought for ZANU-PF's guerrilla army (ZANLA) from 1974 to 1980. Yet the novel makes a vexed presentation of authenticity. Authenticity is equated with explicitness, the kind of detail used to depict excessive, heinous violence, resulting in atrocity. Such unrestrained violence is also presented as belonging to war and hence as beyond explanation and accountability. The novel is framed as an investigation of the "tragic events that happened at Nyamutowa village" (1) but claims to have failed to explain them, even though the reader can discern who is responsible for these events.

The problem is not that war in unnarratable, but that it yields a catalog of events that the novel insists can be considered only holistically as "war" and as that which is "abnormal." The details that Kanengoni offers are incidents from the zone of exception, and, in retrospect, he considers them as events that belong to that other time. Another guerrilla complains to Mao that he fears the war will never end: "I am scared stiff of endlessness; something that goes on and on without any apparent end" (53). Mao offers a reasoned response to reassure Killer that there must of necessity be an end: "there should always be that objective line persisting. For one thing, a thing with a beginning has to have of necessity, an end; that is objectivity" (53). By looking back to the beginning to find the end, Mao restricts himself to a kind of determinism that overlooks the in-between, the part of the story that could explain what happened in the war. This is due to his Marxist rhetoric of "objectivity" that asserts the inevitable people's victory ideologically. Yet clearly this logic is not very convincing to those, like Killer, in the middle of a war who need to understand what happens step by step.

In *Echoing Silences*, published ten years later, Kanengoni focuses on a war veteran haunted by the memory of an atrocity he committed. In this novel the experience of the war spills over into the period after with disastrous effects. Munashe's war trauma results in his suicide, forcing us to confront more directly the enduring impact of the war experience.

Munashe's induction into war is traumatic. Because he is educated, he faces discrimination from the commanders, who mistrust intellectuals. Thus, when caught reading a novel, he is severely tortured and forced to kill a "sellout" (a woman and her infant) using a hoe (Kanengoni, *Silences* 9). Kanengoni presents Munashe as a victim-perpetrator by carefully organizing the narrative order of events to foreground Munashe's trauma alongside his victims' suffering. The novel begins with a narration of the atrocity, but interrupts the account in order to present Munashe first as a victim of torture and as someone who, in crossing the border into Mozambique through the jungle, suffers an "ordeal in the forest" (11–12). In the novel's opening Munashe is haunted by the woman's pleading eyes and her baby's crying before we learn why (5). The scene of the atrocity resumes twenty-five pages later, after the account of Munashe's torture and "ordeal in the forest." Munashe's hesitations and doubts are foregrounded:

> he feared that the woman might ask him why he was about to do what he was about to do and he would not be able to give her any answer at all because he did not know what the talked-about revolt was all about. He knew that he was merely caught up in it. (30)

Before he strikes, his vision fails and the woman's figure:

> lost its shape and its edges got torn and the baby on her back became a protrusion of her hunched back and then he swung the hoe, and he heard the blade swishing furiously through the air and he thought of the sound from the enormous wings of the bateleur as it took off from the towering mukamba tree at the mouth of the cave on the side of the mountain and the foul smell from the inside as Gondo groaned, decaying, dying. The war was an insatiable incinerator that would burn them all up, one after the other. (30)

The directness of the narration at first seems unflinching, until the focus on the woman blurs and we escape into Munashe's interiority, which brings up memories of a bird of prey hovering near his dying comrade, who has a putrid wound. These images, reinforced by the allusion to the cave, which is a setting associated with the guerrillas and the war front, take the focus away from the civilian victims and place it instead on the guerrillas' suffering. The image of war as "an insatiable incinerator that would burn them all up, one after the other" fails as the kind of displacement that would reveal the "song of my country" because it deliberately masculinizes and militarizes the story of war privileging the suffering of combatants over that of civilians.

Munashe's thoughts allude to the symbolism of the religious life. Such symbolism is lacking in the gruesome killing of the peasant woman, except as it is evoked in association with Munashe's memory of his comrade. The spirit mediums were said to have guided the guerrillas in interpreting animal behavior in the forest, and thus an eagle flying in distress was thought to signify danger (Lan 157–58). The bateleur flying up and away from the cave signifies Comrade Gondo's death and places it on the order of the spiritual. The sounds of Munashe's hoe swooshing as he strikes his victim blends with the sounds of the bird's wings in his mind, obfuscating his action and enabling a kind of dissociation from it. The reader's doubts are confirmed because the accusations against the woman are speculative. Thus linking the death of Munashe's comrade to the killing of the sellout as crime and punishment (for her presumed betrayal of the guerrillas to the Rhodesians) is forced and unconvincing. The woman cannot defend herself; her infant is an innocent victim and the manner of killing particularly cruel. More importantly, Munashe cannot repress his own awareness of these facts.

In *When the Rainbird Cries* the white man is the originator of violence. The settler, represented by the sadistic Kruger, is evil, and all the unfortunate incidents of the war occur under the pressure of that original violence. The liberation war is necessary to destroy evil, and the war must be pursued till independence, the ultimate destruction of the original evil. This is asserted with a kind of determinism; it must happen whatever the cost. In *Echoing Silences* war itself is the source of evil, and Munashe "wondered why he had joined the struggle to land himself in such a mess" (10). The guerrilla (and later veteran) is presented as a victim of the leaders of the struggle. To develop this characterization, Kanengoni makes several historical references to the assassination of Herbert Chitepo, an intellectual and the chairman of ZANU. Chitepo was assassinated on March 18, 1975, and to this day there is no solid evidence about the identity of his murderers, despite conflicting confessions to the murder (White 9). His assassination was an important turning point in the war, after which there was increased civil strife.

Key to the understanding the novel is a scene at the end, where Munashe undergoes a spirit possession to communicate with the dead. Primorac interprets the spirit possession as Munashe's attempt to recover from his war trauma (Primorac, *Place of Tears* 139–40). Munashe witnesses Chitepo giving a speech and "angrily" recounting a "series of monumental historical betrayals" (Kanengoni, *Echoing Silences*131). Chitepo's anger, moreover, casts a shadow on the sentimental and conciliatory tone of Munashe's reunions with the dead. Accompanied by his lover, Munashe sees his victim and her child among the dead. His lover reassures him that the woman "has forgiven you" (130). But forgiveness is asserted rather than shown, since there is no exchange of words between Munashe and his victim. Thus this assurance of forgiveness is not really satisfactory and does more to draw attention to the silenced stories of the victims of atrocity.[23]

Kanengoni's division of his fictional world into two spheres (the living and the dead, or spirit world) prevents closure. Munashe's wife hopes that with his suicide "the war has at last ended for him" (134). Hers is an empathetic response to Munashe's inability to recover from trauma. Yet it is unclear whether the war has ended for anyone else, including the reader, who has been privy to the rousing anger of the dead Chitepo. The critique of the war repurposes it for a new generation. Haunted by a "ngoze, an angry spirit of an unjustly killed person, seeking revenge" (Primorac, *Place of Tears* 136), Munashe is unable to overcome his predicament. He is permanently subject to the violent eruption of the supernatural in his life, which leads him to despair and suicide. In the aftermath of atrocity, Munashe is thus beyond repair, lacking any potential for a "personal emergence" (137). However, although Munashe is dead, the ending of the novel is located in the temporality of postponed fulfillment and renewed promise of revolution. The picture it offers is one of failure, which requires a return to the struggle as opposed to building on peace.

The masculine story of war and trauma takes a radically different form in Shimmer Chinodya's *Harvest of Thorns*, even though his novel similarly focuses on a young combatant brutally inducted in war. Chinodya has stated that he thinks "the war is just a back-drop in the novel" and that *Harvest of Thorns* is "much more than a war novel" (quoted in Primorac, *Place of Tears* 125). In such statements Chinodya seeks to distance himself from the nationalist war literature and to announce that his novel incorporates the war of liberation into a longer and more comprehensive historical timeline. Moreover, the portrayal of war in *Harvest of Thorns* reflects anti-war sentiment in a universal way, not specific to the liberation war but to war in general. War is shown to cause enormous suffering, but it also corrupts moral and political purpose. There is nothing redeeming about war and no desire at the end to return to the struggle. Instead, Chinodya posits the family as national allegory for hope in the future. To arrive at this point, however, requires the insight of retrospection, the laying out of the cause-and-effect sequence that unfolds from Benjamin's failed *Bildungsroman*, which is interrupted irrevocably by war.[24] The young combatant's story is once again the story of the interrupted education. Moreover, similar to *Echoing Silences*, we encounter a novel structured as a flashback from the moment of the warrior's return that seeks to tell a life by fitting pieces into a puzzle, revealing the new person who has emerged from the conflict.

Chinodya sees independence in bleak terms, but his protagonist, Benjamin, is ultimately not defeated by this disillusion and demonstrates a lesson about citizenship absent in Kanengoni's work. Although the novel explores the theme of wounded masculinity by focusing on the relationship of the young male to authority, it ends with an investment in the allegory of the family as nation absent from the other novels of the Second Chimurenga.

Benjamin's story, furthermore, bridges the bifurcated narrative of war: he moves into the forest from the township, and there he becomes acquainted with the life of the peasantry. He returns to the township bringing with him his forest wife and thus establishing a new continuity between the rural and the urban. His disillusion with independence is sharp: "The worse thing is to come back and find that nothing has changed" (Chinodya 243). In the township, where economic opportunities are few, the war seems to have been pointless, because the economic inequality between whites and Africans has remained essentially unchanged.[25] This sameness of the before and after is only partial, however, because Benjamin himself has changed and brought with him his experience of the war and his new wife, forcing on his family at least a recognition of the war's impact. Thus the novel concerns itself very much with change, recounting and taking stock of events whose implications continue to reverberate after the war.

Benjamin's return from war is rocky from the start. He makes himself ineligible for veterans' benefits by leaving the camps for veterans without his discharge papers, protesting the abominable conditions there. His family is ambivalent about his return and retreats in his presence because, as his mother says, "This whole family is damned by all the blood on your hands" (22), making him realize that "a guerilla is only a hero while the war is raging" (245). Against the bleak backdrop of the present, the novel unfolds its distinctly unheroic retrospective account of the war, since Benjamin is no hero in his own eyes. The child of what he calls "exaggerated Christians" (244), Benjamin was brought up in a harsh, disciplinarian home where the legacy of colonialism was his parents' conversion to evangelical Christianity and the self-hatred and sense of inferiority it bred in them. Bullied at school because of his parents' religion and taunted with the epithet "sellout," Benjamin unsurprisingly takes on the name "Pasi Nema Sellout" in the war.

Benjamin reaches the forest a teenager, and he is twenty when the war is over. His education is split between his early years in school and church and the forest. In a pattern recognizable from the child-soldier narratives, he is propelled into the forest by a traumatic event that brings his family into a crisis and sets him adrift. In his case, the event is a gruesome accident in which Benjamin severs his brother's leg. For this he is shamed and punished very harshly in his church, pushing him to run away. Thus his decision to join the guerrillas is not deeply political, but rather driven by a personal crisis.

Like Munashe, the defining event in the war for Benjamin is an atrocity that he was forced to commit by his commander when he was seventeen.

He and one other member of his unit are ordered to beat to death a woman accused of poisoning the guerrillas. This episode takes on added importance because Chinodya uses it as a vehicle to examine how the historical memory of events is encumbered with silences and distortions. Benjamin's perspective as a seventeen-year-old is inadequate to take into account the full significance of events such as this atrocity. Unlike Munashe, his thoughts center less on what he had to do than on his resentment of the older members of his unit:

> Mai Tawanda's death had not at first worried him. She was a traitor and she had to die. The horror of it he could suppress; he never allowed himself prolonged thoughts about it, though the incident had sought out a corner of his mind and pitched a little tent there. And now Baas Die's [the guerilla commander's] laughter had triggered off his anger. That the older members of the group had not taken part in the killing, that he himself had been hurtled into that first act of punishment filled him with bitterness. (211)

Benjamin sees himself as a victim of the older men of his group, but also acknowledges the need for someone to perpetrate the killing ("she had to die"). His participation in the killing becomes part of his own story of suffering, the source of his "bitterness," obscuring that of the woman's suffering. The vivid description of the killing shows Benjamin is quite capable of perpetrating it, complicating the reader's empathy for Benjamin as a teen being manipulated by his commander.

After ordering the beating, Baas Die rouses a hesitant crowd of villagers to chant and ululate as Benjamin and the other guerrilla, apparently without hesitation, beat Mai Tawanda. Chinodya emphasizes the focus and effort, the deliberate actions needed to kill someone with sticks and branches, improvised weapons. Baas Die pushes them to the end: "There are no second chances in this war. . . . Finish your job," and Benjamin

> threw down the broken root. His hands were damp. He walked towards a tree. The crowd scrambled back. A woman pulled up her cloth from his boot. A woman snatched up a child from his boot. He walked up to a tree and reached up with his hands to a branch.
>
> He swung the branch sideways until it broke and fell to the ground. He put his foot on the branch and stripped off the leaves. (186)

Benjamin's momentum seems unstoppable here. With a similar weapon, the other guerrilla cracks Mai Tawanda's skull. On the ground with her legs spread out and exposed, her figure reminds Benjamin of his mother, whose legs he saw as a child when he crawled under the table (194). He averts his gaze, therefore, from the woman's head and legs and, focusing on her waist, strikes her and breaks her spine. By fragmenting the body in his perception of it (head, legs, waist), Benjamin represses the disruptive memory of his mother and accomplishes what is required of him. Benjamin only has to look at the part of her he needs to break. Her splayed-out legs suggest, moreover, the vulnerability of women to rape in war. At this time Benjamin is still a virgin, unaware of the extent to which the other guerrillas routinely violate the prohibition against sexual intercourse. This killing is a rite of passage for Benjamin, and its sexual undertones resonate with a gendered logic of perpetrator and victim.

But what of his victim? The disjunction between Benjamin's resentment of those in authority who coerced him and his own clarity about the necessity of the action (somebody would have had to kill the woman) brings the reader to an impasse. The abuse of his commander makes Benjamin into the object of an injustice, but the woman also demands the reader's recognition. How to recover Mai Tawanda's story out of this account of events? This is a question in the novel because Chinodya devotes considerable effort to address it, not satisfied like Kanengoni with claiming the victim's forgiveness of her killer. If Benjamin wants his own victimization as a child soldier to be recognized, it must be paired with a recognition of the injustice done to women such as Mai Tawanda. How to tell the whole story of the war, not war from the perspective of the combatants alone, is the challenge.

Chinodya raises doubts about Mai Tawanda's guilt, and we learn that the poisoning she is accused of could have been accidental (180). Targeted through rumor, she serves as a pretext for Baas Die to terrorize the villagers. He addresses the villagers "like a teacher in the classroom" about the consequences of being a "sellout" (182). Benjamin convinces himself of Mai Tawanda's guilt. Moreover, because the beating is referred to as a "lesson," it is paired with an earlier moment when the guerrillas teach the villagers the history of white settlement and the First Chimurenga. The novel's title comes from this scene, although it acquires its own ironic meaning when placed in the context of Benjamin's return after the war. The guerrillas explain to the villagers that a "harvest of thorns" was reaped by the peasants on the inferior land they were forcibly removed to by white settlers (160–61), hence leading them to rebel heroically. The history lesson about the First Chimurenga is used to inspire the villagers' loyalty to the guerrillas. It evokes nostalgia for a spontaneous unity of purpose that seems harder to achieve in the present.

The mythmaking of repeating chimurengas obscures the specifics of the war. For example, when Chinodya narrates the "battle on the hill," a presumably famous battle of the Second Chimurenga, he stresses "that many stories have been told about that battle . . . some true, some not so true" (190). This battle ensued when, frightened by the killing of Mai Tawanda, the headman of the village betrayed the guerrillas to the Rhodesian forces. The mythology of the battle weaves speculation about the identity of the woman killed (was she a witch?) with beliefs about Nehanda's intervention on behalf of the guerrillas and the martyrdom of the guerrillas killed in a bombing raid. The narrator's repeated use of questions to structure his account shows how myths are made from the effort to comprehend what happened according to already given narrative structures. Folding one narrative into the other obfuscates the specific, troubling details, such as the persistent questions about Mai Tawanda's guilt that need to be resolved to produce a just account of the war.

The guerrillas also participate in their own mythmaking as they explain their role to the villagers by alluding to the First Chimurenga and Nehanda. In one such moment, a consciousness-raising exercise, the guerrillas talk to a very old woman about 1896. The events of that time slowly come back to her as a dim memory of having been hidden by her mother in a cave (133). It is difficult for the woman at first to comprehend what the guerrillas are telling her so that when she finally remembers the past, her memory does not feel very authentic, shaped as it is through the leading comments of the guerrillas.

Chinodya's painstaking account of the construction of multiple stories about the "battle on the hill" shows the reader that what most people believe is neither entirely true nor entirely false. The novel tells a story about people's stories from which the reader deciphers an account of the war. Thus we come to understand that Mai Tawanda probably poisoned the guerrilla accidentally, she was not a witch, and had no deliberate intent to harm the guerrillas in this instance. But she had betrayed the guerrillas' location once under duress, when the Rhodesians threatened to kill her son (a policeman) if she did not cooperate. The story of a mother coerced into revealing the movements of the guerrillas in order to save her son and brutally killed by her own people as a result is the story of a victim of war's messy alliances, where it is not possible to retrieve pure innocence, but, at the same time, guilt is not simple, either.

The narrator stresses the importance of finding concrete evidence, but the guerrillas are not similarly worried about evidence. Their suspicions suffice for them to justify killing Mai Tawanda. They debate what to do and decide, "'She has to go.' 'She's a goner.' 'She has to go fast, before she does us all in,'" and they dismiss fears that she will become a "ngozi" and haunt them: "She is a traitor! Forget the ngozi nonsense." They make instrumental use of the fabulous beliefs in Nehanda's interventions and have no fear of a "ngozi" (180). Hence they appear cynical about these traditional beliefs. The headman's call for mercy contrasts with the attitude of Baas Die, who urges the crowd to cheer on the killers (186). Baas Die, the heroic commander, comes across as evil, and the traitorous headman (the betrayer who caused the "battle on the hill") as humane. These types of reversals typify war's upside-down world, unsettling our moral certainty.

The story of Benjamin's war wife provides an additional perspective on the rural population's suffering in the war. She too is a victim of an atrocity: her village was razed and burned by Smith's forces, setting her adrift. Benjamin is cast as a protector of the people, the one who "let her cry and hold on to him . . . and they hung together, swaying together at the center of her razed homestead" (228). He is also a moral witness to the destruction of his wife's village and the worst atrocity of Smith's forces, their use of napalm: "The forest was strewn with bodies and pieces of clothing. A woman wrapped in a blanket ran into him, hands clamped to her head screaming and stamping the ground with her feet. A naked boy lay on the rock, clasping an arm half-eaten away by napalm" (130). These details are historically accurate; napalm was used on attacks in the forest (Mtisi et al 149). The reference to napalm and "hands clamped to her head screaming" also function as allusions to the Vietnam War and its images, placing the Zimbabwean conflict in a broader context of modern warfare and signaling Chinodya's ambition to address war in more universal terms.

When Benjamin comes out of the forest he brings the reality of the villages and their suffering in the war with him to the township, joining in one narrative the bifurcated reality of the war. Through the bond with his wife, moreover, he gains a new masculine identity as husband and father that enables him eventually to distance himself from the identity of veteran. The child motivates Benjamin anew, despite the bleak circumstances of his poverty: "He's only twenty and he has no job or house of his own yet but he tells himself he'll do all he can to raise the little bundle of humanity in the cot" (Chinodya 248). The novel's last words, "He tells himself he'll do it," contrast sharply with the despair of Munashe, who clearly felt he could not do it. But they also underline the impression that we have of Benjamin's isolation; he is very much on his own, unsupported by any social (national?) structures. The message is one of self-reliance. This is

Chinodya's response to the desire for a dignifying closure to the liberation war. Although many of the painful details he excavates contribute to Benjamin's sense of shame as a veteran and complicate his adjustment to civilian life, Chinodya resurrects the family allegory as an enabling myth because it gives Benjamin a role as an individual.

Moreover, Benjamin's thoughts reveal a striking lack of liberation rhetoric. He is not fighting to take back the land but to end the war: "you'd know that there is no other way but this," fighting to bring an end to war (131). Such scenes delineate the liberation war from myth so that it can be surmounted, gotten past, and normal life can return, a life that as we saw will show that little has changed as a direct result of the war, underscoring once again that the war was pointless. In contrast to Kanengoni, who ends *Echoing Silences* renewing a commitment to the struggle and the incomplete project of land reclamation, Chinodya commits his protagonist fully to civilian life, imagining a future beyond the rhetoric of chimurenga.

Bringing Women into History: Bones *and* Without a Name

Echoing Silences and *Harvest of Thorns* both feature prominently scenes in which a woman is killed by guerrillas. What follows is an examination of novels that take the perspective of similar female victims and tell the story of the liberation war from their perspective. This is complicated by their marginal status, shown as a function of their illiteracy and poverty, their wounds that incapacitate them, or the fact that they have been killed and their voice must be improvised. The criticism of the heroic is implicit here, although some of these women are also mothers of guerrillas. As Chinodya's novel illustrates, criticism of the heroic narrative aims to bring the people into history, and by focusing on the plight of women, Hove and Vera try to achieve this.

Hove has stated explicitly his intention to speak from the people's perspective. Reflecting on his experience as a teacher in a rural village during the liberation war, he explained:

> When you are with them you see their problems, you attend a funeral for some who have been massacred and so on. And then you begin to understand what it is to be without a gun between two people who have guns. (Quoted in Veit-Wild 5)

The insecurity of the people caught in the crossfire generates the perspective of Hove's narrative. His insight suggests a different identity for the heroic; we begin to see it not as an attribute of those who are armed, but of those who must cope with the threat of violence.

Thus *Bones* (1988) reinvents the heroic, feminizing it and identifying it with endurance in order to incorporate the point of view of the people and criticize the abuses of the war. In contrast to Chinodya's concern with wounded masculinity, Hove's novel focuses on women's suffering and identifies the people broadly with the plight of women. As we saw, Vera sought to reclaim Nehanda's story as a woman's story. *Bones*, published six years before *Nehanda*, anticipates this project by setting up an analogy between Nehanda's physical suffering and the suffering of all women, and the people, by extension. The guerrillas are referred to as "children" (an allusion to their identity as children of the soil) and portrayed only indirectly as the lost sons of grieving mothers. The novel, set during the transition from the war to independence, focuses on the gap between the trauma of the war in rural areas and the city's more distanced perspective on the war. It tries to bridge this gap by demonstrating the women's ability to identify with each other's stories as women across the social divides of a bifurcated nation. Thus like Benjamin's story, *Bones* attempts to synthesize the rural and urban experience of the war.

Because the novel's title alludes to the prophecy from the First Chimurenga, Nehanda's "My bones shall rise," Hove clearly places his work in conversation with the literature of the heroic. He refers to Zimbabwe as the "land of rising bones" in "The Spirits Speak: 1897," a chapter that interrupts the narrative to rehearse the Nehanda prophecy (Hove, *Bones* 52). Hove refers to the year after the uprising (1897 instead of 1896) so as to stress the aftermath rather than the rebellion itself. He inserts into his text a Nehanda poem that speaks of linkages between the unfinished work of the First Chimurenga and the Second. Hove describes the land in 1897 as literally full of bones: livestock has died in large numbers from disease, locusts have destroyed the crops, and the people have died both from famine and resisting the settlers (52–53). Hove's use of the Nehanda material appears conventional except for his use of the more intimate pronouns "you" and "me" and the second person:

> . . . you can torture me,
> spread my bowels for the jackals to eat
> and tear them to pieces,
> mutilate my body with your anger,
> throw my brains to the vultures,
> leave the remains of my body in the playground
> for your children to play with,

cut my ears to decorate your own ears,
cut my fingers
use them to wipe your own sweat . . .
my bones will rise in the spirit of war. (53, ellipses in the original)

The voice then warns the torturer that "they" (her children) will take arms again and:

My bones will rise
with such power
the graves will be too small
to contain them.
The ribs of the graves
will break when my bones rise,
and you stare in disbelief,
not knowing if your hunger for war
can stand up to it.

As a poem, this text, inserted into the novel and describing Nehanda's torture, performs the "song of my country" motif. Torture and its victim stand in for the larger entities of war and nation. The one-sided violence of torture will be reciprocated when the "bones will rise" and defy belief. The intimacy of the poem, the way it personalizes the conflict with its second-person address, stages a competition of perspectives that alludes to the reciprocal injuring of war.[26] Although Nehanda was hung, there is no historical evidence that she was tortured, however. The catalog of injuries that Nehanda speaks about is representative of the sufferings caused by colonization and is part of the narrative of conquest, imperialism, and resistance to it. As we saw in *An Ill-Fated People*, Zimbabweans associate colonial and settler rule with the abuses of torture. Thus when torture stands in for war more generally and its story is cast as the "song of my country," we also have a revision of the story of colonial rule that incorporates it into an extended narrative of the liberation war. Colonial rule is not the peace before the war, but part of the war itself, fought against the African through torture. The poem uses a rhetoric of war to dignify the victim and present her as a powerful agent. By inserting the poem in his novel, Hove creates the expectation that there is an analogy between Nehanda and the women who suffer from violence in the war. This analogy, however, does not hold because, whereas the rhetoric of war may serve the nationalist goal, the women's stories introduce dissonance into the nationalist rhetoric.

In *Bones*, violence, especially rape, is rendered very intimately, which contrasts with the conventional, heroic stories of Nehanda that safeguard her dignity and do not speak of the body. By having Nehanda refer to her own physical suffering in the poem, Hove enables by analogy the articulation of the intimate stories of women's suffering. Thus the explicit treatment of the body in Hove's Nehanda poem invites us to compare her suffering to that of the women raped in *Bones*, one by a settler, the other by an African. These two rapes draw attention to the parallel violence done to African women by both white and African men and help Hove focus on the ways in which the violence of war turns inward, disrupting the nationalist narrative. The suffering of women, moreover, has a larger resonance as the suffering of the ordinary people left out of the gains of independence.

The novel deploys multiple narrators who create a network of interlinked stories of suffering that unfold not in the battlefield or the forest, but on the periphery of war. Hove prefigures what Nuruddin Farah does in *Links*, writing a novel that demonstrates how stories form links among people that have the potential to transform the political landscape. The chapter "The Spirits Speak: 1897" is followed by a dialogue between a husband and wife. The wife is referred to as "unknown woman" and is thus opposed by allusion to the Unknown Soldier of Heroes' Acre, the monument to the liberation heroes built by Mugabe just after independence in 1981 (Meredith, *Mugabe* 77). Heroes' Acre (and the national holiday Heroes' Day) exemplify "the new rulers' use of the war to legitimate themselves and the new nation" (Kriger 64).[27] The manner of commemoration reflects the desire to transform the guerrillas into soldiers and accord them the kind of memorial that soldiers of a national army would receive (64). Not only does Hove's "unknown woman" feminize this identity of the unknown hero, but she also demilitarizes it. The three figures of the monument at Heroes Acre (one of which is a woman) are a militant representation of the people, a representation that Hove's novel subverts. Through the figure of the "unknown woman," Hove critiques the appropriation of the people's story by a state that betrayed them.

Speaking to her husband, the "unknown woman" reflects mournfully on the killing of the "children," or guerrillas. The husband, a doctor, works in a government hospital and wants no part in the conflict so as not to jeopardize his job. He believes the whites cannot be defeated and scolds his wife for her "evil Zapu spirit." Alluding to the weakness of Nkomo's party (ZAPU), he asks her, "Do you think a few armed gangsters will fight a whole army and win?" (Hove, *Bones* 55). The husband even goes so far as to threaten to report his wife to the police for her sympathy for the guerrillas so that "they will come and tear you to pieces" (55). "Tear you to pieces" is similar to the wording describing torture in the novel's Nehanda poem cited earlier.

The couple represents the educated, urban class, but between them we see a political rift caused by the wife's sympathy for the nationalist cause and the children of the soil. When the husband is killed in suspicious circumstances, the woman pleads, "who will tell me exactly what happened, the way things actually happened?" (58). The "unknown woman" must piece together an account of what happened from various bits of information garnered through conversations. Thus she shares in the predicament of the powerless, left uninformed on the margins and needing to be told what happened. Her need for the truth ("the way things actually happened") underscores the importance to her of the specific details that pertain to her husband's circumstance, the particularity of his story. Yet these details also render the story untellable, presumably because of its brutality. The husband betrayed the guerrillas when they came secretly to the hospital and asked him for medicine and was killed because of it: "My ears have heard things that no tongue can say in the open" (58–59). The "unknown woman," burdened by her secret, finds comfort in the stories of other women's suffering, spoken surreptitiously on the bus, a space in the margin occupied by women who are "inconsequential" subalterns. There, on the bus to Harare, she meets Marita, the central figure in the novel. The war has ended, and Marita is traveling to the capital in hope of finding her son, who had joined the guerrillas and might be among those returning to the city after the war.

The "unknown woman" and Marita are chance acquaintances; the bond between them is forged through Marita's narration of her story on the bus, which she tells the "unknown woman" because "'You people of the city do not know what war was all about'" (75). Thus, like *Harvest of Thorns*, *Bones* attempts to link the bifurcated narrative of the nation by joining the lives of the villagers to those of the city. Over the entire novel Hove in fact weaves together the retrospective meditations of several women, all of which are linked to Marita as listener and storyteller. Marita's own story is a story of torture and rape, the punishment inflicted on her by her employer, a white settler, for having a son who joined the guerrillas.

The "unknown woman's" empathetic identification with Marita makes her loyal to her so that when Marita dies in the city, the "unknown woman" attempts to retrieve her body for burial, worried that Marita, "the woman whom nobody knows" (76), will not be properly buried. The bifurcated narrative of the nation that keeps peasants and educated city dwellers in different spheres is momentarily overcome by the "unknown woman's" demonstration of solidarity and deep identification with Marita's woman's story of war. However, the "unknown woman's" solidarity moves her into the same space of invisibility occupied by the peasant Marita and costs her her life. Her request for Marita's body is refused. The "unknown woman" persists in asking for it, defying the authority of the soldier in charge who, infuriated, beats her to death. Ironically, the "unknown woman" ends up unclaimed in the morgue, suffering the fate she tried to save Marita from. The "unknown woman's" killing is explained away as "a bad day" in a soldier's life and is thus inconsequential (104).

Although the women can repair the nation's bifurcated narrative through their solidarity, the militarized, masculine actors brutally and at the same time almost casually blot out their lives, unmasking the schism between the state (constituted by the war's victors) and its people. However, the networks of conversation among women and, by extension, the networks among the readers of Hove's novel hold the potential to create a constituency that claims a dissenting war narrative that exposes such atrocities.

Hove carefully excavates layers of repressed stories to get at the truth of these women's experiences. The attachment the "unknown woman" feels for Marita originates from the story of suffering, but does not express itself in a sentimental manner:

> Imagine, just think of it, a woman who gives me so much of what is inside her heart without crying. . . . The mind is a hidden thing. The heart is also a hidden thing. Do they not say the mouth is a small cave with which to hide the things of inside [*sic*]. Many burdensome things which weigh inside the breast of a person. Marita showed me all the burdens I have inside me, but she did so *without shedding even a little tear or making me feel sorry for her*. (69, emphasis added)

Marita does not narrate her sufferings to get pity, but to illuminate and promote understanding. Moreover, by revealing herself she helps the "unknown woman" see within herself, thus creating the kind of correspondence that leads to recognition and solidarity.

The story of the war leads to self-examination, but the "unknown woman's" courageous commitment to Marita's memory results, as we saw, in her tragically duplicating Marita's circumstances. It does not bring a widening of the base, the shared story, but a violent stamping out that snuffs out the "unknown woman's" life so that hers too is now an unremembered life. Interestingly, when the "unknown woman" attempts to explain Marita's story at the mortuary in order to claim her body, she does not recount Marita's personal history, but the larger story of the suffering of the rural villages in the war, stressing the context within which Marita's story unfolded. She has understood the broader implications of a personal history. By beating the "unknown woman," the carrier of this testimony, to death the soldier stamps out the memory of the war, not just Marita. Hove's simile in the earlier quote, which compares the mouth to a cave, resonates with the stories of persecution from the First Chimurenga, where the villagers hid in caves. Caves, like mouths, hold the words or testimony to this historical experience, just as all Zimbabweans potentially hold their own history in their mouths.

Bones has been criticized for romanticizing traditional Africa and reducing the complexity of modern identities (Veit-Wild 5). However, although Hove is concerned with creating authentic voices, his aim is primarily to deconstruct violent identities, which he perceives as having been falsely legitimated as authentic. When the novel won the Noma Award for Publishing in Africa in 1989, it garnered attention for its unusual narrative method, which rendered its protagonists as "voices locked in conversation" (Gunner 83). Written for the most part in the second person, the novel demonstrates the ways in which a personal narrative is a surrogate for the stories of others, of the community. The teller bears testimony for others and places her own experience in a context created by the experience of others. Shuttling between narrators, Hove creates characters whose lives mirror each other's. The repetition of similar experiences underscores that there is a phenomenon that we can name "the condition of the people" and promotes its recognition.

Hove's concern with authenticity led him, like other writers before, to improvise a style that is an invented "Africanized English," his translation of Shona idiom into English (Veit-Wild 7). Critics have noted the irony of a writer who tries to capture the perspective of peasants and ends up creating a difficult literary language, a criticism that was also lodged against Saro-Wiwa for *Sozaboy*. However, the point is to draw attention to difference, not to assimilate, but to "bring educated readers up against the fact that African peasants think and react differently from themselves" (Calder 40). This "invention of a rural idiom" in literary form is necessary to "give voice to the peasantry" (Sibanyoni 64).

The language Hove is imitating is already in a sense literary, as his women characters speak in the style of Shona prophecy, in the manner of the stories of Nehanda. Moreover, as Matthew Engelke argues, Hove's identification of peasants with nature, farming, and the soil is "a performative cultural identity," an aspect of their negotiation of modernity, and hence historical rather than essentializing (Engelke 31).[28] Hove's voices in conversation are not "fused," as Veit-Wild claims (Veit-Wild 7), but remain distinct as responses to each other. He creates the possibility for subaltern subjects to speak, but this is always presented as a literary exercise, an imaginative interpolation of possible voices, distinct from the historical reality itself where subalterns are silenced.

An example of the way in which the stories of the women are interlinked and hence claimed by all communally is captured by the manner in which the reader comes to know the details of Marita's story of rape. Although we know that Marita tells this story to the "unknown woman" on the bus, we do not know the details until another woman, Janifa, tells us this story. Janifa is a young woman who is attached to Marita's son, the guerrilla. Figure 3.6 attempts to show the way the second-person narration in the novel creates an axis going in two directions, away from the center (Marita) and connecting potentially ever more people in the chain of linked testimonies, except that the violence silences the stories at either end.

The story of Marita's rape, narrated by Janifa, captures through second-person narration Marita's "existence dictated from the outside" (DelConte 205). Thus we are not privy to Marita's interiority. The narration is an account of what Janifa sees when she comes upon Marita in the aftermath of the assault. One woman bears witness to another's rape by reading the

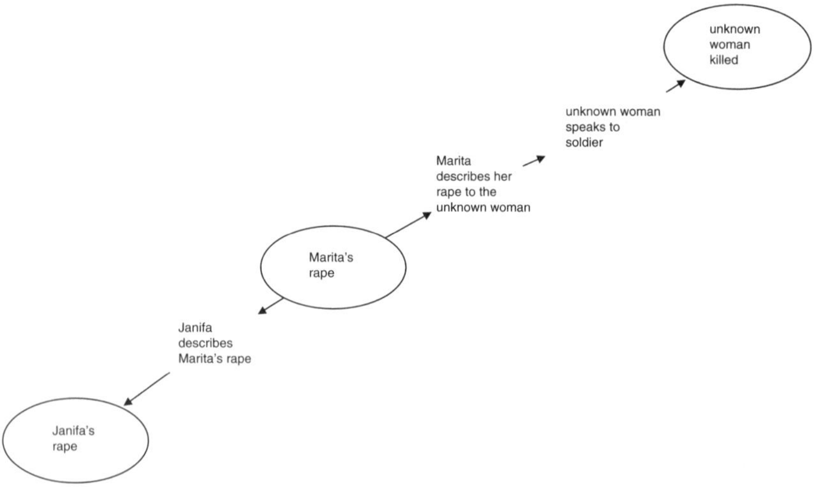

Figure 3.6. Chenjerai Hove's novel *Bones* (1988) examines how the lives of two women, Janifa and Marita, intersect and how their lives are affected by the violence against civilians perpetrated during Zimbabwe's liberation war. Narrative diagram created by the author.

signs on the victim's body after the attack and addressing the victim herself with the account of her own story. This narrative, whose details are already known to the narratee (the victim), is told in order to acknowledge that which is unspeakable and to resist the silencing of rape. If rape is violence "dictated from the outside," its story, told by an empathetic female witness, provides a new "outside," a protective circle around the victim.[29]

The pattern of mirroring and duplication that haunts the women's narratives of war recalls the ever-present danger of the inconsequential woman I identified in the novels of the Nigerian civil war. Following this pattern, Janifa herself is raped after she gives testimony to Marita's rape. Like the "unknown woman" who seeks to bury Marita and is herself killed, Janifa's life ends up imitating Marita's. These two women, Janifa and Marita, are linked by their connection to Marita's son, who, before joining the guerrillas, wrote Janifa a love letter (Hove, *Bones* 5). In the absence of her son, Marita, who is not literate, repeatedly seeks Janifa to read her the letter just so she can hear her son's voice through his letter. Janifa, who is abused emotionally by her own mother, is drawn to Marita because of her mother's love for her son. This attachment shapes the sympathetic attitude through which we learn of Marita's rape and torture: "If eyes could die after seeing bad things, mine would have died after seeing you the way you were, Marita. . . . Heavy things come out of our heart in such times, Marita. Heavy things that words cannot name. Words are weak, Marita. Very weak" (60–61). Although we learn of "heavy things that words cannot name," these heavy things are articulated, albeit in a marginal space, the space created rhetorically by the shared reading of the love letter. A bond cultivated through reading (achieved despite the illiteracy of one participant) stands as paradigmatic of what a literature that empathizes with the people can achieve, facilitating the articulation and acknowledgment of the "heavy things" by creating an empathetic space in which they can be revealed.

Janifa's worry "that words cannot name" reflects on the capacity of language to express emotion appropriately. This anxiety captures the subalterity of her point of view and its ability to signify only indirectly and by surrogate means. Because of the circularity of the second-person narration, Marita's story becomes the prism through which Janifa experiences her own rape. Marita's survival of her rape is in fact a powerful inspiration to Janifa, who survives her attack by thinking of what Marita went through. Janifa feels that her life is deeply entangled with Marita's, even more so because Marita inadvertently exposes Janifa to her rapist.[30] Marita becomes Janifa's interlocutor in her mind, sustaining her in the mental institution where she is placed until, and here the novel's ending is ambiguous, either Marita's son returns from the war (now a disabled veteran) and they marry, or Marita fantasizes about such an outcome.

Like *Harvest of Thorns*, *Bones* ends with hope for the future invested in a young family, but the fragility of the spouses' mental and physical states renders this ending (either as reality or hope) poignant. We are confronted with the clash between the aspiration for a future symbolized by this union (and its allegorical implications for the nation) and our more realistic (and by now historically informed) awareness that the desired future will likely be much more difficult, thus creating the effect of "poignancy."[31] "Poignancy" brings a painful realization that the aspiration of another (that we also see as our aspiration for that other) is "blocked," unrealizable (Mohamed 149). We desire the happiness and healing of Janifa and her lover returned from war, but the novel suggests a very fragile vision of such a future before it pierces us with the disappointing realization that political and historical forces are stacked against them. The activist response then is to find a way to unblock this potential, to help make real the future that our imagination has made us desire.

Overcoming the bifurcated narrative of the nation is also a central concern of Vera, who develops the plots of *Without a Name* and *The Stone Virgins* along an axis from the village to the city. In *Without a Name* the story of atrocity is brought to Harare almost literally on the body of the protagonist, Mazvita, a victim of rape. The pain remains private and turns inward, leading Mazvita to commit infanticide. *The Stone Virgins*, Vera's last novel, is set on a larger canvas, taking on the proportions of a national narrative and striving to expose atrocity to public view. In this novel Vera navigates both the world of private thought, where trauma takes on highly individualized meaning, and the more distanced display of atrocity as spectacle, meant to expose evil, to show how it happened.

Hove, who deeply influenced Vera, was concerned with how to create a space within which to give voice to the people's history. He delved into the private thoughts and intimate conversations among traumatized women, symbols of the subaltern more broadly, to tease out a narrative that captures their resilience, but also the scope of the suffering. In Vera's *Without a Name* this history still needs excavating. The reader must follow deep into the thoughts of the protagonist and follow her private actions to understand the impact of the war on her. Hove's method, second-person narration, deftly kept at bay the problem of a politics of pity. Vera's free indirect discourse places the reader as a witness to Mazvita's intimate thoughts.

Without the use of the first person, however, the narrative remains an observation of Mazvita rather than her voice addressing the reader. The technique is similar in *The Stone Virgins*, although the narrative in this novel is focalized through multiple characters. The politics of pity are evoked in the reception of the story of suffering but also in the examination of atrocity as event, its exposure to public view. Vera's description slows down the action to a step-by-step account of what happened that is rendered in language whose focus is so microscopic that it seems abstract. Her style has been often misread as imprecise and overaesthеticized.[32] Yet, as I will show, it is an extension and variation of the naturalism typical of the war novel.

In Vera's novels women are doubly victimized: by the colonial order and by the masculinist ethos of the liberation struggle. This idea of a double victimization is the premise for *Without a Name*, set in 1977 during the Second Chimurenga. Mazvita remembers her rape by a guerrilla as an attack from the land itself. Hidden in the grass, her attacker rises like the mist that was coming off the land (Vera, *Without a Name* 29–30). Thus "she connected him only to the land. It was the land that had come toward her" (37). The rapist claims her as his "sister" (35), insisting on a political fraternity to which he violently inducts her. Because land was "the central value in nationalist conceptions of identity," Mazvita's rape "left her hating what her attacker was fighting for" (Hunter, "New War" 175). Thus Mazvita associates the liberation struggle with her victimization, and her identity as a rural woman comes into crisis when the land is linked to rape. She seeks to solve her crisis of identity by escaping to the city, a place with no memory. Harare, she believes, "is the perfect place to begin. . . . You can forget anything in the city" (Vera, *Without a Name* 30). Moreover, the opposition of the rural and the urban is posited in gender terms by Vera. Mazvita's lover, a farmer, refuses to join her in the city, not wanting to abandon the land he loves while also associating the city with (cultural) death: "The city will bury us," he claims (31).

Cities are particularly potent symbols of liberation for rural women in Vera's fiction because they promise an escape from traditional roles and more autonomy. Yet, invariably, the women fare badly in the city. Largely unaffected by the guerrilla war, Harare is enjoying the optimism of a new era, evidence of the country's bifurcation: "freedom has already arrived" (30). But although Mazvita is "ready to claim her freedom" in Harare, she is shut out of its promise (64). The narrator's cynical perspective on the city's optimism conveys Vera's bitterness over the unequal experience of the war, reflecting the nation's bifurcation:

> everyone was an overclad and spearless revolutionary. Magazines showed former slaves with a new gospel of truth and freedom. . . . Thus clad, they asserted an inchoate independence. Independence was memory and style. Black had never been as beautiful as when it married slavery with freedom. (55)

Vera's riff on "black is beautiful," a slogan from the 1970s, is caustic. The "inchoate independence" ahead of the completion of the war points an accusing finger at the urban classes that escaped most of the hardship of war. The anonymous, uncaring environment of the city leaves Mazvita vulnerable to exploitation. The man who takes her in has no use for her when he finds out that she is carrying someone else's child and casts her out. Mazvita's tragedy culminates in her act of infanticide, a desperate attempt to erase her past and start over. This act remains private and unrecognized. The "inconsequential" woman murders without anyone noticing, demonstrating that her child is even more inconsequential than herself. Out in the open in the city's streets but out of everyone's view, Mazvita's circumstance captures symbolically the relationship between the rural and the urban in the war. Rural Zimbabwe is consumed in violence, while the city averts its gaze.

Most importantly, Vera presents the infanticide as a radical subversion of the heroic war narrative. Mazvita's resolve and deliberation, the immense grit that she has to muster to kill her child and to survive in the city, are rendered as impossibly heroic.[33] Mazvita kills as if she is pushed by the city's ethos, the same way that violence on the battlefield is unleashed relentlessly in the false hope that something will be resolved. As she readies to kill her child, the narrator describes "sobs that rendered her body into half, in sobs." At the same time she was in a "violent but calculated trance," acting carefully, deliberately: "[she] sought her freedom in slender and fragile movements, finely executed" (107). The word "freedom" is revelatory: that killing brings freedom is the distorted logic of the liberation struggle. Mazvita blindfolds the child before she snaps its neck: the "baby remained blinded and trusting" (109). Vera is unsparing in the details, describing the killing explicitly and providing a version of the accounts of atrocity we encountered in Kanengoni and Chinodya's novels.

The style is naturalistic, driven by a strange determinism. It draws minute attention to the victim's body, details that stand as accusations against the mother, here a victim turned perpetrator: "She felt the neck break and fall over her wrist. She felt the bone at the bottom of that neck tell her that the child had died. The bone broke softly" (109). The emphasis on the tactile, on what Mazvita *feels* as she murders her child, demarcates what Vera is doing as different from Kanengoni and Chinodya, whose victim-perpetrators mentally escape to some other place (myth, childhood memory) as they kill.

Mazvita stays focused, becoming the witness to her own actions. The tactile places the body, two bodies, in fact, at the center of Vera's aesthetic. The child's muteness, its unresponsiveness to the violence ("her boldness had brought a terrible silence to the room" [109]) chillingly registers the absoluteness of Mazvita's power over its life. If the aesthetic of naturalism requires a more robust presence of the suffering body, Vera's text here seems to fail. Yet the identification between mother and child is already in place. The mother internalizes the child's death, its silence and immobility: "There was absolutely no movement, no movement even from her own arms. She noticed first the stillness in her arms. She noticed her arms" (109). The preposition change ("*from* her own arms" to "*in* her arms") signals that Mazvita has internalized the child's death; the tactile feel of its dead body has traveled up her arms. Death inhabits her body now. Haunted by what she has done, she will not recover from it.

Mazvita's delusion that this action is necessary for her "freedom" is apparent in the text that immediately precedes the description of the killing:

> Her determination was amazing. She stood outside her desire, outside herself. She stood with her head turned away from this ceremony of her freedom, from this ritual of separation. She saw nothing of the wildness of her actions, of the eyes dilating, of her furrowed brow, of her constricted face, of her elongated arms, of her shoulders stiff. She mistook her resolve for kindness. She saw nothing of her tears, yet she cried desperately in that triumph of her imagination, in that rejection of the things that were hers, that were of her body. Her forehead broke into ripples. Water fell from her forehead to her eyes, and blinded her. (108–9)

Although undeniably real, the narrator characterizes the murder of the child as the "triumph of her imagination" and thus a symbolic, rather than a real, act for Mazvita. "Triumph," moreover, puts the emphasis on overcoming, and the passage explicitly opposes the mind and the body: she triumphs over her body and the "things that were hers" associated with the body. We are once again confronted with the problem of poignancy, of potential blocked. Mazvita's murder of her child is also a form of self-destruction that occurs in the absence of a more fruitful path for her struggle to emerge as a self. Ato Quayson has discussed Mazvita's inability to focus on the literal as a "symbolization compulsion" that stems from the trauma of her rape and leads her to "act out" rather than "work through" her loss and suffering (Quayson, *Calibrations* 90). As symbolic narrative the allegory implicit in the scene above is somewhat obvious. A symbol of the victimized peasantry, Mazvita stands in for the struggle that devours its own children in the name of freedom. Mazvita's false conviction that violence is necessary is analogous to the factionalism that undermined the struggle. Mazvita attempts to gain autonomy as a woman, but her valid struggle for personal autonomy is perverted by the logic of violent national struggle that invades her imagination.

Thus the infanticide is at once an appropriation and a subversion of the heroic. Mazvita's ultimate aim is self-determination in a situation where she has been robbed of autonomy. Rape, flight from the war, her degradation in the city exacerbated by giving birth to an unwanted child have impossibly narrowed her sphere, hemmed her in to the extent that her only agency, she believes, is to destroy what is hers, the marks of her unfreedom. After the killing, Mazvita is filled with remorse, "a fathomless and heavy guilt," which she seeks to alleviate by burying her child in her native village, returning to the land from which she fled (Vera, *Without a Name* 110). If in her delusion "she was winged and passionate," poignant in the fullness of her problematic aspiration, in the aftermath she is crippled, broken (109). The return to the village is a version of what we saw earlier, an attempt to overcome the bifurcation of the nation, but such resolution is not possible here, where the infanticide itself symbolizes the violence that has stymied the nation's future.

In the passage I quoted earlier, the narrator refers to Mazvita's perception that her decisive action to kill the child by breaking its neck was a form of "kindness" ("She mistook her resolve for kindness"), sparing the child more drawn-out suffering. Yet this is an error, we are told. It is "resolve," a consideration of expediency, rather than concern for the child, and hence it reflects back on Mazvita, typifying the dynamics of pity in the spectatorship of suffering, dynamics that are driven by the considerations of the observer. Moreover, Vera disrupts our perception of Mazvita herself as pitiable by deliberately confusing the chronology of events so that the reader is not confronted with a cause-and-effect sequence that maps onto her victimization and actions. It is imperative that we see Mazvita as an agent, tragically executing these actions.

The novel begins with a description of Mazvita wandering aimlessly in the city after the infanticide. The reader at this point does not know what Mazvita has done. We are given a portrait of her suffering without an explanation of the incriminating facts. The text creates its own spaces of denial through metaphor and circumvention and evokes empathy for the lone figure of a broken woman, homeless in the city. The city itself seems to be on trial, an inhumane place analogous in its violence and disregard for dignity as the battlefield. Mazvita bent over because "her back was so much broken," sightless as a result of a self-willed blinding, having "injured herself irreparably" (8). Only later, through our own efforts to reorder the chronology of her story, do we understand that Mazvita's back is not broken; that she is not blind; that she has injured her baby, not herself. She has become the physical embodiment of her crime. Pitying Mazvita as we do at first draws us into a violent narrative that equates progress with violence:

> It was nothing to be sorrowful. The city was like that. There was a uniformity about suffering, a wisdom about securing your own kind of suffering, your own version of going forward. The idea was to go forward, even those who had died in the streets knew that, they crawled toward the alleys.
>
> Death, properly executed, could be mistaken for progress. (43)

It is the imperative "to go forward" that leads to denials and repression.

Vera's portrait of Mazvita, however, does not end with the condemnation of the city. Mazvita returns to the village to bury her child and give herself yet another new beginning, this time "without a name" so that nothing will recall her past (115). This is a form of denial that draws from a nostalgia of the rural and is always lurking in the persistent dualism of city and village, which sets the poor bouncing back and forth between the two. The bus journey that takes Mazvita back to the village reveals the totalizing insecurity of war. "Traveling," the narrator tells us, "was a suspension of all pretense to freedom," especially as the bus moves precariously on a road "cluttered with dead bodies." The narrator calls this road "another manifestation of death" (87). Confronted with death outside the bus, the passengers cluster in the intimate space inside where, listening to an elderly man playing the mbira (the national instrument of Zimbabwe), they exist in harmony, suggesting the potential for reconciliation and rebuilding of community.[34] Mazvita thinks to herself that:

> the mbira was a splendid remembrance. She fought for a memory brilliant as a star, but there was darkness so deep and silent, and now, this glorious searching sound visited her, sought her out, found parts of her which were still whole, which held some sweetness and longing. (79)

The music is able to awaken a capacity for wholeness, to tap into the potential to overcome the trauma of the war. Similar to allusions to an "eternal landscape," music stands outside historical time and mediates a shared experience of national belonging. But the landscape here is unavailable, usurped by violence.

The chaos of war shields Mazvita, making her own violence complicit with its violence. Although she is carrying the dead baby with her, no one has noticed. The one passenger who becomes suspicious is killed in an attack on the bus before she exposes Mazvita. The text explicitly associates Mazvita with the violence of the war: "1977. Everyone was an accomplice to war" (88). Although Mazvita returns undetected, the village has been destroyed, and there is little there to justify the nostalgia she had felt. The last line of the novel ("the silence is deep, hollow, and lonely") suggests utter emptiness. In this barren place a lone figure and a dead baby hold little optimism for a new beginning.

Mazvita's story has been a stripping down, a sequence of multiple losses that unfolds with a determined inevitability. Yet the novel, like the dialogues between women in *Bones*, gives Mazvita her name, makes her visible, and situates her story in the broader narrative of the war. The infanticide that takes place in the city can only be fully understood if placed within the context of the war raging outside the city. The madness of Mazvita's act provides a window on the war's impact and argues for the ways in which the war's brutality permeates Harare. Vera shows how private anguish and the cover provided by the city's anonymity correspond to a hidden domain of war that is the order of experience for much of Zimbabwe's people. The bleak ending of *Without a Name* is a function of the closed space around Mazvita, the loneliness and isolation of her experience. Never being found out underscores her (and the people's) invisibility in the national story.

Harvest of Thorns ends with a father's hope for his infant son and for himself because of his new identity as father. Moreover, Benjamin has found an interlocutor, his brother-in-law, in whom he confides his story of the war. The women in Hove's novels also find interlocutors. Mazvita has none. Although this is certainly a dimension of Mazvita's tragedy, it does not completely preclude possibilities for surpassing the bifurcated imagination of the nation. The novelist's intimate observation of Mazvita and her deployment of indirect discourse collapse the distance between Mazvita and the reader without effacing the role of observer. This up-closeness and immersion in Mazvita's world claims a stake in her story without couching the real differences that remain in idealizations or romanticized notions of authenticity.

Atrocity and National History: The Stone Virgins

Vera breaks the mold of the Zimbabwean war novel more definitively in *The Stone Virgins*, where she explores many of the themes I have already touched on: the focus on atrocity, the unraveling of the heroic narrative, the attempt to bridge the rural-urban divide, and the persistent evocation of Nehanda. In this novel Vera overcomes a different bifurcation that separated the man- and woman-centered texts of the war. She places the women's narrative of war and the veterans' (here portrayed by a "dissident") in dialogue, inviting the reader to examine a more comprehensive picture of the national history. Moreover, she explores the repression of Matabeleland in 1981–86, silenced in the official record, and takes on a politically risky topic, especially for Vera, who wrote the novel while living in Bulawayo and working as director of the National Gallery. The novel is a "direct indictment of government-sponsored violence in postindependence" (Primorac, *Place of Tears* 164).

The target of government repression was ostensibly the "dissidents," former ZIPRA guerrillas who fought for Joshua Nkomo. The dissidents, who never numbered more than a few hundred men, were guerrillas who returned to the forest after the end of the liberation war out of fear of persecution by ZANU and because they were not successfully integrated in the Zimbabwean army at independence. Historians understand the return to the forest as an act of desperation rather than a political decision: "For many, becoming a dissident was perceived primarily as a means of protecting one's life, a response to patterns of government repression and friction within the army." Moreover, their decision to take arms again was "rarely . . . politically motivated" (Alexander et al 196). The dissidents' presence in Matabeleland was used as a pretext by Mugabe to destroy Nkomo's stronghold in Matabeleland, setting a pattern of violent repression of his political opposition that continues to this day. Under the guise of being the people's protector, Mugabe set out to hunt down the dissidents, whom he portrayed as rogue terrorists. Vera focuses in particular on the atrocities perpetrated by Mugabe's Fifth Brigade, a special forces unit of the Zimbabwean military, trained in secret by North Korea. Also known as the Gukurahundi, or the storm, the Fifth Brigade "acted as an army of occupation, committing atrocities at will" (Meredith, *Mugabe* 67). Their violence was "uniquely humiliating, tribalistic and political" (Alexander et al 204). The people of Matabeleland, subject to the rogue attacks of the dissidents, were also victims of the systematic brutalization of the Fifth Brigade in a campaign that remained for a long time largely unacknowledged, both in Zimbabwe and internationally.

Hove treats this period in *Shadows* but stays focused on the more politically safe topic of the violence of the dissidents, making no reference to the actions of Mugabe's security forces. He portrays the people's confusion about being caught in the middle of warring factions of Zimbabweans *after* liberation. The dissidents are "the new ones who came to fight in anger.... They were angry children, saying all the things we had heard before. It was the same words. They said the enemy had changed his colour, that was all" (Hove, *Shadows* 96). The logic of the liberation struggle has gone awry, and, when Hove's characters resist the pressure to be politicized, they are victimized as sellouts by the dissidents.

When *The Stone Virgins* appeared in 2002, Ranger praised the novel for showing the scale of Mugabe's repression in Matabeleland: "having read Vera no one can ever again say that in comparison with other African slaughters 'not too many people' were killed in Matabeleland in the 1980s" (Ranger, "History Has Its Ceiling" 212). To expose these events is one of Vera's tasks, but central to her ambition for this novel is the effort to flesh out the full context, to explain the historical identities of those victimized by the state in an effort to create a shared understanding of this history so that it can be a bulwark against state repression. Thus Vera presents a detailed indictment of Mugabe, albeit in a highly allusive, poetic style that deemed her "inauthentic" to some readers (Primorac, *Place of Tears* 7).

Two atrocities structure the narrative: the attack by a dissident on two sisters (Thenjiwe and Nonceba) in the rural village of Kezi and the destruction of the same village by the Fifth Brigade. To connect the dots between these two atrocities, Vera suggests, we need to know the background of the dissident, Sibaso, who perpetrates the atrocity against the sisters, and the entanglement in this history of another male character, who stands as the dissident's antithesis, Cephas, an archivist working in Bulawayo. These two men, a destitute traumatized former guerrilla and an urban, educated, idealistic nationalist, share a common preoccupation with the national past, and both idealize woman as an allegory of Zimbabwean nationalism. This common ground gives the reader pause, showing the need to consider the lives of real women and how they figure in the material history of the nation.

But it is not only people's stories that reveal the meaning of the past. The imagination of place is very rich in this novel because place is a repository of historical memory. Bulawayo, Zimbabwe's second city, the "rural enclave" of Kezi (Vera, *Stone* 17), and the caves in the Matopos hills with their prehistoric paintings, places where the guerrillas and now the dissidents find refuge, function as a visual text containing the past. Thus Bulawayo is the place to escape to from the regressive violence of the rural. It is modernity, the future, but it also registers the mixed legacy of colonialism. A colonial city with majestic boulevards, buildings, and plantings, it weds the discipline of the colonial order with a rioting energy that escapes its limits. The jacaranda trees that line the boulevards (and were planted by the British) are bursting through the pavement. Their roots "bulge off the earth where they meet rock, climb over, then plunge under ground" (3). In Vera's detailed mapping of the "colonial city space," we come to see not only the materiality of the city, but the way it shapes identity (Nuttall, "Inside" 188). Just before independence, Africans occupy non-spaces within the segregated city: they congregate on corners, basements, the road to Johannesburg. Their presence is marked less by their bodies than their music, which resonates throughout.

On the other hand, the description of the village of Kezi, lying beyond the end of the road to the big city, gives the impression of neglect, epitomized by the telephone booth without a telephone (Vera, *Stone* 22–23). But there are trees here, too, trees whose roots don't need to "plunge under ground," but spread "large, wide, plastered against the smooth surface, the roots are hard as stone, each is a gleaming gray, peeling firm" (18). The landscape of Matabeleland (the Matopos, in particular), is a highly significant place, a deeply contested symbol of the nation as it evokes both Zimbabwe's spiritual history and its colonial past. The landscape figured prominently in the white settlers' national imaginary as African nature that they brought under their control; Rhodes was buried there (Ranger, *Voices* 11). For the Ndebele, it is the place of burial of their ancestors, dotted with significant shrines. For Zimbabwean nationalists, it is closely identified with Zimbabwe's war history, since its caves were the location of much of this contest.

Through the figure of Cephas, the archivist, Vera tries to link an intimate account of the suffering in Matabeleland to the broader national narrative. Cephas is on a quest to get to know his country. He comes from the east, from Chimanimani, but is working in Bulawayo. He travels to Kezi in order to get to know this part of the country: "Cephas wanted to see Kezi, to see more than Bulawayo, after coming all the way from Chimanimani; he wanted to see the mopani shrubs, the Mtshwankela, the Dololenkonyane, the balancing Matopo hills, the gigantic anthills of Kezi" (41). Cephas is on a pilgrimage, in search of the eternal landscape, evoking this motif of war fiction, which will reveal Zimbabwe to him. His journey in fact links two distinctive landscapes associated with the national—his native Chimanimani and the Matopos—as part of one national imaginary. Chimanimani, on the border with Mozambique, is a significant farming area with a national park. It was settled by white pioneers who came to farm in the 1890s. Before that it had attracted the abaGaza, a Zulu people who fled north from South Africa during the *mfecane* (the scattering) in the first half of the nineteenth century (Godwin 50–51). The novel begins with an idyll, a love affair between Thenjiwe, a woman from Kezi, and Cephas, her chance acquaintance. Between them Vera stages a meeting of different regionalisms, beyond the reader's immediate association of the rural and the city.

Vera suggests a melding of regions through the symbolism of distinctive landscapes, the dry rocky landscape and the deep forest. Thenjiwe and Cephas's lovemaking stands for the making of Zimbabwe as nation as it takes place on the eve of independence. Moreover, Thenjiwe's beauty has an archetypal quality that appears already familiar to Cephas, recognizable: "he remembers this woman as though he has met her before" (Vera, *Stone* 33). The past hangs over this moment in a different way, as well. Thenjiwe and her sister, Nonceba, are orphans, and allusions are made to their family's suffering during the liberation war. Thenjiwe "has a lot to forget" (36).

Past and future collapse into each other as Cephas's observations about Thenjiwe's body allude to Nehanda. His comments turn into a prophecy that inscribes Thenjiwe's future in Zimbabwe's war past. Cephas admires Thenjiwe's bones, an odd preoccupation except in the literature of Zimbabwe, where bones carry nationalist resonance. Thus Cephas unknowingly foreshadows Thenjiwe's death when he describes her bones:

> You are in this bone, and it is my most precious memory. When you move, its motion tells me something intimate about your mind. I am inside you. If you die in my absence and I find that you have already been buried, I will dig your body up to the moonlight, so that I can touch this beautiful bone. Touch it, touch it, touch it, till you are alive. (45)

By telling Thenjiwe that "you are in this bone," Cephas renders Thenjiwe into a manifestation of the national aspiration for a rising Zimbabwe. Like the bones of Nehanda's prophecy, Thenjiwe can inspire life, resurrection, the enduring nation. The "bones shall rise" is made manifest to Cephas in Thenjiwe's body, capturing the meaning of an achieved independence. Cephas's recognition is shaped by his vocation as an archaeologist, and he is unaware that this liberation is only incompletely achieved, the war not over. Susceptible to the optimism of the moment because of his educated, urban background, Cephas is a believer in the promise of independence. Importantly, his interpretation of Thenjiwe's symbolic meaning is resisted by Thenjiwe herself, who remains suspicious of Cephas and refuses to marry him and follow him to Bulawayo.

The passage above gains much greater poignancy after Thenjiwe's violent death, where poignancy once more marks the tragic realization of aspiration blocked. That which independence promised has turned out to be very different. Although Cephas does not act on his intention to dig up Thenjiwe's body, the suggestion lingers provocatively as a material possibility rather than a metaphor for resistance. In the aftermath of atrocity, the evidentiary power of bones indicts. Exhumed remains potentially restore the victims' stories through forensics and, in this sense, the bones rise again to indict the perpetrators (Dawes 198–99).

The reader's perspective on the attack on the two sisters comes from the surviving sister, Nonceba. The story of violence renewed after the peace is deeply disconcerting and shatters the sense of hope associated with liberation. Sibaso is a traumatized veteran who, unable to transition back to civilian life, is portrayed by Vera as the warrior who has become war incarnate, unleashing a compulsive violence that he cannot stop: "If he loses an enemy, he invents another. This is his purge" (Vera, *Stone* 83). He decapitates Thenjiwe, assaults and maims Nonceba. Thinking back on Sibaso's assault, Nonceba is bothered by his lack of hesitation, his determination, what she calls his "obedience" (162). During the attack she recognizes that she cannot hope for "pity" from Sibaso, but speculates whether he might feel "something akin to kindness" and spare her suffering (67). Nonceba has already witnessed Sibaso's decapitation of her sister and wonders if he is capable of pulling back and reflecting on the moment, whether "he, too, may be stunned by his own dramatic presence" (67). What she is looking for is the restraint that we have noted referred to in other novels and that marks the hero, although in most cases the novels (as Vera does here) note the absence of restraint. Nonceba concludes that Sibaso is incapable of "kindness." Vera uses the word "kindness" to stress the identification with another as kin and hence draws attention to Sibaso's lack of a sense of kinship, or civic bond, with Nonceba.[35] Nonceba comes inevitably to the conclusion that in this moment they are not of a kind at all: "He is a predator, with all the fine instincts of annihilation. She, the dead, with all the instincts of the vanquished" (69). After raping Nonceba, Sibaso slashes her mouth and cuts her lips, silencing her.

This spectacular act of violence has two consequences, both of which allow Vera to explore the politics of pity. The Fifth Brigade descends on

Kezi and destroys the village (more on this episode later), and Cephas reads about the attack on the sisters in the newspaper and is spurred to intervene to help Nonceba. Nonceba is at first mistrustful of him and tries to find the right word to describe his intentions, but gets stuck: "Not kindness, perhaps. Something else" (161). Is pity the word she is looking for? Vera does not use the word here. In her interior monologue Nonceba wonders if Cephas's intervention to take her away from a place of the dead, the destroyed Kezi,[36] does not reflect a power analogous to that of armed men who stand on the "faint line between life and death" (162). She processes the encounter with the man who wants to help her by analogy to her encounter with her attacker. In reference to Cephas, she dismisses kindness, the term stressing kinship and identification, and evokes pity instead, the relation of the powerful to the weak. She expects a kind of historical accountability from Cephas, who represents the authority of the city and the educated—the authority of the recognized powers. Although it is not his crime or deed, she hopes Cephas will explain to her why someone would kill her sister, "cut her up like a piece of dry hide without asking himself a single question about his own actions." This echoes her thoughts during her rape, when she wondered whether Sibaso was capable of self-reflection (162). It is Cephas's burden to explain Sibaso. This is a daunting responsibility that reveals Vera's own sense of what the duty of the historian is.

But what is Cephas's sense of obligation toward Nonceba? Is it more than personal, and can it be construed as political? He first learns of the attack as an instance of "distant suffering" that turns out to be personal (Boltanski 3). Although he had not met Nonceba, who was away earning her teacher's certification during the time of his affair with Thenjiwe (another poignant detail of aspiration blocked), he feels compelled to intervene. Risking a "politics of pity," Cephas seeks to overcome the bifurcation of urban and rural Zimbabwe and reach out to the surviving sister. But his offer of help to Nonceba is also an act of atonement, as he feels guilty about Thenjiwe's death, wondering if she would still be alive had he not left. Cephas's sense of guilt is misplaced; Thenjiwe refused to marry him, and he respected her autonomy. Yet this sense of responsibility revives the longing for national wholeness, an idea unraveling violently during the time he was pursuing his archaelogical project on the town founded by King Lobengula. It is the comparative fates of two places within the same nation that shock Cephas.

In an effort similar to what Diop called the "resurrection of the living" necessary in post-genocide Rwanda (181), Cephas returns to Kezi, retrieves the injured Nonceba, and devotes himself to her care. He struggles to name what he is doing in relation to Nonceba. As he removes the bandages from the reconstructive surgery he arranged for her, he wants to bear her pain, relieve her of it: "Closely he searches her eyebrows, her cheeks, her stillness. If there is to be pain, he must be the one to bear it" (183). Cephas wants to be Nonceba's "co-sufferer," but he doubts himself. Arendt distinguishes pity from compassion by suggesting that compassion evokes "co-suffering," that it is particular, occurring between two individuals, and equalizing (Arendt, *On Revolution* 80). She explains compassion thus: "Its strength hinges on the strength of passion itself, which, in contrast to reason, can comprehend only the particular, but has no notion of the general and no capacity for generalization . . . to have compassion with all men in their singularity, that is, without lumping them together in some such entity as one suffering mankind" (80). The private nature of the relationship between Cephas and Nonceba, his individual act of rescue and intense personal involvement, speaks to Arendt's concept of "co-suffering," in intention at least. However, the pain of others, as Scarry has argued, reveals to us the limits of our ability to take on the other's point of view (4). Cephas does not dramatize it as his own poignant narrative of sacrifice: "It is not much to sacrifice love; he does not deserve the term at all. He is not a martyr" (Vera, *Stone* 183). He effaces himself to care for Nonceba, but his act remains individual, its broader political implications unexplored, unless we see these in Vera's insistence on the space for the individual.

Arguably, Cephas has a stake not only in what has happened to the two sisters, but also what has happened to Kezi as a place. This sense of responsibility comes from his prior interest in the village, when he traveled there to get to know his country. Now, however, Cephas's return to the destroyed village to retrieve Nonceba brings into focus the overlapping of Sibaso's crimes and the brutality of the Fifth Brigade. Kezi has been laid to waste by the Fifth Brigade after Sibaso's attack. The violence of the Fifth Brigade bursts to the foreground of the novel as an interruption, and thus the episode reads like a narrative interlude, or separate narrative. The Fifth Brigade targets the heart of the community, the general store, which has become a place for returning guerrillas to congregate and which, as the social and commercial hub of the community, links itself to Bulawayo and places elsewhere. In the novel we see that the persecution of dissidents victimizes the people, while dissidents like Sibaso act with impunity. The village of Kezi, emblematic of rural Zimbabwe, is left a "naked cemetery where no one is buried and everyone is betrayed" (159). The traumatized population is like the walking dead; they stay behind, too fragile psychologically to move on. Thus Nonceba finds herself the victim of a compounding violence from which there is little hope of escape before Cephas reaches her. Kezi, "a place for the trapped" with only "boulders, ruins, burned villages, the dead, a naked sky," must be abandoned if there is any hope to transcend its history (153).

By narrating the violence attributed to the Fifth Brigade, Vera balances the historical record in which dissidents have been blamed disproportionately (Alexander et al 192). She depicts the torture of the storekeeper in great detail, a death that, she tells us, "would not be registered. There would be no memory desired of it" (Vera, *Stone* 133). (In contrast, as I noted, the attack on Thenjiwe and Nonceba by a dissident was reported in the newspapers.) Mahlathini's horrific death is an attack on the most public person in the most public place of the community, the store, and it was meant to terrorize and silence the community. Mahlathini, however, is not silent when his skin is burned, "perforated like lace": "[he] howled like a helpless animal" (134). Afterward no one dares go to the site of the burned-down store to retrieve the bodies; most flee the town, finding it unbearable to confront what happened. Vera's account of torture and death and her attention in particular to the victim's screams produces another instance of the "song of my country," a resistant narrative that pulls torture into the narrative of war and transforms its victim into a voice that speaks to the collective witnessing of this act at some distance or, most likely, indirectly.

How Vera renders visible the suffering of a community through the story of an individual's torture is crucially important to her effort to embed victims' stories in a larger canvas. Mahlathini's torture is experienced by all and destroys the community; everyone bears the trauma. Moreover, Vera's description of the atrocity is intent on attributing moral culpability and echoes Card's terms for the definition of evil, "foreseeable intolerable harms by culpable wrong doing":

> anything that had happened so far had not been random or unplanned. Atrocious, yes, but purposeful. They committed evil as though it were a legitimate pursuit, a ritual for their own convictions. Each move meant to shock, to cure the naive mind. The mind was not supposed to survive it, to retell it, but to perish. (135)

Vera stresses premeditation, the intentional infliction of harm and the embrace of evil as "a legitimate pursuit." She clarifies that atrocity is not mere lack of restraint. Moreover, the atrocity is a colossal betrayal of the people by their government. Thus Mahlathini refused to look in the faces of his attackers: "he avoided encountering, right before his own eyes, that sort of betrayal" (132). The members of the Fifth Brigade remain anonymous and faceless, known only through their actions. They do not have a point of view and are portrayed collectively as evil.

In contrast, Vera's portrayal of the dissident is intimate and individual. She probes his state of mind with care, claiming him as part of her country's war history. Vera introduces the resurgence of conflict in 1981 with an explicit allusion to the Nehanda prophecy, although she signals its misappropriation in a war that is unjustified and shameful, not heroic: "The cease-fire ceases. It begins in the streets, the burying of memory. The bones rising. Rising" (65). Juxtaposing "the burying of memory" and the "bones rising" in this sequence without a conjunction, Vera renders ambiguous how to relate one to the other. If the new violence is a burying of the young memory of independence and peace, then the "bones rising" are a prophecy once again of war without the prospect of liberation this time.

The intricately choreographed episode of Sibaso's attack on the sisters risks being parodic of the earlier intimate scenes in the novel, the lovemaking of Cephas and Thenjiwe, where the emphasis was on a (figurative) fragmenting of Thenjiwe's body.[37] Cephas's desire to capture "the deepest part of her, the most prevailing of her being, beyond death, a fossil before dying [her bones]" acquires violent undertones through its juxtaposition with Sibaso's actions (37). Both men are literalists of sorts and make the Nehanda prophecy seem confining, oppressive.

Sibaso, like Cephas, is inspired by Zimbabwe's past. He is sentimentally attached to his copy of *Feso*, which he retrieves after the war from his family's former home in the city, now occupied by others. It is ancient history, however, that speaks to him more immediately. He knows the landscape of the Matopos from experience, having hidden in its caves during the Second Chimurenga just like the fighters from 1896. Even though he has a traumatic memory of being in a bombed-out cave amidst the dead during the war, he returns there as a dissident. No longer feeling constrained by tradition now that he is alone, he trespasses, entering a cave that is considered off-limits, sacred. There he sees prehistoric paintings, and one in particular captures his attention. It depicts women dancing in a circle at the funeral of a king, and Sibaso wonders whether it depicts the sacrifice of the maidens or their suicide (103–4).[38] Because the image is not well preserved, the women appear fragmented, their heads floating above their bodies, their feet missing (104). Sibaso tries to hold one of the images by placing his hand on the woman's hip and, in language that alludes both to Cephas's obsession with Thenjiwe's hip and to the association between wind and Nehanda's prophecy, he reflects, "I place my hand over the waist of the tall woman, on an inch of bone, yet forty thousand years gather in my memory like a wild wind" (104). The reader, therefore, recognizes that Sibaso's attack on the sisters acts out this ancient painted scene.

Sibaso's efforts are not spontaneous, but a thought-out attempt to insert himself in the heroic narrative of the king's funeral. At his funeral the king receives the sacrifice of young life. War has exacted sacrifices from Sibaso, as well. Can he similarly demand the sacrifice of others, therefore, in a ritual honoring himself? His delusion renders him into a figure analogous to the king and perversely attempts to complete the imperfectly achieved struggle of a failed quest for the people's restitution.

Sibaso's struggle to reclaim a historical identity begins with the reclamation of his proper name and his rejection of the war names he had adopted:

> My name is Sibaso. I have crossed many rivers with that name no longer on my lips, forgotten. It is an easy task to forget a name. Other names are assumed, temporary like grief; in a war, you discard names like old resemblances. . . . During a war it is better to borrow a name, to lend an impulse to history. (82)

The crossing of rivers is a traditional reference to encounters with death (Ranger, *Revolt* 18). As a guerrilla Sibaso discarded his name and all the ties to community that a name implies. However, reclaiming his name is not an attempt to return to civilian life. He takes his real name and reenters the forest, coming in on his own, no longer fighting war *for a cause*, but for himself: "I want to risk my mind, to be implicated in my own actions, having taken a personal resolve against personal harm" (Vera, *Stone* 141). This is a defensive measure ("against personal harm") responding to extreme insecurity, but its no-holds-barred attitude turns Sibaso into a rogue menace.[39]

By returning to the caves, Sibaso must also confront his own war trauma, however, and in particular an atrocity that haunts him: "I buried him in water, inside the cave. He could not survive. I placed a rock above him and he lay still" (142). Unable to cope with this memory, Sibaso reinvents himself as war incarnate: "I endure the war anew. I am an instrument of war. I lose all sight of pity for myself" (141). This loss of self and its transformation into an "instrument of war" instantiates the motif of the male warrior as war personified. Nowhere except in Vera do we see this as part of a psychological justification of a character, evidence of the acting out of trauma. Nonceba wondered how Sibaso could act with no moral restraint, with no ability to see his own actions. He can because they are not his, but war's. Having no "pity" for himself, he can risk everything, or "endure," as he says, in a special state called war. By calling himself an "instrument of war" he acknowledges precisely what Nonceba accuses him of. Moreover, when Sibaso slices Nonceba's mouth so that she "cannot call out his name" (110), he preempts her from identifying him. He is not afraid of being found out; rather, he does not want her to name him and make a claim on him. A claim on him as "Sibaso" would render him into an individual with responsibility for his actions. He would no longer be an "instrument of war" without a self, and thus would be risking what he called his "personal resolve against personal harm."

Vera's female characters are more resistant to national mythologies and to the historical narratives that seem to justify them. Thenjiwe mistrusts the identity that Cephas wants to impose on her. She resists turning into a national allegory. Nonceba asserts her autonomy and her desire for a future she will shape, not one Cephas might choose for her. Vera does not give in to clichés about romantic plots, nor does she offer us an allegory of the family. Cephas's romantic intentions toward each of the sisters are frustrated. Such plots seem spent.

Yet Cephas remains engaged by history, and this seems appropriate to Vera. He takes up again his archaeological project after Nonceba is healed, because a "new nation needs to restore its past" (184). He is building a model of a pre-colonial village by recreating the traditional "beehive hut," work that Vera characterizes as "deliverance," the novel's last word (184). Cephas's project aims at the reinvention of the rural and its reincorporation into the national identity. Cephas's caring for Nonceba's wounds recalls J. M. Coetzee's Magistrate in *Waiting for the Barbarians* who searchingly explores the blind girl's scars in order to uncover a history of torture she refuses to disclose. Cephas pulls back when he becomes aware of the danger of becoming "too involved in replicating histories" that might end up trapping Nonceba (184). The Magistrate is not as successful in this regard, but, like Vera's Cephas, he turns to archaeology to find an alternative relation to the past. The magistrate excavates an ancient site outside the borders of the garrison where he has found hieroglyphics. He tries to translate these, an arduous task that requires a lot of historical imagination. The hope is to reinvent life on the frontier according to its ancient ways and thus circumvent the history of empire, which has turned this into a place of horror and violence. Adichie picks up on this theme with Richard in *Half of Yellow Sun*, as I show in Chapter 4. The archeological interest in the pre-colonial is Richard's way of creating a new identity for himself outside his complicity with empire as an Englishman. But the project remains unfinished and transforms instead into the people's history, handed down to Ugwu, an exceptional figure that Adichie chooses to represent the rural poor.

Conclusion

I began this chapter by bringing into question the figure of the hero and ended with an analysis of a male character that could represent a different type of hero. Cephas exercises restraint in his relationships with both Thenjiwe and Nonceba in *The Stone Virgins*, respecting these women's autonomy in situations where he could have asserted the authority of his urban identity and masculinity. In both instances he respects the limits the women place on his relationship with them. From the outset of my analysis of the Zimbabwean novels, heroism and restraint have been intertwined. In *The Contact*, a novel that answers back to the Rhodesian discourse that demonized the guerrillas, restraint is what shows them as idealized figures. In *Pawns* the public and private perceptions are split. Fangs, a veteran, was a hero during the war for killing unrestrainedly, yet in one instance he registers the humanity of his victim and hesitates, allowing for a glimpse of his private sense of restraint, which, once violated, brings him remorse and shame after the war. Cephas's restraint is contrasted to Sibaso's uninhibited violence, which is "justified" aesthetically (although not morally) by Vera's engaged account of his history as a traumatized combatant (Mda, "Justify" 42). Moreover, Cephas's restraint remains a matter of private conscience, and it is unclear from the novel how it can be realized as a broader principle of social conduct.

When the figure of the hero is tarnished in these novels, he comes through as an individual, not a type, and acquires the fuller dimensions of a fictional character. Such characters make it possible, perhaps paradoxically, since they are more individualized, to imagine new collective identities that are truer to historical experience instead of the idealized identities of nationalist history. Because the novels I examined in this chapter are intensely focused on revising and rendering more capacious and complex the narratives of Zimbabwe's past, taking into account as fully as possible the lived historical experience of its people, they constitute good examples of what I have been calling an introverted literature—this despite the fact that, for the most part, my examples are drawn from canonical texts and internationally acclaimed authors such as Hove, Chinodya, and Vera. If the hero is a figure that answers back to the denigrations of colonial attitudes, then it makes sense that the dissatisfaction with this figure would stem from an impulse to address other Zimbabweans about a shared historical memory, as in Evan Maina Mwangi's paradigm of Africa writing "back to self." Moreover, although I address only novels written in English, other scholars have drawn attention to the extensive Shona and Ndebele language literatures of Zimbabwe and the synergy among the three literatures that provides for a rich intertextuality. Furthermore, Zimbabwe had, especially before the last decade, a strong publishing industry and a sizeable urban readership. The Zimbabwean International Book Fair successfully showcased African publishers and cultivated African readerships, giving special prominence to Zimbabwean writers (Larson 97).

In the war novels of Zimbabwe we find a persistent questioning of the official constructions of history and a desire to find new narratives. At the end of *Harvest of Thorns* Benjamin tells his brother-in-law, "When you are trying to piece together the broken fragments of your life it hurts to think back" (Chinodya, *Harvest* 243). Recollection is not merely putting events in order, coming up with a sequence that can stand for a whole; it is also thinking and feeling. The association here among memory, reason, and feeling sheds light in very simple terms on the difficulties of remembering war, especially atrocity in war. The motifs of the "song of my country," the "ordeal in the forest," and the "male warrior as war personified" help draw our attention to this effort to find new ways to tell the experience of war. Thus Nehanda is reinvented as a fictional character whose death by hanging is cast as the nationalist "song of my country," not by deflecting her physical suffering, but by exploring how it is possible that her death could be written out of the popular memory. In *Echoing Silences* Munashe's "ordeal in the forest" before he commits his atrocity severs him from the civilian life without hardening him into a combatant. It creates a kind of liminality that allows for a new perspective on the combatant's experience. In what follows I turn to novels published since 2000 where the motifs are one element among others that indicate how these novels build on the war novel as a distinct tradition in African fiction.

CHAPTER 4

Contesting the New Authenticity: Contemporary War Fiction in Africa

The claim that the war novel presents us with an introverted genre might seem surprising to readers of recent African fiction. Since approximately the mid-1990s there has been an explosion of African war fiction published by both established and emergent writers, many of whom live and write in the West.[1] In addition to fiction, there has been a proliferation of memoirs of war (including former child soldier Ishmael Beah's bestselling *A Long Way Gone*, 2007 and Nega Mezlekia's *Notes from the Hyena's Belly: An Ethiopian Boyhood*, 2001) and fiction about war in Africa written by authors from outside Africa who assume the perspective of Africans (for example, Dave Eggers's *What Is the What*, 2007, and Gil Courtemanche's *A Sunday at the Pool in Kigali*, 2003).

Arguably, war has emerged problematically as the new authenticity out of Africa, and much of it contributes to a phenomenon that works at cross-purposes with the material I recover in the main body of this study because it addresses an international audience shaped by a humanitarian ethos that sees Africa through the lens of "distant suffering." Although the seeds for this new writing can be found in key texts from the earlier period, the newer literature reflects the opening of a literary market for African writers in what critics have identified as "an emerging global subgenre" of human rights fiction (Dawes 190) at a time when publishing in Africa has declined, economic conditions for writers have become extremely difficult, and African universities are also in crisis (Larson 147).

All the same, this newer literature includes several important works that extend the genre that I discuss in this study. The literary history that I recover enables us to see both how the war novel interrupts the monolithic impression of the canonical "extroverted" African novel and how it constitutes the antecedent for the newer literature about war, marketed once again extrovertly and riding a wave of interest in human rights narratives. This chapter foregrounds the ways in which the texts by Adichie and Farah intervene and disrupt the renewed interest in Africa as "heart of darkness" while they engage with key arguments of human rights discourse. The child-soldier fictions of Emmanuel Dongala, Ahmadou Kourouma, Chris Abani, and Uzodinma Iweala provide a counterpoint to the novels of Adichie and Farah, but both bodies of work draw from the war fiction that came before, although they (especially the child-soldier novels) are often read as if they represent a new literary phenomenon with no antecedent.

Elsewhere I have drawn attention to the problem of arrested historicization in child-soldier fiction, which exhibits a lesser engagement with history than the war novels from the colonial and immediate postcolonial periods because of the way the human rights frame is applied to the child-soldier identity and shapes his story through the genre of the recovery narrative (Coundouriotis, "Child Soldier Narrative" 192). The recovery narrative individualizes the child soldier and shifts attention away from social and political conditions that brought on his circumstances in the first place. Kourouma's *Allah n'est pas obligé* (2000) is an exception. The irreverent Birahima speaks mockingly as an expert witness but engages directly with the difficulties of constructing a historically accurate account that attributes the war's excesses to political decisions and actors. Moreover, his obsessive parsing of words such as "humanitarian peacekeeping," "ethics," and "decency" destabilizes the genre (Kourouma 126–27). The ending of the novel surprises the reader by revealing its circularity and frustrating the expectations of a linear narrative. Birahima's account concludes where he begins; the text at the end is identical to the beginning and launches the narrative again. This circularity subverts the structure of the recovery narrative, which attempts to set the interrupted story of education typical of the young combatants throughout the literature (such as Njoroge, Mene, and Benjamin) back on track.[2] Moreover, it evokes Charles Mangua's *A Tail in the Mouth* and its pun, which equates the account of war with the tale in the mouth.

The frame of the interrupted novel of education is also highlighted in Dongala's *Johnny chien méchant* (2002), although here it is potentially renewed at the end as a promise for the future of Laokolé's adopted child. The interrupted education is a significant marker of poverty in the contemporary novels, and although education has been the focus of much anxiety over the colonization of identity, it is clear in these novels that the absence of education is devastating. What links Dongala's two sixteen-year-old antagonists (the vicious Johnny and the innocent Laokolé) to each other is their shared experience of poverty, not only in individual but also in national terms. They are children born into the precarious economy of an underdeveloped nation. Laokolé's interest in and talent for science, moreover, make the point that the education missed is not only the education in the colonizer's culture, but the scientific education. Johnny's most cherished possessions are the books he collects as war booty, an eccentric choice in his circumstances, but one that hints at the potential for his reform, a possibility never actualized.[3]

In the novel's climactic confrontation when Johnny and Laokolé finally meet, Johnny tries to deny to Laokolé that he is a murderer by calling himself an intellectual and showing her his books. Laokolé flings a Bible at him and stuns him enough to gain the advantage in their fight and eventually kill him.[4] The heavy-handed symbolism in this confrontation of good versus evil is perhaps less stable than it first appears. While arguably Johnny gets punished by a higher power (the Bible), it is also possible to see the Bible, turned into a weapon of opportunity, as emptied of all its content, its moral and cultural authority debunked. It, too, does violence in the war. By flinging a Bible, which is the only heavy object she can find, Laokolé is hence freed from the moralizing authority of the colonial culture's Christianity, which would expect her to remain nonviolent or even to turn the other cheek.

Laokolé's capacity to act decisively in her own defense and surprise us by effectively eliminating the unrestrained, fearsome Johnny is brought forth by her passage through an "ordeal in the forest." Dongala's particularly vivid evocation of this motif reveals the ways in which his novel sits between the war novel and the child-soldier narrative. By doubling his narrative (good girl/bad boy), evoking the humanitarians in a bad light and depicting naturalistically how the body breaks up under the violence of war, Dongala creates a dialogue between the older and the newer literature.[5] When Laokolé enters the forest she loses her fears and inhibitions, eager to escape the immediate dangers of the war: "I was no longer thinking of the snake that could bite me, of the scorpion that could sting me with its poisonous tail, of the gorilla I might encounter" (Dongala [2006]: 272). Soon, however, she is overwhelmed by the enormity of the rain forest and the force of nature. During a thunderstorm she imagines herself at the beginning of time:

> I felt as if I had been transported back to the primeval age when the planet was being formed, millions of years before paltry *Homo sapiens* appeared on the scene—the age in which thunder and lightning, water and clay, nitrogen and oxygen all tumbled around in the primordial soup. . . . I saw myself as small, insignificant, no bigger than a flea, a speck of atomic dust whose disappearance wouldn't alter the total mass of the universe by even a single femtogram. (274)

"As if" a witness to creation and in a time outside history, Laokolé comes to a new sensibility of what it means to be human in the cosmos. Before leaving the forest she must fight a pig, "roll[ing] around in the muck," in order to get to some bananas and eat. The experience is demeaning: "I staggered to my feet, winded, furious, and ashamed" (277); however, she prevails over the pig, just as she will over Johnny. Laokolé's "ordeal in the forest" enables her to shed the restraints on her identity that made her obedient. Although her experience in the forest might seem regressive, juxtaposed to the violence of the war, it is not savagery but survival, basic to all humans, and different from the fundamentally purposeless violence of the war. Moreover, Dongala's evocation of the thunderstorm in the forest provides us with a view of an imposing and unchanging landscape that works like another of the motifs of the war novel, the eternal landscape. It is precisely the ambiguous status of this landscape as pure nature and/or national symbol that functions restoratively to open up a new vista in the bounded and claustrophobic space of war. Dongola's Republic of Congo is renowned for its rain forests, as is of course the neighboring Democratic Republic of Congo. This is a transcendent landscape that appeals to a larger sense of our human belonging on earth, much like Diop's evocation of Rwanda's hills does.

Kourouma's and Dongala's texts deliberately challenge the contours of the child-soldier narrative as it has been shaped by the interaction of international organizations and NGOs with real-life child soldiers. Kourouma and Dongala take what is already a discourse formed by the effort to try to explain African realities to the outside world and attempt to turn that discourse inward by engaging with a tradition of writing about war shaped in Africa. The literary tradition is the platform for the self-critical introversion. Whereas undoubtedly these texts are published with international audiences in mind, they have significant potential to engage readers in Africa, as both authors' previous works are seminal critiques of the nation.

So far I have sought to delineate instances of people's history of the war that do not overlap with the nation states' histories because of the bifurcation of the postcolonial state as described by Mamdani. This focus exposed the need for developing a more nuanced discussion of class in the analysis of African fiction. Discontent with the humanitarian discourse about Africa and the ways in which it focuses on the continent's most vulnerable populations has created a renewed desire by novelists to engage with the problem of representing the people, and specifically the people's interface with the political structures that leave them so vulnerable. In a circuitous way at least for some authors, the genesis of their introverted works in the 2000s is facilitated by their location outside Africa, in the diaspora of African intellectuals, and by their exposure not only to the production of the humanitarian discourse about Africa but also its reception. I am not only alluding to Farah's explicit acknowledgment of his own position as an exile who writes to keep his nation alive, but to something different, a new effort to write back to the humanitarian and human rights responses to Africa. This writing back is seen, however, as an intermediate step to be overcome or made obsolete when the national political discourse is restored through democratic reform that will bring the people more fully into the nation. Thus these texts evoke the people's history in order to propel such democratization.

As I turn my attention to Adichie and Farah in what follows, it will become clear that national history is in contention. The two authors share a number of key preoccupations for my study. Both Adichie and Farah respond explicitly in their novels to the work of journalists who reported on the Biafra war and Somalia's two-decades'-long civil war. They reflect on the relationship between reportage and historical retrospectives, problematizing all along the contours of historical fiction. Their range of reference is also marked by a keen awareness of a national literature and the African novel more broadly, thus performing the paradigm of Africa writing back to self. Moreover, both authors' experiments with the genre of the domestic novel (Farah does this in *Knots*, the middle novel of his trilogy, *Past Imperfect*) allude once again to national allegory. Distinguishing their approach to that of previous writers, they resist explicitly the naturalistic aesthetic. The reasons for this are complicated, as I will try to show, and stem in part from their deployment of a different notion of resistance than the pure negativity that Lazarus identified with African naturalism. Moreover, folded within their larger canvases are stories of child soldiers, which they situate within the more expansive narratives of family and community. Adichie and Farah may seem strange bedfellows, and what follows is not so much a comparative reading as a detailed engagement, taking each author in turn, with the most significant contemporary writers on war.

The Domestic Novel as War Novel

Half of a Yellow Sun is a novel that reinvents the genre of domestic fiction by using it to tell the story of war. My discussion of Adichie's novel could have just as easily been placed at the end of Chapter 2 as the capstone of the analysis of the novels of the Nigerian Civil War. But this is also very much a novel of the new wave of historical novels and novels of war appearing in the twenty-first century, and discussing it in this chapter helps foreground the ways in which it breaks up the monolithic impression that all novels of African war are child-soldier narratives.

The child soldier's story is embedded in the history of Odenigbo's and Olanna's educated middle-class family through the figure of their servant Ugwu. Unlike Adichie's first novel (*Purple Hibiscus*, also a domestic fiction), *Half of a Yellow Sun* does not look to the feminist African *Bildungsroman* as a model.[6] Instead, Adichie extends the tradition of the narratives of woman's war in Nwapa and Emecheta, her female predecessors among the novelists of Biafra. She also looks to the extended tradition of Igbo writers on the war and to the journalists who reported on it, many of whom she cites at the end of her novel.

Following in Emecheta's footsteps, Adichie's project is the feminization of the war novel, but also its domestication, by which I mean its submission to the moral and political authority of women's points of view—women whom the novel imagines in relation to their familial identities (as mothers, daughters, wives). The political implications of domestic fiction as genre, the claim that it strengthens women's political identity by demonstrating how they reform men, has been central to revisionist approaches to the genre (Nancy Armstrong, *Desire* 251). Thus Adichie writes outside the paradigm of the war novel. In her novel we no longer find the four motifs or the naturalistic aesthetic. On the other hand, Adichie insists on the centrality of the people's history, although with mixed results, as I will show.

Adichie braids the domestic novel together with the story of the peasant boy turned servant, then child soldier, and finally (and most surprisingly) historian of the people. She shows that the two cannot be disentangled, gesturing, therefore, to the allegorical meaning of home as nation, even though in her work home is never devoid of its particularity, is always rich in realist detail, and is anchored firmly in the novel's mainstream storytelling practices. The home does not transmute into a symbol of the nation. Rather the nation folds into the home and is brought into the fold of the home's richly imagined relations to be legitimated. Thus Adichie powerfully reconfigures the people's history, although ultimately her project is not without some troubling implications, especially as it pertains to her delineation of Ugwu's identity.

The multiple strands of Adichie's plot create several pairings with rich symbolic import. The novel is not only the story of Odenigbo and Olanna's household, but, stepping back one generation, it compares this household to Chief Ozobia's home (the father of Olanna and Kainene). Thus the novel follows the fate of two generations as the war progresses. It also follows two sisters with contrasting temperaments, one toward the domestic and the other toward greater autonomy, and the romantic relationship of each. The novel, furthermore, introduces an English character, Richard, who becomes Kainene's lover, as a key point of view and as a counterpoint to Odenigbo. Both men are intellectuals and attracted to strong, independent women. But between them they traverse the divide of colonialism and attempt to override it, ultimately with little success. A third man, Madu, competes with them, but he is not an intellectual. He is a military man, reminding the reader of the crisis of masculinity that the war posits. Another pairing in the novel sets Olanna and Kainene's family, which is urban and politically influential, against Odenigbo's, which is provincial and has closer ties to the peasantry. Finally Ugwu, the servant, is paired with Odenigbo, his master, but also with the Englishman, Richard, who is for a while his surrogate master. Both men are also Ugwu's tutors. Furthermore, Odenigbo and Ugwu are both guilty of rape, a link that spells out their bond as men in a patriarchical culture and highlights war as a crisis in the ethics of masculine identity (Cooper 143).

These intricate pairings, which shift as if in a dance and invite the reader constantly to rethink the relation of the parts to the whole, illuminate the "links" that tie people together through shared stories and memories. I am purposefully using Farah's term "links" to draw an analogy between the two novelists. The multiple ways in which the reader can relate characters to each other (staged almost like a drama in a series of conversations in

Links) speak not only to the ties that bind, but to the importance of narration in making these ties conscious and in working against the destructive force of war.

Adichie is interested in portraying ordinary lives in time of war: the quotidian existence of relationships, domestic life, and career ambitions. War is not a total environment that includes everything in its determinism, but a complication superimposed on normal life, engulfing the family incrementally and with increasing crescendo, but against which the ordinary continually reasserts itself (Adichie, "African 'Authenticity'" 53). In an interview Adichie complained that the earlier novels of the Nigerian civil war were more "interested in the larger and grander narratives than in the small things that make up day-to-day life," implying that the literature lacks a certain intimacy in its treatment of the war. In contrast, she wants "the reader to feel what Biafra was like for ordinary middle-class men and women" (Adichie, "Brief" 5).

The domesticity of Odenigbo and Olanna's middle-class home survives the war in the sense that the family stays together despite the stresses of the war. However, the home itself, both as a structure and as an environment affording a certain type of lifestyle, is destroyed. Odenigbo's living room, his intellectual salon, as well as his library and research, are all casualties of the war. At the beginning of the novel the values of open debate and critique associated with the ethos of "sincerity" flourish in this home.[7] This setting illustrates in a microcosm the ideals of a tolerant, open, and democratic society, whereas outside the home, the nation, whether it be Biafra or Nigeria, is undemocratic and violent and does not come anywhere close to being a convincing double for this home. It is necessary to find some process that will make it possible to generalize from Odenigbo's home to society at large, to spread the values of open exchange, gender equality, tolerance of ethnic difference, and a democratic nationalism that we find in the home to the broader social reality. This process is the education of the peasant, Ugwu, and by extension the people. However, Adichie also seems to project the people's history beyond the end of the novel, when Ugwu will complete his book. In the novel she gives us instead a more partial history of the war that foregrounds the family itself (and Ugwu's story living among this family) as the domestic fiction of the war. The domestic fiction privileges the private life, the plot's narratives of desire and sexual relations, conventionally viewed as occupying a sphere apart from politics but given political implications as elements of domestic fiction.

One possible critique of Adichie is that her "middle-class men and women" are clearly a few cuts above middle class. The sisters, Olanna and

Kainene, are daughters of a wealthy Igbo businessman, Chief Ozobia. They move in the upper circles of society, and the opportunities they have are out of reach for most middle-class Nigerians in the 1960s or today. The family is clearly part of the postcolonial elite. Moreover, by making the character of the father a chief, Adichie is identifying him explicitly with the remnants of the colonial political structure.[8] Indeed, Adichie locates Olanna and Kainene within the kind of privilege whose hold onto power is regressive. But the daughters are rebels. Olanna chooses her "revolutionary lover," an academic and a Biafran nationalist, and lives within his means, bringing her closer to the middle-class stereotype, although her freedom is still predicated on her elite background. This is even truer of Kainene. Kainene behaves like a son, following in the family business and holding her own professionally. She is sexually liberated and exercises autonomy in her relationships with men.

Thus Adichie blunts some of the regressive political implications of Chief Ozobia's identity by giving him daughters and no sons.[9] Western-educated daughters occupy a unique social position in the immediate postcolonial period, just as Emecheta illustrated in her fiction before Adichie. Their privilege can be deployed toward progressive ends, as their education enables them to take the lead in a revolution of gender identities with broad implications for the reform of society.

The changed parameters of Adichie's deployment of domestic fiction are apparent in her treatment of rape. In one of its two instances in the novel, rape ironically turns the household into a family. Born of violence, this family is an avatar of the nation that will be stitched back together after the civil war. Rape also brings the people into the fold of the family, although the problem of the inconsequential peasant woman remains. Dissatisfied with her son's choice to live with the apparently barren Olanna, Odenigbo's mother brings a peasant from their village and thrusts her at her son. Odenigbo falls for the sexual trap, and, ignoring the woman's unresponsiveness, he rapes her. Olanna, grieving her own barrenness, decides to raise Baby, the child of the rape, and assumes some of the responsibility to atone for Odenigbo's crime, which she perceives not only as a gender crime but also as a class crime. This development in the plot sets the tone for the new parameters of the domestic fiction, with an empowered woman as the moral arbiter who keeps the common-law marriage together because it enables her to get something out of it.[10] The family we end up with bears the marks of both the traditional failings of the African man (with the abuses of polygamy in the background) and the strong corrective action of the woman, who, as a classic domestic woman, uses her power to create and define the family.[11] All of this happens under the shadow of the inconsequential woman, the victim of rape.

Individuated through desire, Olanna and Kainene can be said to have a middle-class ethos in conformity with the genre of domestic fiction that they inhabit. The domestic here, even when under extreme stress, holds onto the wholeness of family, keeping at bay the "unhomely" dissolution of the boundary between home and world (Bhabha). The main household of Olanna, Odenigbo, Baby, and Ugwu survives the war, proving the resiliency of the private sphere, despite the disorder of the political.

The second instance of rape belongs to the child-soldier narrative. Ugwu, the servant, is abducted and forcibly inducted into the war. His unwilling participation in a gang rape has traumatized him and put him in a similar position as characters from the earlier novels that are haunted by a particular atrocity. Taunted into joining the assault on a young peasant woman by the other men's mockery of his manhood ("aren't you a man?" [Adichie, *Half* 365]), Ugwu participates in the rape, but is deeply affected by his victim, who stared back at him with "dead hate" (397). Later, when he is planning his history, he takes Frederick Douglass's "sad and angry" book as an inspiration for his own writing and associates "sad and angry" with his victim's gaze, vowing to "atone for what he had done" by writing this history (397).

The history's genesis and, more significantly, Ugwu's discovery of his vocation as people's historian, is not only a part of the novel's plot but is reflected in its structure. There we find inserted an outline of the people's history in eight numbered sections interspersed throughout the novel, representing a "book within a book," entitled "The Book: The World Was Silent When We Died." Seeking to place Adichie within the tradition of the Nigerian novel, Susan Z. Andrade links this "conceit of a book within a book" to the ironic ending of *Things Fall Apart*, where the District Commissioner's text describing the suicide of Okonkwo is alluded to as an alternative to the novel's account, capturing ironically the inadequacy of the colonial perspective (Andrade, "Adichie's Genealogies" 92). In Adichie's novel this "book within a book" is also ironic, because the reader assumes until the end that the text is written by Richard, the Englishman, when its author turns out to be Ugwu.

Adichie has said that her novel is anchored in three points of view, those of "a university instructor (Olanna), her houseboy, and an Englishman" (Adichie, "Brief" 5). The Englishman, Richard, is ostensibly the historian in the novel, a character similar to Vera's Cephas. Richard comes to Nigeria before the war to research and write about ancient Igbo pottery. Plagued by doubts about what kind of book he should write, he makes several false starts, including trying to write a "speculative novel where the main character is an archaeologist digging for bronzes who is then transported to an idyllic past" (Adichie, *Half* 72). The present takes over, however, and any contemplation of such an "idyllic past" seems like a holdover of a passé attitude where the European is the discoverer of Africa.

Richard comes to self-identify as a Biafran, showing that one can become Biafran and that the identity is not based on ethnicity, but on a shared identification with a particular place and experience. Aware that he is becoming part of history, part of the creation of a new nation and society, Richard makes his commitment:

> It was not only because secession was just, considering all the Igbo had endured, but because of the possibility Biafra held for him. He would be Biafran in a way he could never have been Nigerian—he was there at the beginning; he had shared in the birth. He would belong. (168)

Willing this identity does not necessarily make it real, and Richard is repeatedly reminded that he does not count as Biafran. Madu, Kainene's former lover, urges him to write for the "Propaganda Directorate": "They will take what you write more seriously because you are white. Look, the truth is that this is not your war" (305). Madu urges Richard to be a moral witness, a role more fitting to an outsider: "If you really want to contribute, this is the way that you can. The world has to know the truth of what is happening, because they simply cannot remain silent while we die" (305). Richard is haunted by Madu's phrase ("they simply cannot remain silent while we die"), and, in fear of being among those who remain silent, he begins to write for the Biafran government. This he does to acclaim, putting emphasis on the cultural achievements of the Igbo and portraying them against the stereotype of anonymous, starving masses or spectral humans in the war.[12] Drawn in to contribute to the ideological work of the Biafran regime, Richard finds that "he felt a part of things."

But this conviction fades by the end of the war. Richard reads Ugwu's first attempt at writing, his record of Olanna's testimony of her flight from the north and, impressed with Ugwu's writing, admits that "the war isn't my story to tell, really." Ugwu nods in agreement: "he [Ugwu] had never thought that it was" (425). Thus Richard cedes the role of historian of the war to Ugwu, and Ugwu makes a strong claim of this role for himself and his people. This change brings crashing down the dream of an inclusive, non-essentialist, Biafran nationalism in which one could become African. Such an ideal now appears as a casualty of Biafra's collapse, but perhaps one that, Adichie suggests, we can accept if the tradeoff is the celebration of the peasant turned people's historian, an inclusion with much larger implications for the democratic future of Nigeria.

When we learn that Ugwu is the author of the "book within a book," we are caught in having made the wrong assumption about historiographic authority. In the novel's opening scene, Ugwu is an illiterate peasant boy, but, by the novel's end, he has supplanted Richard as the designated historian.[13] Following Adichie's habit of fleshing out her characters by analogy to each other, she depicts Ugwu's struggles to find his writing voice just as she did with Richard. Ugwu first intends to write the "Narrative of the Life of a Country" (424), a title inspired by Frederick Douglass's autobiography, which Ugwu reads while he is fighting in the war. This title signals that he is writing a national history. He revises his title, however, borrowing from Richard, and writes "The World Was Silent When We Died." The change of title also substitutes "world" for "country" in Ugwu's first title. The project thus no longer has an introverted focus, and it acquires the intimations of an unsettled worldliness. The world it refers to has betrayed the people by not intervening effectively to stop the famine. "We" and "world" are opposed, and the "country" of Ugwu's original title stands in relation to the world and not as a context of its own.

Until Ugwu is conscripted to fight, he has experienced history vicariously through his master's family. Although he does not choose freely to be a soldier, fighting in the war is a circumstance that sets him on the historical stage, where he must come to terms with his own agency. The history he plans to write, however, does not suggest that it will contain much self-disclosure. What we see is a sketch or outline that, for readers familiar with the historiography of the war, rehearses received truths about Nigeria's colonial and postcolonial history, a history Ugwu learned by reading his master's books and listening to the conversations in his master's intellectual salon. "The Book" begins with a scene of the returnees from the pogroms, but then goes back in time to give a history of colonialism, ethnic division, decolonization, political instability in the postcolonial period, and finally the genesis of Biafra. Thus the outline is a sketch for one of the "larger and grander narratives" that Adichie complains about and that she intentionally sought to revise with her novelistic account (Adichie, "Brief" 5). The war takes up two chapters of Ugwu's text and is observed from a distance: "He writes about starvation. Starvation was a Nigerian weapon of war. Starvation broke Biafra and brought Biafra fame and made Biafra last as long as it did" (Adichie, *Half* 237). He uses the title of the book: "He writes about the world that remained silent while Biafrans died. He argues that Britain inspired this silence. The arms and advice that Britain gave Nigeria shaped other countries" (258). Ugwu accuses the British and other nations of not intervening to help the starving and of arming Nigeria to continue the war. This is the thesis of Dan Jacobs's widely read book on the war, *The Brutality of Nations*.

The derivative nature of Ugwu's book sits uncomfortably with the claim that the people's history posits a distinct point of view. The sketch of Ugwu's book provided in the novel glosses much of the existing historiography of the war, which Adichie, furthermore, cites in the bibliography at the end of the novel. In contrast, Adichie's domestic fiction makes a different historiographic point, seeking to give a sympathetic account of the Igbo intellectuals' support for Biafra and their commitment to this nationalist dream. She wants to answer the question of how it is possible that they endorsed what turned out to be a catastrophic political agenda.

Ugwu is located at the juncture of multiple influences, each powerfully symbolic. A member of the peasantry, he represents the people. Educated under Odenigbo's guidance, Ugwu is shaped by the Westernized intellectual class of Nigerians who were the product of colonialism's modernizing cultural policies. His model of authorship is Richard, a white European, who cedes his own epistemic authority as an Africanist scholar to Ugwu. Moreover, Ugwu is a rapporteur who has his own experience as a child soldier to draw on.

However, Ugwu's identity as a servant, which he never seems to outgrow, troubles Adichie's vision of a people's history.[14] The novel's closing line is a quotation of the dedication in Ugwu's book: "*For Master, my good man.*" Read through the lens afforded by this sentiment, the novel's class politics become clearer. The phrase expresses a servant's gratitude and enduring devotion to his master, even as it acknowledges a change in the relation between master and servant. The servant, now an author of a people's history of the war, addresses the master in the terms the master formerly addressed him. Throughout the novel, Odenigbo addressed Ugwu as "My good man," an affectionate gesture to the boy servant he helped raise and whom he refused to call "boy." Ugwu, who accepts the paternalistic logic of this benign master-servant relation throughout the novel, recognizes the debt owed to his master and pledges his sincere and enduring allegiance, even after he has acquired the status to address his master as his "good man."

In this closing line of the novel Adichie packs all her nostalgia, a form of mourning for the lost promise of the early postcolonial period and an expression of fear that its corrosive politics have destroyed much of civil society. At the end of the novel, gone is the university, the poets, the intellectual milieu of Odenigbo's home. But this nostalgia is also intended to rekindle the desire to reinvent in the present the cultural life of such a broad, literate, and modernized middle class. Contemporary Nigeria, in other words, has a usable past to evoke. Ugwu is the custodian of this legacy, the holder of its memory, and his education in Odenigbo's household holds the promise for a more democratic realization of an enlightened, intellectual middle class.

All the same, "*For Master, my good man*" is jarring in its insistence on Ugwu's continued subordination to his "Master." Ugwu's "sincerity" lacks the appropriate capacity for critique. Perhaps this is a manifestation of the specter of a continued patriarchy. By being himself guilty of rape, Ugwu can be accommodating of Odenigbo's greatest failing. The two men, who occupy such different social positions, are equalized as men guilty of violating women. "My good man" proclaims Ugwu's awareness of his emotional connection with Odenigbo and resonates with the echo of a master's benevolence. But it could also be Ugwu's signature (as opposed to referring to "Master"), since this was his name, what Odenigbo called him, and insofar as Ugwu retains this as his name, it reflects his consent to the continuation of the existing terms of their relation.

The servant, a well-established literary trope, confirms the master's status and moral standing, and Ugwu never outgrows this role. Servants in the novel have usually functioned to occlude the people rather than give them prominence (Robbins, *Servant's Hand* x–xi). The figure of the servant is pivotal in anchoring the domestic ethos of Adichie's book. Eager for learning, hardworking, and an intelligent observer, Ugwu puts a legitimating stamp of approval on the protagonists' lives. He also functions with a servant's "comic instrumentality" (6) as he adapts to his new environment, especially early in the novel. He reminds us that the class gap is also a culture gap.

Ugwu thus echoes another figure in African fiction, Tambu in Tsitsi Dangarembga's *Nervous Conditions*. Daughter of uneducated peasants, Tambu moves in with the family of her educated uncle to take her brother's place after he dies unexpectedly. She is educated and is given the opportunity to assimilate into the modern colonial culture. Although not a servant as such, Tambu has a second-class status in her uncle's home because she is the recipient of his charity. But as Slaughter has noted, Tambu grows up to realize the limits of her education and its failed promise to incorporate her as an equal in a community of rights holders. In articulating this impasse, the *Bildungsroman* in its postcolonial form becomes "dissensual," a conflicted and divided form (Slaughter, *Human* 256). This is the move that Adichie's novel tries to buck by imagining for Ugwu a more secure place, recognized by his new role as a writer. With war and dissolution in the background, the ending of *Half of a Yellow Sun* puts emphasis on survival and resilience, on enduring attachments that hold the promise of orderly human relations and democracy, the political order to which they aspire. Adichie gives testimony to "that stubborn unreasonable love that holds people together" (Adichie, "Brief" 5) with the stuff of domestic fiction and, more, as "unreasonable love" spills out of the home and into the public sphere to forge social ties. Women, moreover, Olanna and Kainene in particular, are transformative forces because they inspire and nurture love, all kinds of love. Olanna accepts Baby as a daughter, treats Ugwu like a member of the family, inspires Odenigbo, and finally mourns her sister. Kainene brings Richard into the fold of Biafra, devotes herself to humanitarian work, and sacrifices her life to feed her family.

In sum, what does Adichie really tell us about the genre of a people's history? The reader's surprise at the end of the novel is twofold. We have been led to believe that Richard is writing "The World Was Silent When We Died." Instead we learn that Ugwu is the author and that the contents of the book are different from the other book we thought Ugwu was writing. The first impression we get of Ugwu as a writer is when he records Olanna's testimony of her traumatic experience returning home with the refugees from the North. Olanna had visited her aunt's family and witnessed their demise in the ethnic violence. When she escapes back "home" to the East, Olanna finds herself in a train crowded with refugees sitting next to a woman who was traveling with her daughter's severed head in a calabash (Adichie, *Half* 82). The sight is deeply shocking and traumatizes Olanna, who remains mute for some time and is only able to tell Ugwu what she saw much later. Empathetic and accepting, Ugwu is an ideal listener for Olanna. When he records what he heard, he discovers his ability as a writer and his desire to write more. Thus, in a sense, Olanna is his muse, giving him a view of the people's suffering. Richard, as already noted, reads Ugwu's account and is so impressed that he gives up writing a history of the war himself. All these details lead us to believe that Ugwu's book will be a narrative, even novelistic, history collected from witness accounts and his own experiences as a child soldier, the type of another genre of war writing. Yet the narrative outline in eight parts shows the book is going to be quite different. It will focus on the distant facts of the war and not the intimate details that a servant could reveal and that have been the subject Adichie's novel. Ugwu's history will not describe his own experience as a soldier, either. The people's story of the war as we have come to know it through the main plot of *Half of a Yellow Sun* is not going to figure in the text by the historian from the people. This disjunction between the two books, the novel and the "book within a book," either invites us to substitute one for the other (take the domestic fiction and diminish the importance of the history as secondary) or to see both as somehow incomplete, hiding an unresolved difficulty, which, I would suggest, pertains to the women's story of the war that is even here, in this domestic fiction, hemmed in by the negative influence of patriarchy.

When Kainene disappears at the end of the novel in search of food, Olanna, in her desperation to know what happened to her sister, consults a dibia and declares against reason that "I believe in anything that will bring my sister home" (433). Like Nwapa's Kate, Olanna turns to the healing powers of traditional beliefs, but they fail to resolve her grief. Kainene's disappearance leaves unfulfilled this desire to return "home" that held the promise of resolving the crisis of the ethnic violence and giving the Igbo a protected space of their own. The uncertainty of the political landscape at the war's close is reflected in the lack of closure for the family's grief over Kainene, bringing the meaning of "home" into crisis. Kainene in life had rejected domesticity by refusing marriage and motherhood. She was also always skeptical of Biafran nationalism, and the last image of her is her departure across the border out of Biafra to go on "attack trade" to get food. Of all the characters in the novel, she is the one who would have taken this border the least seriously and seen it as artificial. Yet she dies crossing the border, and her death, unwitnessed and unconfirmed, inconsequential in the larger narrative of the war, bodes ill for the future of the reunified Nigeria. What Kainene symbolizes as a fiercely independent woman makes this death, moreover, a deeply cautionary moment about women's plots.

Olanna's despair at the loss of her sister and her grief's hollowing out the sense of home are offset by the conciliatory tone of Ugwu's dedication to his master, the novel's closing words. Immediately above the novel's last words, Odenigbo is kissing and consoling a grieving Olanna. The servant's devotion in these hard times sheds a favorable light on the masters, helping to stabilize the idea of domesticity. They have overcome the damage of their past infidelities (both Odenigbo's and Olanna's, who had a relationship with Richard, betraying her husband and sister). The war is over and the nuclear family is still here, having outlasted the fraternal bond and the bond between sisters, between women.

Despite authorizing Ugwu with the task of writing history, Adichie herself is not really writing a people's history, at all, but rather proposes a domestic novel as a corrective to what she sees as the failed project of people's history, a body of work that does not look at "every day life" but constructs overly general, "large narratives." We can find the people instead within the domestic and its entanglements. Thus Adichie seeks to blunt the divisive class conflict implied in people's histories. Some tension still persists in Adichie's juxtaposition of her own domestic narrative and Ugwu's proposed other text. Ugwu is, as we saw, conciliatory, but his proposed history with its reference to the world intimates a First World/Third World argument that hints at the fragility of the wholeness of the domestic fiction Adichie foregrounds. Several critics have described Adichie as being a realist in Georg Lukacs's sense of the term, constructing the world of her novel so as to lend it the appearance of totality and objectivity (Andrade, "Genealogies" 91; Hawley 20). Lukacs contrasted this type of historical realism with naturalism, an aesthetic he rejected as not properly historical and too deterministic. Thus when Hawley describes *Half of a Yellow Sun* as putting the emphasis on love stories and rendering the war "with comparatively little gore" (Hawley 21), he is reacting out of the expectation that he might find the kind of naturalism that is typical of the literature. These questions of genre, the relation among domestic fiction, the war novel, realism, and naturalism, show that the novel's relationship to the project of a people's history is vexed because it always begs the questions of who is speaking, for whom and to whom.

The City in War: Farah's Novels of Mogadiscio

Adichie moves beyond the paradigm of the war novel by adapting the domestic novel, a genre that Farah also turns to, as we shall see, in *Knots*, the middle novel of the *Past Imperfect* trilogy. Like Adichie, Farah seems particularly resistant to the naturalist aesthetic, preferring instead to rethink and reaffirm a critical, historical realist aesthetic. His *Past Imperfect* trilogy declares its interest in the past in its title, but its pun on the grammatical term draws attention equally to narrative method. Time and space, the two parameters of the realist novel, show their resilience despite being tested by war's disordering of the novelistic chronotope. Farah probes the chronotope of war fiction and how we have come to depend on the visual for the real, offering a conversational narrative as an alternative way to reengage historical memory.

I mean to bring attention to the ways in which Farah problematizes visuality as a mode of understanding, by asking, "what is war?" in his fiction.

He began this exploration of the visual with *Maps* (1986), the first novel of *Blood in the Sun*. This novel about the Somali-Ethiopian War (Ogaden War) of 1977 queries the boundaries of Somali nationalism and its political implications through an extended metaphor on maps. Here I situate those of Farah's novels that trace the violent dissolution of Somalia after the fall of Siyad Barre in 1991 in the context of the contemporary writing on war in order to explore what is original about Farah's approach as well as discuss how it draws from the tradition of African war writing. My focus is primarily on *Links* and *Knots*, with a brief glance back at *Secrets* (the last novel of *Blood in the Sun*), where Farah's depiction of the dissolution begins. *Crossbones*, the novel that completes the most recent trilogy, sketches Farah's response to the international (especially media) accounts of Somali piracy. I link it to my readings of the other novels methodologically without giving it a full account here.

In Farah's novels war no longer looks like what we expect. Civil strife in Somalia has created a new paradigm, referred to as "dissolution."[15] In "dissolution," the arena of war is quotidian civilian life. There is no battleground, but insecurity pervades the everyday so that every aspect of the quotidian is transacted in conditions of constant danger. Looking is key to navigating dangerous situations, but under the conditions of "dissolution" we are not always sure of the meaning of what we see. Furthermore, what Farah's characters see is conditioned by what they are prepared to understand and, even more importantly, what they are prepared to question.

Visuality informs Farah's understanding of the aesthetic, as well. He compares his novelistic discourse to a "broken mirror," an allusion to the often used metaphor of the mirror as a metaphor for realism, and he discovers truth in distortion:[16]

> I spot the fractured quality of souls deflected in the looking glass: I see amputated limbs and am consequently overwhelmed with images suggesting Guernica. Since I am speaking in the tongue of images, my most recurrent vision remains one full of rifts: the rift between the text and its author, the rift between the text and its interpreter, the rift ultimately, between myself and my country! (Farah, "Country in Exile" 713)

Broken souls become a dominant motif in *Links* (2004), in which Mogadiscio is superimposed on Dante's city in the *Inferno*.[17] Thus images in Farah's distorted mirror are not mimetic, but recall works of art (Picasso's painting, Dante's poem). Farah has used intertextuality to "dissociat[e]" readers from the immediate historical context and to help them see through art "the utopian possibilities of society" (Gikandi, "Postcolonial Textuality"

753). The "rifts" Farah alludes to above suggest dissociation. Such intertextual references continue to bridge those divides in *Past Imperfect* and are powerful reminders of a literary tradition of war writing.

The visual references in the novel, therefore, are made by borrowing from other visual references. This technique is not alien to realism. As Nancy Armstrong has shown in her revisionist history of English realism, the visuality of the novel after 1850 is largely shaped by images already in cultural circulation.[18] The difference is that for Farah this visual archive, and in particular the media images of Somalia, are a hindrance rather than a help. *Links*, the first novel of the *Past Imperfect* trilogy, draws from the media directly by commenting on the text and the movie *Black Hawk Down*. Mark Bowden's text is markedly visual and depicts the experience of the American troops in Operation Restore Hope as conditioned by how they saw Somalia through the optics of military technology, their training, and ideology. The film by Ridley Scott (2001) creates a visual aesthetic based on a perception of Somalia as a place that looks like permanent war. *Links*, on the other hand, attempts to show how limiting the visual archive is in helping us understand Somalia, without, however, positing some kind of authentic "seeing" in its place. Instead, Farah rejects the usefulness of metaphors of visibility as explanations of civil war. Furthermore, *Crossbones* (2011), the third novel of the trilogy, uses more conventional novelistic devices to undermine the obfuscating journalistic accounts of piracy.

The real in Farah reveals itself over time as a system of relations. Relations need to develop, to unfold, before their meaning is manifest. The titles of his novels that concern me here (*Links*, *Knots*, *Crossbones*, as well as the earlier novel *Secrets*) gesture to connectedness, to interdependence, but also to intersecting flows. Retrospection and analysis discover value in secrets, links, and knots. The distance of retrospection in Farah is balanced by the intimacy of personal history. The city is the space that holds this history together, and even in "dissolution," it can provide a stage where relations are played out. In *Knots* (2007), the stage becomes quite literally the theater as the novel culminates in the staging of a play. A variation on the domestic novel, *Knots* is both the story literally of the reclamation of a particular family home from the warlord who has appropriated it and an exploration of the privatization of the public sphere, a kind of inversion where the social life outside the home now takes place inside private spaces, whereas the outside (the street and other public spaces) has succumbed to the insecurity of dissolution. The unscripted, improvisational lives of Farah's characters in *Knots* find solace in the disciplined, collaborative creativity of the theater.

In *Past Imperfect* the Somali civil war, ongoing since the fall of Siyad Barre in 1991, has brought war to the city. Most of my focus in this study has been on war in rural settings, away from the city. Yet there were exceptions to this, as in the numerous references to the evacuation and destruction of cities in Biafra, important events that captured the imagination of that war's storytellers as its big, traumatic events. But there is little sustained focus on what the city in war looks like until Farah's novels. Vera, for example, who describes Bulawayo and Harare extensively, distinguishes them as spaces spared the direct brunt of war. Beginning with *Secrets* (1998), the last novel of *Blood in the Sun*, Farah chronicles the war closing in on the city.[19] *Secrets* takes place at a threshold, before "absolute total anarchy" (Farah and Coover, "Saving the Soul" 123). In the novel Farah relies heavily on the motif of the car ride to register the transformation of the urban into an arena of war. The rider in a car looks through the windshield as through a lens framing the urban as a scene. However, he is not always able to recognize or understand what he sees. Driving as the war closes in on Mogadiscio, Kalaman recounts:

> I get into my car and drive, with no idea at all where I am headed. I can see smoke in the distance as I drive north, smoke spiraling upwards. What I cannot tell is whether, as a result of a militia attack or a reprisal by Siyad's regime, a bombshell has struck home and in a deadly way, setting people's houses alight, or whether it is wood smoke rising. Like a cow knowing where it is going after a day's grazing in the green grass on the outskirts of a village, my car leads me somewhere but I know not where. (Farah, *Secrets* 62)

Driving his car, Kalaman has lost his volition and is aimless and disoriented, not understanding what he has seen ("smoke," but what kind?). From the car he can see, but seeing does not help him understand. In *Secrets* the city exists on a trajectory of rural to urban along which the main characters travel numerous times. The pastoral analogy ("like a cow") compares the car to a cow, leading the herdsman along; the driver does not direct the car. The image underscores Kalaman's confusion about the new relation of the rural to the urban, increasingly likely to be cut off from each other so that the city in war will become a world of its own, an island. All the same, the car is comforting as it propels him somewhere. Movement is better than stasis.

Traveling back and forth between Mogadiscio and Afgoi "on a road which for thirty-odd years had seen [him] come and go," Kalaman maintains a sense of who he is (94). The road is not impassable and the two locations crucial to the novel's exploration of identity remain connected, despite numerous checkpoints (93, 232). It is the traffic between places that helps map the personal onto the national. The nation exists along the axes that connect different places and depends on the traffic to and from to cohere. The civil war disrupts the mobility of citizens to move about the country, seriously impeding their ability to hold the nation in the imagination.[20]

In *Secrets* war closes in on the city: there are checkpoints, bombings, carjackings, murders. In *Links*, the war is of the city, permeating all its space and creating a new novelistic terrain. Indeed, Farah has called the city his "principal character" in the novel (Appiah, "Nuruddin," *Bomb* 87:58). *Links* takes us to Mogadiscio in the aftermath of the United Nations–sanctioned American intervention, Operation Restore Hope, in 1992–93. The protagonist, Jeebleh, is a successful expatriate academic teaching in New York who returns to Somalia around 1994, after an absence of twenty years, to bury his mother, now dead for seven years. His return, however, has an additional objective. It is a rescue mission, a timely intervention in the lives of those closest to him in Somalia. He has learned that the niece of his closest friend has been abducted, a victim of the political violence. Knowing only what he has been able to glean from newspapers and television, Jeebleh comes to Somalia thinking he can rescue the missing girl from her captors. Thus Farah explores what motivates this risky mission as well as what makes it succeed in a context pervaded by the failure of intervention. He sets Jeebleh off on his own Operation Restore Hope, since the girl's name, Rajo, means hope (Farah, *Links* 53).

A city in war is not an easy city to see. It lies hidden behind its destroyed architecture, its people in retreat. In *Links*, civil war permeates every aspect of quotidian living, every inch of space. It is an inescapable, total condition, and thus it is difficult to achieve the appropriate distance from which to observe it. The city's "prevailing obfuscation" creates problems for the novelist working in a tradition that has put its faith into the explicatory power of metaphors of visibility (Farah, *Links* 32). Conventionally, the novelistic whole functions as a metaphor for the whole of a nation or culture: "the promised unity of the *book*" is held up as a sign for the "unity of the social domain it represented" (Buzard 39). In his years of exile Farah has admitted writing within this paradigm, hoping to keep his country alive, whole, through his fiction (Farah and Coover, "Saving the Soul" 116), while fearing that civil war would unravel the metaphor.

Like Farah himself, Jeebleh has an idea of Mogadiscio in his mind, shaped through his childhood memories:

> Jeebleh's Mogadiscio was orderly, clean, peaceable, a city with integrity and a life of its own, a lovely metropolis with beaches, cafes, restaurants, late-night movies. It may have been poor, but at least there was dignity to that poverty, and no one was in any hurry to plunder or destroy what they couldn't have. He doubted if there was enough space in people's minds for the pleasures he had enjoyed when living in Mogadiscio. (Farah, *Links* 35)

The city is autonomous, dignified, yet worldly. In this nostalgic description, Mogadiscio at once belongs to history and the past and is out of history, because its condition as a colonial city is not referred to.

Jeebleh's childhood memories of Mogadiscio make the most powerful reference to a sense of place in the novel and constitute Farah's version of the restorative eternal landscape. Whenever these memories surface, however, they put Jeebleh in danger. Such memories inspire him to seek out his old haunts and take risks in his movements through the city, which expose him and render him a target. Jeebleh follows his nostalgic yearning to repeat his childhood swims and goes to the beach, now eerily deserted. He enters the water, only to realize that he is being watched and that it might not be safe to come out of the water (123). He swims out as far as he can and stays in the water for an hour with just sea and sky, making himself invisible from land, but also blinding himself to the place he nostalgically sought. Instead of looking out at the landscape, he turns inward to think: "he lay on his back, contemplating the blue sky, thinking" (124).

What he recollects is his New York apartment and the moment he watched the TV footage of the American marines "alighting from their amphibious craft" to do "God's work," which he remembers his wife questioning. Jeebleh's retreat mentally to another place (New York) through which to see Somalia (on television) illustrates the failure of the present to make itself intelligible as visibility. It also raises the possibility that Jeebleh has come to Somalia because, after viewing the U.S. troops on television, he identified with them and their intervention. When Jeebleh gets out of the water, cowering in his exposure (a scene that is almost a parody of the widely televised marines' landing), he wonders, "was he being paranoid?" (125).

There are two recurring motifs of the visual in the novel: references to television footage of the American intervention (the marines landing but also the atrocity of the U.S. Ranger's body that was dragged through Mogadiscio), and descriptions of the devastated city that Farah gives us as Jeebleh's witness. The car ride once again provides a vantage point from which to take stock of the changed landscape and social relations of the city. Farah assumes the reader knows the television footage and thus describes it only minimally, although he alludes to it frequently. The cityscapes, however, are a different matter. Here Farah borrows from the visuality of a different text, pairing his sparse descriptions of the city with references to Dante's "suffering city" in the *Inferno*. Although he is riding in the car looking at the city, Jeebleh mediates what he sees through his memory of Dante's landscape of death, which helps make what he sees intelligible. Thus each section of the novel is prefaced by a passage from the *Inferno*, such as Dante's evocative lines from the opening of Canto III, "Through me the way into the suffering city, / Through me the way into eternal pain, / Through me the way that runs among the lost," which Farah uses at the beginning of Part I.[21] Mogadiscio is no longer a city; it is death itself. Vultures, for example, are everywhere:

> From where he sat in the back of the car, Jeebleh saw vultures everywhere he turned: in the sky and among the clouds, in the trees, of which there were many, and on top of buildings. There were a host of other carrion-feeders too, marabous, and a handful of crows. Death was on his mind, subtly and perilously courting his interest, tempting him. (69)

Soon after this passage, one of the novel's few sustained descriptions of the city, Farah makes several allusions to other places that help establish the reality of Mogadiscio: American slums, Virgil's warscapes, Rwanda, Liberia. The description emphasizes the state of mind of the city's residents:

> What Jeebleh had seen of the city so far marked it as a place of sorrow. Many houses had no roofs, and bullets scarred nearly every wall. In contrast to the rundown ghetto of an American city, where the windows might be boarded up, here the window frames were simply empty. The streets were eerily, ominously quiet. They saw no pedestrians on the roads, and met no other vehicles. Jeebleh felt a tremor, imagining that the residents had been slaughtered "in one another's blood," as Virgil had it. He would like to know whether, in this civil war, both those violated and the violators suffered from a huge deficiency—the inability to remain in touch with their inner selves or to remember who they were before the slaughter began. Could this be the case in Rwanda and Liberia? Not that one could make sense of this war on an intellectual level—only on an emotional level. Here, self-preservation helped one to understand. (70)

Just as people have vacated their former selves psychologically, so has the city been vacated as a place and marked by signs of its erasure. Farah's efforts to connect what Jeebleh sees to other places, histories, and literatures puts civil-war Mogadiscio in an expanded context, both geographically and historically: "he is deterritorializing Somalia as a national project and re-territorializing it as a place that belongs with the world" (Myers 145–46). The reality in front of him corresponds to his reading and other visual archives, and where it does not match up, it leads him to question what he sees some more.

Bowden in *Black Hawk Down* describes the U.S. troops' impression of Mogadiscio as the "postapocalyptic world of Mel Gibson's *Mad Max* movies, a world ruled by roving gangs of armed thugs" (Bowden 10). Bowden has borrowed this analogy from Daniel R. Bolger, who used it before (Bolger 273). This way of viewing the devastation gives the city a minimalist moral compass that is to Farah a dangerous way to orient oneself as an intervening force. In their mission to "restore sanity and civilization," the U.S. troops were charged with the task of using the most lethal power, to be "the baddest boys on the planet" who would "clean things up" (Bowden 10). Jeebleh's view of the abandoned city at street level signifies through the sign of absence. For Farah, what is meaningful is what is missing. In contrast, the Mogadiscio conjured up by Bowden to capture what the American Rangers saw from their helicopters is chock-full, a "clotted" space of destruction:

> Mogadishu spread beneath them in its awful reality, a catastrophe, the world capital of things-gone-completely-to-hell. It was as if the city had been ravaged by some fatal urban disease. The few paved avenues were crumbling and littered with mountains of trash, debris, and the rusted hulks of burned out vehicles. Those walls and buildings that had not been reduced to heaps of gray rubble were pockmarked with bullet scars. Telephone poles leaned at ominous angles like voodoo totems topped by stiff sprays of dreadlocks—the stubs of their severed wires (long since stripped for sale on the thriving black market). . . . Every open space was clotted with the dense makeshift villages of the disinherited, round stick huts covered with layers of rags and shacks made of scavenged scraps of wood and patches of rusted tin. From above they looked like an advanced stage of festering urban rot. (Bowden 7)

As an aerial view, Bowden's description is made through "imperial eyes," or what Mary Louise Pratt calls the commanding point of view of the "monarch-of-all-I-survey" (Pratt 201). As if in a tit-for-tat, Farah placed a very different aerial photograph on the title page of the novel that shows Somalia from space, making visible only its geographical outline. The strong geometric lines in the satellite picture render the image very abstract, the opposite of realistic.

Bowden's biological metaphors of disease describe the deterioration of the city. Thus Bowden's description is a naturalist description of war. The humanity left here (the "makeshift villages of the disinherited") is also a symptom of rot, and the city appears beyond redemption, its fate sealed through its identification with war and its characterization as "catastrophe." The view from above establishes in advance the futility of American intervention for Bowden. Unlike Pratt's explorers, who appropriated what they saw because they could reinvent it at will, Bowden's Rangers see Somalia as a wasteland, too far gone, as that which is not worth saving.[22]

As a highly visual narrative, Bowden's book attempts a full reflection in a mirror that Farah feels compelled to complicate and show that it can only ever be a partial reflection. Farah does this by jostling visuality against (fictional) testimony, pictures (albeit pictures in words) against narrative. Farah does not dismiss the media story and sees its wide dissemination as an opportunity to intervene in how Somali history is told.[23] If *Black Hawk Down* narrates break-down and failure, then *Links* goes against the grain, attempting to synthesize or *link* up many different perspectives on what happened and, more importantly, to show what it means for what happens next. Farah does not so much write back to Bowden as create a companion text, another voice in the conversation, albeit a more authoritative voice, for portraying the Somali point of view. This project could be located in the extroverted tradition of the African novel, except that the literary map is now different and more capacious.

Farah's most extended response to Bowden's book is the testimony of Dajaal, a character who fought the Americans. In multiple conversations with Dajaal and his family, Jeebleh creates a companion story to the media story of *Black Hawk Down*. As if to stress this parallelism, the cover of *Links*, which shows a photograph of a Somali militia fighter, is a quotation from Bowden, who reproduced the same photograph from the *Philadelphia Inquirer* in his text, where it is one of only two pictures of Somalis. The other picture shows the violent mob dragging the Ranger's body (Bowden 134, 260). The cover of *Links* reproduces the picture of the Somali fighter in duplicate, two of the same image side by side, suggesting an infinite series of the same image and a monolithic view of what a Somali fighter is. Despite the fact that Bowden names the man (Mohammed Shiek Ali) and gives a short narrative of his participation in the battle (179–81), Farah seems to be commenting on Bowden's collectivizing portrayal of Somalis: they are fearless; they do not value their lives and are willing to risk them repeatedly: "the volume of fire was terrifying. Yet Somalis seemed to be darting across streets everywhere" (Bowden 117).

Dajaal's version of this key incident is the story of a missed opportunity: when the United States wiped out most of the leaders with whom they could have negotiated in an aerial attack in July 1993 (Farah, *Links* 72–73). Aiming at General Mohammed Farrah Aidid, who was believed responsible for the killing of twenty-four Pakistani peacekeepers, the Americans bombed a gathering of clan leaders, missing Aidid, who was not there, in fact. The meeting was being held without his knowledge to discuss his increased confrontational attitude toward the UN. Close to a hundred men representing a wide spectrum of leaders (elders, intellectuals, militia leaders), "the best educated members of the clan," were at the meeting (Bowden 72). Seventy-three people were killed, including women and children who were in or near the house (Bolger 303).

Bowden describes the destructive effects of the missiles that hit the house and the carnage they left behind in naturalistic detail (Bowden 73–74). Dajaal conveys the intensity of the attack to Jeebleh more economically: "I felt hell was paying us a visit. . . . I remember thinking, 'Here's an apocalypse of the new order'" (Farah, *Links* 72) and explains that this was a gathering of leaders to discuss a "peaceful way out of the impasse between the American in charge of the UN Blue Helmets, and Strongman South and his militiamen" (71; Strongman South is the fictional figure of Aidid).[24] By impeding these types of conversations, the American intervention deepened the violence in the region. Dajaal regrets that the Americans pulled out immediately after the downing of the two helicopters, because even then "some of us would've liked to talk things through" (269). He suggests that the Americans could have found partners to work with, alluding indirectly to a widely held view, with which Bowden concurs, that the Americans were too focused on their goal of eliminating Aidid and blind to the existence of other leaders (Bowden 91). Talks could have enabled a new leadership to emerge from those Somalis who opposed the mob action against the Americans. In an interview with Kwame Anthony Appiah in 2003, Farah talked about the importance of listening when brokering peace: "When you listen, you arm yourself against your enemy" and "If you listen you won't need to pull out your gun" (Appiah, "Nuruddin," *Bomb* 87:58).

Farah uses Dajaal's perspective to change the perception of what a Somali fighter is and suggest that he might have a just cause. Thus Dajaal claims that "justice," not "rage," motivated him when he fought the Americans: "I was prone to fear, like the Marines, and alone in my fear too. But I wasn't in a strange country, I knew *why* I was doing what I was doing and I knew *where* I was, even in the dark! That was the difference between our situation and that of the young Americans" (Farah, *Links* 269). Dajaal's language is telling here. By knowing where he is "even in the dark," Dajaal illustrates that knowing is not a function of seeing, but of belonging. Hence the view from the outside is inevitably disorienting. The Americans, dependent on their aerial views, lacked the necessary knowledge and did not help themselves by not listening. Dajaal's claim that he fought the Americans out of a sense of justice for his people constitutes Farah's revision of Bowden's account; Bowden, assuming the perspective of one of the Somali survivors of this attack, says "the sight filled him and his friends with rage . . . this was too much" (Bowden 74). Farah emphasizes the legitimacy of fighting back by stressing justice over rage.

The story of the civilian trauma from this same episode is recounted by Dajaal's daughter-in-law, who explains how before the fateful crash, two American helicopters had landed near her house, creating panic, especially among the children. This perspective from below is not afforded at all by Bowden. We learn that in the confusion, her one-year old child got away and was caught up in the dust raised by the helicopters. The mother, interrupted in her nursing and thus bare-breasted, cried desperately for her child and, when the American soldiers saw her, they humiliated her by making lewd gestures at her nudity. Her daughter became mute and deaf after the incident (Farah, *Links* 275–76).

This scene directly echoes a detail in Bowden's text. In his narrative of the events that preceded the downing of the helicopter, Bowden describes the landing (also by helicopter) of the Delta forces in a crowded city setting: "the crowd spooked . . . wind from the powerful rotors knocked some people down and tore the colorful robes off some of the women" (Bowden 13). The phrase "colorful robes" betrays Bowden's othering of the Somalis and prepares us for what happened next: "A few of the Rangers, still high overhead, spotted people below gesturing up at them eagerly, as if inviting them to come down to the streets and fight"(13). From up high, the reality on the street is "as if" menacing. The women in colorful dress (or undress) are a mere detail, their terror muted.

The swooping helicopter is a recurring motif in Bowden's visualization of Mogadiscio. Thus we have the following description, which also seems to have inspired Farah's account:

> They flew in groups, at all hours of day and night, swooping down so low they destroyed whole neighborhoods, blew down market stalls, and terrorized cattle. Women walking the streets would have their colorful robes blown off. Some had infants torn from their arms by the powerful updraft. On one raid, a mother screamed frantically in flex cuffs for nearly a half hour before a translator arrived to listen and to explain that her infant had been blown down the road by the landing helicopters. The residents com-

> plained that pilots would deliberately hover over their roofless outdoor showers and toilets. Black Hawks would flare down on busy traffic circles, creating havoc, then power off leaving the crowd below choking on dust and exhaust. Mogadishu felt brutalized and harassed. (75)

The helicopter terrorizes the population without even using its artillery. From above, the civilian life of the city is exposed, and this exposure, like a form of undress, invites the teasing, humiliating attention of the more powerful. Most striking here, however, is the tension in Bowden's account between an intentional voyeurism and an obliviousness to what is actually there: the helicopter pilots spy on those showering, but they don't see the mothers and children that their engines terrorize. This inconsistency is a result of the slipperiness of point of view. Although Bowden's third-person narrative focalizes interchangeably through the Somalis and the American Rangers, Somali "characters" never speak. Their "tagged speech" (Chatman 198) is not in the text. Thus the conceit of the woman's testimony that Farah's text presents us with (as well as Bile's and that of the others who speak to Jeebleh) removes Farah from the situation of having to create a different conceit—that of the omniscient narrator who has a superior knowledge of Somalia. For Bowden the aerial views provide the only knowledge of Somalia that matters, and even when these views prove inadequate, it does not lead him to ponder "what is Somalia," but to disengage, to leave and not come back. Bowden's narrative is a story without a prelude or a conclusion. The Americans arrived not knowing anything about the place they were going to fight in (Bowden 10) and returned unsure of their experience (346). Jeebleh's return to Somalia, however, is an encounter with people's words that is transformative of his own identity. He sets out to listen before he acts, intervening by arranging the killing of the warlord responsible for much evil.

An Encounter with People's Words

Jeebleh declares that "despite the prevailing obfuscation, I've come to assess the extent of my culpability as a Somali" (Farah, *Links* 32). Because he claims an identity as a Somali, Jeebleh feels implicated in the civil war. Part of the difficulty, however, lies in answering the question, what exactly he is culpable of? Identity for Farah is closely tied to the problem of moral agency. And moral agency is determined by what he calls "links," the ties that bind us to those closest to us, those with whom we have shared a history of intimacy. "Intimates," a favorite word in the novel, indicates a level of human association that binds through shared experience and love, not ideology or clan. Moreover, "links" are expressed most powerfully in stories (memories) shared by "intimates." On the last page of the novel, Farah describes Jeebleh and his friends as "forever linked through the chains of the stories they shared" (334). Farah also broadens the question of responsibility to ask it of the world: as people around the world watch Somalia descend into chaos, whose responsibility is it to help? What links, or chains of stories, connect us to a place like Somalia and consequently reveal our culpability in what is happening there? In *Crossbones*, where he seeks to explain the international ties of Somali pirates and piracy, Farah comes the closest to making concrete these culpable links.

Rather than the narrator's words, Farah privileges the spoken words of his characters, what Seymour Chatman calls their "tagged speech," speech reported in quotation marks and modified by phrases such as "she said," "he shouted" (Chatman 198–209). Most of the novel is devoted to Jeebleh's conversations with people in the city. Indeed, the preponderance of dialogue in the novel makes it a difficult work to classify narratologically. Gérard Genette describes a genre he calls the "dramatic novel" when he discusses Ernest Hemingway's "Hills Like White Elephants," which is all dialogue and the closest thing to "purely objective narrating" (Genette 187). *Links* is definitely more hybrid, blending features of the "dramatic novel" with what Genette calls "simultaneous narration," where narrative is "in the present contemporaneous with the action" (217). Thus in *Links* events in the novelistic present (Jeebleh's return, his search for his mother's grave, for the girls, his moral dilemma about how to intervene) constitute the main plot line, and they are not rendered retrospectively. Yet "simultaneous narration" does not quite capture what happens overall in the novel, because the role of memory in the novel is important and the conversational passages are mostly retrospective. These are stories of remembrance, and hence of "subsequent" narration, or "past tense narrative" (217).

The conversational form of the novel demonstrates a political point: how an informal network of associates develops a consensus about action. In conversation key events and players are recast in new, differently nuanced moral terms. The conversations set the stage for political action, and Farah renders in fiction something similar to what Margaret E. Keck and Kathryn Sikkink describe in their analysis of how "transnational advocacy networks" emerge and operate; they stress the importance of such networks as mechanisms for "information exchange" that enable a new "framing" of the sociopolitical situation and the emergence of new ideas for action (Keck and Sikkink 2). Although they stress the informality and flexibility of such networks, what Keck and Sikkink describe is much more organized than what Farah is getting at. However, their analysis captures the political value of talk, a useful emphasis for reading *Links*. The reliance on conversation, moreover, is a narratological feature typical of political novels. André Malraux's protagonist in *The Conquerors*, for example, meticulously records the conversations he hears. Although initially overwhelmed by the magnitude of the historical events that are unfolding, his attentiveness to the talk of others serves as his entry into the world of political action (Howe 207–8). In war fiction, furthermore, conversation directly opposes war (Odenigbo's salon, for example, or Hove's women in conversation). War is an impasse, a point at which discussing differences has given way to violence. Conversation, listening and responding, is opposed to the violence of reciprocating rounds of fire.

Not surprisingly, *Links* begins with a sentence in quotation marks—"Guns lack the body of human truths"—spoken by Af Laawe, a stranger to Jeebleh who turns out to be Jeebleh's first interlocutor upon his return. This enigmatic statement raises questions about materiality and meaning. The "lack" in guns is ambiguous, empowering because it could be freeing or dangerous because, subject to its power, one has no recourse to oppose the gun. In the first sentence of the novel, therefore, Farah has posited the problem of agency: guns don't act on their own. Rightly suspicious of Af Laawe, Jeebleh questions him, but fails to elicit the truth about his identity. Jeebleh must piece together from many more conversations a history that places Af Laawe on the political and moral map of mid-1990s Somalia, especially because Af Laawe is Bile's antagonist and Jeebleh has returned to Mogadiscio to rescue his friend Bile's niece.

The scene is set for Jeebleh to enter a network of humanitarian actors when he learns that Bile is running a humanitarian organization, the Refuge, with the help of a mutual Irish friend from their university days in Italy. Having fled Ireland's civil strife and its tragic toll on his family, Seamus has committed himself to Somalia because of his friendships (his links) with Somalis. Someone with a "good measure of cosmopolitanism" and a past as an Irish nationalist, Seamus does not want a new country (unlike Richard in *Half of a Yellow Sun*), but to do something out of love: "good, plain, old-fashioned, sixties-style personal commitment to love" (Farah, *Links* 189). Bile, a doctor, tries heroically to save lives, yet his reputation (based on talk) suffers because his source of funds is suspect.

The first conversation between Jeebleh and Af Laawe concerns the matter of legitimacy—why Bile has "detractors" (5–6). Indeed, Af Laawe tries to smear Bile's reputation, to plant the seeds of mistrust in Jeebleh before the two friends reunite. Af Laawe strongly implies that Bile's niece and another girl have been abducted in an attempt to avenge Bile's purported crimes of robbery and murder. As the narrator explains, in civil war "no one . . . is deemed to be innocent . . . everyone is potentially guilty" (218). Because Bile spent almost the entire time of Jeebleh's exile imprisoned in solitary confinement, Jeebleh is uncertain of his mental state. Moreover, Jeebleh is dependent on Af Laawe, who becomes his guide through the city, providing the armed escort necessary in a city in civil war. Thus Jeebleh's physical safety depends on his assenting to Af Laawe's truth. If Jeebleh questions Af Laawe's version of Bile's story, he will also lose Af Laawe's protection. Words and material conditions are linked in the fundamental problem of security.

Jeebleh's conversations with his former intimates help foreground the role of capital in the war, reframing the explanation of the war. He comes to understand that the question of whether Bile's action is theft puts the emphasis on the wrong ethical issue. Bile had a compelling moral reason to take the money and use it to do good.[25] Af Laawe himself turns out to be the one who profits from war. Jeebleh learns that Af Laawe's rival humanitarian organization, which provides proper Islamic burials to the dead abandoned in the city, is a front for a business that sells human organs to an illicit international market (209). Af Laawe's crime is particularly heinous, rendering the bodies of Somalis into commodities in a global market. Jeebleh learns in conversation with Bile's sister how money runs the war and that there is a "cartel" of business interests to whom clan is just a facade (208).

For Farah language is at the forefront of civil war's battlefield. It is used to coerce allegiance. In the novel the narrator offers many definitions of civil war that demonstrate this idea. Civil wars, we are told, "produce a multiplicity of pronominal affiliations, of first-person singulars tucked away in the plural, of third-person plurals meant to separate one group from another" (41). Bile goes further than Jeebleh to say that civil war "was language," the language that serves to identify your clan as your identity and deny your individuality (119). Civil war is likened to madness and disease, which are manifested by the different use of language (68). In civil war. moreover, "you are killed by a person with whom you've shared intimacies" (137); the Somali expression for civil war ("*dagaalka sokeeye*") is "warring against an intimate" (138). Mutually incompatible identities are asserted: "everyone was victim, seldom a culprit" (52), and, as previously noted, "no one . . . is deemed to be innocent . . . everyone is potentially guilty" (218). If language is used by Somalis to collectivize identity, in the novel it is used subversively to uncover individuals. Conversations, together with the individual testimonies given to Jeebleh, work against the instrumental use of language in civil war.

The novel tries to connect words to actions by exploring the meaning of the word "intervention." Upon arriving in Somalia, Jeebleh makes an important realization about the dysfunctional setting he is about to enter: visibility is death. At the airport he witnesses the arbitrary shooting of a boy killed for fun by some young thugs just because they could aim at him. If you can be seen, you can be shot. But not only is becoming visible risky; if you look, you acquire the responsibility to act. As his discussion with Af Laawe at the scene of the shooting indicates, Jeebleh feels compelled to intervene. Af Laawe explains to Jeebleh moments before the shooting what he thinks the present danger is about:

> "It's a sport to them, a game to play when they are bored. The one who hits the target is the winner."
> "And that's what they are doing now?"
> "I suspect so."
> "Can't we intervene?"
> "I doubt it."
> "What if I talk to them?"
> "Why take unnecessary risks?"
> "Because somebody has to."
> "If I were you, I wouldn't." (16)

Immediately after this exchange and before Jeebleh has a chance to decide what to do, the shooting occurs. Jeebleh is left "shocked that no one in the crowd of people still milling about had been willing to confront the gunmen" (17).

In the city streets Jeebleh decides to intervene on behalf of an epileptic who is having a seizure. An unsympathetic crowd has gathered around him. In a rare instance when he draws attention to himself, Jeebleh chastises the crowd for their coldness. The man is unknown to them, they declare, hence they are not obligated to help (196). In response, Jeebleh asserts, "But he is a human being like you and me! . . . Do you need to know his clan family before you help him? What's wrong with you? You make me sick, all of you" (199). Jeebleh expresses his indignation and shames the crowd into letting him help out, but only after he has identified himself as Bile's friend. Hence his intervention is not that of an outsider, and it does not change the crowd's attitude that they help only those they know, which remains unchanged. They allow Jeebleh to help the man when he is no longer an unknown. The only conclusion Jeebleh can draw is to scale back his universalist claims and focus on the real conditions of Mogadiscio: "People living in such vile conditions were bound to lose touch with their own humanity, he thought; you couldn't expect an iota of human kindness from a community coexisting daily with so much putrefaction" (201). War induces a loss of self. The only imperative, as noted earlier by Jeebleh, is "self preservation" (70). But intervention must risk "self-preservation."

The idea of intervention is also explored through the novel's allusion to the convention of the captivity narrative. Jeebleh has returned to Mogadiscio to rescue Bile's niece (Rajo, whose nickname is Raasta, referring to her curls) and her companion, Makka, who is a younger child with Down's syndrome. Raasta "intimates care," we are told by Bile, and Makka is "boundless, generous love" (161). The girls are innocents, angels in the devastation of Mogadiscio. Farah's characterization here is strained, sentimental. Raasta, who inspires asexual male devotion, seems like a type borrowed from nineteenth-century fiction (Stowe's Little Eva or Dickens's Nell). As a figure from the captivity narrative (a subgenre of the sentimental), she is rescued to preserve hope in a future, represented here by the vitality of the Refuge, where she spends all her time. Sentimentalism in *Links* is located outside of a traditional household in the alternative home of the Refuge, a shelter for the displaced. The captivity narrative as genre gains its poignancy from how it responds to the disruption of the household (Nancy Armstrong, "Why Daughters Die" 30–31), marked in this case by Raasta's misrecognition of who her father is. Instead of bonding with her biological father, she has bonded with Bile, who attended her birth as a physician and was the first to claim her in a paternal embrace. The patriarchical order central to Armstrong's argument is confused in Farah's rescue narrative. Jeebleh and Seamus are two more paternal figures for the girls. Many fathers are needed to rescue the innocent (female) children, whereas in *Knots*, Cambara figuratively adopts the male child soldiers.

Raasta speaks in a different register. She has a poetic gift, an ability to "giv(e) shape to the links between words and their meanings" (Farah, *Links* 303). For Farah, both the girls are a means of opening up his novelistic discourse to a sense of possibility that the rest of the novel's realism seems to foreclose. In *Knots* the girls have gone overseas and all the male characters, especially Bile, are falling apart. The girls provide an emotional sustenance on which the men have become entirely dependent. Even Seamus has described his commitment to Somalia as his love for Raasta, the "good, plain, old-fashioned, sixties-style personal commitment to love" (189).

Rescuing the girls is not Jeebleh's only intervention. If this is unambiguously a mission of peace, Jeebleh's other intervention is ethically more problematic. Jeebleh comes to the conclusion that he needs to orchestrate the killing of the novel's chief villain, Caloosha, who is one of those archetypal characters of "war personified." In the novel he is portrayed as physically repulsive and morally degraded, a warlord living in looted property with a girl forty years his junior, whom others refer to as his sex slave (313). He is responsible for imprisoning Bile, his half-brother, and for the abduction of Bile's niece and friend. He is also suspected of having killed Bile's father when they were children. Farah carefully avoids describing Jeebleh's plan as vengeance and justifies it by recourse to the literary conventions of the war novel in Africa: he stages an ordeal for Jeebleh, not in the forest, but in a cemetery, and enhances Jeebleh's capacity for action. The trip to the cemetery is charged with emotion, and Jeebleh's anxiety becomes very elevated because of his difficulty in reading the terrain.

To bring the novel to a resolution, Farah shows that Jeebleh must be transformed from a nonviolent intervener to one willing to kill, or at least consent to killing. Farah resorts to "magic" in order to bring this transformation about. Af Laawe's men bring Jeebleh to what they tell him is his mother's grave, and, in a surprise attack, they inject Jeebleh by force with a mysterious drug. The purpose of this action is not entirely clear, other than it seems intended to intimidate him. However, the opposite happens. After this he is able to carry a gun and plan the assassination of the novel's villain.

This scene can be read as an allusion to *Chaka*. At the gravesite of his father and under the influence of the sorcerer Isanusi, Chaka is "innoculated" with medicines that make him a powerful warrior. The scene in *Chaka* stages a reconciliation between Chaka and his father's spirit, allowing Chaka to overcome his sense of having been disowned by his father and to find his motivation to reclaim his title as chief of his people. The problem of restored legitimacy applies to Jeebleh, as well, who feels guilty about his mother's unmourned death and his lack of knowledge about where her body is. Finding the gravesite enables him to complete his reconnection with Somalia and to find his bearings. In this scene he is actually being prevented by Af Laawe from finding the real grave; the injection is an attempt to "obfuscate" his understanding of where he is. The literary allusion to *Chaka* is not meant to create an exact parallel, but to situate his text in the tradition of the war novel in Africa, extending its rich literary history. The motif of the ordeal asserts the determinism of war by bringing Jeebleh into its sphere more completely. The ordeal also allows for him to act in a decisive way, although it makes it imperative that Jeebleh plan his exit from Somalia before he is drawn in more deeply.

Jeebleh gets lost in the cemetery and is purposely misled looking for his mother's grave, bringing him to a breaking point. The search for the mother's grave in order to give her a proper funeral and honor her memory is an errand that offers itself too easily to an allegorical reading for us to overlook it. The exiled Jeebleh returns to a war-torn and unrecognizable Somalia in dissolution, symbolically to the "mother," to bury her and make his peace with the situation. Instead of resignation and the tame satisfaction of filial duty fulfilled, he commits to justice and an active role in resolving the family (i.e., national) crisis. The ceremony for his mother turns into a hope-filled family reunion that opens a vision for the future. The sentimental and the allegory of family as nation are aligned to break the naturalist determinism of war.

The moral question that haunts *Links* is the one Jeebleh is asked: "Are you prepared to kill and to be killed?" Jeebleh appears to equivocate when he answers that it would depend on "what's at stake" (217). However, after arranging for the secret killing of Caloosha, Jeebleh is at ease with his conscience, having resolved his moral dilemma thus:

> Given the choice, Jeebleh would oppose all forms of violence. But what is one to do when there is no other way to rid society of vermin? Which would he rather be, someone who minds the opinion of others and advocates for peace, or someone who does what he can despite the risks—to improve the lives of many others? (332)

Caloosha is the "vermin" that Jeebleh refers to. Jeebleh justifies his decision by seeing it as the only way out of an impasse: "there is no other way." The purpose of his intervention is to prevent further wrongdoing on behalf of Caloosha, who is unstoppable by other means. Jeebleh evokes Thomas Jefferson, quoting him: "The tree of liberty must be refreshed from time to time with the blood of patriots and tyrants. It is its natural manure" (332). Farah is careful to focalize these thoughts entirely through his protagonist, thus stopping short of endorsing them directly. Jeebleh might feel that he has resolved his moral hesitations, but has Farah? Are we supposed to be a little uncomfortable when the narrator states, "Jeebleh was all for justice, by any means possible" (332)? Not surprisingly, Bowden also refers to Jefferson. Writing through the perspective of one of the Somalis he is profiling (young, American-educated Yusuf), Bowden questions, "did the Americans expect Somalia to suddenly sprout full-fledged Jeffersonian democracy?" (Bowden 75). The implication is that the path to democracy in Somalia may also lead through war first, before democracy can be achieved. Violent struggle sharpens the desire for liberty; the two are interdependent, according to Jefferson. Moreover, it is hard to miss the irony of Jefferson's naturalist imagery, where the "blood of patriots and tyrants" is the "manure" for liberty's tree. Arranging for Caloosha's murder is an action that reflects this logic, but this action does not necessarily have to lead to endless war and dissolution. It can sprout a tree (or a "grain of wheat" or "bones" that will rise again), all in the name of liberty. Jeebleh concludes, "there is no other way" but to kill Caloosha, and this should be a step toward killing war itself, since Caloosha is war personified.

Domesticity Restored

When we arrive in the world of *Knots*, the second novel in the trilogy, we question the efficaciousness of Jeebleh's intervention. Farah provides a gloss on *Links* in this sequel that unsettles any optimism one might have been left with at the end of the first novel. Once again Farah sends a Somali expatriate (a woman this time) to intervene. Jeebleh, we are told in *Knots*, had visited and "set off a tremor that became an earthquake. Death called, and Bile's half-brother answered" (Farah, *Knots* 326). Seamus, Bile, Dajaal all reappear in *Knots*, but their living conditions and their persons (especially Bile and Seamus) are squalid. Physically they have deteriorated enormously.[26] Bile is deeply depressed and barely functioning, making Cambara think "she is bearing witness to the birth of a terrible ugliness, the start of a gradual falling apart of a giant man who is otherwise famous . . . for his inner strength. . . . She thinks Bile is caving in" (318). The girls Raasta and Makka have left for school in Europe, and, bereft of their presence, the Refuge has closed down (326). Seamus refers to the Refuge as "our own paradise in a country that has gone to hell" (329). Jeebleh's visit seems to have unmoored the characters, and although the girls are undoubtedly in a better place, those left behind are unable to cope with the changes. Seamus pessimistically reports to Cambara that "no do-gooders can do as much as it will take to reconstruct" Somalia (329).

The middle novels of each of Farah's trilogies have all featured a woman protagonist, and *Knots*, like *Gifts*, is a love story with a happy ending, despite the environment of the "wounded city" (Myers 141). Farah borrows again from the conventions of sentimental literature. Cambara has returned to Somalia to restore domesticity: fleeing her own home in North America that has been shattered by the drowning death of her son, she wants to retrieve her family property in Mogadiscio, appropriated illegally by a warlord. After Jeebleh's just but apparently inefficacious intervention, Farah seems to be asking what difference gender can make. Cambara intervenes in the lives of many men (and boys) from disparate groups, men whose degraded existence might be turned around through her feminine intervention. Farah is explicit about Cambara's mission: "she thinks herself as a frontierswoman come to reclaim these men from their primitive condition" (Farah, *Knots* 103). The allegory of nation is still at work here as Cambara alludes to the Somali diaspora, its role in sustaining the national identity, and its potential to bring it back to Somalia. Although *Links* attempts to hold off the deterministic logic of war, in *Knots* the city has deteriorated back to the primitive and needs to be "reclaim[ed]."

Cambara helps restore the figure of the "mother" to dignity. The warlord who has taken over her house has enslaved a young woman who has borne him, and perhaps the other men who have gang-raped her, several children (178–79). When Cambara meets her in the family property, Jiigo is pregnant. Cambara removes her from the home and arranges for her to be in the hospital to give birth. Jiigo is freed of the warlord because he is killed in the intervention to restore the house to Cambara. The tale of property restored is also national allegory, part of the sentimental convention of the return of the daughter and restoration of the home in the literature of the frontier (Nancy Armstrong, "Why Daughters Die" 30–31). When Jiigo tells Cambara her story, Cambara thinks of Jiigo's emblematic status as a representative of the nation. "It is the way Jiigo talks," Cambara notes, "the way she lets go of her words with a baffling ease, telling as she does a tale, her own and the nation's" (Farah, *Knots* 179).

Farah gives Cambara unconventional characteristics, as well. She is physically fearless, an accomplished martial artist who dons a veil to walk the streets of the city and, although uncomfortable, relishes the protection it provides. She is also by profession an actress who sees her ability to survive in Mogadiscio as an improvisational performance. There is no script, but the opportunity to invent one is there, and Cambara takes it. She recovers her property with the help of many Somalis who seem eager to set things right for someone who presents to them a refreshing idealism. She also saves Bile and gives Seamus new purpose through her ministrations of care but also, more importantly, through the staging of a play.

Indeed, in a surprising twist, it turns out that Cambara wants the family property not for a conventional purpose but as a safe venue to turn it into a theater where her play, a rendition of a Ghanaian folktale, can be staged.

The national allegory of the restoration of property is overshadowed in significance by a different allegory: the process of producing the play is an allegory of emergent democratic politics. Cambara successfully draws all the people who have helped her or whom she has befriended to participate in the creation of the play. The emphasis is on collaboration, discussion, responsive leadership, willingness to change direction, and creativity. The play's production is made possible by the sponsorship of a political organization called the Women's Network. In the devastation of war, the opportunity to collaborate on something creative is exhilarating. Farah makes a passionate case for the arts' ability to revitalize political culture. The play's opening is deemed significant enough to draw hesitant, exiled Somalis to return and stage a reunion of family and "intimates" in Mogadiscio. Moreover, the play itself comes to be an example of cultural syncretism: it is a modernized recreation of a West African folktale, and the performance includes masks designed by Cambara but sculpted by Seamus. The play itself is allegorical, an animal tale, although Cambara "altered its drift" so that it is not moralizing like traditional folktales but "intense, provocative, complex, and a touch modernist" (387). It is also not realistic, which means that it addresses issues of contemporary relevance indirectly in ways that make them fresh and open up them again for reflection.

The establishment of a safe space is crucial for such creativity. In *Knots* the world of the street recedes as Cambara's efforts to establish a home succeed. Outside the house she "is always in some car, being ferried there and back; constantly in the sight of a gun, never mind if it is friendly; always under someone's constant supervision purportedly for her safety; sentries at the gate, either granting or denying her entry; armed youths to ensnare her" (322). Even from the safety of the hotel she is not protected from the city's squalor, where those less fortunate than her, with less protection, fend for themselves, homeless:

> She stands directly behind the window, looking out and surveying a wasteland of heartbreaking ugliness: trees that have not grown to their normal height, scraps of wood and metal thrown any which way, children rifling in the arid waste all around, as though in search of something precious that they can sell. The fact that she sees adult men squatting and defecating in full view of the road . . . troubles her no end. (188)

The most striking passages in the novel describe Cambara as a pedestrian, partly blinded by the veil while navigating the confusing streets of this desolate place. The danger is always palpable, as in the episode where she confronts armed youths in the street: "her knife in her left hand, hidden from view by a shopping bag, she moves away from them with the slowness of a huntress in a territory familiar to her" (163).

It is from all this that her family compound insulates her, its architecture such that you enter it behind a courtyard, leaving the street and its sites away.[27] When there is a will, security can be established, and thus Cambara's seemingly impossible mission is accomplished because of the will to change that she inspires in others through her determination and example of caring. Farah situates this novel historically in the transition between the rule of warlords and the Islamists (the Islamic Court Union) who controlled much of Somalia for a short period in late 2006 and returned Mogadiscio to normalcy temporarily (135). Peace seemed possible. Acting, in the double sense of political action and performing, is important for daring to find a way to peace.

When Cambara listens to Jiigo's testimony of her suffering, Cambara thinks of her as "another actor, raw, untrained"; she watches Jiigo "reinvent herself right there and then" (179). The conversation between Cambara and Jiigo is reminiscent of the women in dialogue in Hove's *Bones*. Speaking to another woman, Jiigo "reinvents" herself. Farah wills this to happen, because, in Seamus's words, there is a need "for more universal commitments . . . [to] reorient the people of this nation so they may find their proper bearing" (329). Individuals like Jeebleh, Bile, Dajaal have been betrayed by the wholesale failure of leadership of the "cowardly intellectual class" (329).

Conclusion

The contemporary novels of war place children and women at the center of their stories. In the examples I have stressed, the authors insist on finding a message of hope by identifying areas of agency that escape the all-determining force of war. The interrupted childhoods of young soldiers retain aspects of the unruliness of children that can, as we see with Birahima, escape the bounds of the adult world through wit and subversive language. Kourouma's playfulness with language is a literary conceit that demonstrates the importance placed on invention and improvisation, afforded by an aesthetic project (the novel), to buck a reality of war that is represented as going in circles, repeating itself. The young girls are innocents who surprise by being stronger and more agentic than one would think. The kidnapped girls in *Links* simply reappear and resolve the complication of their abduction, miraculously unsullied by their experience. Dongala's Laokolé is not ineffectual when confronted by evil. She kills Johnny and saves herself without losing her goodness. The novelists thus invest in the children for a vision of the future.

Women as mothers, daughters, wives keep the home and, by implication, the nation viable. Even in "dissolution" it is possible to see the nation's skeleton ready to be revived. The home is a collaborative space of committed relationships under the aegis of women who are against war. The concern for the people evident in the war literature as a whole finds its manifestation here in the alliances that women form with one another on the basis of their shared understanding of domesticity, which surpasses class difference. Cambara identifies with Jiigo, reviving the communion of women depicted in the earlier literature as a metaphor for the overcoming of the bifurcation of the nation.

Whereas in the novels of Mau Mau, Biafra, and Zimbabwe the novelists wrote against an effort to silence or avoid the histories of war, the contemporary novelists are writing against the tendency to see Africa only through the lens of war. This inevitably turns their novels into the extroverted project of answering back, although they are now placed differently than in the literature of the immediate postcolonial era. Novelists today are writing with awareness of the context of a world novel rather than with the reference back to the imperial centers. This worlding of the novel has occurred, while national readerships that sustained the literatures of Kenya, Nigeria and Zimbabwe are under significant economic stress. The novel does not reach down as deeply, especially as it competes with other media. The contemporary novel of war does not fall entirely outside the paradigm of introversion, however. Written as it is in the shadow of a long tradition of African war fiction, it extends introversion into a kind of intertextuality, finding the reference to itself in literary terms from where it hopes to sustain a national, even if more broadly African, imaginary.

Afterword

The ambition of this study is shaped by two somewhat contradictory impulses. The first is to use the novel of war in Africa as a case study to say something broader and bigger about the war novel as a genre, across literary traditions, and reaching backward and forward in history. The second is to deepen our understanding of the novel in Africa by doing a literary history of the genre of the war novel that has been overlooked in relation to the more widely read and canonized *Bildungsroman* form. Pulling in two different directions, one toward a more global context and the other inward to the specificities of a particular tradition, I placed stress on the convergence of two sensibilities: the naturalist aesthetic and a humanitarian ethos that takes up the responsibility for the suffering of others. Both these sensibilities are present in culturally hybrid forms in the African war novel, reflecting its syncretism as a narrative practice engaged with the colonial and postcolonial history of the continent. Moreover, I would argue, the narration of war evokes by itself some form of these two sensibilities of naturalism and humanitarianism, gesturing toward a universal statement about the experience of war.

I began my study with attention to the historical convergence in nineteenth-century Europe of a naturalist aesthetic to describe the wounds of war and a humanitarian sense of responsibility to lift the suffering of others. Dunant's *Un souvenir de Solférino* had a profound impact on how the story of war is told. In sync with the emerging aesthetic of naturalism, Dunant shifted the focus of the narrative of war from an account of the battle (which he delivers quickly, with ample gore but great economy) to the protracted narrative of the aftermath, showing in detail the appalling degree of suffering caused by the fourteen hours of fighting. The transformed setting after the battle, now littered with destroyed and abandoned property and the dead and dying, becomes the narrative's focus (Dunant 35). The aftermath is presented as an entirely new time and place, the landscape of emergency, where there is no norm and the extant communities must reinvent themselves as emergency care centers. Thus in Dunant's text we discover a historical account that stresses not the strategy of the battle or the execution of the fighting, but the consequences of the battle. Much of the war fiction examined in this study echoes this representational strategy, especially as it tries to integrate the experiences of combatants and civilians.

The novel of war as we have seen, however, departs from Dunant's method by being more explicit about its struggle to balance the universal and the historically specific. When the narrative of war is moralized it tends to be discussed in general terms. Particular conflicts are brought under the rhetoric of war so that their destructive aspects can be fully recognized. Details inflect the narratives of particular conflicts, but often the emphasis is on how all war is similar and brings human beings to the brink of losing their humanity. In Dunant's description of the fighting at Solferino, it is beasts who are fighting ("un combat de bêtes féroces, furieuses et ivres de sang," [8]), and it matters little who is on which side or what the reason for the fighting is. War is a limit case with its own time outside of normal temporality.

However, the war novel exhibits a tendency toward historical specificity, as well, and, because of this, it engages a problematic at the core of humanitarian discourse. Because humanitarianism is a response to the reality of war, it describes humanity as mired in negative formulations of limits and thresholds, constraining any sense of potentiality. As Ruti G. Teitel argues most cogently about humanitarian discourse:

> . . . the meaning of humanity lies not in aspiration but on its underside, in the practices reflecting the degradation of the human, "man's inhumanity to man." This understanding is customarily revealed by practices stuck in

> the crucible of conflict—norms which have escalated in recent times of enduring conflict. Here, paradoxically, humanity is defined by its breach, constituting only a bare limit on the waging of violence. (Teitel 225)

Humanitarianism is formulated reactively as a response to war and attempts to curtail war's most atavistic elements. In seeking a remedy, humanitarian discourse veers to sentimentality. Dunant's fighting beasts turn human again only when their wounds are cared for and when, even as they appear monstrous in their extreme disfigurement, they express gratitude for the care given them by a concerned volunteer (Dunant 66). The presence of the concerned volunteer, the attention to the aftermath of battle, is one of the ways by which war can be regulated, its release of violence harnessed back so that its narrative can conclude with a sense of restoration.

The literature I examine in this project, with its claim to a right, strains not toward the "bare limit" referred to by Teitel, but to fullness. The right to the novel proclaims a right of inclusion and recognition in the narrative of the nation and seeks to resist the blurring enacted reactively to the horror of war. War fiction peels back from the "bare limit" to which Teitel refers. The war novel's focus on the agency of ordinary people resists the distanced portrayal of them as victims, even though humanitarian narratives are victims' stories deployed to elicit an empathetic response. We might be reminded of Fassin once more who tells us that humanitarianism addresses "those who can generally be constituted as victims of an overwhelming fate" (Fassin 4). The effectiveness of humanitarian narratives is mired in controversy: is the objective to lift the victim or to create the savior?[1] As I demonstrate, the war novel in Africa is instead a genre of protest that aims to mobilize a democratic ideal of a people's right to history—the making and claiming of historical narration. The novel must accommodate the individual and the collective and amplify, even exaggerate (as in the naturalist tradition) its portrayal of humanity as humanity, as feeling bodies and thinking minds, in order to resist being reduced to the "bare limit."

The attention to historically particular conflicts is reflected onto what I have called the genre's introverted orientation toward national and sometimes continental (African) readerships. Evan Maina Mwangi's paradigm of a writing "back to self" for African literature since 1980 captures a similar emphasis, especially as he foregrounds the intertextuality of African novels with each other, bringing to the fore the "metafictional" character of his examples (Evan Mwangi 6). My argument for this introversion goes beyond a self-referentiality that applies to the literary and addresses the politics of the nation state. I began this study by putting heavy emphasis on Mahmood Mamdani's description of the bifurcation of African states, the structural abandonment of the people at the state's margins of poverty and geography to a condition outside full citizenship. What my study tries to capture is the awareness of African writers that they must speak for and with the people against their condition of abandonment. As we saw in Ekwensi's *Divided We Stand*, the novel stages a scene of recognition in which the journalist protagonist understands that he, too, is in the war and a potential victim, just like the ordinary people of Biafra that he has been reporting about, counting (and exaggerating) the number of casualties for his newspaper. Telling the story of war opens up the potential for the narration of a collective experience with powerful resonances for a democratic future.

Ironically, the condition of abandonment is what makes it challenging to develop a truly national readership in Kenya, Nigeria, and Zimbabwe (the three countries of my case studies) because of low literacy rates spread over a number of different languages (English, Swahili, and indigenous languages). As one scholar of the Kenyan publishing industry put it, "'The publisher in Africa publishes for only about twenty percent of the population,'" who may or may not buy books (quoted in Larson 101). This does not change, however, the fact that we find a literary conceit deployed in the novels I examine of a national audience, a "we" who experienced the war and must come to recognize the correspondences across the many and varied stories of the war. Most effectively in the works of popular writers such as Cyprian Ekwensi, these novels affirm an ownership of the war's stories in a collective consciousness that is distinct from official discourses.

The educational market has predominated in African publishing because it alone can be predictably profitable (Larson 104), and several of the novels I discuss were marketed as secondary school texts (*Taste of Death*, for example). This gives the narrative of interrupted education of many of these novels' protagonists added poignancy and displays the continued hope invested in the socially and politically transformative effects of education. There are some ironic moments, however, on that score. My reading of Wachira's *Ordeal in the Forest* demonstrated how Wachira displaced the young person with the father figure in his novel, situating the former teacher and officer of the guerrilla force as the person who accedes to the full citizenship of the matured individual envisioned as the culmination of the conventional story of education instead of the character who is the student at the beginning of the novel. The downward pressure on the people in the postwar settlements is noted with acuity by Wachira and others through this subversion of the *Bildungsroman* form, which challenges the robustness of the narrative of education as a harbinger of progress and development.

Women authors play a large role in broadening the scope of the war novel. More than the male authors, perhaps, they are intent on the project of testimony, of shaping their fiction through the heightened rhetoric of testimonial discourse. Thus they foreground the experience of war and its impact on personal lives (families, love relationships). But they also significantly give us the sweeping vistas of the destruction of cities and villages. It is in the works of Nwapa, Adichie, and Vera that the accounts of the destruction of public space, war's toll on civilian infrastructure, comes across most clearly. This enables the women writers to make a claim on that space of the city or the village and burst out of the confines of a feminine domestic fiction with new authority to intervene in the public sphere.

The people's right to the novel, a phrase I borrowed from the nineteenth-century manifesto of naturalism, ties my study to the long and transnational history of naturalism as a form. The phrase refers, perhaps disappointingly, not to a right of access (as readers and writers, presumably) but to a right to be represented in the novel. This right of inclusion, I claimed in the introduction, gains deeper resonance from the novel's role in national formation. Anti-colonial discourse and nationalism have been linked, most notably by Barbara Harlow, to a discursive model of "resistance literature" that is shaped by a collective consciousness of displacement from the land and opposition to an occupier (Harlow 2). The cultural expressions of such resistance are viewed as playing a central role in the politics of resistance (9). My discussion of torture as a motif in the war narrative and my focus in particular on the witness's understanding of the screams of the victim as the "song of my country" comes closest to capturing how the discourse of resistance collectivizes individual experience and mobilizes it. More can be said here on that score by returning to Djebar's novel and reading it alongside Alex La Guma's *In the Fog of the Seasons' End*, where torture and war also map onto each other. The "song of my country" motif applied to La Guma's text of resistance foregrounds the analogy of torture to war, showing it to be more than a rhetorical emphasis. The motif allows us to read along the grain of Elias's (La Guma's protagonist's) thinking and substantiate more fully the implications of his resistance. What resistance literature aims for, "the passage from genealogical or hereditary lines of filiation to the collective bonds of affiliation" (Harlow 116), it achieves by borrowing, as we see in the final stages of Elias's torture, the rousing rhetoric of war. Yet the war novel shows us repeatedly that war fails to create lasting "bonds of affiliation," or perhaps, more accurately, it reveals new fissures, resistance to which can articulate broader democratic ideals. Torture as a motif captures the rifts between the resistance literature and the war novel.

Powerless to intervene and change the course of the torture, Salima, in Djebar's novel, pays close attention to the sounds of torture in order to intuit from them a vision, or conviction, about the nation. A similar expansiveness occurs in La Guma's text, where torture becomes metaphorically a scene of war. Through Elias's thought process the torture chamber transforms into a historic battlefield; Elias recalls his Zulu ancestors and the Anglo-Zulu wars. As he is being electrocuted, he is hearing, "Far away the tramp of thousands of feet drummed on the crackling earth, the rattle of spears and shields came across the long, hazy distance with the cries" (La Guma 172). In a place where the individual stands most alone, an army enters and, just as torture accomplishes its ends ("his flesh burned and scorched and his limbs jerked and twitched and fell away from him, jolting and leaping in some fantastic dance which only horror linked to him" [173]), the narrative postpones the resolution of the conflict to a future war that will carry on the unfinished business of national becoming: "*Uya kuhlasela-pi na?Where wilt thou wage war?* The ghosts of his ancestors beckoned from afar" (174). There is no honor or glory in the war of the torturers, nothing to compare to Elias's yearning to join his ancestors' continuing war, "spears sparkling like diamonds in the exploding sun" (175). As I noted with other texts, this type of renewal and postponement of the fulfillment of the resistance to the struggle grows out of the prophetic rhetoric of liberation movements that are the subject of Wenzel's study.

In the torture chamber this historical recollection posits the struggle against apartheid not as a new episode in South Africa's history, but as a chapter of an ongoing war against white oppression. South Africa of the late 1960s was, according to La Guma, in an unofficial war. The torture chamber thus takes on a surrogate role as the battlefield, a role to which it is not easily suited because of the extreme unevenness in power that defines this space. But the torturer also recognizes this as a war, which makes the scene in La Guma's novel all the more persuasive because it establishes a reciprocal understanding. The Major torturing Elias declares, "It is my duty to destroy your organization. Already you people are on your knees; soon you will be on your bellies. Soon we will stamp you out altogether. We know all about you" (5). The major's collective reference ("you people") encompasses all black South Africans, and Elias's fate becomes the example of the destruction of a people. Toward the end of Elias's ordeal, his frustrated torturer, nicknamed by La Guma "the sportsman" for the pleasure he takes in the exertions of inflicting pain, reveals what drives him to kill Elias: "He's making a bladdy fool of us. . . . We are at war, and your life really means nothing to us" (174). The torturer's admission that this is war reveals that war licenses the killing of Elias from beyond the torture chamber. With its walls metaphorically broken and exposed to view by the narrator's intrusiveness, the torture chamber can no longer be used to uphold an ideology of separation that hides the actions of the terroristic state. The unambiguously nationalist character of Elias's imaginings, therefore, foreground the collective implications of his individual suffering, made more robust by the expressed intentions of his torturer.

As J. M. Coetzee has commented, La Guma's "achievement it is to demystify the torture chamber, inner sanctum of the terroristic state" (Coetzee, *Doubling* 358). La Guma's text represents an effort to neutralize the effects of what Henry Shue has called "terroristic torture," torture that seeks to intimidate a larger community and discourage insurgency. Shue contrasts this to "interrogational torture" that assumes a "constraint of possible compliance," which means that the torture occurs under the assumption that if the victim complies and provides information, the torture will stop (Shue 245). In La Guma's novel interrogation is used as a pretense to terrorize; the victim is noncompliant, but the intent is to kill him regardless. What Coetzee calls the "terroristic state" of apartheid South Africa aims to establish through torture the total domination of a people; in the words of Pierre Vidal-Naquet, "The essential feature of the practice of torture is that one man or one class of society claims absolute power over another" (Vidal-Naquet 195). Moreover, in the case of La Guma, once exposed, torture takes on a new guise and becomes a scene of war.

The comparison of the torture chamber and the battlefield implicit in La Guma's representation echoes Shue's philosophical argument against torture in which Shue compares the confrontation of enemies in war to torture, which is then defined by analogy to war as a "cruel assault upon the defenseless" not permitted in just war (Shue 243). Shue explains that "torture begins only after the fight is—for the victim—finished. Only losers are tortured" (243). By giving Elias a collective rather than individual identity, La Guma forestalls the inevitability of the outcome of terror; the people have not lost yet. Moreover, La Guma renders the singular event of Elias's martyrdom hidden out of sight in the torture chamber through the prism of a much larger narrative, that of the Zulus's (a symbol of a broader African nationalism) struggle against white rule. A situation of extremely uneven power is recast as a situation of reciprocal struggle through the rhetoric of war.

In his internal thought process Elias is able to transport himself spiritually to his ancestors, which enables him to regain control over the terms of his own death and locate it within an economy of signs belonging to his people against his racist denigration by the torturers. Leading up to the climactic scene of Elias's electrocution, Elias's memories become increasingly collective. Early in the torture, Elias thinks of his childhood: "Far away, he was suddenly a child again and he had fallen into the dam and was drowning" (La Guma 7). Later, when he is barely aware of being alive because of the pain, he has a happy childhood memory: "he was a child and they all ran along the railway tracks through the dust. . . . Then it was autumn. The grass was still green, and at that time the evenings were best. . . . They were sitting around the fires in front of the homesteads" (169). The normalcy of the everyday contrasts sharply with Elias's present moment. Nostalgia for the homestead leads not to resignation but to a recommitment to struggle.

If La Guma manages "to demystify the torture chamber," as Coetzee argues (Coetzee, *Doubling* 358), this is not only because the violence is exposed. It is also because its relevance is widened. When he is still able to, Elias speaks out during his torture: "You shoot and kill and torture because you cannot rule in any other way a people who reject you. You are reaching the end of the road and going downhill toward a great darkness" (La Guma 6). These words typify the rhetoric of denunciation that characterizes war literature (Fréris 85). Although Elias's words may seem ineffective (they don't forestall his death), that is hardly the point. They constitute his response to the torturer's denigration of him (and his people) and establish the moral superiority of his cause, exhibiting the key function of resistance literature.

Djebar, as we saw earlier, uses the torture chamber like La Guma as a place from which to stage the collective commitment to resistance. The scene ends as Salima grieves the loss of the voice, now silenced because the man she presumes has died (Djebar 113).[2] Salima, who is unmarried, comes to see her relation to the voice as analogous to the experience of the wives in her neighborhood who exist in the "shadow" of their husbands' secretive activities in the war against the colonizer, unable to share fully in their husbands' experience. She thus comes to see herself as a surrogate for a community of sequestered women who have watched their husbands go to fight. Women's sequestration, like the walls of the prison that keep the torture out of view but within earshot, place women intimately close to war while also keeping them separate from it. In the gender-segregated world Salima lives in, the war has been taking place at a distance, in the hills outside the city. From the opening sequence of the novel, we know that women are located as spectators watching the action from their windows in the city (2). As Salima surrenders to the screams of torture, the sounds "form a long chant, a threnody" that, as I noted, she recognizes as the "song of my country" (112–13). Through Salima, Djebar is able to create an affiliation among women, who, as witnesses of the war's impact, can speak to the nation and give it a different, more expansive sense of its experience.

The novels by Djebar and La Guma exemplify the ways in which the narrative of the torture of an individual takes on the burden of narrating the conflict of the war more generally. Djebar's description of the screams of the torture victim as the "song of my country" is an emplotting device for the nationalist narrative of resistance. The four motifs I named in my study (the "song of my country," the ordeal in the forest, the male warrior as war personified, and the eternal landscape) reveal the ways in which these works form a coherent body of literature that is distinct. The motifs can also be used to comment on the war novel as a genre more broadly, reaching back to open up earlier examples of the form to new readings or traveling through a comparative methodology across other narrative traditions and forms. The ordeal in the forest is perhaps the most evocative of these motifs outside its immediate context of African literature. As a closing gesture for this study, I want to hint at the possibilities that such readings hold by turning to two exemplary war narratives from the United States: Stephen Crane's *The Red Badge of Courage* (1895) and Francis Ford Coppola's *Apocalypse Now* (1979). Thinking about war, although always urgent, has become particularly pressing in our post 9/11 reality. Crane and Coppola, separated by almost a century and addressing two wars that were crucibles in America coming to terms with itself, both teach us to view war critically and with detachment, in particular with reference to nationalism or a sense of the heroic. The juxtaposition of them with the African texts helps perhaps to reveal the particularity of their (Crane and Coppola's) dissidence in a fresh way and to bring the African writers more robustly into the conversation about war.

In Crane's classic war novel, the youth, Henry Fleming, deserts the battlefront and runs into a "thick wood," where at first the beautiful nature gives him some solace (Crane 46). The escape is illusory, however, because deep in the wood the ordeal manifests itself when Henry encounters the shocking corpse of a soldier, rendered thus through Crane's naturalism: "The eyes, staring at the youth, had changed to the dull hue to be seen on the side of a dead fish. The mouth was open. Its red had changed to an appalling yellow. Over the gray skin of the face, ran little ants. One was trundling some sort of bundle along the upper lip" (Crane 46). More than anything he sees on the battlefield, Henry is affected by this encounter, made unexpectedly when he considered himself away from the scene of war, safely nestled in the "chapel"-like space of the close wood with its "religious half light" (45). The dead man is a synecdoche for death itself, war's inevitable outcome. This is a transformative experience that imprints on the youth the impossibility of moving beyond the space of war in the time of war.

The experience, however, also accelerates Fleming's capacity to deal with war. This is where the motif of the ordeal is most pertinent. Consistent with the motif, Fleming's encounter with the dead soldier results in his intensified involvement in war and not his retreat.[3] Immediately after leaving the wood "he began to run in the direction of the battle" and not away from it, as he had been when he entered the wood (47). We learn that, transfixed by death, he returns intent to see how the battle, like a "terrible machine," could "produce corpses" (48). To observe killing becomes an activity of war. Because he is a survivor, the youth is positioned as the surrogate: "his essential experiences are of seeing other men dying or dead" (Kazin xvi).

The motif of the male warrior as war personified has been associated with the lore of "the heart of darkness."[4] The tendency to metaphorize and psychologize the heart of darkness has allowed for it to be transposed onto war as a general condition. A very resonant example is *Apocalypse Now*, Coppola's adaptation of Joseph Conrad's *Heart of Darkness* into a film about the Vietnam War. This film is contemporaneous with much of the literature examined in this study, a variant that captures something about the global phenomenon of narrating war at a time (the late 1970s) when recently decolonized societies are struggling under the influence of the new empires and the Cold War. In Coppola's film Kurtz is no longer associated with the lie at the heart of the civilizing mission but with the mystification of "war personified" that follows from the confrontation with this figure. War is the way of empire, according to Coppola's critique. Africa as a specific referent for the heart of darkness is not at play here, as Coppola's adaptation develops the forest motif in the setting of Vietnam. And as we saw, the heart of darkness is resisted overtly by the African writers when they narrate the ordeal in the forest and stress that the ordeal occurs because the guerrilla fighter finds the forest alien and challenging.

In Coppola's adaptation of Conrad, the encounter with war personified in the figure of Kurtz takes place during an ordeal in the forest, bringing the two motifs together. In the bleak territory that Coppola takes us to, we have dispensed with references to a civilizing mission, and the alternate reality of Kurtz's inner station is better understood not as his alternative "civilization" but as the logic of war exposed. The place is littered with death, dying, and suffering, all under the auspices of the powerful figure who evokes evil and has adopted the eccentric appearance (in voice, as well) of a self-fashioning that reflects his immersion in violence.

Walter Kurtz is a renegade colonel who has gone rogue, amassing his own "army" and crossing over into Cambodia to kill the Viet Cong. Willard (the Marlow figure in the film) is sent not to bring Kurtz out of the jungle, as he is supposed to in Conrad's novel, but to assassinate him. Willard is himself complicit in war's violence; after all, he is selected for this mission precisely because of his record as an assassin—and, in this degree of experience, he is very much unlike Crane's Fleming. But the film shows us that Willard must accede to a different order of violence in order to complete his mission. Willard's capacity to turn Kurtz's brutality against him is awakened through the transformative experience of the ordeal, which culminates in Kurtz's torture of him. Willard's willingness to swing a machete and cut up Kurtz, presented as the only action that can possibly defeat him, is brought out by the experience of the ordeal whose core is the confrontation with war personified in the figure of Kurtz. Before meeting Kurtz, Willard learns about Kurtz's standing as a highly decorated officer and develops a fascination for him. Duplicating the mirroring effect that Conrad creates in Marlow's confrontation with Kurtz, which becomes both a confrontation with a truth about another and a confrontation about the self, Coppola turns Willard's fascination with Kurtz into horror, but not without recognizing its echoes in himself first and his own complicity in war. Willard succeeds in leaving the heart of darkness alive and, like Conrad's Marlow, will undertake the double gesture of revealing (in his first-person voiceover) and concealing what he saw, to protect those outside war from seeing war personified (Coundouriotis, "Congo Cases" 137).

This reading of *Apocalypse Now*, however, hits a wrong note in that the ordeal in the forest, while it always represents an intensification of the protagonist's engagement with war (evident here by Willard's use of a machete to kill), is not necessarily represented as a form of corruption or contamination by evil. The ordeal in the forest bucks the tendency of the naturalist narrative to devolve toward atavism. It is part of the tug and pull of the literature's engagement with and resistance to naturalism.[5] In several instances—for example, Laokolé in *Johnny chien méchant* or Jeebleh in *Links* (who experiences a variant of the "ordeal" in the cemetery)—the ordeal represents a necessary shift in involvement that pushes the protagonist to confront and resolve a pressing danger. It awakens the character to his or her capacity to act violently. For Laokolé being implicated in killing is required for her survival. Not so for Jeebleh, who plans Caloosha's murder to achieve a sense of justice. Willard, of course, is far from naïve in war, yet the logic of the ordeal in the forest might in fact still apply to him insofar as there is valor in killing Kurtz. Does the emphasis in the film's ending (ambivalent, as it is, in fact, a double ending) fall on the impact this experience has on Willard, who might be viewed now as irreparably sullied, or is it on how the elimination of Kurtz authorizes the continuation of the war as a legitimate conflict? As Coppola leaves this unresolved, it demonstrates a degree of detachment on his part and his desire to provoke the viewer to think critically about war. Furthermore, it distances his adaptation from readings of Conrad that see his narrative as endorsing Marlow's lie instead of exposing it and thus extending the logic of empire.

The reading of Coppola's film also raises a question about the fourth motif, the landscape of eternity. The landscape speaks loudly in Coppola's film as the threatening jungle, mastered only elusively from above and requiring penetration from the ground and intimate contact with its recesses to achieve a resolution, which is, moreover, equivocal, as we saw. Coppola's warscape represents the invader's point of view. The violence exerted against Vietnamese villagers speaks for Coppola's critique of American power and its scopic invention of spaces of evil that call forth a violent response, even though the evil contained in these spaces, personified in Kurtz, is a seed of the empire itself. Coppola's landscape does not align itself with the motif of the landscape of eternity, therefore. The motif puts in play ideas of nature that transcend human history and remind the protagonist of his or her connection to the earth and capacity for harmony with it. In Diop's *Murambi: The Book of Bones* this comes in the form of a distantly evoked pastoral, recovered through the recollection of a childhood experience shared with the grandfather. Nwapa's lake in *Never Again* promises through its unspoiled and enduring beauty to be the source of spiritual renewal after the war. The African novelists address the land in a reclamation that intends to be unifying and reassuring against the turbulence of war and nationalist projects that have exposed deep rifts. In this attitude of reverence toward the land, furthermore, one can detect an environmentalist consciousness. Nobel Peace Prize winner Wangari Maathai's Green Belt movement, founded in 1977 and thus taking shape contemporaneously with this literature, exemplifies the trajectory from a childhood experience of war (the Mau Mau conflict) to environmental activism. The tragic example of Ken Saro-Wiwa also endures. What Rob Nixon has called the "environmentalism of the poor" develops from an awareness of enduring insecurity and, while constituted by transformative practices of struggle, its momentum, I would argue, is shaped at least in part by the people's awareness that emerged in reaction to the wars of decolonization and the early independence years (Nixon 128–29). The motif of the landscape of eternity thus presages the way that an environmental connection to the land can inspire a collective movement of the people to resist their abandonment by the nation state and global interests. By recuperating the non-canonical novels and recontextualizing the more widely read texts in this war literature, I hope *The People's Right to the Novel* provokes us to think some more about the relationship between narrative and the experience of war and the contributions of African writers to this rich vein of inquiry.

NOTES

INTRODUCTION: NATURALISM, HUMANITARIANISM, AND THE FICTION OF WAR

1. The *Bildungsroman* held out a promise to colonial subjects that they would belong to its legal regime through assimilation. Joseph Slaughter locates the postcolonial novel of education in the trajectory of the emergence of a global human-rights discourse and explains how African writers engaged with and dissented from their colonial culture, giving shape to a literature of disillusion he characterizes as *dissensual* (Slaughter, *Human Rights* 267).

2. Examples of studies that organize war literature historically around particular wars are Margaret Higonnet's anthology of women writers of World War I, *Lines of Fire*, and Gareth Thomas's *The Novel of the Spanish Civil War (1936–1975)*. Kate McLoughlin's *Authoring War: the Literary Representation of War from the Iliad to Iraq* attempts a broad definition of war writing, but looks at all literary genres, not just the novel. McLoughlin places less emphasis on the historical and more on the universals of war. All writing about war, she argues, is plagued by a sense of its secondariness, the fact that it can't capture the experience, and marks "a transition into falsehood" (2). Her *Cambridge Companion to War Writing* contains an extended section on "Poetics" that is organized topically by specific wars.

3. Harry Levin notes, for example, that "class struggle is inherent in the naturalistic universe" as part of its treatment of capital as an all-encompassing and inescapable environment (Levin 335).

4. Dunant's exhaustive account of the suffering of the wounded created a sensation that led to the founding of the International Committee of the Red Cross and the birth of the modern humanitarian movement (Fassin and Rechtman 192). For a comprehensive institutional history of the founding and early years of the ICRC, see Forsythe 19–23.

5. Beyond Arendt, Luc Boltanski and Fassin have elaborated on this idea of distance as constitutive of a humanitarian consciousness; see Boltanski, *Distant Suffering*, which focuses on the figure of the spectator and, unlike Arendt, posits distance in terms of geography rather than class (Boltanski 7).

In *Humanitarian Reason*, Fassin tries to do both: to look at France internally and the West as a spectator of the suffering of distant others. He identifies the emergence of "humanitarian reason" in the late twentieth century as a type of governmentality that seeks to alleviate suffering: "Humanitarian government is indeed a politics of precarious lives" (Fassin 4). Social inequality is expressed in the language of suffering, turning politics into a redress of suffering (23). See also an important revision of Boltanski's theory in Lilie Chouliaraki, *The Ironic Spectator*. I return to all three theorists in some detail later in my study.

6. Arendt speaks of a moral distance, but this distance is often articulated as also physical, or geographical, distance, best illustrated by Boltanski's idea of "distant suffering" whose archetypal situation is the middle-class European household sitting down in front of the television and viewing the suffering of the Third World poor (Boltanski 7).

7. The distinction between humanitarian and human rights discourses is that humanitarianism seeks to alleviate suffering, whereas human rights discourse makes rights claims (Wilson and Brown 11).

8. McLoughlin discusses the war as environment and argues that it creates "zones" that help us perceive how alien or unassimilable war is (*Authoring* 18).

9. When the Goncourts declared after the success of the novel that they were done with the people, Zola expressed his distress. He sarcastically commented that the Goncourts gave the people the right to the novel and then abandoned them. For Zola, the poor, urban and rural alike, were a complex subject that would consume a career rather than just a single work (Zola, *Roman* 263).

10. In *Inventing Human Rights*, Hunt explains the rise of sentimentality as the invention of the category "human" that enables the creation of human rights.

11. Perhaps Laqueur's insistence on the term "ordinary man" and its allusion to the division among the privileged and the not-privileged is more closely aligned with Richard Rorty's account of how our sentimental education predisposes the well-off to identify with people that are far away and different (Rorty 122–23). For both Laqueur and Rorty the emphasis remains on a notion of us and them, even when the gap can be bridged through the imagination.

12. Dave Eggers riffs on "war is war" with the title of his novel *What Is the What*. This is not a question but a statement that announces how the novel will solve the riddle of "what is the what." Yet, because of the absence of the question mark, the statement becomes a tautology that explains nothing. The reader of this text, which is deeply invested in the ameliorative logic of humanitarianism and the power of witness to achieve such goals, can choose

either to see this as nonsensical or to answer affirmatively by reading along the grain of hopefulness that the unknown possibilities of the future might indeed bring good.

13. Zola anticipates this difficulty in his own war novel, *La Débâcle*, which was the most widely read of his works during his lifetime. In this work he demonstrates that war is one manifestation of the total social environment. *La Débâcle* is both a novel of the Franco-Prussian War (1870–1871) and of the collapse of the Paris Commune (1871), a history that intertwined war and political revolution.

14. This is from Iyayi's novel *Heroes* (28), which I discuss in Chapter 2. The best-known example of a naturalist war novel is Stephen Crane's *Red Badge of Courage*.

15. Lazarus is not looking at war novels specifically, although there is some overlap. He mentions as examples of naturalism the works of Dambudzo Marechera and Mongane Serote, as well as Mwangi. There is also an alternative canon of naturalist African novels. Zola's depiction of the miners' strike in *Germinal* is considered an important influence behind Sembène's *God's Bits of Wood*; see Darbouze. Alex La Guma's *Walk in the Night* is also widely recognized as a naturalist text; see JanMohamed, "Alex La Guma," 275.

16. Mamdani explains the origins of this division as part of the colonial political culture: "there was a real internal difference between civil power over citizens and customary power over free peasants. That difference turned more on the political than on the economic. It was not a difference between capitalist and precapitalist or market and premarket formations. The free peasantry lives neither outside market relations nor simply within it. It lives, rather, on the interstices of the market and direct compulsions. The internal difference between civil society and the free peasantry, however, lay in the mode of rule characteristic of each: whereas civil society was governed directly by a civil power enforcing a civil law claiming to guarantee rights, the free peasantry was ruled indirectly through Native Authorities whose claim was to enforce custom through a customary law" (Mamdani, *Citizen* 183).

17. Speaking of Kenya specifically but in ways that resonate throughout this literature, Tirop Simatei describes the problematic remembrance of war: "as the moment and site in which the memory of the war of independence is enacted, the postcolonial moment is itself a painful inversion and denial of the objectives of war. In other words, the ironies and paradoxes that circumscribe the postindependence moment tend to question the success of decolonization in general and armed struggle in particular" (Tirop Simatei 90).

18. According to Lazarus, Fanon's theory is multifaceted, and postcolonialists have gravitated away from his "Third-Worldist formulations" such as the one on violence and more toward his theory of identity and race as

developed in *Black Skin, White Masks* (Lazarus, *Postcolonial Unconscious* 165). In making this point, Lazarus follows the argument of Fanon's biographer David Macey, who explores the reception of Fanon's thought and its influence on postcolonial studies (Macey 25–26). Lazarus derives from Macey a distinction between the "revolutionary Fanon" and the "post-colonial Fanon" (Lazarus, *Postcolonial Unconscious* 163–69).

19. African history was represented in a cluster of four essays by Alessandro Triulzi, Shula Marks, Richard Rathbone, and Robin Law. The essays address methodological issues: decolonizing the study of African literature, what constitutes a people's history of South Africa, slavery and pre-colonial Africa, and the methods of Marxist historiography.

20. Samuel differentiates between people's history and Marxist history, although he calls for a closer synergy between them. Marxist history is methodologically central to the development of African history. According to Samuel, however, people's history is "affirmative," and Marxist history tends to be critical. This divergence stems from people's history's aim to "celebrat[e] the creative power of the masses while ignoring (so it is alleged) the imperatives under which they labour." Although Samuel is clearly in disagreement with the idea that people's history overlooks the material conditions of labor, he does acknowledge the strength of Marxist history that looks at the "totality of social experience." He also notes at the same time that Marxist history is suspicious of the word "people" because of its association with "bourgeois democracy" (Samuel xxviii).

21. See, for example, two authoritative works: Gérard Prunier, *Africa's World War* (2009) and René Lemarchand, *The Dynamics of Violence in Central Africa* (2009).

22. James Buzard in *Disorienting Fiction* claims that the novel is an autoethnographic form helping to invent Englishness. Patrick Parrinder's literary history *Nation and Novel* also tracks how the novel shaped ideas of Englishness (Parrinder 15).

23. See, for example, Christopher Miller, *Theories of Africans*; Abiola Irele, *The African Experience in Literature and Ideology*; and Eleni Coundouriotis, *Claiming History: Colonialism, Ethnography and the Novel.*

24. For nationalism as a borrowed discourse, see Benedict Anderson, *Imagined Communities*; Partha Chatterjee, *Nationalist Thought and the Colonial World* and *The Nation and Its Fragments*; Terry Eagleton, Fredric Jameson, and Edward W. Said, *Nationalism, Colonialism, and Literature*; andMamdani, *Citizen and Subject.*

25. See, for example, my discussion of Paul Hazoumé's *Doguicimi* in *Claiming History*. Other early and influential examples are the South African novels *Chaka*, by Thomas Mofolo, and *Mhudi*, by Sol Plaatje.

26. Julien notes that many of the "extroverted" novels have enjoyed large African audiences because they have become the canonical texts promoted by the literary establishment both within and outside Africa. The "extroverted" novel thus speaks to "a nation's 'others' and elites in terms (which is to say, about issues and in a language and style) they have come to expect" (683). The growing scholarship on African popular literature (by scholars such as Stephanie Newell, Karin Barber, and Wendy Griswold) indicates a widening recognition of other fictional conventions. Julien also highlights the instability of the adjective "African" when she disavows the term both as "*the* African novel" and as the "African" novel (Julien 667–68n1).

27. Agamben aligns the "people" with "bare life" and "People" with "political existence" or *bios*. I discuss Agamben's terms "bare life" and *bios* later (Agamben, *Homo Sacer* 177).

28. Agamben acknowledges, however, that it is compatible with Marxian "class conflict," which he calls the "civil war that divides every people" (*Homo Sacer* 178).

29. See Mamdani's critique of Basil Davidson's *The Black Man's Burden*. Mamdani says of Davidson that he "uses the concept of 'civil society' as many have 'socialism,' prophetically and not analytically, as promise and not reality, as programmatic and not actually-existing, just as he employs 'modern tribalism' as a semi-caricature, throwing to the winds his otherwise sure inclination for a contextualized and nuanced understanding of historical phenomena" (Mamdani, *Monthly Review* essay).

30. Dangarembga's novel is the key text in Slaughter's argument about the creation of dissensual subjects in the colonial *Bildungsroman*.

31. Primorac also notes Dangarembga's lack of attention to the guerrilla war but links the focus on gender in the novel to nation making and hence does not agree with the implications of Dangarembga's critics that she eschews politics (Primorac, *Place of Tears* 105).

32. Two critics are particularly compelling on this point. Lazarus, also a Marxist, sees in Jameson a defender of Third World literature who is trying to tap into its liberationist aspiration as "national" literature in a context of resistance to colonialism (Lazarus, "Fredric Jameson" 57). He seeks in particular to discredit Aijaz Ahmad's argument that Jameson's attitude is "colonialist" (47). Similarly, Jameson is important to Susan Andrade for portraying "sympathetically" the "historical investment in nationalism" in the decolonization effort and for positing that in Third World fiction the breach between private and public "is fictionally reconciled" and national allegory "functions as a passage between the two spheres" (Andrade, *Nation* 25).

33. Jameson looks at the way in which Lu Xun describes the writer's dilemma in a hopeless political situation and quotes the following: "Imagine

an iron house without windows, absolutely indestructible, with many people fast asleep inside who will shortly die of suffocation. But you know that since they will die in their sleep, they will not feel the pain of death. Now if you cry aloud to wake a few of the lighter sleepers, making those unfortunate few suffer the agony of irrevocable death, do you think you are doing them a good turn?" (quoted in Jameson, "Third-World Literature" 75).

34. For a contrasting situation, see Jameson's discussion of *Heart of Darkness*, a novel that presents a situation in which one can only designate the inside from the outside, radically limiting the implications of interiority. Kurtz's "the horror" transforms a historical circumstance into a "mood," a matter of interiority. The real horror of Leopold's Congo "can only be designated by recourse to an aesthetic *expression*—the unspeakable, *unnameable* inner feeling, whose external formulation can only designate it from without, like a symptom" (Jameson, "Third-World Literature" 70–71). Instead of imploding and bringing down the oppressive system of imperial exploitation, the aesthetic representation exposes it as private and "recontains" it, taming its unsettling energy for the political.

35. Darius Rejali in *Torture and Democracy* shows that "virtually all the techniques used in conflicts in Afghanistan, Iraq, Algeria, and Northern Ireland, as well as in prisons in France, England and the United States, are descended from these procedures or subsequent variants." In addition to French and British colonial practices, he cites British military punishments and torture in the context of American slavery (Rejali 4).

36. For example, Chaka struggles with the decision whether to kill his lover, Noliwa, as Isanusi suggests he do with the promise that he will be rewarded with unlimited power (Mofolo, *Chaka* 123, 125–26).

37. Mofolo deploys an agricultural metaphor for mass extermination that correlates with what Ben Kiernan identifies as genocidal ideology's "fetish for agriculture" (Kiernan 2).

38. The three novels in the trilogy are *Links*, *Knots* (2007), and *Crossbones* (2011).

39. On human rights history as genre, see Coundouriotis, "Congo Cases: The Stories of Human Rights History."

40. The most frequently discussed of these texts are Nuruddin Farah's *Links*; Emmanuel Dongala's *Johnny chien méchant*; Ahmadou Kourouma's *Allah n'est pas obligé*; Uzodinma Iweala's *Beasts of No Nation*; Chris Abani's *Song for Night*; and Chimamanda Ngozi Adichie's *Half of a Yellow Sun*. In addition are the texts from the Rwanda Memory Project, which include Boubacar Boris Diop's *Murambi, livre des ossements*.

41. This was the case in the nineteenth-century European naturalist novel, as well. The preface of *Germinie Lacerteux* proposed a "mixture of

styles" in order to allow the suffering of the people to be portrayed with seriousness (Auerbach 496). The novel was perceived as the successor to classical tragedy. Ironically, the provocative nature of the naturalist aesthetic registered the writer's sense of alienation from his public, bringing into doubt the ability of the work to gain enough political traction to achieve its goals.

1. "NO INNOCENTS AND NO ONLOOKERS": THE USES OF THE PAST IN THE NOVELS OF MAU MAU

1. The meaning as well as the origin of the name "Mau Mau" is still debated. Maughan-Brown cautions against using the term because it carries with it the negative characterizations attributed to the movement by the British (Maughan-Brown 16). In his autobiography, Josiah Mwangi Kariuki offers an explanation of the term that connects it to children's word games. Making anagrams was commonplace. Mau Mau is, according to Kariuki, an anagram of Uma Uma (he does not give the meaning of Uma Uma). Mau Mau was used, according to Kariuki, by a loyalist, Parmenas Kiritu, to portray the movement as childish (Kariuki 23–24).

2. Elkins does not cite literary sources, although she makes extensive use of Kariuki's autobiography, *Mau Mau Detainee*, which she says "is one of the few autobiographical documents that give us a vivid picture of the world behind the wire" enclosure of the detention camps (Elkins 160).

3. Ngũgĩ also cowrote, with Micere Mugo, *The Trial of Dedan Kimathi* (1977), a play. His novel *Matigari* (1989), in which he disclaims historicity, is the story of a former Mau Mau who decides to return to the forest to renew the struggle for justice. The novel was immediately censored by the Moi regime.

4. Daniel Branch adds to this picture by emphasizing that many Gikuyu were indiscriminately arrested and that there was significant "retrospective politicisation" of this population, some of whom undoubtedly were radicalized by the experience of detention itself (Branch 181).

5. Elkins's and David Anderson's books were reviewed mostly as a pair. A. J. Stockwell's review typifies the skepticism with which Elkins's book was received in Britain, which contrasts with the more positive reception of Anderson's book in the United States. Stockwell faults Elkins's account of British policy, which, he says, overstresses its coherence and its deliberate intent. In contrast, Stockwell finds Anderson's attention to "sins of omission as well as those of commission" by the British as more persuasive (Stockwell 582). Kenyan historian Bethwell A. Ogot also expresses a preference for Anderson's book. He is critical of Elkins's reliance on interviews with camp survivors fifty years after the events and wonders to what degree she can rely on the authenticity of their accounts (Ogot, "Britain's Gulag" 493).

6. Anderson's account of Dedan Kimathi's case, in particular, has resonance for the literary renditions of Mau Mau, as Kimathi is the most often referred-to figure in the literature. Anderson explains how Kimathi came to be regarded as one of the most charismatic and dominant personalities among the Mau Mau commanders whose memory "remains potent today in Kenya" (David Anderson 287). For literary versions of Kimathi's life, see the play by Ngũgĩ and Micere Githae Mugo and Samuel Kahiga's novel *Dedan Kimathi: The Real Story*, which I discuss later in this chapter.

7. Class is key to this discourse. Writing more than twenty years after Maughan-Brown, Branch concurs that more analysis is needed of the intersection of class and ethnicity in Kenya, especially as it determines the "dichotomies of landed/landless, wealthy/poor, and labourer/idle" that have shaped Kenyan political debate since the Emergency (Branch 207).

8. By placing the discussion of the "novels of the freedom" first and the discussion of Ngũgĩ second in his study, Maughan-Brown obscures the actual literary history. Ngũgĩ's novels are the earliest in the group, written before there was any significant body of literature on the Mau Mau other than autobiography and colonialist treatises. A more appropriate comparison would be between *Petals of Blood* (1977) and "the novels of the freedom," works that are roughly contemporary. Once again Ngũgĩ takes a different course. As Carol M. Sicherman has argued, *Petals of Blood* uses the memory of Mau Mau to press for economic rights and places the Emergency in a longer historical frame that extends back to pre-colonial and colonial history (Sicherman, "Kenyan History" 349–50), sharpening the contrast with the "novels of the freedom," which, in order to reinforce a "fragile 'national consensus'" after independence, seriously curtailed the historical scope.

9. The genre of Elkins's text is more properly understood as human rights history and not conventional African or imperial history. It narrates the Emergency through the lens of the legal obligations that were violated. For a definition of human rights history as genre, see Coundouriotis, "Congo Cases," 133.

10. "Principles of International Law Recognized in the Charter of the Nüremberg Tribunal and in the Judgment of the Tribunal, 1950" can be found at http://www.icrc.org/ihl.nsf/full/390, accessed 1 May 2012.

11. Anderson also refers to the "civil war" between the Gikuyu Home Guard set up by the British and the Mau Mau and indicates that the British encouraged this because the conflict seemed like less of a "race war" (David Anderson 240).

12. The official reclaiming of Mau Mau by Kibaki's regime was politically instrumental, in part a response to Mungiki, a group "made up of discontented, unemployed youth from Nairobi" who use the memory of Gikuyu

armed revolt to threaten Gikuyu elite who have not done enough to redistribute wealth (Branch xiii). The official embrace of Mau Mau as a national narrative is an attempt to "delegitimize Mungiki" by claiming the legacy of Mau Mau for the state and deflecting attention from class differences (xiv).

13. Elkins allowed the occasion of her book's publication to become an official government event in which two ministers, later charged with corruption, spoke (Branch xv). Moreover, Branch discusses the negative reviews that Elkins received, and although he faults her for a monolithic account of the Gikuyu, he credits the attention given to her work with energizing the field (xv). Another reviewer, Philip Murphy, notes Elkins's methodological shortcomings, such as using census data to estimate the numbers killed by the British. Yet, although he sides with Elkins's detractors on this point, Murphy still credits Elkins with producing a study of "considerable value as a chronicle of such abuses." Although much of the evidence for this history has been available in the National Archives, Murphy claims that Elkins is the "first scholar to have brought these various strands of this 'dirty war' together in a single, powerful narrative" (Murphy 427). Kennell Jackson draws attention in contrast to the systematic destruction by the British of their colonial record in Kenya and lauds Elkins for painstakingly piecing together this silenced history (Jackson 159).

14. Elkins regrettably makes no reference to Ngũgĩ. Fiction and history are not interchangeable, but they can be read together fruitfully. For a discussion of Ngũgĩ's work in relation to that of professional historians, see Sicherman, who explains Ngũgĩ's critique of neocolonial attitudes in their work, especially in Ogot, whom I cited earlier as one of Elkins's reviewers (Sicherman, "Kenyan History" 353–57). James Ogude discusses Ngũgĩ's fiction of the Mau Mau as an intentional response to "Kenya's pioneer historians Ogot, Were, Muriuki, and Ochien," whom, Ogude argues, Ngũgĩ wanted to surpass by focusing on the "marginalized" or "subaltern" ignored in their histories (Ogude 9).

15. The creation of a consensual historical narrative can be a human rights project that aims to "unite the often unfulfilled promises of rights with the aspirations of conflict resolution" (Barkan, "Redress" 4). Such projects complement the work of tribunals and truth commissions by addressing the "long-term memories," events from which the primary actors and victims might be dead but whose resonance still haunts and divides a community. From such projects, a "new shared historical identity" can emerge (Barkan, "Historians" 903). Before Elazar Barkan, Lonsdale had also expressed the desire for a history that can strengthen "the negotiated bond of responsible nationhood" to replace the "codes of oblivion" devised instead by Kenyans (Berman and Lonsdale 267, 265).

16. Ngũgĩ names *Mau Mau Detainee* and the following: Muga Gacaru's *Land of Sunshine*; Mugo Gatheru's *A Child of Two Worlds*; Waruhiu Itote's *Mau Mau General*; and Grace Waciuma's *Daughter of Mumbi* (Ngũgĩ, *Homecoming* 70–71). Another important autobiography, which appeared subsequently, is Muthoni Likimani's *Passbook Number F.47927: Women and Mau Mau in Kenya*. Ngũgĩ also mentions fictional works (*Ordeal in the Forest* and the stories by Leonard Kibera and Samuel Kahiga in *Potent Ash*) that, in addition to *Carcase for Hounds* and *Dedan Kimathi* (both published after the essays in *Homecoming*) and Ngũgĩ's own very widely read fiction, constitute the core of a body of literature on the Mau Mau.

17. According to Sicherman, Ngũgĩ was "preoccupied with history from the beginning," and the "major theme" of his writing has always been "the history of resistance" and the ways in which it has been occluded (Sicherman, "Kenyan History" 349, 354).

18. The same visit that began in triumph with a welcome for Ngũgĩ "bigger than a presidential visit" ended in violence as Ngũgĩ and his wife were attacked in their hotel (Diawara 74). In the attack, his wife was raped. For Ngũgĩ's reflections on the "political" nature of the attack, see his interview with Manthia Diawara (78). Ngũgĩ's visit also coincided with the publication of his critique of the Moi dictatorship, a novel written in Gikuyu, *Murogi wa Kagogo* [*The Wizard of the Crow*] (Gikandi, "Winter" 76).

19. Gikandi has discussed a different way of addressing this impulse to make whole again in Ngũgĩ's early works, or his desire for an "autochtonous African culture" to respond to colonialism and become the "foundation of the new nation." Gikandi, moreover, takes note of Ngũgĩ's ambivalence toward traditional culture (Gikandi, *Ngũgĩ* 58).

20. These two novels focus on torture and detention, which is why I discuss them. The memory of Mau Mau is also important in *Petals of Blood*, as noted above. Ngũgĩ's *Matigari* (1989) could also be considered a Mau Mau novel. It tells the story of a forest fighter who returns to civilian life, is appalled by the injustices he sees, and tries to take up the armed struggle again, only to be killed. This novel examines the enduring impact of the conflict in the postcolonial era, when its memory was suppressed. It does not depict the Mau Mau conflict directly, however. Ogude has noted this shift in Ngũgĩ's depiction of the Mau Mau: "whereas in the earlier novels Ngũgĩ captures the moral complexity of the historic war, in the later works the Mau Mau war is singularly seen as the ultimate expression of Kenya's anti-colonial struggle—a class war against the colonizing oppressor" (Ogude 13).

21. Similarly, Elkins writes, "The Gikuyu soldiers who returned from war would galvanize popular discontent" (Elkins 23). These Gikuyu veterans

had acquired a more worldly perspective (having learned of India's successful independence, for example) and saw "their British counterparts receiving demobilization support from the colonial government," whereas their own families had been further pushed into poverty (24).

22. Branch notes Kariuki's importance as a politician and his role in trying to advance reconciliation between loyalists and Mau Mau, though he was a "champion of the poor and landless." A successful and wealthy man, Kariuki had an "unimpeachable" standing as a Gikuyu nationalist, but was not a radical. He was assassinated in 1974 (Branch 204–5).

23. Elkins explains the meaning of land ownership in Gikuyu society and the reasons alienation from the land was infantalizing and demeaning. She calls this the "social consequence to the British landgrab" and explains, "To be a man or a woman—to move from childhood to adulthood—a Gikuyu had to have access to land. . . . Land and family entitled him to certain privileges within Gikuyu patriarchy; without land a man would remain socially a boy" (Elkins 14).

24. English was taught only beginning in standard seven, which meant that the vast majority of those who went to school never learned English (JanMohamed, *Manichean* 190). Independent schools defied the British and taught English earlier, but in 1952 all independent schools were closed because of the Emergency (191).

25. For example, in Chapter 3, I discuss a scene in *The Stone Virgins* where Nonceba ponders her attacker's capacity for mercy.

26. Oathing was viewed as one of Mau Mau's more controversial practices. It was used to unite people and connect them to the movement. Elkins describes what is known about the oaths (Elkins 25–28). Kariuki gives a detailed account of the two oaths he took, which he likened to a spiritual rebirth (Kariuki 27–31). The British considered the oath to be one of the movement's most primitive aspects, and rehabilitation in the detention camps consisted of forced confessions (often under severe torture) of the oath; see Elkins's chapter on rehabilitation (Elkins 91–120).

27. The reader does not learn this until after Ngotho dies. The torture scene leads us to believe that Howlands stops when he gets frustrated with Ngotho's endurance, but it turns out that he stops because he knows that Boro killed Jacobo.

28. As a student Ngũgĩ had been an admirer of Paton's novel, calling it "my Bible, a noble book" (quoted in Sicherman, "Ngũgĩ's Colonial" 15). But in *Homecoming*, he criticizes Paton's erasure of the black man's political and economic claims (Ngũgĩ, *Homecoming* 43).

29. Tirop Simatei discusses the conflicting perspectives on the land held by Howlands and Ngotho as a way of inscribing the potential violence of the

colonial relationship onto the land itself and foreshadowing the violent revolt to come (Tirop Simatei 86–87).

30. Written after the Emergency was over and during the period of self-government that immediately preceded independence, this novel is surprisingly "pessimistic" and does not "generate a celebratory narrative," because the scale of violence that the Emergency inflicted on the Gikuyu people "called into question the nationalist romance of restoration" even as independence was becoming reality (Gikandi, *Ngũgĩ* 72–73).

31. The regressiveness of colonialism is a key argument in *Facing Mount Kenya*, Kenyatta's dissertation at the London School of Economics, written under Bronisław Malinowski's mentorship, originally published in 1938 and republished in 1965. Ngũgĩ wrote *Weep Not, Child* before his disillusionment with Kenyatta (Gikandi, *Ngũgĩ* 113). Of particular interest is Kenyatta's attention to the British suppression of Gikuyu democratic forms of governance and his detailed explanation of the establishment of "itwika" ceremonies for passing the privilege of governance from one generation to another. Kenyatta repeatedly characterizes the proceedings as "national" in character (Kenyatta, *Facing* 183, 185). Itwika, he explains, regulates "the changing of government in rotation through a peaceful and constitutional revolution" (189). This passage of political authority from fathers to sons has been disrupted, creating conditions for regression.

32. Sicherman speculates (citing a colonial official by the name of T. C. Colchester) that this is legend, rather than fact, because the Gikuyu did not have a tradition of burial, so any kind of burial of the body would have seemed to them traumatic, like being buried alive (Sicherman, "Kenyan History" 360).

33. The influence of Fanon on Ngũgĩ's choice of epigraphs in the novel is apparent in the following: "National consciousness, instead of being the all-embracing crystallization of the innermost hopes of the whole people, instead of being the immediate and most obvious result of the mobilization of the people, will be in any case only an empty shell, a crude and fragile travesty of what it might have been" (Fanon 148).

34. Kariuki in his autobiography corroborates this by asserting that he knew detainees who had been castrated (41).

35. Sexual fear of Africans contributed as well to the frequency of male rape (Elkins 208). Of course, women too were raped. Elkins documents assaults on women in the enclosed villages in particular (Elkins 244–48). In the novel, Ngũgĩ renders a sexual episode between a loyalist and Kihika's sister, Mumbi, as consensual, even though the psychology is highly ambiguous. Karanja, who has vowed not to rape Mumbi, seduces her when he brings news of her husband's, Gikonyo's, release. The narrator rather unconvincingly ex-

plains that she sleeps with Karanja out of a sense of "submissive gratitude" for the good news (Ngũgĩ, *Grain of Wheat* 150). Karanja then humiliates her. She recalls, "I could see he was laughing at me with triumph" (151). Mumbi defies Karanja earlier in the novel, calling him a woman for becoming a loyalist (148). Mumbi's compromised status is important so that she is not a perfect victim and is analogous to Mugo and Gikonyo.

36. Atrocities in Kenya's camps did attain notoriety, and eventually public opinion forced the British to curtail their actions in Kenya; see Elkins, Chap. 10, "Detention Exposed." Ngũgĩ may be drawing here specifically from an incident that occurred in 1959 in Hola camp, where the warders beat eleven prisoners to death. Margery Perham, the most vocal member of the British parliament against the Emergency, refers to this incident as a turning point in public opinion in Britain in her "Foreword" to Kariuki's autobiography (Perham xii).

37. Not surprisingly, participants in these oathing rituals give a different account. In his memoir Kariuki explains that the only oaths he knew as legitimate were the kind that were administered to himself: one for binding him to the movement and a second, more rigorous ritual that he underwent because he was expected to fight for the movement. His detailed descriptions include the use of a sacrificial animal (a goat) and the consumption of the raw meat of the goat (Kariuki 27–31). Furthermore, Kariuki discredits any information on the oaths gained by the British through coerced confessions, because detainees would say whatever the interrogators wanted to hear (33).

38. Carothers's *The African Mind in Health and Disease* was mainly responsible for characterizing Mau Mau as a mental illness (Elkins 106). His 1954 report to the British government cited in note 22 helped the government justify its policy of rehabilitation through confession. Carothers referred to "'public confession as performed in Kikuyu law'" (quoted in David Anderson 283). Anderson concurs with Elkins that Leakey was the one "who argued that 'confessions were essential if the curse inflicted by having taken the oath was to be lifted'" (283).

39. Kenyatta discusses a Gikuyu practice of oath taking in contrast to colonial practices. He puts oath taking in the context of good governance and conflict resolution. Oaths bind people to be honest and facilitate the prosecution of those who violate their agreements (Kenyatta, *Facing* 214). The British discouraged traditional oath taking and substituted it with the gestures of "raising hands or kissing the Bible" that, Kenyatta explains, were meaningless to Africans who did not feel bound by them. These new gestures, therefore, undermined the authority of the courts (216). He also makes a passing reference to confession when he discusses the authority of native courts: "the fear of [the oath] prevented people from giving false evidence, and helped

to bring the offenders to justice through guilty conscience and confession" (214). Here confession means confession of the crime, not confession of the oath.

40. Harriet Beecher Stowe's *Uncle Tom's Cabin* is the most celebrated instance in literature of such rhetoric where the slave masters' Christian conscience is appealed to for recognition of the slave's humanity. As I show in my discussion of the "novels of the freedom," the rhetoric of abolition was used repeatedly to describe Kenya's freedom after independence in ways that would be politically unifying. For a discussion of the appropriation and revision of Christian ideas and texts by the Mau Mau, see Berman and Lonsdale, 442–47.

41. The work of Wachira, Mwangi, and Kahiga (all published in Kenya) reflect the cultural influence of their intended audience: Kenya's educated in the immediate post-independence period. Mwangi's *Taste of Death*, in particular, was written for adoption by "lower and middle secondary" education classes and hence for a limited audience of young readers (Maughan-Brown 218). Maughan-Brown sees the novel as propagandistic. These students, by the time they read this book, "will already have been securely enough formed in alienation from their historical identity as to be incapable of recognising that the price of this reading of 'Mau Mau' is nothing less than the acceptance of self-hatred, the surrender of all conscious control over past and future" (218). Maughan-Brown assumes, in his Marxist terms, that there is a single, authentic historical identity to be retrieved.

42. For a discussion of how Leavis's aesthetic value of moral seriousness and emphasis on the individual's struggles against an alienating world shaped Ngũgĩ's early fiction, see Gikandi in *Ngũgĩ* (106).

43. Achebe's "The Novelist as Teacher" is an eloquent defense of didactic literature; see *Morning Yet on Creation Day* (1975).

44. Whether decolonization is or not a human rights movement has been the matter of much debate. Samuel Moyn (2010) argues against conflating the two because decolonization is less concerned with individual rights and more with the collective self-determination of emergent nation states. In contrast, Roland Burke (2010) sees decolonization as a key episode in the evolution of the human rights movement.

45. Peter Simatei faults Wachira for adopting a critical stance toward the fighters that confirms the settler and colonial racist hysteria over their purported savagery and undermines the nationalist dimensions of their struggle (Peter Simatei 154).

46. The colonial view of the Mau Mau and the pseudoscientific reasoning that supported it is evident in J. C. Carothers, *The Psychology of Mau Mau*, a study commissioned by the colonial government. L. S. B. Leakey was also

very influential in shaping colonial thinking about the Mau Mau in three published studies and his participation as an expert witness and Gikuyu translator in Kenyatta's trial (David Anderson 282–83). For an analysis of Leakey's thought, see Berman and Lonsdale, "Louis Leakey."

47. War reveals a common humanity through suffering, obliterating social differences, yet survival demands selfishness. War's homogenizing force is captured beautifully by Barbusse: "The frightful narrowness of communal life compresses us, adapts us and blends us into each other. It is like some kind of fatal contagion, with the result that one soldier looks like another, even if you do not observe us from such a distance that we are only a few grains of dust rolling across the plain" (Barbusse 18).

48. For a discussion of Chaka's transformation, see Coundouriotis, "Child Soldier Narrative," 198–99.

49. Maughan-Brown interprets the novel's ending as Mwangi's deployment of "stock images from British public school pseudo-classicism by transforming Elysian fields into 'cool dark jungles.'" He also compares the ending to *Wuthering Heights* (Maughan-Brown 222).

50. The novel is full of the larger-than-life heroics of the forest fighters, punctuated by several escapes. However, the forest war is shown as unwinnable. Thus, although the captured Leader is rescued in a daring and improbable mission, he is shot shortly after and dies anyway.

51. For example, on the novel's opening page, Moira is on the train from Mombasa to Nairobi, hung-over and penniless. His companion, George, addresses him brusquely using recognizable Americanisms: "Oh shut up. You talk too blinking much. Who told you we had dough in common? It's my dough. You don't have a cent to your name" (Mangua, *Tail* 7).

52. "Impaired citizens" is a term used by Ariella Azoulay in discussing Israeli soldiers: "the soldiers were made impaired citizens by their own regime" when they were ordered (in her specific example) to invade and take possession of the homes of Palestinians. The soldiers' efforts later to "reframe" the photos they took on that occasion in an effort to speak out about their experiences show them "rehabilitating their civil fitness and regaining the rights of which they had been robbed by the regime" (Azoulay, "Photography Without Borders" 679). She has elaborated more fully her theory of citizenship in Chapter 1 of *The Civil Contract of Photography*.

53. The exception is Ngũgĩ, who wrote a play (with Micere Mugo) about Dedan Kimathi in 1974; his other plays also make reference to the conflict and to the popular memory of Kimathi. See, for example, the way references to the struggle for land are posed in *I Will Marry When I Want*. As we saw, he alludes to real figures from the war and incorporates, with the example of Kihika, a "histor[y] of the hanged" in *Grain of Wheat*.

54. Peter Simatei tackles this metanarrative aspect of Kahiga's text by arguing that Kahiga's "real story" is real because it takes on the pervasive "Dedan Kimathi/Mau Mau narrative" rather than attempting to reconstruct the actual figure (Peter Simatei 154). Simatei outlines the historiographic debates that surround Mau Mau and claims that Kahiga "tries to negotiate the middle course" (156).

55. For example, when the fighters burn down a house with thirty people in it, the victims are portrayed as "howling inside" and we learn that "By the time the roof caved in there was not a single sound, just a stench that reminded Theuri that, after all, men were animals" (Kahiga 162).

56. Anderson draws contrasting portraits of these two figures in similar terms (David Anderson 248–49). His use of memoirs by men under the command of Mathenge and Kimathi as his sources points to another body of narrative literature that could be usefully reread as a context for the fiction of Mau Mau. In his account of Kimathi's trial and execution, Anderson recounts how he converted to Catholicism (290).

57. Evan Maina Mwangi makes note of other Kenyan writers during Moi's rule who had to veil their political messages to "elude the censors" (46).

58. Longman picked up the novel in 1994 for its African Writers series; the Nigerian edition of *Sozaboy* appeared in 1985.

59. The passage from Matthew 5:13 is the first verse of the Sermon on the Mount: "You are the salt of the earth: but if salt have lost his savour, wherewith shall it be salted? It is thenceforth good for nothing, but to be cast, and be trodden under foot of men."

2. TOWARD A PEOPLE'S HISTORY: THE NOVELS OF THE NIGERIAN CIVIL WAR

1. Wendy Griswold identified twenty-nine novels about the war (Griswold 206). At least three more have appeared since her study: Uzondinma Iweala's *Beasts of No Nation* (2005); Adichie's *Half of a Yellow Sun*; and Chris Abani's *Song for Night* (2007). These novels demonstrate the continued relevance of the war to a new generation of Nigerian writers raised after the war.

2. Frederick Forsyth and John De St. Jorre wrote as journalists. Dan Jacobs worked first for UNICEF and then as director for the Committee on Nigeria-Biafra Relief. His history was not written until the mid-1980s, whereas the journalistic accounts are more or less contemporary to the war. David Forsythe's history of the ICRC documents how Biafra brought to a crisis the composition and structure of the ICRC's leadership as well as its mission of neutrality (Forsythe 63). The ICRC came to see its leadership as too "amateur" and to understand retrospectively that they had too few knowl-

edgeable people in Nigeria and an inadequate understanding of the conflict (65). The crisis over neutrality came to a head out of the political complications of executing relief operations, which threatened to render the ICRC essentially ineffective. The ICRC, following the Geneva Conventions, would enter Biafran territory only with the permission of Nigeria, since Nigeria was the recognized sovereign state. The crisis resulted in Bernard Kouchner's defection from the ICRC and the creation of Doctors Without Borders (Forsythe 66).

3. Born in 1931, Nwapa published *Never Again* in 1975 and a collection of stories, *Wives at War*, in 1980. Her work was followed by Emecheta's *Destination Biafra* in 1982 and Adichie's *Half of a Yellow Sun* in 2006. (Emecheta was born in 1944 and Adichie in 1977.) The conventional periodization of Nigerian literature divides writers into a first generation that published right before or right after independence, a second generation that published after the civil war, and a third generation of writers born after independence and beginning to publish in the mid-1980s (Hewett 76–77).

4. At independence Nigeria had been divided into three regions, the North, the West, and the East, each dominated by political parties defined along ethnic lines, divisions largely cultivated by the British in the transition to independence.

5. Biafra was recognized by four African nations: Côte d'Ivoire, Gabon, Tanzania, and Zambia. France provided weapons to the Biafrans, but did not recognize their independence. Broader international recognition was never achieved. Nigeria did not lose recognition as the sovereign nation-state, although it was criticized for blockading Biafra and using famine as a weapon of war. It continued to receive international military aid, especially from the British (Jacobs 246–47).

6. The *Biafra Newsletter* from 24 November 1967, for example, describes horrific acts of violence against civilians and concludes, "Wives were forced to witness the slaughtering of their husbands and children and compelled to ask 'why was this mass killing carried out?' The simple answer is 'for no other reason than that the victims were Biafrans. For the same ethnocentric reason that the Nazi regime sought to exterminate the Jewish race.' This is Genocide" (Nwankwo 8).

7. The leader of the Federalists and Nigeria's postwar president, Yakubu Gowon, was held in high regard for his immediate postwar leadership, especially for what was perceived as his even-handed treatment of the defeated side. Much of the criticism directed against him during the war was silenced after the war. However, problems emerged for Gowon when he declared that Nigeria was not ready for civilian rule in1974; he was deposed in a coup in 1975.

8. Ken Saro-Wiwa makes the most compelling case for the Eastern minorities in his memoir of the war, *On a Darkling Plain*. His portrait of the Biafran leader, Ojukwu, is particularly scathing and contrasts sharply with the favorable portraits in the pro-Biafran accounts of the war (especially Forsyth and Jacobs).

9. Achebe also suffered considerably in the war, although he did not discuss it in personal terms. His family were "returnees," and his wife miscarried while fleeing from the North. During the war he was displaced several times, including when the university at Nsukka was destroyed; his house was bombed, his books and some manuscripts destroyed. He also lost several relatives (Ezenwa-Ohaeto 117, 129, 155). He wrote poetry and a few short stories, but no novel on the war. His poetry from the period, collected in *Beware, Soul Brother* (1971), depicts the suffering of the people and was intended for a popular audience, using "simple language" that is easily understood by the people (quoted in Ezenwa-Ohaeto 162).

10. Nwapa fled Lagos in the violence that preceded the war and lived in Biafra throughout the war. After the war she worked in the government of East Central State (which had been part of Biafra) and dedicated herself to reconstruction and reconciliation (Wilentz).

11. For example, Nwapa depicts the effects of the regime's criminal lying, which kept everyone guessing about what was really going on. People in the cities were repeatedly not given enough warning to evacuate because the regime would not acknowledge that it was about to lose more territory. And Nwapa depicts Kate anxiously identifying contradictions in Radio Biafra reports. A report lauding Biafran bravery against the "vandals" ("'The gallant Biafran soldiers wiped out the Vandals in Ugwuta sector'") leads her to wonder whether the wounded, sorry-looking soldiers her husband has seen could possibly defend their town (Nwapa, *Never Again* 29). The radio played a big role in spreading Ojukwu's propaganda, especially among the educated. It had a more limited influence over those who either did not own a radio or who were not literate enough to understand the broadcasts (Harneit-Sievers et al 58).

12. Nwapa takes rumor as her subject in her short story "Wives at War," where language expresses the peoples' delusions and their fragile mental state. In the story, a rumor circulates that Queen Elizabeth has secretly invited Biafran women to meet with her in London so she can plan relief for Biafra. This rumor becomes the cause of extensive squabbling among women's organizations, who are offended at not all being included in such an invitation (Nwapa, "Wives," in *Wives* 9). The rumor itself is ironic, since despite humanitarian protest, the English were helping arm the Federalists.

13. Readers of *Efuru* are familiar with Nwapa's investment in the lake goddess Uhamiri. Nwapa structured the ending of *Efuru* with masterful irony so that the goddess accommodates rather than represses a more flexible definition of womanhood. The narrator in that novel wonders how come the goddess of the lake, a protectress of childless women, is wealthy when childlessness in this society is seen as a curse. Moreover, women who ask Uhamiri for a child remain barren, an irony Nwapa exploits to suggest that women can have alternative identities and sources of authority within tradition; motherhood is not the only one.

14. Andrade places *Efuru* differently than Griswold. She sees the novel as hampered by having to conform to male versions of the national imaginary. Interestingly for my grouping of novelists, Andrade discusses *Efuru* in relation to Ekwensi's popular novel *Jagua Nana*, an urban story of a prostitute (Andrade, *Nation* 56–57).

15. In contrast to "Girls at War," *Efuru*, and Nwapa's fiction more generally, illustrates that "it is primarily when women take on spiritual power, and therefore, according to convention, discard their sex roles, that they are able to enter a sphere where male authority has little effect" (Boehmer, *Stories of Women*, 101). Gladys, seen only through Nwankwo's eyes, remains wedded to her sexed identity.

16. Ekwensi is one of the most widely read Nigerian novelists, having sold 640,000 books by 1990 (McLuckie 16). *Survive the Peace* was a bestseller (McLuckie 31). McLuckie argues that Ekwensi is an example of the cultural project discussed by C. Chinweizu et al in *Toward the Decolonization of African Literature*. They describe the development of "an extensive audience, a nationalist, right-minded one that would displace the Western audience" for African literature along with a "mass public education" that could play a significant role in shaping the nations of post-independence Africa (McLuckie 17).

17. Agamben develops the idea of the "bare life" from the Greek distinction between *zoe* ("the simple fact of living common to all living beings") and *bios* ("the form of living proper to an individual or a group") (Agamben, *Homo Sacer* 1). His terms evoke a distinction between biology and culture. In the classical distinction Agamben explains that *zoe* is outside politics, but in modernity, he argues, the creation of "bare life" politicizes *zoe*, which becomes the "nucleus of sovereign power" (Agamben, *Homo Sacer* 6).

18. Telling the stories of the war is itself an assertion of subjectivity and agency outside the purview of Agamben's thought in *Homo Sacer*, where he refers to resistance only once and in terms of muteness and silence when he alludes to Robert Antelme in a discussion of the *Muselmann* (the Muslim), a

Nazi camp prisoner rendered totally apathetic by his trauma. Agamben wonders if the apathy isn't a "silent form of resistance," a refusal to recognize the law by "mov(ing) in an absolute indistinction of fact and law, of life and juridical rule, and of nature and politics" (Agamben, *Homo Sacer* 185). The apathy also displays an absence of a sense of self-preservation; if it is in fact a form of resistance, it originates in despair at the betrayal of the promises of juridical rule—a despair not shared by Ekwensi, however trenchant his critique.

19. In his other war novel, *Survive the Peace*, Ekwensi presents similar circumstances (a visit to the morgue) very differently, focusing less on what his protagonists see (to provide the visual record of atrocity) and more on what they feel. Thus Odugo in *Survive the Peace* covers up the nakedness of the body he has come to find and reflects on the oddness of people's embarrassment when facing death (Ekwensi, *Survive* 42–43). He becomes an "introspector," commenting on his own reaction to the suffering of others.

20. Ernest N. Emenyonu describes Ekwensi professional positions during the war slightly differently. He says Ekwensi was chairman of the Bureau for External Publicity for Biafra from 1967 to 1969 and then controller-general of the Broadcasting Corporation of Biafra for a few months before the war ended (Emenyonu 6–7). Achebe describes him during this period as a "roving ambassador for the people" of Biafra and says that he traveled with him on several "diplomatic voyages" (Achebe, *There Was* 109).

21. Griswold discusses *No Longer at Ease* as a novel of the "culture of disappointment" that punctuates the protagonist's "lack of a sense of center" as a result of his failure in the city and his loss of a traditional identity (Griswold 222–23).

22. The distinction between a time and space of war is widely recognized in war narratives. McLoughlin names "space" and "time" as two of the six challenges involved in the narration of war, alongside the challenges of "epistemology" (the believability of the narrative), "scale" (the details of the account), "language," and "logic." The problem of space finds expression in the delineation of "zones," which demarcate war as an alien environment; time, on the other hand, challenges our notion of duration and asks when it will end (McLoughlin, "Authoring War" 17–18).

23. Fírinne Ni Chréacháin argues that Iyayi's adoption of the point of view of the common soldier is a direct response to the proliferation of memoirs by generals in the war and one text in particular, Olusegun Obasanjo's *My Command*. Obasanjo claims to have been responsible for the recapture of the West, a major turning point in the war in favor of the victorious Federalist side. Chreachain reads *Heroes* alongside the general's memoir to demonstrate how Iyayi "rewriting history from below makes articulate the silences in Obasanjo's text" (Ni Chréacháin 52).

24. These images, where he "could see the long sticks that had been driven through the women's vaginas" as well as the decapitated corpses of the victims, are particularly shocking to Osime (Iyayi, *Heroes* 63). The figure of the impaled woman is significant here, as she prefigures her prominence in later testimony, such as texts from the Rwanda genocide (Coundouriotis, "Rape and Testimony" 377ff).

25. Diff en: Compare Anything; Centrifugal Force vs. Centripetal Force, http://www.diffen.com/difference/Centrifugal_Force_vs_Centripetal_Force, accessed 22 May 2013. Alluding to the place "*where nothing holds*," Iyayi is also making an intertextual reference both to Yeats's "Second Coming" and to Achebe's *Things Fall Apart*, whose title comes from Yeats's poem. In Yeats, the centrifugal image is more explicit: "the center cannot hold."

26. Iyayi's Marxism inclines him to collective portrayals of the people's condition and makes him the paradigmatic naturalist among the war novelists.

27. These are characteristics of his naturalism. As Moglen has noted, in naturalist fiction characters "make choices and take actions," but "these only drive them further into the destructive social mechanisms that constrain and mangle their lives" (Moglen 183). Moglen argues this is a characteristic of both the European naturalists "from Zola to Hardy" and their American followers like Crane and Norris, who are associated more directly with the war novel as a genre (183). Iyayi is explicit about being influenced by American writers, especially John Steinbeck's *Grapes of Wrath* (Iyayi, "Freedom" 414). Moreover, writing in the mid-1980s from a position of strong dissent to Nigeria's military government, Iyayi uses the war as allegory for the political culture of militarism more generally.

28. Szeman, seeing the novel as another example of the "intellectual novel" (Griswold 210), argues that Ofeyi stands in for the figure of the writer (142–43). The novel depicts the failure of "national literary politics," rather than the failure of national politics (148). However, as I argue later, Ofeyi could also be loosely based on Ojukwu himself and a characterization of his rhetorical powers.

29. The punishing details of Soyinka's descriptions and his way of melding the body with the ground are echoed in Yvonne Vera's fiction, which I discuss in the next chapter.

30. Like Soyinka, Nuruddin Farah in *Links* resorts to Dante's *Inferno* to frame the portrayal of a society at war, but Farah's reference is also more specifically to a city state (Florence and Mogadishu).

31. Despite the difficulty that readers have had in placing Soyinka's novel in relation to the other novels of the war, its influence on the corpus of war writing is palpable, as two recent examples of Nigerian fiction illustrate: *Beasts of No Nation*, whose title echoes Soyinka's novel, and *Song for Night*,

where the mute peasant of Soyinka's fiction returns as a ghost. The mute peasant is now a mute child, but the figure of the child has become the new figure of the people in the child-soldier narratives that have proliferated since the late 1990s. After a period of almost twenty years, during which the war stopped being a prominent subject of Nigerian fiction (approximately 1987–2005), there has been a recent resurgence of interest in the war instigated perhaps by the wars of the 1990s in West Africa. Both Iweala and Abani's novels are child-soldier narratives. As critics have noted, Iweala's novel is stylistically imitative of Ken Saro-Wiwa's *Sozaboy*.

32. Novels with a focus on humanitarian crises have been cast as thrillers with some regularity. In popular works such as John Le Carré's *The Constant Gardener*, for example, the "human rights detective" enters a scene of humanitarian crisis with a mandate for "unmediated intervention" (Bain). There are similar figures in the fiction of Michael Ondatjee and Nuruddin Farah (Bain). That Iroh's work prefigures this subgenre is not clear, although his satire clashes with their sincerity.

33. It is possible that Iroh based his character on Colonel Rolf Steiner, a German who was a former Foreign Legionnaire. He led a mercenary unit for Biafra (De St. Jorre 325).

34. Emecheta makes rape the centerpiece of her treatment of the war as a woman's narrative. Both Iroh and Emecheta connect rape to their depiction of humanitarian actors in the field, a curious congruence in texts that are tonally very different.

35. The fuller analysis of child-soldier narratives is in Chapter 4. *Beasts of No Nation* very self-consciously imitates Saro-Wiwa's literary "rotten English." *Song for Night* and francophone texts such as *Allah n'est pas obligé* and *Johnny chien méchant* are important examples of this genre. The popular success *A Long Way Gone*, which is also indebted to Saro-Wiwa's text, has helped disseminate the genre as a form of human rights narrative. Both of the novels by Nigerians (Iweala and Abani) have an unspecific setting like *Sozaboy*, although Iweala and Abani use Igbo names for their characters.

36. Saro-Wiwa became known internationally for his activism in the Movement for Survival of the Ogoni People in the 1990s. The Ogoni, a minority of about half a million in population, are traditionally fishermen and depend on the waters of the Niger Delta for their livelihood. This area has been catastrophically degraded by the oil industry and in particular the Anglo-Dutch corporation Shell. His execution by Sani Abacha's military dictatorship in 1995 created a worldwide outcry and ushered environmentalism to the forefront of the human rights movement.

In contrast, neither *Season of Anomy* nor *Destination Biafra* is in print. This is especially surprising for Emecheta, whose other fiction is widely taught in the United States, whereas Soyinka is mostly taught as a dramatist and essayist (Adams 296).

37. Although he came from a poor community, Saro-Wiwa was educated at Nigeria's most prestigious schools, Government College, Umuahia, and the University of Ibadan (Okere 255).

38. Manmuswalk is reminiscent of Isanusi in *Chaka*. When Chaka first meets Isanusi he sees him transform from evil to good in the blink of an eye. Both characters come from nowhere and belong only to war.

39. Yet he clearly understood that literature was not a substitute for political action. Saro-Wiwa's life project was to see an Ogoni homeland come into existence (Okere 259). Ogoni nationalism was "an article of faith" since his primary school days. Although this is not explicit in the novel, his biographers have shown that Saro-Wiwa understood the civil war as the moment when Ogoni nationalism gets in motion (quoted in Ojo-Ade xiv). Thus Ogoni nationalism against the neocolonial regime and world capital becomes real (is "actualized") as a political movement during the civil war and is imagined as the necessary, other space for the achievement of the people's freedom.

40. This was a common practice late in the war, depicted also by Nwapa in *One Is Enough*, where she refers to it as "attack trade" (Nwapa, *One* 4). In *Half of a Yellow Sun*, "attack trade," a desperate measure of last resort, costs one of the protagonists her life.

41. The war brought more, not less, British involvement in Nigeria. Jacobs draws a damning picture of British complicity, especially their heavy involvement in supplying the Nigerians with arms. The British, moreover, knew, according to Jacobs, that Nigerians had a deliberate policy to starve Biafra that was put in place three months before Biafra seceded (Jacobs 26, 32–33).

42. It is probably not accidental that Debbie's circumstances parallel Ojukwu's. Ojukwu also joined the army against his parents' wishes (his father was, like Debbie's, a successful businessman). The army appealed to him because "it was organized along the lines of a unified nation" (Jacobs 23).

43. Mutua, for example, sees humanitarianism as an extension of colonial ideology: "The human rights corpus . . . falls within the continuum of the Eurocentric colonial project, in which actors are cast into superior and subordinate positions" (Mutua 204). This "colonial project" is the "Eurocentric civilizing mission" (210). Emecheta seems very aware of this pitfall and its implied structural inequality, something her novel tries to undermine.

44. Most of Nigeria's oil reserves are in the East, although not in traditionally Igbo areas (Falola and Heaton 175–76). As a major shareholder in Shell-BP, the British government had a direct financial interest in the oil reserves of the East (Nugent 95). Moreover, the British felt more secure with

their established ties in Lagos and did not support a rebellious Biafra. Thus they armed the Federalist side (Jacobs 68). Although the political leadership of Biafra was in Igbo hands, the oil was in territories traditionally populated by other groups who ended up stuck on the Biafran side and were only halfhearted supporters of the cause. Saro-Wiwa's account of the war in *A Darkling Plain* explains the minorities' hesitation to support Biafra.

45. Emecheta's portrayal of rape in war is particularly important for its resonance in the discussions of women's real-life testimony. I place Emecheta's novel against real testimony and engage with the changing international law on rape as a war crime in Coundouriotis, "Rape and Testimony" (373–74).

3. "WONDERING WHO THE HEROES WERE": ZIMBABWE'S NOVELS OF ATROCITY

1. Examples of works that fit this description are: Edmund Chipamaunga's *A Fighter for Freedom*; Solomon Mutswairo's *Mapondera: Soldier of Zimbabwe*; Garika Mutasa's *The Contact*; and Charles Samupindi's *Death Throes.*

2. "Patriotic" history has given "war veterans" a new identity. The war veterans' group that emerged since 2000 has important historical links to actual veterans, but is also in significant ways transformed and includes many who were too young to have fought in the war (White 95). Until the late 1990s the war veterans were a discontented group that felt insufficiently recognized and even betrayed by Mugabe. The veterans came to prominence under the leadership of Chenjerai Hunzvi, an activist with only dubious credibility as a veteran who propelled himself to prominence by aggressively pressing for the veterans' demand for land (Meredith, *Mugabe* 134–35). After 2001 and Hunzvi's death, they adopted an "inclusive war narrative" and portrayed themselves as a group wronged by the British in the Lancaster House Agreement that ended the "anti-colonial" war in 1979 (White 95). The agreement guaranteed the land rights of the white farmers for ten years and provided for the protection of private property that was bought after independence. Hence, it was perceived that the agreement robbed veterans of the land that should have been given to them in reparation. Mamdani, a critic of this agreement, asserts that it resulted in "qualified majority rule at best" (Mamdani, "Lessons"). Mugabe failed to make adequate reparations to veterans in the 1980s. The farm invasions begun with Hunzvi were only subsequently endorsed by Mugabe, who rewarded the veterans with farms when they helped him terrorize the opposition in the 2000 parliamentary elections and the 2002 presidential elections (Meredith, *Mugabe*, 194).

3. In the novels bones are also a biblical reference. To mission-educated writers (as were most of the first generation of Zimbabwean writers) bones

allude to the passage from Ezekiel (37:1–14) in which rising bones are explicitly linked to the return of the land of Israel (Ez 37:12–14). For a discussion of the biblical reference, see Primorac, *Place of Tears* 5. Mugabe was also educated by Catholic missionaries (Meredith, *Mugabe* 19).

4. Ranger provides a slightly different explanation. He asserts there were two connected systems: the Mhondoro cult, whose medium communicated with the dead, and the Mwari or Mlimo cult, whose medium communicated with the divine (Ranger, *Revolt* 17). Ranger also provides an extensive explanation of how the spirit mediums exercised their political influence. This is especially clear in his account of Kaguvi's rise to power and role in the uprising (212ff).

5. In their analysis of the contemporary discourse about land in Zimbabwean politics, Chan and Primorac argue that we need to be reminded of this spiritual dimension. They turn to early Zimbabwean novels to demonstrate how the discussion of land is tempered and complicated by the inclusion of a consideration of its spiritual dimension. They date the emergence of an instrumental and purely economic, resource-driven policy on land to the 1980s (Chan and Primorac 65–67).

6. Farm "invasions" and forceful evictions began after the defeat of the proposed constitutional reforms in 2000, which were meant to secure Mugabe's power for the foreseeable future. In the proposed constitution Mugabe had included an amendment that allowed for the requisition of land without legal consultation (Meredith, *Mugabe* 164). He had hoped that this provision would buy him rural votes. When the referendum failed to pass, he made the policy of forced evictions the centerpiece of his presidential reelection campaign and the Third Chimurenga in 2002. The policy ("Fast Track Land Reform") also gave Mugabe ideological cover to attack his political opposition (191). For an account of the impact of these policies on Zimbabwe's economy and society and especially its food crisis, see Howard-Hassmann, 906ff. The political consequences have been complex. By drastically curtailing white ownership of land and crushing white farming, Mugabe enabled the emergence of a new victim narrative, the white farmer's (Raftopoulos 216).

7. In 2004 Ranger warned of the demise of academic history in Zimbabwe and urged academic historians to find a response to the distortions of "patriotic" history (Ranger, "Nationalist" 234). The collaborative project *Becoming Zimbabwe: A History from the Pre-Colonial Period to 2008* (reviewed by Ranger in 2010) is the beginning of such a project, but it had to take shape outside Zimbabwe in Cape Town, South Africa, because of the dire deterioration of the University of Zimbabwe.

8. Peter Godwin describes watching "Comrade Chinx," a war veteran on Zimbabwean TV in 2008, "exhorting the viewers to 'war,'" and insisting,

"We are not *ex*-fighters, . . . we are current freedom fighters—*current*. I don't want anyone to call me an *ex*-freedom fighter" (Godwin 40–41).

9. *Feso*, written in Shona and published in 1956, is considered the first novel by a Zimbabwean. Mutswairo published an English version in 1974. The novel was widely read and even adopted as a school text before being banned by the Rhodesian authorities. Set in seventeenth-century Zimbabwe, *Feso* depicts the sufferings of the Vanyai, a peace-loving agricultural people under the incursions of the Pfumojena. It is thus a story of the occupier and the occupied, a thinly disguised allegory of white conquest. Nehanda is invoked after a scene that depicts the devastation of war. The poem expresses the yearning for freedom. In the late 1950s and 1960s, Zimbabweans recited this poem in nationalist rallies that took place in the townships and, as a result, the book was banned (Ranger, "History Has Its Ceiling" 213).

10. Wenzel cites such rhetoric used in anti-colonial struggles as typical of the prophetic, hence the title of her study makes reference to warriors' claims to be "bulletproof" (Wenzel 4).

11. Lobengula, last of the Ndebele kings, was defeated by the British in 1893 and died the following year under mysterious circumstances. Seeking at first to cooperate with the British South Africa Company, he granted them the right to occupy Mashonaland. Ndebele discontent over the terms of this agreement led to war in 1893 and Lobengula's defeat (Ranger, *Revolt*, chap. 3).

12. Commenting as an academic historian, Ranger notes that *Nehanda* was written without any awareness of what historians or anthropologists had written about the First Chimurenga and the "rituals of possession by a senior ancestral spirit." Ranger, however, deeply admires Vera's accomplishment, her "extraordinary feat of imagination" in which "[she] had set out to imagine from the ground up and from the sky down what it would mean for a girl to make herself open to the ancestors" (Ranger, "History Has Its Ceiling" 203). Although one would not want to argue against the historian's appreciation of how the imagination can contribute to historical understanding, I doubt that Vera was as naive of academic history as Ranger assumes. In addition to Ranger's *Revolt in Southern Rhodesia, 1896–7*, which was published in 1967, Vera would also have had access to Lawrence Vambe's *An Ill-Fated People: Zimbabwe Before and After Rhodes* from 1972.

13. Bryce has written persuasively that Vera's hermeneutics are based on her visual imagination and the claim that she gains her inspiration by visualizing a "'moment'" that she places in front of her as if "'it were a photograph'" (quoted in Bryce, "Snapshots" 39).

14. Interpreted through what Ariella Azoulay calls the "social contract" of photography, this image demands we recognize the appeal made to us by the figures in the photograph. Azoulay provides us with a theoretical model

for what "writing beyond the photograph" means: not casting aside the photograph, but examining it for what it has to suggest beyond the bounds of a strict indexicality. This is a method of reading the photograph historically and transactionally, taking into account the encounter among the photographer, the subject, and the viewer (Azoulay, *Civil Contract* 18–20).

15. The creation of an African police force and the hut tax were the two most hated aspects of white rule after 1893 (Lawrence Vambe 105). Not only were the Zimbabweans resentful of being policed, but the policemen were invariably abusive, wielding their sjambok (a leather whip with which they were officially armed) with impunity (106–7).

16. Lessing witnessed the torture of an African cook unfairly accused of stealing soap. In an effort to get him to confess to this act, he was tied to a tree and beaten, dragged by a horse, and subjected to other punishments, then returned to his compound at night and beaten again the next day. The man continued to proclaim his innocence, and when the settler realized that the man would not confess, he claimed to have taught the man "to be honest," disguising his cruelty as an act of the civilizing mission.

17. This is the language on the ICTY's website, http://www.icty.org/sections/AbouttheICTY, accessed 16 March 2011. Similarly the word "atrocity" is eschewed at the International Criminal Tribunal for Rwanda, whose statute (United Nations' Security Council Resolution 955) refers instead to genocide, crimes against humanity, "other inhumane acts," violations of Geneva Conventions; http://www.un.org/ictr/english/Resolutions/955e.htm, accessed 16 March 2011.

18. I must clarify that in the prosecutions of particular cases at the ICC, of course, individuals are held accountable for mass crimes, and distinct incidents or events become the focus of the trials. The ICTY, for example, states emphatically that "guilt should be individualized"; http://www.icty.org/sections/AbouttheICTY, accessed 16 March 2011.

19. She defends the term in response to the controversy it raised in the sequel, *Confronting Evils: Terrorism, Torture, Genocide* (2010); see chap. 1. Her concern is to better distinguish "evils from lesser wrongs," a nuance that philosophers have neglected, she claims (Card, *Confronting* 6–7). Moreover, she consistently understands evil as secular and widens the scope of her study to look at "collectively perpetrated evils" (4).

20. Regrettably, the revision of her theory has softened this stance. Card has changed her definition of atrocities by substituting "inexcusable wrongs" for "culpable wrongdoing" (Card, *Confronting* 16). "Inexcusable" puts the emphasis on an external judgment of atrocity, whereas "culpable" allowed for self-reflexivity. This shift reflects the greater emphasis in Card's recent thinking on collectively perpetrated evils.

21. The emphasis on atrocity circumscribing a particular space and gaining its features from its relation to that space is reflected perhaps unconsciously in Card's presentation of her three extended examples of such violence: war rape and domestic violence (which she characterizes as public versus private, respectively [Card 5–6]) and "gray zones," which, in its paradigmatic setting of the concentration camp described by Primo Levi, is a space that is circumscribed like a private space, but in it privacy is thoroughly violated.

22. As Godwin explains, "The 'land issue' was about so much more than land. It was about breaking up the million-strong voting bloc of black employees who worked on the farms, and who had voted for the MDC. Mugabe wanted to shatter that bloc. And they became the main, though largely unsung, victims of the land takeovers" (Godwin 31).

23. We might infer from this scene that Kanengoni is also casting doubt on Mugabe's rhetoric of reconciliation at independence, which shaped his public image. Desmond Tutu, for example, praised Mugabe as a model of reconciliation and held him up as an example for South Africa's own efforts with truth and reconciliation. In *No Future Without Forgiveness*, the text in which he set out to explain the work of the Truth and Reconciliation Commission, Tutu singled out Mugabe's rhetoric as paradigmatic of *ubuntu*, the ethos of understanding one's humanity in relation to one's understanding of the humanity of others: "But in Zimbabwe, after one of the most bruising bush wars, Robert Mugabe on the night of his election victory in 1980 amazed all by talking about reconciliation, rehabilitation, and reconstruction. That was ubuntu at work" (Tutu 32). Hove and Vera, as I show later, are concerned very specifically with the voices of victims, such as the woman and her child.

24. Whether *Harvest of Thorns* is or is not a *Bildungsroman* has been discussed extensively. Primorac insists that it is and disagrees with Flora Veit-Wild, who does not see the novel as a *Bildungsroman* because Benjamin, in her view, fails to mature, or arrive at a new understanding of himself (Primorac, *Place of Tears* 129; Veit-Wild 324–25).

25. Mamdani makes a similar point when he tries to explain why Mugabe has endured: "Southern Rhodesia became Zimbabwe in 1980, but the social realities of the newly independent state remained embedded in an earlier historical period," with land and business largely in white hands. Writing in 2008, Mamdani concludes that "the people of Zimbabwe are likely to remember 2000–2003 as the end of the settler colonial era" because of the farm evictions (Mamdani, "Lessons").

26. In contrast, the poem in *Feso* is an appeal to Nehanda by the people: "Where is our freedom Nehanda? / Won't you come down to help us?"

(Mutswairo, *Feso* 66). Mutswairo seems to be borrowing a motif from Christian prayer: the people abandoned by God seek to understand their faults and regain his protection. Thus they ask Nehanda, "What foul crime have we committed / That you should abandon us like this?" (67).

27. Every year the national holiday is marked at Heroes' Acre, and those deemed national heroes after their death are buried there (about fifty at the time Kriger published her study). National heroes can be selected either from those who were dedicated to the "national liberation cause" or "'contemporary sons and daughters of Zimbabwe of the same calibre as those fallen heroes" of the liberation war. The monument was built by North Koreans on fifty-seven hectares a few kilometers outside Harare. Its main symbols are the eternal flame and the Tomb of the Unknown Soldier, which is a statue of three figures (one is a woman) that symbolizes the "freedom fighters and 'freedom loving people.'" On either side of the tomb is a mural depicting scenes from the struggle (Kriger 64–65).

28. Engelke borrows the term from Tejumola Olaniyan, who applies it to his analysis of plays by Wole Soyinka, Amiri Baraka, and Derek Walcott and their enactment of "black anti-imperialist cultural identity." Olaniyan puts the emphasis on theatrical practice, where "identity is conceived as open, an articulation, interculturally negotiable and always in the making: a *process*" (Olaniyan 116). This is useful for thinking of *Bones* because the second-person narration (and in one instance the extended dialogue) gives the novel a theatrical feel, and identity unfolds in the novel as part of the open process of articulation.

29. Chisaga, the rapist, has his own narrative in the novel.

30. Marita had promised to sleep with Chisaga in exchange for money that would enable her to go to the city and find her son. Marita, who never intended to follow through on her promise, leaves for the city before meeting Chisaga, who then attacks Janifa to revenge the snub. Marita's agency ironically sets in motion Janifa's victimization, which is also facilitated by Janifa's mother, who is eager to win Chisaga's good graces and gives him access to her daughter.

31. Feisal Mohamed explains that "Poignancy—arising from the Latin *pungĕre*, "to puncture or stab"—pierces us to the quick with its striving for sublimity and beauty blocked" (Mohamed 149). He argues that poignancy is a key feature of human rights aesthetics.

32. Quayson places too much emphasis on the stylistic difficulty of Vera's writing and erroneously equates it with imprecision. To be metaphorical requires precision, which we find in Vera in the form of a myopic and thus somewhat disorienting attention to detail. Other readers of Vera respond so strongly to her realism that they warn against finding any allegory in her

writing (Gunner and Kortenaar 3). This, too, is an extreme position when, in the context of Zimbabwean literature, Vera responds to longstanding allegorical uses of woman as symbol of the peasantry at large, the same as we have seen in Hove's work. Another criticism has been that Vera's writing is not "Shona enough" because it is too influenced by Western feminism (Primorac, *Place* 6).

33. Hunter also links Mazvita to the heroic narrative, but claims that Vera creates alternative heroes in women (Hunter, "New War" 176). I would argue instead that Vera uses Mazvita's story to question the very idea of heroism and what it implies. The parallels to heroism undermine the idea of heroism.

34. Vera returns to this motif in *The Stone Virgins*, where the bus linking Bulawayo to Kezi is described as a lifeline; she stresses its economic and cultural importance. But the war destroys this link, dooming Kezi to being a place of death, a place from which one must flee.

35. The OED defines kindness as "natural affection arising from kinship."Annie Gagiano interprets Vera's use of the word "kindness" in a similar way by linking it to humanity, the "familial relatedness (like a kinship) of all human beings" (Gagiano 69).

36. Kezi is destroyed by the Fifth Brigade in response to the "dissident" attack on the sisters. Thus Nonceba is victimized twice.

37. Vera introduces Sibaso as he stands behind Thenjiwe, approaching the sisters' home. Nonceba spots them coming just as Sibaso decapitates Thenjiwe. This is followed by his macabre dance with the headless body and his rape and mutilation of Nonceba.

38. In *Voices from the Rocks*, his cultural history of the Matopos, Ranger discusses the scenes depicted in the prehistoric paintings and draws a parallel between their attempt to illustrate man's domination over nature and the similar impulse much later of the white settlers in their topographic paintings of the Matopos (Ranger, *Voices* 16–17).

39. I am responding here to Gagiano, who complains that the novel has been read too often as only interested in the female point of view. Although Gagiano correctly shifts attention back to Sibaso, her reading of Sibaso as a victim perhaps goes too far. She describes Sibaso as "one of Africa's unaccommodated millions" (68), seeing him as typical of the people. This is too skewed, as the majority of people are the victims of men like Sibaso, rather than perpetrators themselves.

4. CONTESTING THE NEW AUTHENTICITY: CONTEMPORARY WAR FICTION IN AFRICA

1. The most frequently discussed of these texts are Emmanuel Dongala's *Johnny chien méchant*, Ahmadou Kourouma's *Allah n'est pas obligé*, Uzodinma

Iweala's *Beasts of No Nation*, Chimamanda Ngozi Adichie's *Half of a Yellow Sun*, and Chris Abani's *Song for Night*. In addition are the francophone texts from the Rwanda Memory Project (including Diop's *Murambi, livre des ossements*) and Nuruddin Farah's *Past Imperfect* trilogy of Somalia's civil war. I have discussed the novels of the Rwanda Memory project in Coundouriotis, "'You Only Have Your Word': Rape and Testimony."

2. John Walsh describes Kourouma's novel as a "deformation of the African *Bildungsroman* in French" not only because of Birahima's interrupted education, but also because of Kourouma's unaccommodating attitude toward assimilation, reflected in his irreverence toward the French language (Walsh 185).

3. Odile Cazenave sees humor in the novel as a way of exposing Johnny's childishness. Humor is a type of "echoing" that "exposes Johnny Chien Méchant's flaws, his weakness, his truancy, his false excuses, etc. In doing so, Dongala deconstructs the whole process of de-humanization of children turned adult soldiers: at heart, Johnny Chien Méchant is still a boy, a child, who does not want to confront certain realities, who wants to pretend he is a real chief, a real 'Chien Méchant,' when his first nickname is 'Gazon' (lawn) and the members of his gang are contesting his authority" (Cazenave 63).

4. Dongala is very explicit about Laokolé's fury. She beats Johnny to death, avenging his violence against women in particular: "I began stomping, crushing, kicking with all my might, aiming my blows at those genitals that had humiliated so many women. I thought of the twelve-year-old girl in the camp; I thought of my daughter [a child she adopts], whom he'd nearly flayed alive with lashes from his belt; and I rammed him ceaselessly between the legs. I trampled, pounded, pulverized his groin" (Dongala, *Johnny Mad Dog* [2006]: 320).

5. Dongala depicts the humanitarians (the UN and NGOs) in a particularly negative light. In the novel they are identified primarily by barriers, gates, and walls that close off their compounds and arbitrarily select whom to save and whom to abandon. They are collectively incapable of fulfilling the promises they hold out and, hence, they are cruel (Dongala, *Johnny Mad Dog* [2006]: 67, 157–59).

6. The most important influence on *Purple Hibiscus* is Tsitsi Dangarembga's *Nervous Conditions*, which controversially avoided all reference to Zimbabwe's liberation war that was raging during the years the novel was set. Primorac argues in defense of Dangarembga's choice in *Place of Tears* (Primorac, *Place of Tears* 105ff).

7. My reference to "sincerity" draws on Amanda Anderson (166), as discussed more fully in Chapter 2. We see this through the perspective of the servant, Ugwu, who eagerly listens to the debates about Biafran nationalism

and the war as he observes the intellectuals who come to the house. Ugwu quickly realizes that "he was not a normal houseboy" because he was given a bed to sleep on, books to read, and greater autonomy and decision making in his job (Adichie, *Half* 16–17).

8. Chiefs were appointed by the British as instruments of indirect rule and had authority over customary law, the type of power exercised most exclusively in rural areas and over peasant populations. The persistence of the chiefs' authority in the postcolonial era and their continued use of customary law has been a key complicating factor in the efforts of African countries to democratize (Mamdani, *Citizen* 23, 286–88).

9. The daughters' refusal of the more regressive implications of their elite status is apparent when, unlike their parents, they refuse to leave Nigeria during the war. Their parents, who live in Lagos, escape to London. Both daughters remain in Biafra, refusing even the distance of Lagos (outside Biafra). Each sister has different political views, however. Olanna is more persuaded by Biafran nationalism, whereas Kainene maintains a cynical distance from nationalism and politics in general. Although she is deeply identified with the East as a region, she opposes secession and the war. All the same, she throws herself into the humanitarian effort.

10. Compared to Nnu Ego in Emecheta's *Joys of Motherhood*, for example, Olanna is empowered through her unconventional motherhood. The stark difference is based on socio-economic status, of course.

11. This kind of feminization of the home, wresting it away from patriarchy, is key to the creation of a middle-class identity, which is one of Adichie's projects: to create through fiction an imaginative construct of an African middle class. As Nancy Armstrong tells us about the British novel, "middle-class authority rested in large part upon the authority that novels attributed to women and in this way designated as specifically female" (Nancy Armstrong, *Desire* 4). Adichie has acknowledged the influence of British fiction on her work (Adichie, "African 'Authenticity'" 44).

12. Writing about the fall of Onistha, Richard stressed that "the Nigerians had tried many times to take this ancient town but the Biafrans fought valiantly, that hundreds of popular novels had been published here before the war, that the thick sad smoke of the burning Niger Bridge had risen like a defiant elegy" (Adichie, *Half* 305). The literature he refers to is the Onistha Market literature, an important antecedent to the modern, anglophone Nigerian novel.

13. Ugwu's aunt brings him to work for Odenigbo, a bachelor in need of domestic help (Adichie, *Half* 3–4). When Olanna arrives, Ugwu is nervous about the prospect of a woman mistress in the house and at first treats her

with suspicion: "he did not want to share the job of caring for Master with anyone, did not want to disrupt the balance of his life with Master" (25).

14. Cooper gives a different but similarly critical reading of Adichie's treatment of Ugwu by focusing on his guilt as a rapist and the reassertion of patriarchy that this indicates. She remains unconvinced that Ugwu's vocation as people's historian is "atonement," as he claims, for his crime (Cooper 143).

15. See for example Anna Simons, *Networks of Dissolution: Somalia Undone*, whose particular focus, like Farah's, is Mogadiscio. Simons explains Somalia's dissolution in terms of the politicization of clans during colonialism and Somalia's particular colonial history, one nation divided among several colonial powers (39). Somalia in independence was never able to hold together its own idea of its different regions being one nation.

16. A well-known example is George Eliot's metaphor of the "defective mirror" for realism in Book 2, Chapter 17 of *Adam Bede*.

17. I use Farah's preferred spelling for the city's name, as opposed to Mogadishu.

18. Nancy Armstrong argues in *Fiction in the Age of Photography* that in the second half of the nineteenth century, "the kind of visual description we associate with realism refers not to things, but to visual representations of things, representations that fiction helped to establish as identical to real things and people" (3). Photography, "new technologies of seeing," Armstrong says, exerted a powerful influence: "revers(ing) the traditional relationship between image and object observed," making the "material world" known through images rather than direct observation (4–5).

19. *Secrets* is the last novel of the *Blood in the Sun* trilogy. The first two are *Maps* and *Gifts*. *Maps* is about the Ogaden War, Somalia's failed attempt to reclaim the Ogaden from Ethiopia. This was a war conducted at the height of the Cold War, from 1977 to 1978. Farah extends in the novel his critique of totalitarian governments and their manipulation of nationalism from his first trilogy, *Variations on the Theme of an African Dictatorship*, setting these against the politics of the Cold War and the shifting alliances of Somalia and Ethiopia. The trilogy's second volume, *Gifts*, focuses on humanitarian aid. It should be noted that all three novels of *Blood in the Sun* examine the way the national imagines the relation between Mogadiscio and Somalia's various regionalisms.

20. Kalaman is traveling to Nonno's estate, which is located in Afgoi by the Shebeele River, an agricultural area in the eastern outskirts of Mogadiscio. In the immediate postcolonial years (until the mid-1980s), when Mogadiscio grew rapidly, Afgoi became more of a suburb. In *Secrets*, Farah constructs Afgoi as a place where Somalia's three populations (pastoralists,

agriculturalists, and city dwellers) all have a presence. Critics have questioned the accuracy of this portrayal (Samatar 139), but it is an important fictional construct for Farah, a way of positing the wholeness of the nation before the war.

21. Dante also provides another way to think of the conversational structure of the novel, since it imitates the relationship between Dante's poet and guide.

22. Nor was it worthwhile for their own country. Speaking of the troops who fought, Bowden says, "they returned to a country that didn't care or remember" what they did. He continues, "Their fight was neither triumph nor defeat; it just didn't matter. It's as though their firefight was a bizarre two-day adventure, like some extreme Outward Bound experience where things get out of hand and some guys got killed" (Bowden 346). The Americans' distanced view of the Somalis is amply evident here, as is the prism through which they viewed the country.

23. Bowden's is an American perspective, but he is not unsympathetic to the Somalis. He articulates his criticisms of American policy through the perspective of Somalis who know the realities on the ground better than the Americans, thus giving some authority to the Somali point of view (Bowden 71–76). But his goal is to show how the Americans experienced the battle.

24. Bowden does acknowledge that "some in the crowd at Abdi House were there to argue for peace" (Bowden 72).

25. Bile's account of himself (Farah, *Links* 113ff) is given to Jeebleh in a conversation. Bile explains how he found one million dollars in cash in the abandoned house in which he took refuge when Siyad Barre was driven from the city and the prison doors were opened. He says he decided to "appropriate" the money and "use it for other people" (118) rather than let looters get to it. Bile insists he is not a thief. His intention had been to turn over the money to the government, not realizing (because he had been in prison) that there was no government.

26. For example, Seamus is introduced as follows: "Seamus, she thinks, has the look of an exhausted beast of burden that is carrying more than twice its weight and rises to its diminished height, knees burdensomely bent and aching, gaze wary, and mouth pouting, as if annoyed" (Farah, *Knots* 222). There are also references to his dirty, unkempt nails and beard (223). When Cambara meets Bile the second time, she finds him semi-conscious on the floor of his filthy apartment with excrement in his pants and vomit dried up around his mouth (313).

27. In *Crossbones* the safe bounds of the home restored in *Knots* fall away as the home becomes the locus of one of the novel's key scenes, a botched,

violent home invasion in which the perpetrator is a very young child recruited by the Islamists. Furthermore, Farah's novelistic nation bifurcates, because this is the tale of two Somalias, Mogadiscio and the northern area of Puntland.

AFTERWORD

1. In his widely read critique, Makau Mutua rejects humanitarian discourse as self-serving for the savior and debilitating for those deemed victims. A more sympathetic rereading of this dynamic, which draws on Dunant's text, is offered by Slaughter. Putting the emphasis on the reader as savior (constituted through the moral journey of sentimental reading), Slaughter warns that "this divisive map of suffering and sympathy contains the seeds of its own undoing and undercuts the patronizing sense of moral superiority and cosmopolitan largesse that it seems to encourage on the part of the rich, safe, and powerful readers" (Slaughter, "Humanitarian Reading" 105). He urges an ethic of impartial reading, akin to the impartiality advocated by Dunant's humanitarianism, which responds to the victims' address to the reader by recognizing that being thus addressed, the reader is invited into the community of humanity. This is a reversal of the dynamic that posits a reader who initiates the gesture to include the other. Slaughter proposes a figure of the reader who responds to an invitation embedded in the narrative of suffering.

2. Salima witnesses torture without seeing the victim because she is listening rather than watching. Thus Djebar's account subverts the intent of "clean" or "stealth" torture—torture, such as electrocution, that does not leave marks on the body. The Algerian conflict has a special place in the history of torture practices because the French enlarged significantly the repertory of such "clean" tortures (Rejali 163). As Rejali points out, "torture victims have always authenticated their claims by describing their wounds," and stealth torture effectuates a further disempowerment of the tortured individual by staging the erasure of wounds (164).

3. John Carlos Rowe notes this as well: Fleming "initially flees from battle to face existential dread and then returns curiously transformed into a daring leader of his Union regiment" (Rowe 817). Rowe's "curiously transformed" signals Crane's ironic treatment of Fleming, or perhaps the reader's suspicion that it must be ironic.

4. Elsewhere I have written about the appearance of the heart of darkness motif in human rights narratives; see Coundouriotis, "Congo Cases: The Stories of Human Rights History."

5. Donna Campbell identifies the pull toward atavism with the idea of "devolition" in the context of American naturalism: "Naturalistic writers saw

that the untrammeled nature within human beings—sometimes selfish, often violent, and always driven by desire—made “devolution” (a scientifically dubious concept suggested by the connotations of progress within the word “evolution”) and atavism as likely as the transcendentalists’ vision of human perfectibility” (Campbell 501).

WORKS CITED

Abani, Chris. *Song for Night*. New York: Akashic Books, 2007.

Abrams, M. H. *Glossary of Literary Terms*. New York: Holt, Rinehart, and Winston, 1988.

Achebe, Chinua. *Arrow of God*. 1964. New York: Anchor, 1989.

———. *Beware, Soul Brother*. Enugu, Nigeria: Nwankwo-Ifejika, 1971.

———. "Chinua Achebe on Biafra." *Transition* 36 (1968): 31–38.

———. *Girls at War and Other Stories*. London: Heinemann, 1972.

———. Morning Yet on Creation Day. Garden City, N.Y.: Anchor, 1975.

———. *No Longer at Ease*. 1960. Oxford: Heinemann, 1987.

———. *There Was a Country: A Personal History of Biafra*. New York: Penguin, 2012.

———. *Things Fall Apart*. 1958. New York: Anchor, 1959.

Adams, Ann Marie. "It's a Woman's War: Engendering Conflict in Buchi Emecheta's *Destination Biafra*." *Callaloo* 24, no. 1 (2001): 287–300.

Adichie, Chimamanda Ngozi. "African 'Authenticity' and the Biafran Experience." *Transition* 99 (2008): 42–53.

———. "A Brief Conversation with Chimamanda Ngozi Adichie." *World Literature Today*, March–April 2006.

———. *Half of a Yellow Sun*. New York: Knopf, 2006.

———. *Purple Hibiscus*. New York: Anchor, 2004.

Agamben, Giorgio. *Homo Sacer: Sovereign Power and Bare Life*. Translated by Daniel Heller-Roazen. Stanford: Stanford University Press, 1998.

———. *State of Exception*. Translated by Kevin Attel. Chicago: University of Chicago Press, 2005.

Ahiara Declaration: The Principles of the Biafran Revolution. http://www.biafraland.com/Ahiara_declaration_1969.htm. Accessed 13 June, 2011.

Ahmad, Aijaz. *In Theory: Classes, Nations, Theories*. London: Verso, 1992.

Alden, Patricia, and Louis Tremaine. "How Can We Talk of Democracy? An Interview with Nuruddin Farah." In Wright, *Emerging Perspectives*, 25–46.

Alexander, Jocelyn, Joann McGregor, and Terence Ranger. *Violence and Memory: One Hundred Years in the "Dark Forests" of Matabeleland*. Oxford: James Currey, 2000.

Amadiume, Ifi. "The Politics of Memory: Biafra and Intellectual Responsibility." In *The Politics of Memory: Truth, Healing and Social Justice*, edited by Ifi Amadiume and Abdullahi An-Na'im, 38–55. London: Zed, 2000.

Amuta, Chidi. "The Nigerian Civil War and the Evolution of Nigerian Literature." *Canadian Journal of African Studies* 17, no. 1 (1983): 85–99.

Anderson, Amanda. *The Way We Argue Now: A Study in the Cultures of Theory*. Princeton: Princeton University Press, 2006.

Anderson, Benedict. *Imagined Communities: Reflections on the Origin and Spread of Nationalism*. New ed. London: Verso, 2006.

Anderson, David. *Histories of the Hanged: The Dirty War in Kenya and the End of Empire*. New York: Norton, 2005.

Andrade, Susan Z. "Adichie's Genealogies: National and Feminine Novels." *Research in African Literatures* 42, no. 2 (2011): 91–101.

———. *The Nation Writ Small: African Fictions and Feminisms, 1958–1988*. Durham: Duke University Press, 2011.

Anthony, David. "South African People's History." *Radical History Review* 46 (1990): 411–19.

Apocalypse Now. Directed by Francis Ford Coppola. Written by John Millius and Francis Ford Coppola. Paramount Pictures, 1979. DVD.

Appiah, Kwame Anthony. "For Nuruddin Farah." *World Literature Today* 72, no. 4 (1998): 703–5.

———. "Nuruddin Farah." *Bomb* 87 (2004): 54–59.

Arendt, Hannah. *On Revolution*. New York: Viking, 1969.

———. *The Origins of Totalitarianism*. New York: Harcourt, 1976.

Armstrong, Andrew. "Speaking through the Wound: Irruption and Memory in the Writing of Ben Okri and Festus Iyayi." *Journal of African Cultural Studies* 13, no. 2 (2000): 173–83.

Armstrong, Nancy. *Desire and Domestic Fiction: A Political History of the Novel*. New York: Oxford University Press, 1987.

———. *Fiction in the Age of Photography: The Legacy of British Realism*. Cambridge, Mass.: Harvard University Press, 1999.

———. "Why Daughters Die: The Racial Logic of American Sentimentalism." In *Burning Down the House: Recycling Domesticity*, edited by Rosemary Marangoly George, 23–46. Boulder: Westview, 1998.

Atieno-Odhiambo, E. S. "Democracy and the Ideology of Order in Kenya." In *The Political Economy of Kenya*, edited by Michael G. Schatzberg, 177–201. New York: Praeger, 1987.

Atieno-Odhiambo, E. S., and John Lonsdale, eds. *Mau Mau and Nationhood*. Oxford: James Currey, 2003.

Auerbach, Eric. *Mimesis: The Representation of Reality in Western Literature*. Translated by Willard R. Trask. Princeton: Princeton University Press, 1953.

Azoulay, Ariella. *The Civil Contract of Photography*. New York: Zone, 2008.

———. "Photography Without Borders." In *Handbook of Human Rights*, edited by Thomas Cushman, 669–81. London: Routledge, 2012.
Bain, Alexander. "A Constant Engagement: John Le Carré's Humanitarian Interventions." Paper delivered at "Comparative Human Rights: Literature, Art, Politics," University of Illinois, 6 February 2009.
Barber, Karin. "African Language Literatures and Postcolonial Criticism." *Research in African Literatures* 26 (1995): 3–30.
Barbusse, Henri. *Under Fire* [*Le Feu*]. 1916. Translated by Robin Buss. Introduction by Jay Winter. New York: Penguin, 2003.
Barkan, Elazar. "Can Human Rights Be Local?" *Raritan* 28, no. 1 (2008): 135–55.
———. "Historical Reconciliation: Redress, Rights and Politics." *Journal of International Affairs* 60, no. 1 (2006): 1–15.
———. "Introduction: Historians and Historical Reconciliation." *American Historical Review* 114, no. 4 (2009): 899–913.
Barker, Francis, Peter Hulme, and Margaret Iversen. *Cannibalism and the Colonial World*. New York: Cambridge University Press 1998.
Beah, Ishmael. *A Long Way Gone: Memoirs of a Boy Soldier*. New York: Farrar, Straus and Giroux, 2007.
Benthall, Jonathan. *Disasters, Relief and the Media*. 1993. Wantage, UK: Sean Kingston, 2010.
Berman, Bruce. *Control and Crisis in Colonial Kenya: The Dialectic of Domination*. London: James Currey, 1990.
Berman, Bruce, and John Lonsdale. "Louis Leakey's Mau Mau: A Study in the Politics of Knowledge." *History and Anthropology* 5, no. 2 (1991): 143–204.
———. *Unhappy Valley: Conflict in Kenya and Africa*. London: James Currey, 1992.
Bevington, David, ed. *The Complete Works of Shakespeare*. Updated 4th ed. New York: Longman, 1997.
Bhabha, Homi K. "DissemiNation: Time, Narrative and Margins of the Modern Nation." In *Nation and Narration*, edited by Homi K. Bhabha, 291–322. London: Routledge, 1990.
———. "The World and the Home." *Social Text* 31–32 (1992): 141–53.
Boehmer, Elleke. "Motherlands, Mothers, and Nationalist Sons: Representations of Nationalism and Women in African Literature." In *From Commonwealth to Post-Colonial*, edited by Anna Rutherford, 229–47. Sydney: Dangaroo Press, 1992.
———. *Stories of Women: Gender and Narrative in the Postcolonial Nation*. Manchester, UK: University of Manchester Press, 2005.
Bolger, Daniel P. *Savage Peace: Americans at War in the 1990s*. Novato, Calif.: Presidio, 1995.

Boltanski, Luc. *Distant Suffering: Morality, Media, and Politics*. Translated by Graham Bruchell. Cambridge: Cambridge University Press, 1999.

Bowden, Mark. *Black Hawk Down: A Story of Modern War*. New York: Penguin, 2000.

Branch, Daniel. *Defeating Mau Mau, Creating Kenya: Counterinsurgency, Civil War, and Decolonization*. New York: Cambridge University Press, 2009.

Brown, Homer. "Why the Story of the Origin of the (English) Novel Is an American Romance (If Not the Great American Novel)." In *Cultural Institutions of the Novel*, edited by Deidre Lynch and William B. Warner, 11–43. Durham: Duke University Press, 1996.

Bryce, Jane. "Imaginary Snapshots: Cinematic Techniques in the Writing of Yvonne Vera." In Muponde and Maodzwa-Taruvinga, *Sign and Taboo*, 39–56.

———. "Interview with Yvonne Vera." In Muponde and Maodzwa-Taruvinga, *Sign and Taboo*, 217–26.

Burke, Peter. "People's History or Total History." in Samuel, *People's History*, 4–9.

———. *What Is Cultural History?* Cambridge: Polity, 2004.

Burke, Roland. *Decolonization and the Evolution of International Human Rights*. Philadelphia: University of Pennsylvania Press, 2010.

Butler, Judith. *Precarious Life: The Powers of Mourning and Violence*. London: Verso, 2004.

Buzard, James. *Disorienting Fiction: The Autoethnographic Work of Nineteenth-Century British Novels*. Princeton: Princeton University Press, 2005.

Calder, Angus. "The New Zimbabwe Writing and Chimurenga." *Wasafiri* 22 (1995): 35–42.

Campbell, Donna. "The Rise of Naturalism." In *The Cambridge History of the American Novel*, edited by Leonard Cassuto, 499–514. New York: Cambridge University Press, 2011.

Card, Claudia. *The Atrocity Paradigm: A Theory of Evil*. Oxford: Oxford University Press, 2002.

———. *Confronting Evils: Terrorism, Torture, and Genocide*. Cambridge: Cambridge University Press, 2010.

Carlyle, Thomas. *The French Revolution*. 3 vols. New York: Putnam's Sons, 1902.

Carothers, J. C. *The Psychology of Mau Mau*. Nairobi, 1954.

Cazenave, Odile. "Writing the Child, Youth, and Violence into the Francophone Novel from Sub-Saharan Africa: The Impact of Age and Gender." *Research in African Literatures* 36, no. 2 (2005): 59–71.

Chan, Stephen. "The Memory of Violence: Trauma in the Writings of Alexander Kanengoni and Yvonne Vera and the Idea of Unreconciled Citizenship in Zimbabwe." *Third World Quarterly* 26, no. 2 (2005): 369–82.

Chan, Stephen, and Ranka Primorac. "The Imagination of Land and the Reality of Seizure: Zimbabwe's Complex Reinventions." *Journal of International Affairs* 57, no. 2 (2004): 63–80.

Chatman, Seymour. *Story and Discourse: Narrative Structure in Fiction and Film*. Ithaca: Cornell University Press, 1978.

Chatterjee, Partha. *The Nation and Its Fragments: Colonial and Postcolonial Histories*. Princeton: Princeton University Press, 1993.

———. *Nationalist Thought and the Colonial World: A Derivative Discourse?* Minneapolis: University of Minnesota Press, 1993.

———. "Reflections on 'Can the Subaltern Speak': Subaltern Studies After Spivak." In Morris, *Can the Subaltern Speak*, 81–86.

Chinodya, Shimmer. *Harvest of Thorns*. Portsmouth, N.H.: Heinemann, 1989.

Chinweizu, C. "Time of Troubles." *Times Literary Supplement*, 26 February 1982.

Chinweizu, C., et al. *Toward the Decolonization of African Literature*. Washington, D.C.: Howard University Press, 1983.

Chipamaunga, Edmund. *A Fighter for Freedom*. Gweru, Zimbabwe: Mambo, 1983.

Chouliaraki, Lilie. *The Ironic Spectator: Solidarity in the Age of Post-Humanitarianism*. London: Polity, 2013.

Christiansen, Lene Bull. "Yvonne Vera: Rewriting Discourses of History and Identity in Zimbabwe." In Muponde and Primorac, *Versions of Zimbabwe*, 203–15.

Cobban, Helena. "The Role of Mass Incarceration in Counterinsurgency: A Reflection on Caroline Elkins's Imperial Reckoning in Light of Recent Events." *Radical History Review* 96 (2006): 112–36.

Coetzee, J. M. *Doubling the Point: Essay and Interviews*. Edited by David Attwell. Cambridge, Mass.: Harvard University Press, 1992.

———. *Waiting for the Barbarians*. New York: Penguin, 1980.

Conrad, Joseph. *Heart of Darkness and Selections from the Congo Diary*. Introduction by Caryl Phillips. New York: Modern Library Paperback Edition, 1999.

Cookman, Claude. "Gilles Caron's Coverage of the Crisis in Biafra." *Visual Communication Quarterly* 15, no. 4 (2008): 226–42.

Cooper, Brenda. *A New Generation of African Writers: Migration, Material Culture and Language*. Suffolk, UK: James Currey, 2008.

Coundouriotis, Eleni. "The Child Soldier Narrative and the Problem of Arrested Historicization." *Journal of Human Rights* 9, no. 2 (2010) 191–206.

———. *Claiming History: Colonialism, Ethnography, and the Novel*. New York: Columbia University Press, 1999.

———. "Congo Cases: The Stories of Human Rights History." *Humanity: An International Journal of Human Rights, Humanitarianism, and Development* 3, no. 2 (2012): 133–53.
———. "Self-Inflicted Wounds in Yvonne Vera's Butterfly Burning." *World Literature Today* 79, nos. 3–4 (2005): 64–67.
———. "'You Only Have Your Word:' Rape and Testimony." *Human Rights Quarterly* 35, no. 2 (2013): 365–85.
Courtemanche, Gil. *Sunday at the Pool in Kigali*. Translated by Patricia Claxton. Edinburgh: Canongate, 2003.
Cowell, Alan. "Britain to Compensate Kenyan Victims of Colonial-Era Torture." *New York Times*, 6 June 2013.
Crane, Stephen. *Red Badge of Courage*. 1895. Introduction by Alfred Kazin. New York: Bantam Classics, 2004.
"Cry That Will Be Heard." *Life Magazine*, 12 July 1968.
Dangarembga, Tsitsi. *Nervous Conditions*. Boulder: Lynne Rienner, 2004.
Darbouze, Gilbert. "Les Bouts de bois de Dieu d'Ousmane Sembène: L'ésthétique naturalist d'Émile Zola dans un roman sénégalais." *Excavatio: Émile Zola and Naturalism* 11 (1988): 182–87.
Davidson, Basil. *Black Man's Burden: Africa and the Curse of the Nation-State*. New York: Random House, 1992.
Dawes, James. *That the World May Know: Bearing Witness to Atrocity*. Cambridge, Mass.: Harvard University Press, 2007.
De Man, Paul. "The Rhetoric of Temporality." In *Blindness and Insight*, 187–228. Minneapolis: University of Minnesota Press, 1983.
De St. Jorre, John. *The Nigerian Civil War*. London: Hodder and Stoughton, 1972.
De Waal, Alex. *Famine Crimes: Politics and the Disaster Relief Industry in Africa*. Bloomington: Indiana University Press, 2009.
DelConte, Matt. "Why You Can't Speak: Second-Person Narration, Voice, and a New Model for Understanding Narrative." *Style* 37, no. 2 (2003): 204–19.
Diawara, Manthia. "Who Is Afraid of Ngũgĩ?" *Black Renaissance/Renaissance Noire* 7, no. 3 (2007): 74–78.
Diop, Boubacar Boris. *Murambi: The Book of Bones*. [*Murambi, le livre des ossements*]. 2000. Translated by Fiona McLaughlin. Bloomington: Indiana University Press, 2006.
Djebar, Assia. *Children of the New World* [*Les Enfants du nouveau monde*]. 1962. Translated by Marjolijn de Jager. New York: Feminist Press, 2005.
Dongala, Emmanuel. *Johnny Mad Dog* [*Johnny chien méchant*]. 2002. Translated by Maria Louise Ascher. 2005. New York: Picador, 2006.
Dunant, Henri. *Un Souvenir de Solférino*. 1862. Geneva: Comité International de la Croix Rouge, 1990.

Eagleton, Terry, Fredric Jameson, and Edward W. Said. *Nationalism, Colonialism, and Literature*. Minneapolis: University of Minnesota Press, 1990.
Eggers, Dave. *What Is the What*. New York: Vintage, 2007.
Ekwensi, Cyprian. *Divided We Stand*. Enugu, Nigeria: Fourth Dimension, 1980.
———. "Interview." in Lindfors, *Dem-Say*, 24–34.
———. *Jagua Nana*. 1965. London: Heinemann, 1975.
———. *Survive the Peace*. London: Heinemann, 1976.
Eliot, George. 1859. *Adam Bede*. Oxford: Oxford World Classics, 2008.
Elkins, Caroline. *Imperial Reckoning: The Untold Story of Britain's Gulag in Kenya*. New York: Henry Holt, 2005.
Ellison, Ralph. *Invisible Man*. New York: Vintage, 1995.
Emecheta, Buchi. *Destination Biafra*. 1982. Glasgow: William Collins Sons, 1983.
———. *Joys of Motherhood*. New York: George Braziller, 1979.
Emenyonu, Ernest N. *The Essential Ekwensi*. Ibadan, Nigeria: Heinemann, 1987.
Engelke, Matthew. "Thinking about the Nativism in Chenjerai Hove's Work." *Research in African Literatures* 29, no. 2 (1998): 23–42.
Ezeigbo, Theodora Akachi. "War, History, Aesthetics and the Thriller Tradition in Eddie Iroh's Novels." *African Literatures and Cultures* 4, no. 1 (1991): 65–76.
Ezenwa-Ohaeto. *Chinua Achebe: A Biography*. Bloomington: Indiana University Press, 1997.
Falola, Toyin, and Matthew M. Heaton. *A History of Nigeria*. Cambridge: Cambridge University Press, 2008.
Fanon, Frantz. *The Wretched of the Earth*. Translated by Constance Farrington. New York: Grove, 1968.
Farah, Nuruddin. "A Country in Exile." *World Literature Today* 72, no. 4 (1998): 713–15.
———. *Crossbones*. New York: Riverhead, 2011.
———. *Gifts*. 1993. New York: Penguin, 1999.
———. *Knots*. New York: Riverhead, 2007.
———. *Links*. New York: Riverhead, 2004.
———. *Maps*. 1986. New York: Penguin, 1999.
———. *Secrets*. New York: Arcade, 1998.
———. *Yesterday, Tomorrow: Voices from the Somali Diaspora*. London: Cassell 2000.
Farah, Nuruddin, and Robert Coover, moderator. "Saving the Soul of the Nation." In *The Writer in Politics*, edited by William H. Gass and Lorin Cuoco, 110–32. Carbondale: Southern Illinois University Press, 1996.
Fassin, Didier. *Humanitarian Reason: A Moral History of the Present*. Berkeley: University of California Press, 2012.

Fassin, Didier, and Richard Rechtman. *The Empire of Trauma: An Inquiry into the Condition of Victimhood.* Translated by Rachel Gomme. Princeton: Princeton University Press, 2009.

Feierman, Steven. "African Histories and the Dissolution of World History." In *Africa and the Disciplines*, edited by Robert H. Bates and Valentin Y. Mudimbe, 167–212. Chicago: University of Chicago Press, 1993.

Foner, Eric. "Zinn's Critical History." *Nation* 290, no. 7 (2010): 6.

Forsyth, Frederick. *The Biafra Story: The Making of an African Legend.* 1969. Barnsley, South Yorkshire: Leo Cooper, 2001.

Forsythe, David P. *The Humanitarians: The International Committee of the Red Cross*. Cambridge: Cambridge University Press, 2005.

Fréris, Georges. "Le Roman de guerre: Discours autobiographique, expression d'une collectivité ou d'une identité a-nationale." *Neohelicon* 23, no. 2 (2004): 77–89.

Gagiano, Annie. "Reading 'The Stone Virgins' as Vera's Study of the Katabolism of War." *Research in African Literatures* 38, no. 2 (2007): 64–76.

Genette, Gérard. *Narrative Discourse: An Essay in Method.* Translated by Jane E. Lewin. Ithaca: Cornell University Press, 1980.

Gikandi, Simon. "Ekwensi, Cyprian." In Gikandi and Mwangi, *Columbia Guide*, 170–71.

———. "The Embarrassment of Victorianism: Colonial Subjects and the Lure of Englishness." In *Victorian Afterlife: Postmodern Culture Rewrites the Nineteenth-Century*, edited by John Kucich and Dianne F. Sadoff, 157–85. Minneapolis: University of Minnesota Press, 2000.

———. *Encyclopedia of African Literature*. London: Routledge, 2003.

———. "Introduction: East African Literature in English Since 1945." In Gikandi and Mwangi, *Columbia Guide*, 1–22.

———. *Ngũgĩ Wa Thiong'o*. Cambridge: Cambridge University Press, 2000.

———. "Nuruddin Farah and Postcolonial Textuality." *World Literature Today* 72, no. 4 (1998): 753–58.

———. "Pan-Africanism and Cosmopolitanism: The Case of Jomo Kenyatta." *English Studies in Africa* 43, no. 1 (2000): 3–27.

———. "The Politics and Poetics of National Formation: Recent African Writing and Maps." In Wright, *Emerging Perspectives*, 449–67.

———. "Theory after Postcolonial Theory: Rethinking the Work of Mimesis." In *Theory After "Theory,"* edited by Jane Elliott and Derek Attridge, 163–78. New York: Routledge, 2011.

———. "The Winter of Discontent (Book Review)." *Foreign Policy* 147 (March–April 2005): 76–77.

Gikandi, Simon, and Evan Mwangi. *The Columbia Guide to East African Literature in English Since* 1945. New York: Columbia University Press, 2007.

Godwin, Peter. *The Fear: Robert Mugabe and the Martyrdom of Zimbabwe*. New York: Little Brown, 2010.

Goncourt, Edmond, and Jules Goncourt. *Germinie Lacerteux*. 1864. Paris: Flammarion, 1990.
Graham, Lucie Valerie. "Reading the Unspeakable: Rape in J. M. Coetzee's 'Disgrace.'" *Journal of Southern African Studies* 29, no. 2 (2003): 433–44.
Griswold, Wendy. *Bearing Witness: Readers, Writers, and the Novel in Nigeria*. Princeton: Princeton University Press, 2000.
Gugelberger, Georg M., ed. *Marxism and African Literature*. Trenton, N.J.: Africa World Press, 1985.
Guha, Ranajit. *Elementary Aspects of Peasant Insurgency in Colonial India*. Delhi: Oxford University Press, 1983.
Guha, Ranajit, and Gayatri Chakravorty Spivak. *Selected Subaltern Studies*. New York: Oxford University Press, 1988.
Gunner, Liz. "Power, Popular Consciousness, and the Fictions of War: Hove's Bones and Chinodya's Harvest of Thorns." *African Languages and Cultures* 4, no. 1 (1991): 77–85.
Gunner, Liz, and Neil Ten Kortenaar. "Introduction: Yvonne Vera's Fiction and the Voice of the Possible." *Research in African Literatures* 38, no. 2 (2007): 1–8.
Harlow, Barbara. *Resistance Literature*. New York: Methuen, 1987.
Harneit-Sievers, Axel, Jones O. Ahazuem, and Sydney Emezue. *A Social History of the Nigerian Civil War: Perspectives from Below*. Hamburg: Lit Verlag, 1997.
Harrow, Kenneth. "'Un train peut en cacher un autre': Narrating the Rwandan Genocide and Hotel Rwanda." *Research in African Literatures* 36, no. 4 (2005): 223–32.
Hawley, John C. "Biafra as Heritage and Symbol: Adichie, Mbachu, and Iweala." *Research in African Literatures* 39, no. 2 (2008): 15–26.
Hewett, Heather. "Coming of Age: Chimamanda Ngozi Adichie and the Voice of the Third Generation." *English in Africa* 32, no. 1 (May 2005): 73–97.
Higonnet, Margaret R., ed. *Lines of Fire: Women Writers of World War I*. New York: Plume, 1999.
Hove, Chenjerai. *Bones*. 1988. Harare: Baobab, 1990.
———. *Shadows*. Portsmouth, N.H.: Heinemann, 1991.
Howard-Hassmann, Rhoda. "Mugabe's Zimbabwe, 2000–2009: Massive Human Rights Violations and the Failure to Protect." *Human Rights Quarterly* 32, no. 4 (2010): 898–920.
Howe, Irving. *Politics and the Novel*. New York: Horizon, 1957.
Hunt, Lynn. *Inventing Human Rights: A History*. New York: Norton, 2007.
———, ed. *The New Cultural History*. Berkeley: University of California Press, 1989.
Hunt, Nigel C. *Memory, War and Trauma*. Cambridge: Cambridge University Press, 2010.

Hunter, Eva. "New War Stories: Women, Heroes and Violence in Yvonne Vera's Novels." In *Missions of Independence*, edited by Gerhard Stilz, 169–81. Amsterdam: Rodopi Press, 2002.

———. "'Shaping the Truth of the Struggle': An Interview with Yvonne Vera." *Current Writing* 10, no. 1 (1998): 75–86.

Ike, Chukwuemeka. *Sunset at Dawn: A Novel about Biafra*. London: Collins and Harvill Press, 1976.

Irele, Abiola. *The African Experience in Literature and Ideology*. London: Heinemann, 1981.

Iroh, Eddie. *Forty-Eight Guns for the General*. London: Heinemann, 1976.

———. *Siren in the Night*. London: Heinemann, 1982.

———. *Toads of War*. London: Heinemann, 1979.

Iweala, Uzodinma. *Beasts of No Nation*. New York: Harper Collins, 2005.

Iyayi, Festus. "The Freedom and Responsibilities of a Writer." *Landfall* 44 (1990): 493–99.

———. *Heroes*. Essex: Longman, 1986.

Jacobs, Dan. *The Brutality of Nations*. New York: Knopf, 1987.

Jackson, Kennell. "Review of Imperial Reckoning: The Untold Story of Britain's Gulag in Kenya." *International Journal of African Historical Studies* 39, no. 1 (2006): 158–60.

Jameson, Fredric. *The Political Unconscious: Narrative as a Socially Symbolic Act*. Ithaca: Cornell University Press, 1981.

———. "Third-World Literature in the Era of Multinational Capitalism." *Social Text* 15 (1986): 65–88.

JanMohamed, Abdul R. "Alex La Guma: The Literary and Political Functions of Marginality in the Colonial Situation." *Boundary2* 11, nos. 1–2 (1982–1983): 271–90.

———. *Manichean Aesthetics: The Politics of Literature in Colonial Africa*. Amherst: University of Massachusetts Press, 1983.

Jeyifo, Biodun. "The Nature of Things: Arrested Decolonization and Critical Theory." *Research in African Literatures* 21, no. 1 (1990): 33–46.

Johnson, Alex. "Sunset at Dawn: A Biafran on the Nigerian Civil War." *African Literature Today* 11 (1980): 149–60.

Julien, Eileen. "The Extroverted African Novel." In *The Novel, Volume I: History, Geography, and Culture*, edited by Franco Moretti, 667–700. Princeton: Princeton University Press, 2006.

Kahiga, Samuel. *Dedan Kimathi: The Real Story*. Nairobi: Longman Kenya, 1990.

Kanengoni, Alexander. *Echoing Silences*. Portsmouth, N.H.: Heinemann, 1997.

———. *When the Rainbird Cries*. Harare: Longman Zimbabwe, 1987.

Kaplan, Fred. *Sacred Tears: Sentimentality in Victorian Literature*. Princeton: Princeton University Press, 1987.

Kariuki, Josiah Mwangi. *"Mau Mau" Detainee*. London: Oxford University Press, 1963.
Kazin, Alfred. "Introduction." In Crane, *Red Badge of Courage*, vii–xviii.
Keck, Margaret E., and Kathryn Sikkink. *Activists Beyond Borders*. Ithaca: Cornell University Press, 1998.
Keen, Suzanne. *Empathy and the Novel*. Oxford: Oxford University Press, 2010.
Kenyatta, Jomo. *Facing Mount Kenya*. New York: Vintage, 1965.
———. *Suffering Without Bitterness: The Founding of the Kenyan Nation*. Nairobi: East African Publishing House, 1968.
Kibera, Leonard, and Samuel Kahiga. *Potent Ash*. Nairobi: East African Publishing House.
Kiernan, Ben. *Blood and Soil: A World History of Genocide and Extermination from Sparta to Darfur*. New Haven: Yale University Press, 2007.
Kortenaar, Neil Ten. "'Only Connect': Anthills of the Savannah and Achebe's Trouble with Nigeria." *Research in African Literatures* 24, no. 3 (2003): 59–72.
Kourouma, Ahmadou. *Allah Is Not Obliged*. Translated by Frank Wynne. New York: Anchor, 2007.
———. *Allah n'est pas obligé*. Points ed. Paris: Seuil, 2002.
Kriger, Norma J. *Guerrilla Veterans in Post-War Zimbabwe: Symbolic and Violent Politics, 1980–1987*. Cambridge: Cambridge University Press, 2003.
Kunene, Daniel. "Introduction." In Mofolo, *Chaka*, xi–xxiii.
LaCapra, Dominick. *Writing History, Writing Trauma*. Baltimore: Johns Hopkins University Press, 2001.
La Guma, Alex. *In the Fog of the Seasons' End*. 1972. Oxford: Heinemann, 1992.
Lan, David. *Guns and Rain: Guerrillas and Spirit Mediums in Zimbabwe*. Harare: Zimbabwe Publishing House, 1985.
Laqueur, Thomas W. "Bodies, Details, and the Humanitarian Narrative." In Hunt, *New Cultural History*, 176–204.
Larson, Charles. *The Ordeal of the African Writer*. New York: Zed, 2001.
Lazarus, Neil. "Fredric Jameson on Third-World Literature: A Qualified Defense." In *Fredric Jameson: A Critical Reader*, edited by Sean Homer and Douglas Kellner, 42–61. New York: Palgrave, 2004.
———. "The Politics of Postcolonial Modernism." *The European Legacy* 7, no. 6 (2002): 771–82.
———. *The Postcolonial Unconscious*. Cambridge: Cambridge University Press, 2011.
———. "Realism and Naturalism in African Fiction." In *African Literature: An Anthology of Criticism and Theory*, edited by Tejumola Olaniyan and Ato Quayson, 340–44. Oxford: Blackwell, 2007.
———. "Representation and Terror in V. Y. Mudimbe." *Journal of African Cultural Studies* 17, no. 1 (2005): 81–101.

Leakey, Louis S. B. *Defeating Mau Mau*. London: Methuen, 1954.
Lemarchand, René. *The Dynamics of Violence in Central Africa*. Philadelphia: University of Pennsylvania Press, 2009.
Lessing, Doris. "Foreword." In Lawrence Vambe, xiii–xxi.
Levin, Harry. *The Gates of Horn: A Study of Five French Realists*. New York: Oxford University Press, 1966.
Lindfors, Bernth. "Achebe's African Parable." In *Critical Perspectives on Chinua Achebe*, edited by Bernth Lindfors, 248–54. London: Heinemann.
———. ed. *Dem-Say: Interviews with Eight Nigerian Writers*. Austin. Tex.: African and African American Studies and Research Center, 1974.
Lukács, Georg. *Studies in European Realism*. Introduction by Alfred Kazin. New York: Grosset and Dunlap, 1964.
Maathai, Wangari. *Unbowed: A Memoir*. New York: Anchor, 2007.
Macey, David. *Frantz Fanon: A Biography*. New York: Picador, 2001.
Malraux, André. *The Conquerors*. 1928. Translated by Stephen Becker. New York: Holt, Rinehart, and Winston, 1976.
Mamdani, Mahmood. *Citizen and Subject: Contemporary Africa and the Legacy of Late Colonialism*. Princeton: Princeton University Press, 1996.
———. "Lessons of Zimbabwe." *London Review of Books* (4 December 2008): 17–21.
———. "Review of The Black Man's Burden: Africa and the Curse of the Nation State." *Monthly Review* 45, no. 3 (1993): 27ff.
———. "The Politics of Naming: Genocide, Civil War, Insurgency." *London Review of Books* (8 March 2007): 5–8.
———. *When Victims Become Killers: Colonialism, Nativism, and the Genocide in Rwanda*. Princeton: Princeton University Press, 2001.
Mandela, Nelson. *Long Walk to Freedom*. Boston: Little Brown, 1994.
Mangua, Charles. *Son of Woman*. Nairobi: East African Publishing House, 1971.
———. *A Tail in the Mouth*. Nairobi: East African Publishing House, 1972.
Marechera, Dambudzo. *House of Hunger*. London: Heinemann, 1978.
Maughan-Brown, David. *Land, Freedom, and Fiction: History and Ideology in Kenya*. London: Zed, 1985.
Mbembe, Achille. *On the Postcolony*. Berkeley: University of California Press, 2001.
McLoughlin, Kate. *Authoring War: The Literary Representation of War from the Iliad to Iraq*. Cambridge: Cambridge University Press, 2011.
———, ed. *Cambridge Companion to War Writing*. Cambridge: Cambridge University Press, 2009.
McLuckie, Craig W. *Nigerian Civil War Literature: Seeking an Imagined Community*. Lewiston, Me.: Edwin Mellen, 1990.
Mda, Zakes. "Justify the Enemy: Becoming Human in South Africa." *Boston Review*, May–June 2008.

———. "The Pink Mountain: Landscapes and the Conception of a Literature of Public Action." Address delivered at the African Literature Association Conference in Burlington, Vermont, 18 April 2009.

Mellors, John. "Selected Books: Afro-Asiatica." *London Magazine*, April–May 1974.

Meredith, Martin. *Diamonds, Gold, and War: The British, the Boers, and the Making of South Africa*. New York: Public Affairs, 2007.

———. *The Fate of Africa*. New York: Public Affairs, 2005.

———. *Mugabe: Power, Plunder, and the Struggle for Zimbabwe*. New York: Public Affairs, 2007.

Mezlekia, Nega. *Notes from the Hyena's Belly: An Ethiopian Boyhood*. New York: Picador, 2001.

Miller, Christopher L. *Theories of Africans: Francophone Literature and Anthropology in Africa*. Chicago: University of Chicago Press, 1990.

Mofolo, Thomas. *Chaka*. 1925. Translated by Daniel P. Kunene. 1981. London: Heinemann, 1986.

Moglen, Seth. *Mourning Modernity: Literary Modernism and the Injuries of American Capitalism*. Stanford: Stanford University Press, 2007.

Mohamed, Feisal G. "Poignancy as Human Rights Aesthetic." *Journal of Human Rights* 9, no. 2 (2010): 143–60.

Moretti, Franco. *Atlas of the European Novel 1800–1900*. London: Verso, 1998.

———. *The Way of the World: The Bildungsroman in European Culture*. London: Verso, 1987.

Morris, Rosalind C., ed. *Can the Subaltern Speak? Reflections on the History of an Idea*. New York: Columbia University Press, 2010.

Morrison, Jago. "Imagined Biafras: Fabricating Nation in Nigerian Civil War Writing." *Ariel* 36, no. 1–2 (2005): 5–25.

Moyn, Samuel. *The Last Utopia: Human Rights in History*. Princeton: Princeton University Press, 2010.

Msiska, Mpalive-Hangson. "Zimbabwe." In Gikandi, *Encyclopedia*, 92–94.

Mtisi, Joseph, Munyaradzi Nyakudya, and Teresa Barnes. "War in Rhodesia: 1965–1980." In Raftopoulos and Mlambo, *Becoming Zimbabwe*, 141–66.

Muponde, Robert, and Mandivavarira Maodzwa-Taruvinga, eds. *Sign and Taboo: Perspectives on the Poetic Fiction of Yvonne Vera*. Harare: Weaver, 2002.

Muponde, Robert, and Ranka Primorac, eds. *Versions of Zimbabwe: New Approaches to Literature and Culture*. Harare: Weaver, 2005.

Murphy, Philip. "Histories of the Hanged: 'Britain's Dirty War in Kenya and the End of Empire,' by David Anderson, and 'Britain's Gulag: The Brutal End of Empire in Kenya' by Caroline Elkins." *History* 91 (2006): 427–28.

Mutasa, Garikai. *The Contact*. Harare: Mambo, 1985.

Mutswairo, Solomon M. *Feso*. In *Zimbabwe Prose and Poetry*. Introduction by D. E. Herdeck. Washington, D.C.: Three Continents, 1974. 17–120.

———. *Mapondera: Soldier of Zimbabwe*. Harare: Longman Zimbabwe, 1983.
Mutua, Makau. "Savages, Victims, and Saviors: The Metaphor of Human Rights." *Harvard International Law Journal* 42, no. 1 (2001): 201–45.
Mwangi, Evan Maina. *Africa Writes Back to Self: Metafiction, Gender, Sexuality*. Albany: SUNY Press, 2009.
Mwangi, Meja. *Carcase for Hounds*. Nairobi: Heinemann, 1974.
———. *Taste of Death*. Nairobi: East African Publishing House, 1975.
Myers, Garth. *African Cities: Alternative Visions of Urban Theory and Practice*. London: Zed, 2011.
Nance, Kimberly. *Can Literature Promote Justice? Trauma Narrative and Social Action in Latin American Testimonio*. Nashville: Vanderbilt University Press, 2006.
Nazareth, Peter. "Survive the Peace: Cyprian Ekwensi as a Political Novelist." In Gugelberger, *Marxism and African Literature*, 165–77.
Ndlovu-Gastheni, Sabelo J. "Mapping Cultural and Colonial Encounters, 1880s–1930s." In Raftopoulos and Mlambo, *Becoming Zimbabwe*, 39–74.
Nelson, Nici. "Representations of Men and Women, City and Town in Kenyan Novels of the 1970s and 1980s." In Newell, *Readings*, 108–16.
Newell, Stephanie, ed. *Readings in African Popular Fiction*. Bloomington: Indiana University Press, 2002.
Ngũgĩ wa Thiong'o. *Dreams in a Time of War: A Childhood Memoir*. New York: Pantheon, 2011.
———. *A Grain of Wheat*. Oxford: Heinemann, 1986.
———. *Homecoming: Essays on African and Caribbean Literature, Culture and Politics*. 1972. Westport, Conn.: Lawrence Hill, 1983.
———. *Matigari*. Oxford: Heinemann, 1989.
———. *Petals of Blood*. New York: Penguin, 1977.
———. "The Role of the University in Africa Today." Address at Makerere University, Uganda, 8 August 2004.
———. *Secret Lives*. London: Heinemann, 1975.
———. "Tolstoy in Africa: An Interview with Ngũgĩ wa Thiong'o." Reinhard Sander and Ian Munro. 1971. In Sander and Lindfors, *Ngũgĩ wa Thiong'o Speaks*, 43–56.
———. *Weep Not, Child*. 1964. Oxford: Heinemann, 1987.
———. *Wizard of the Crow*. New York: Anchor, 2007.
Ngũgĩ wa Thiong'o, and Micere Githae Mugo. *The Trial of Dedan Kimathi*. Oxford: Heinemann, 1976.
Ni Chréacháin, Fírinne. "History and Radical Aesthetics: A Study of Festus Iyayi's Heroes." *African Literature Today* 20 (1996): 14–24.
Nixon, Rob. *Slow Violence: The Environmentalism of the Poor*. Cambridge, Mass.: Harvard University Press, 2011.
North, Michael. "Ken Saro-Wiwa's Sozaboy: The Politics of 'Rotten English.'" *Public Culture* 13, no. 1 (2001): 97–112.

Nugent, Paul. *Africa Since Independence*. Hampshire, UK, and New York: Palgrave MacMillan, 2004.

Nuttall, Sarah. *Entanglement: Literary and Cultural Reflections on Post-Apartheid*. Johannesburg: Wits, 2009.

———. "Inside the City: Reassembling the Township in Yvonne Vera's Fiction." In Muponde and Primorac, *Versions of Zimbabwe*, 177–92.

Nwankwo, Arthur. "Genocide Not Internal Affair." *Biafra Newsletter* 1, no. 3 (24 November 1967): 8.

Nwapa, Flora. *Efuru*. 1966. London: Heinemann, 1969.

———. *Never Again*. 1975. Enugu, Nigeria: Tana, 1986.

———. *One Is Enough*. Enugu, Nigeria: Tana, 1981.

———. *Wives at War*. 1980. Trenton, N.J.: Africa World Press, 1992.

Nzongola-Ntalaja, Georges. *The Congo: From Leopold to Kabila; A People's History*. London: Zed, 2002.

Obasanjo, Olusegun. *My Command: An Account of the Nigeria Civil War, 1967–1970*. Ibadan, Nigeria: Heinemann, 1980.

Ogot, Bethwell A. "Britain's Gulag." *Journal of African History* 46 (2005): 493–505.

———. "The Construction of a National Culture." In *The Challenges of History and Leadership in Africa: The Essays of Bethwell Allan Ogot*, edited by Toyin Falola and E. S. Atieno Odhiambo, 155–81. Trenton, N.J.: Africa World Press, 2002.

Ogude, James. *Ngũgĩ's Novels and African History: Narrating the Nation*. London: Pluto, 1999.

Ojukwu, C. Odumegwu. "The Ahiara Declaration: The Principles of the Biafran Revolution." 1 June 1969. http://www.biafraland.com/Ahiara_declaration_1969.htm. Accessed 3 June 2009.

———. *Biafra: Selected Speeches and Random Thoughts*. New York: Harper and Row, 1969.

Ojo-Ade, Femi. *Ken Saro-Wiwa: A Bio-Critical Study*. New York: Africana Legacy Press, 1999.

Okere, Augustine C. "The Eternal Sojourner: Ken Saro-Wiwa, The Man and His Fiction." In *Goatskin Bags and Wisdom: New Critical Perpectives on African Literature*, edited by Ernest N. Emenyonu, 255–69. Trenton, N.J.: Africa World Press, 2000.

Olaniyan, Tejumola. *Scars of Conquest/Masks of Resistance*. New York: Oxford University Press, 1995.

Oliver, Kelly. *Witnessing: Beyond Recognition*. Minneapolis: University of Minnesota Press, 2001.

Osaghae, Eghosa E. *Crippled Giant: Nigeria Since Independence*. Bloomington: Indiana University Press, 1998.

"Ouroboros." *Encyclopedia Britannica*. 2008. Encyclopedia Britannica Online. 2 June 2008. http://search.eb.com/eb/article-9057736.

Pajalich, Armando. "Allegorizing Terror: A Comparative Study of Novels by Farah and Soyinka." In Wright, *Emerging Perspectives*, 309–29.

Parrinder, Patrick. *Nation and Novel: The English Novel from Its Origins to the Present Day*. Oxford: Oxford University Press, 2006.

Paton, Alan. *Cry, the Beloved Country*. New York: Scribner, 1948.

Perham, Margery. "Foreword." In Kariuki, *"Mau Mau" Detainee*, xi–xxi.

Pierce, Steven, and Anupama Rao, eds. *Discipline and the Other Body: Correction, Corporeality, Colonialism*. Durham: Duke University Press, 2006.

Plaatje, Sol T. *Mhudi*. 1930. Penguin Global, 2006.

Prashad, Vijay. *The Darker Nations: A People's History of the Third World*. New York: New Press, 2007.

Pratt, Mary Louise. *Imperial Eyes: Travel Writing and Transculturation*. London: Routledge, 1992.

Primorac, Ranka. "Echoing Silences: Zimbabwean Writing Today." *Mazwi: A Zimbabwe Journal*. http://www.mazwi.net/essays/echoing-silences-zimbabwean-writing-today. Accessed 18 February 2011.

———. *The Place of Tears: The Novel and Politics in Modern Zimbabwe*. London: Tauris, 2006.

Prunier, Gérard. *Africa's World War: Congo, the Rwandan Genocide, and the Making of a Continental Catastrophe*. Oxford: Oxford University Press, 2009.

Quayson, Ato. *Aesthetic Nervousness: Disability and Crisis of Representation*. New York: Columbia University Press, 2007.

———. *Calibrations: Reading for the Social*. Minneapolis: University of Minnesota Press, 2003.

Raftopoulos, Brian. "The Crisis in Zimbabwe: 1998–2008." In Raftopoulos and Mlambo, *Becoming Zimbabwe*, 201–32.

Raftopoulos, Brian, and A. S. Mlambo, eds. *Becoming Zimbabwe: A History from the Pre-Colonial Period to 2008*. Harare: Weaver, 2009.

Ranger, Terence. "Constructions of Zimbabwe." *Journal of Southern African Studies* 36, no. 2 (2010): 505–10.

———. "History Has Its Ceiling: The Pressures of the Past in The Stone Virgins." In Muponde and Maodzwa-Taruvinga, *Sign and Taboo*, 203–16.

———. "Nationalist Historiography, Patriotic History, and the History of the Nation: The Struggle over the Past in Zimbabwe." *Journal of Southern African Studies* 30, no. 2 (2004): 215–34.

———. *Revolt in Southern Rhodesia 1896–7*. Evanston: Northwestern University Press, 1967.

———. *Voices from the Rocks: Nature, Culture and History in the Matopos Hills of Zimbabwe*. Oxford: James Currey, 1999.

———. *Writing Revolt: An Engagement with African Nationalism, 1957–1967*. Suffolk, UK: James Currey, 2013.

Rejali, Darius. *Torture and Democracy*. Princeton: Princeton University Press, 2007.

Remarque, Erich Maria. *All Quiet on the Western Front* [*Im Westen nichts Neues*]. 1929. Translated by A. W. Green. New York: Ballantine, 1982.

Robbins, Bruce. "Afterword." *PMLA*. Special issue, *Remapping Genre* 122, no. 5 (2007): 1644–51.

———. *The Servant's Hand: English Fiction from Below*. Durham: Duke University Press, 1993.

Rorty, Richard. "Human Rights, Rationality, and Sentimentality." In *On Human Rights: The Oxford Amnesty Lectures 1993*, edited by Stephen Shute and Susan Hurley, 111–34. New York: Basic Books, 1993.

Rowe, John Carlos. "U.S. Novels and U.S. Wars." In *The Cambridge History of the American Novel*, edited by Leonard Cassuto, 813–31. New York: Cambridge University Press, 2011.

Rutten, Marcel, and Sam Owuor. "Weapons of Mass Destruction: Land, Ethnicity, and the 2007 Elections in Kenya." *Journal of Contemporary African Studies* 27, no. 3 (2009): 305–24.

Said, Edward W. *Culture and Imperialism*. New York: Knopf, 1993.

———. "Permission to Narrate" (1984). In *The Politics of Dispossession: The Struggle for Palestinian Self-Determination, 1969–1994*. New York: Pantheon, 1994.

Samatar, Said. "Are There Secrets in *Secrets*?" *Research in African Literatures* 31, no. 1 (2000): 137–43.

Samuel, Raphael, ed. *People's History and Socialist Theory*. London: Routledge and Kegan Paul, 1981.

Samupindi, Charles. *Death Throes: The Trial of Mbuya Nehanda*. Harare: Mambo, 1990.

———. *Pawns*. Harare: Baobab, 1992.

Sander, Reinhard, and Bernth Lindfors. *Ngũgĩ wa Thiong'o Speaks: Interviews with the Kenyan Writer*. Trenton, N.J.: Africa World Press, 2006.

Sanders, Mark. *Ambiguities of Witnessing: Law and Literature in the Time of a Truth Commission*. Stanford: Stanford University Press 2007.

Saro-Wiwa, Ken. *On a Darkling Plain: An Account of the Nigerian Civil War*. Port Harcourt: Saros International.

———. *Sozaboy: A Novel in Rotten English*. 1985. Essex: Longman, 1994.

Scarry, Elaine. *The Body in Pain: The Making and Unmaking of the World*. New York: Oxford University Press, 1985.

Scheffer, David. "The Merits of Unifying Terms: 'Atrocity Crimes' and 'Atrocity Law.'" *Genocide Studies and Prevention* 2, no. 1 (April 2007): 91–96.

Scheingold, Stuart A. *The Political Novel: Re-Imagining the Twentieth Century*. New York: Continuum, 2010.

Schulz, William E. *The Phenomenon of Torture: Readings and Commentary.* Introduction by Juan E. Méndez. Philadelphia: University of Pennsylvania Press, 2007.
Shue, Henry. "Torture." In Schulz, *Phenomenon of Torture*, 241–48.
Sibanyoni, Mxolisi R. "The Fading Songs of Chimurenga." *African Studies* 54, no. 2 (1995): 52–72.
Sicherman, Carol. "Ngũgĩ's Colonial Education: 'The Subversion . . . of the African Mind.'" *African Studies Review* 38, no. 3 (1995): 11–41.
———. "Ngũgĩ Wa Thiong'o and the Writing of Kenyan History." *Research in African Literatures* 20, no. 3 (1989): 347–70.
Simatei, Peter. "Versions and Inversions: Mau Mau in Kahiga's Dedan Kimathi: The Real Story." *Research in African Literatures* 30, no. 1 (1999): 154–61.
Simatei, Tirop. "Colonial Violence, Postcolonial Violations: Violence, Landscape, and Memory in Kenyan Fiction." *Research in African Literatures* 36, no. 2 (2005): 85–94.
Simons, Anna. *Networks of Dissolution: Somalia Undone*. Boulder: Westview, 1995.
Sithole, Masipula. "Zimbabwe: History and Politics." In *The New Encyclopedia of Africa*, edited by John Middleton, 5:336–39. Detroit: Thomson Gale, 2005.
Slaughter, Joseph R. "Humanitarian Reading." In Wilson and Brown, *Humanitarianism and Suffering*, 88–107.
———. *Human Rights, Inc.* New York: Fordham University Press, 2007.
———. "Master Plans: Designing (National) Allegories of Urban Space and Metropolitan Subjects for Postcolonial Kenya." *Research in African Literatures* 35, no. 1 (2004): 30–51.
Sosnowsky, Alexandre. *Biafra: Proximité de la mort, continuité de la vie*. Paris: Fayard, 1969.
Soyinka, Wole. *Death and the King's Horseman*. New York: Hill and Wang, 1990.
———. *The Interpreters*. New York: Collier, 1970.
———. *The Man Died: Prison Notes*. 1972. London: Rex Collins, 1973.
———. *Season of Anomy*. 1973. New York: Third Press, 1974.
Spivak, Gayatri Chakravorty. "Can the Subaltern Speak?" In *The Postcolonial Studies Reader*, edited by Bill Ashcroft et al, 24–28. London: Routledge, 1995.
Stockwell, A. J. "British Decolonisation: The Record and the Records." *Contemporary European History* 15, no. 4 (2006): 573–83.
Szeman, Imre. *Zones of Instability: Literature, Postcolonialism, and the Nation*. Baltimore: Johns Hopkins University Press, 2003.
Teitel, Ruti G. "For Humanity." *Journal of Human Rights* 3, no. 2 (2004): 225–37.

Thomas, Gareth. *The Novel of the Spanish Civil War (1936–1975)*. Cambridge: Cambridge University Press, 1990.
Tolstoy, Leo. *The Sebastopol Sketches*.Translated by David McDuff. London: Penguin, 1986.
———. *War and Peace*. 1869. Translated by Louise Maude and Aylmer Maude. Oxford: Oxford University Press, 1983.
Tutu, Desmond Mpilo. *No Future Without Forgiveness*. New York: Doubleday, 1999.
Ugah, Ada. "A Reader's Diary of Cyprian Ekwensi's War Novels." In Emenyonu, 52–60. Ibadan, Nigeria: Heinemann, 1987.
Umeh, Marie. *Emerging Perspectives on Buchi Emecheta*. Trenton, N.J.: Africa World Press, 1996.
Vambe, Lawrence. *An Ill-Fated People: Zimbabwe Before and After Rhodes*. London: Heinemann, 1972.
Vambe, Maurice T. "Spirit Possession and the Paradox of Post-Colonial Resistance in Yvonne Vera's *Nehanda*." In Muponde and Maodzwa-Taruvinga, *Sign and Taboo*, 127–38.
Veit-Wild, Flora. "'Dances with Bones': Hove's Romanticized Africa." *Research in African Literatures* 24, no. 3 (1993): 5–12.
Vera, Yvonne. *Butterfly Burning*. 1998. New York: Farrar, Straus and Giroux, 2000.
———. *Nehanda*. 1993. Toronto: Tsar, 1994.
———. *The Stone Virgins*. New York: Farrar, Straus and Giroux, 2002.
———. *Without a Name and Under the Tongue*. New York: Farrar, Straus and Giroux, 2002. Originally pubished in 1994 and 1996, respectively.
Vidal-Naquet, Pierre. "Torture." In Schulz, *Phenomenon of Torture*, 195.
Wachira, Godwin. *Ordeal in the Forest*. Nairobi: East African Publishing House, 1968.
Walsh, John. "Coming of Age with an AK-47: Ahmadou Kourouma's *Allah n'est pas obligé*." *Research in African Literatures* 39, no. 1 (2008): 187–97.
Walzer, Michael. *Just and Unjust Wars: A Moral Argument with Historical Illustrations*. New York: Basic Books, 1977.
Wendt, Albert. "An Interview with Festus Iyayi." *Landfall* 44, no. 4 (1990): 412–22.
Wenzel, Jennifer. *Bulletproof: Afterlives of Anticolonial Prophecy in South Africa and Beyond*. Chicago: University of Chicago Press, 2009.
White, Luise. *The Assassination of Herbert Chitepo: Texts and Politics in Zimbabwe*. Bloomington: Indiana University Press 2003.
Wilentz, Gay. "Flora Nwapa." In *Twentieth-Century Caribbean and Black African Writers*, edited by Bernth Lindfors and Reinhard Sander. 2nd series. Detroit: Gale Research, 1993. See online: "Dictionary of Literary Biography." Vol. 125. *Literature Resource Center*. http://go.galegroup

.com.ezproxy.lib.uconn.edu/ps/start.do?p=LitRC&u=22516. Accessed 16 November 2013.

Wilson, Richard A. *The Politics of Truth and Reconciliation in South Africa: Legitimizing the Post-Apartheid State*. Cambridge: Cambridge University Press, 2001.

Wilson, Richard A., and Richard D. Brown, eds. *Humanitarianism and Suffering: The Mobilization of Empathy*. Cambridge: Cambridge University Press, 2008.

Winter, Jay. "Introduction: Henri Barbusse and the Birth of the Moral Witness." In Barbusse, *Under Fire*, vii–xix.

Winter, Joseph. "The Law of the Gun." *Times Literary Supplement*, April 1, 2005.

Witz, Leslie. "History of the People, for the People and by the People: A Brief Examination of the Development of People's History in South Africa, 1977–1988." *South Africa International* 19, no. 2 (1988): 90–95.

Wright, Derek, ed. *Emerging Perspectives on Nuruddin Farah*. Trenton, N.J.: Africa World Press, 2002.

———. "Nations as Fictions: Postmodernism in the Novels of Nuruddin Farah." *Critique: Studies in Contemporary Fiction* 38, no. 3 (1997): 193–204.

———. *Wole Soyinka Revisited*. New York: Twayne, 1993.

Zabus, Chantal. "Mending the Schizo-Text: Pidgin in the Nigerian Novel." *Kunapipi* 14 (1992): 119–27.

Zinn, Howard. *A People's History of the United States*. 1980. New York: Harper, 2010.

Zola, Émile. *La Débâcle*. 1892. Paris: Garnier Flammarion, 1975.

———. *Germinal*. 1885. Translated by Peter Collier. Oxford: Oxford University Press, 1998.

———. *Le Roman expérimentale*. Paris: Garnier-Flammarion, 1971.

———. "Préface." *Thérèse Raquin*. http://webcache.googleusercontent.com/search?q=cache:http://lettres.ac-rouen.fr/francais/zola/textes/raq-pref.html.

INDEX